Design Principles for Process-driven Architectures Using Oracle BPM and SOA Suite 12*c*

A design handbook to orchestrate and manage flexible process-driven systems with Oracle BPM and SOA Suite 12*c*

Matjaz B. Juric

Sven Bernhardt

Hajo Normann

Danilo Schmiedel

Guido Schmutz

Mark Simpson

Torsten Winterberg

[PACKT] PUBLISHING enterprise
professional expertise distilled

BIRMINGHAM - MUMBAI

Design Principles for Process-driven Architectures Using Oracle BPM and SOA Suite 12*c*

First published: August 2008

Second edition: June 2015

Production reference: 1240615

Published by Packt Publishing Ltd.
Livery Place
35 Livery Street
Birmingham B3 2PB, UK.

ISBN 978-1-84968-944-1

`www.packtpub.com`

Credits

Authors
Matjaz B. Juric
Sven Bernhardt
Hajo Normann
Kapil Pant
Danilo Schmiedel
Guido Schmutz
Mark Simpson
Torsten Winterberg

Reviewers
Kaustav Das
Haitham A. El-Ghareeb
Fabio Persico

Acquisition Editor
Vinay Argekar

Content Development Editor
Shweta Pant

Technical Editor
Humera Shaikh

Copy Editor
Sarang Chari

Project Coordinator
Shipra Chawhan

Proofreader
Safis Editing

Indexer
Monica Ajmera Mehta

Graphics
Disha Haria

Production Coordinator
Arvindkumar Gupta

Cover Work
Arvindkumar Gupta

About the Authors

Matjaz B. Juric holds a PhD in computer and information science. He is a full-time professor at the University of Ljubljana and heads the Cloud Computing and SOA Competence Centre (`http://www.soa.si`). Matjaz is an Oracle ACE Director and has been designated Java Champion and IBM Champion. He has more than 20 years of work experience.

He has authored and coauthored *Do More with SOA Integration: Best of Packt, WS-BPEL 2.0 for SOA Composite Applications with IBM WebSphere 7, Oracle Fusion Middleware Patterns, Business Process Driven SOA using BPMN and BPEL, Business Process Execution Language for Web Services* (both English and French editions), *BPEL Cookbook* (which was awarded the best SOA book in 2007 by SOA World Journal), *SOA Approach to Integration, Professional J2EE EAI, Professional EJB, J2EE Design Patterns Applied,* and *Visual Basic .NET Serialization Handbook.*

He has published chapters in *More Java Gems, Cambridge University Press,* and in *Technology Supporting Business Solutions, Nova Science Publishers, Inc.* His work has also been published in several journals and magazines and presented at conferences.

This book is dedicated to my beautiful daughter, Ela, and my second child, who will be born in July. Big thanks go to my beautiful Eva, my mother, and my grandmother (R.I.P.). I would like to specially thank my team, my friends, and the team at Packt Publishing.

Sven Bernhardt is a leading SOA/BPM architect and works as a solution architect for OPITZ CONSULTING Deutschland GmbH—a German Oracle Platinum Partner. In his role, he follows his passion for designing and building future-oriented, robust enterprise applications based on pioneering technologies. Sven is involved in diverse, large SOA and BPM implementations, dealing with challenges in the areas of business process automation and enterprise application integration. He also has longtime experience as an SOA/BPM coach, trainer, developer, and architect. As a leader of Competency Center for Oracle-based solutions, he develops and prepares implementation best practices and showcases and is responsible for knowledge building with respect to different Oracle technologies in the middleware area. Sven is an Oracle ACE and a frequent speaker at numerous IT conferences.

Hajo Normann works at Accenture in the role of an SOA and BPM's community of practice lead in ASG. Hajo is responsible for the architecture and solution design of SOA/BPM projects, mostly acting as the interface between the business and IT sides. He enjoys tackling organizational and technical challenges and motivates solutions in customer workshops, conferences, and publications. Hajo, together with Torsten Winterberg, leads the DOAG SIG Middleware; is an Oracle ACE Director; and is an active member of the global network within Accenture. Hajo is also in regular contact with SOA/BPM architects from around the world.

Kapil Pant (coauthor of the first edition of this book) is an accomplished BPM consultant and a public speaker with extensive experience in products and professional services consulting. He currently manages Wipro Technologies' BPM/SOA practice in Europe and leads consulting engagements, including business process improvement workshops; BPMS and SOA tools study and recommendations; and the BPM architecture, implementation, and governance.

Over the years, Kapil has been extensively involved in conducting successful workshops on process improvement, requirement analysis, BPM/SOA, and enterprise architecture for clients in the telecom, banking, securities, and insurance industry verticals. He has also worked closely with leading system integrators, such as Wipro, Tata Consultancy Services, HCL, and the then Satyam (now Tech Mahindra), to conduct technology enablement programs for client projects across industry verticals.

As a recognized public speaker, Kapil is known for his well-researched programs delivered in his high-energy, enthusiastic, and down-to-earth style. He has presented keynote speeches, workshops, seminars, and over 40 roadshows across Asia-Pacific, Europe, and the U.S. He was also nominated by the Government of India to lead seminars as a part of a 25-member working committee for E-Governance Enterprise Architecture and Standards Taxonomy.

He has a master's degree in computer applications, a bachelor's degree in business studies, and a TOGAF Certification.

Kapil presently lives in Hampshire, UK, with his wife and enjoys blogging in his free time.

Danilo Schmiedel follows his passion to deliver SOA and BPM solutions based on new technologies and trends. He is one of the leading BPM and SOA architects at OPITZ CONSULTING Deutschland GmbH—a German Oracle Platinum Partner. He is involved in large integrations, business process automations, and BPM/SOA development projects, where he has implemented well-accepted solutions for various customers. Danilo is an Oracle Director (ACE is short for Acknowledged Community Expert); frequent speaker at IT conferences; and author of numerous articles in various technical journals. Before joining OPITZ CONSULTING, he worked as a software engineer in several international projects. The Leipzig University of Applied Science awarded his outstanding work in 2009.

I would like to thank my wife and my little son for their support, patience, and help in producing this book as well as for enduring the many late nights and weekends that I spent working on many different projects over the past few years. In addition, I would like to thank my colleagues as well as the many clients who have provided me with opportunities to expand my knowledge and take on challenging tasks.

Guido Schmutz works for Trivadis, an Oracle Platinum Partner. He has more than 25 years of technology experience, including mainframes, integration, and SOA technologies in financial services, government, and logistics environments. At Trivadis, he is responsible for innovation in the areas of SOA, BPM, and application integration solutions and leads the Trivadis Architecture Board. He has longtime experience as a developer, coach, trainer, and architect in the areas of building complex Java EE and SOA-based solutions. Currently, he is focusing on the design and implementation of SOA and BPM projects using the Oracle SOA stack. A few other areas of interest for Guido are big data and fast data solutions and how to combine these emerging technologies into a modern information and software architecture. Guido is an Oracle ACE Director for Fusion Middleware and SOA and a regular speaker at international conferences, such as Oracle Open World, ODTUG, SOA & Cloud Symposium, UKOUG conference, and DOAG. He is also a coauthor of *Oracle Service Bus 11g Development Cookbook, Do More with SOA Integration: Best of Packt, Service-Oriented Architecture: An Integration Blueprint, Spring 2.0 im Einsatz, Architecture Blueprints*, and *Integration Architecture Blueprint*.

I would like to thank my wonderful wife, Renata, and my family for their love and all the support. Without their help and understanding, such a book project would not be possible.

And, of course, a big thank you goes to the whole team at Packt Publishing for their help and support.

Mark Simpson, in addition to being an Oracle ACE Director, is Consultancy Director at Griffiths Waite, where he leads the UK-based Fusion Middleware development team with a focus on user experience, BPM, and SOA. He has worked with these technologies for over 10 years, having successfully delivered the first UK Oracle BPEL project back in 2004 and then the first BAM dashboard in 2005 for an innovative financial services organization. He is a frequent conference speaker, has received numerous awards, and actively supports the UKOUG and EMEA SOA Community. Recently, Mark was the lead architect on a design-focused ADF and WebCenter project. This project has reignited his passion for great UX and delivering increased customer insight through data visualization using SOA to ensure consistency in processes, services, and data.

I would like to thank my wonderful wife, Laura, and my three amazing boys, Archie, Benji, and Tom, for their patience and support while I juggled the book project, Griffiths Waite commitments, and family life. Also, I must thank my coauthors for their perseverance to get a distributed team pulling in the right direction to get this book completed.

Torsten Winterberg is active in several roles at OPITZ CONSULTING, all with a strong focus on delivering value to the customer. Being part of the business development and innovation department, he searches for and evaluates emerging trends and technologies to deliver innovative and differentiating solutions to customers. As a director of the competency center for integration and business process solutions, he follows his passion to build the best delivery unit for customer solutions in the areas of SOA and BPM. Torsten has longtime experience as a developer, coach, and architect in the area of building complex mission-critical Java EE applications. His competence and passion lies in the design and architecture of complex IT systems with regard to BPMN, BPEL, ESB, BAM, and service-oriented architecture in general. He is a known speaker in the German Java and Oracle communities and has written numerous articles on SOA/BPM-related topics. Torsten is part of the Oracle ACE Director team, is active in Enterprise BPM Alliance, and is responsible for the SOA/BPM topics in the DOAG development community.

Thanks to my wife, Simone, and my wonderful daughters, Johanna and Amelie, for their patience with me when I was spending time with my hobby and job, doing this nerdy IT stuff.

About the Reviewers

Kaustav Das is an Oracle Fusion Middleware consultant with more than 8 years of experience in application designing and implementing and deploying scalable enterprise architectures focused on service-oriented architectures (SOAs), governance, business process management (BPM), and enterprise application integration (EAI). He is an Oracle SOA Suite and Oracle BPM Suite Certified Implementation Specialist and has led multiple successful full-lifecycle projects across different domains.

He currently works as a senior sales consultant at Oracle; prior to joining Oracle, he worked for Accenture as a subject matter expert for Oracle Service Bus and other BEA Aqualogic products.

I would like to appreciate the encouragement I got from my family to achieve many things in my life. A special note of thanks to my wonderful wife, Trishna, for her constant support, cooperation, and patience, without which, it would not have been possible for me to manage my work and life together.

Haitham A. El-Ghareeb is an assistant professor at the Information Systems department, Faculty of Computers and Information Sciences, Mansoura University, Egypt. Haitham is a member of many distinguishable computer organizations; reviewer at different, highly recognizable academic journals; contributor to open source projects; and author of different books.

Haitham is interested in e-learning, enterprise architecture, information architecture, and software architecture, especially service-oriented architecture (SOA), business process management (BPM), business process management systems (BPMS), information storage and management, virtualization, cloud computing, big data, and collaboration with information systems and e-learning organizations and researchers.

Haitham holds a master's degree in science (2008) from the same faculty he is currently working for. His master's thesis was entitled *Evaluation of Service Oriented Architecture in e-Learning*. This thesis was highly recognized and has been published as an international book under the same title (ISBN-10: 3838355385). Haitham holds a PhD (2012) from the same faculty he is currently working for. His PhD dissertation was entitled *Optimizing Service Oriented Architecture to Support e-Learning with Adaptive and Intelligent Features*. This PhD dissertation was highly recognized and has been published as an international book under the title *Optimizing Service Oriented Architecture to Support e-Learning* (10-digit ISBN: 3847311875). Haitham is the author of *Enterprise Integration Opportunities and Challenges* (10-digit ISBN: 3659371793). For an updated list of Haitham's activities and research articles, consider the following websites:

- **LinkedIn profile**: `http://eg.linkedin.com/in/helghareeb/`
- **Personal website**: `http://www.helghareeb.me`
- **Blog**: `http://blog.helghareeb.me`
- **Channel on YouTube**: `http://video.helghareeb.me`
- **List of publications**: `http://scholar.google.com.eg/citations?user=wXaTCaUAAAAJ&hl=en`

Big thanks go to my family, without whom I wouldn't have been where I am today.

Fabio Persico is a senior Oracle Integration Specialist at infoMENTUM Ltd., London. He has almost 10 years of experience in the software development industry, working with services and data integration technologies, such as Java, SOA, BPM, ESB, and ETL.

In his current role at infoMENTUM Ltd., he works on the architecture, design, and implementation of strategic and innovative solutions, mainly based on SOA.

Currently, he is particularly interested in learning DWH and implementing them using Oracle and OBIEE.

Fabio is an Oracle Certified Specialist Consultant in SOA, BPM, and ODI.

You can get in touch with him using the following channels:

LinkedIn profile: `http://uk.linkedin.com/in/fabiopersico`

Blog: `http://fabiopeblog.blogspot.co.uk`

Company website: `http://www.infomentum.com`

I would like to thank my wonderful wife, Giulia, for her patience, support, and help. I wouldn't be where I am without her!

---

www.PacktPub.com

Support files, eBooks, discount offers, and more

For support files and downloads related to your book, please visit www.PacktPub.com.

Did you know that Packt offers eBook versions of every book published, with PDF and ePub files available? You can upgrade to the eBook version at www.PacktPub.com and as a print book customer, you are entitled to a discount on the eBook copy. Get in touch with us at service@packtpub.com for more details.

At www.PacktPub.com, you can also read a collection of free technical articles, sign up for a range of free newsletters and receive exclusive discounts and offers on Packt books and eBooks.

PACKTLIB™

https://www2.packtpub.com/books/subscription/packtlib

Do you need instant solutions to your IT questions? PacktLib is Packt's online digital book library. Here, you can search, access, and read Packt's entire library of books.

Why subscribe?

- Fully searchable across every book published by Packt
- Copy and paste, print, and bookmark content
- On demand and accessible via a web browser

Free access for Packt account holders

If you have an account with Packt at www.PacktPub.com, you can use this to access PacktLib today and view 9 entirely free books. Simply use your login credentials for immediate access.

Instant updates on new Packt books

Get notified! Find out when new books are published by following @PacktEnterprise on Twitter or the *Packt Enterprise* Facebook page.

Table of Contents

Preface

The implementation and optimization of business processes have become high priorities for most enterprises. However, experience has shown that there is a huge gap between the implementation of a single business process and the definition of an enterprise-wide process-driven architecture that will be able to accommodate business processes over time, while ensuring the benefits of concepts and best practices, including reusability, loose coupling, flexibility, discoverability, and so on.

Experience has shown that only projects based on key design principles and best practices are successful. This book presents the key design principles for process architectures in a practical way via examples, using Oracle BPM and SOA Suite 12*c*.

This book is a design handbook. It provides you with the skills to successfully design, implement, and optimize business processes on top of SOA. Starting with business process modeling, it shows design principles to architect sound process architectures. It presents best practices to model business processes using BPMN, together with design principles to design and implement services (SOAP and REST) and extending through to composite applications.

It provides a detailed coverage of how to prepare business processes in BPMN for execution purposes on process servers and when to use BPEL. An in-depth explanation of human interactions is given, including different patterns, escalations, renewals, and other important concepts.

Business rules are covered, including principles and best practices to use rules in BPMN and BPEL processes. For scenarios where classical human interactions and rules are not sufficient, the book explains Adaptive Case Management.

Extending the reach of business processes to mobile devices and ensuring multichannel and omnichannel interactions are covered and explained.

Finally, business activity monitoring, event-driven architectures, and complex event processing in relation to business processes are explained. Here, it is not only shown how to monitor KPIs and do process analytics, but also how to enable integration with events and Internet of Things devices.

The design principles and best practices are demonstrated in a practical way on a rental car use case, called *Rent Your Legacy Car*, which is used for demonstration purposes through the chapters. Each topic is explained in detail and supported by examples that allow you not only to understand the principles and practices, but also to learn how to use and apply them in practice. Each chapter builds on the previous chapter, assuring a continuous flow and coherent reading experience. The reader will not only learn design principles and best practices, but also learn how to apply them through the *Rent Your Legacy Car* use case, which is used in all chapters. In the book, the latest Oracle BPM and SOA Suite 12*c* are used. The principles are, however, relevant for all process-driven architectures regardless of which implementation platform is used, on-premise or cloud based.

In this book, you will learn the following:

- Design principles for modeling business processes and business architectures
- Best practices to produce executable business processes in BPMN
- Principles for designing reusable services and composite applications
- Advanced approaches to human interactions in business processes, including patterns and advanced case management
- Business rule management and principles for rule design and implementation, including using rules in the BPMN and BPEL processes
- Preparing process application for mobile and multichannel/omnichannel
- Business activity monitoring and principles to define and monitor key performance indicators and using these for process optimization
- Extending the processes to Internet of Things devices and processing complex events

What this book covers

Chapter 1, Business Process Management, Service-oriented Architecture, and Enterprise Architecture, discusses the importance of business processes and their relevance to IT, application systems, enterprise architecture, reference models, and modeling principles. It describes the business architecture and enterprise architecture, describes their relation to business processes, and digs into business process management and its life cycle. It discusses the key concepts of process modeling, adaptive case management, and process execution, monitoring, and analytics. It explains process optimization. Finally, it explains how SOA and BPM fit together and discusses new frontiers for SOA.

Chapter 2, Modeling Business Processes for SOA – Methodology, describes strategies and methodologies that can help us realize the benefits of BPM as a successful enterprise modernization strategy. It discusses a set of actions in the course of a complete methodology in order to create the desired attractiveness toward broader application throughout the enterprise. It describes organizational and cultural barriers to apply enterprise BPM and discusses ways to overcome them.

Chapter 3, BPMN for Business Process Modeling, introduces the fundaments of business process modeling using a standard-based approach. It explains the concepts of using Business Process Model and Notation 2, a standard developed by the Object Management Group (OMG). BPMN 2 has gained the capability not only to model, but also to execute processes. From strategy modeling all the way to modeling executable business processes, this chapter discusses best practices to model business processes on different levels of decomposition.

Chapter 4, Process-driven Service Design, discusses best practices and patterns to design services. It explains the guidelines for service design in relation to BPM and demonstrates key service design principles. This chapter discusses service granularity, categories, data in the context of services, and how application services, cloud or on-premise, can be incorporated into your executable process.

Chapter 5, Composite Applications, explains key ways to architect and design the backend services that comprise the composite application. In this chapter, best practices for integration to backend systems, complex orchestrations, data validations, and calculations are explained. Also, some tools, such as templates, are used that help to create a successful solution that follows consistent architecture and design standards.

Chapter 6, Process Execution with BPMN and BPEL, outlines a set of guidelines to actually implement business processes and the associated services. This chapter describes how to define an implementation roadmap, explains how to implement the Service Facade and Delegation patterns in BPEL, discusses the right level of variances, highlights the degrees of coupling between technical components, and sets out a series of best practices, for example, naming conventions for composite partitions.

Chapter 7, Human Interaction with Business Processes, explains in depth what the integration of human actors means for process-driven applications, especially about the challenges from an architectural, conceptual, and technical perspective. Considerations with reference to UI design principles and user experience during development of user-centric processes and the corresponding inbox applications are discussed. The impact of the task-based approach on end users is also considered.

Chapter 8, Business Rules, outlines how a transparent enterprise decision management can be supported by IT by automating business decisions. It describes the characteristics of business rules and their relation with BPM; explains how to identify and assess business rules, that is, business rules candidates; discusses how to design, organize, and implement business rules; and depicts the Oracle Business Rules design time as well as the runtime architecture and its concepts. Finally, it discusses best practice approaches to implement business rules.

Chapter 9, Adaptive Case Management, gives all the overview information that is needed to fully understand the ideas behind ACM. It explains the characteristics of ACM, its relation to business analytics, shows how to model a case, how to build your own UI on top, and presents best practices.

Chapter 10, Mobile and Multichannel, explains the integration of mobile and BPM, provides best practices to design the architecture to enable multichannel access, accesses human tasks and BAM from mobile, and explains best practices for multichannel.

Chapter 11, Event Processing and BPM, explains what event processing is, why it is of interest to combine it with BPM, and how this can be achieved. It answers questions such as what is fast data and what is event processing, explains key elements of event processing and the different types of event processing, and compares event processing with Business Rule Management Systems (BRMS). It provides conceptual architecture for event processing and explains how event processing fits into a modern architecture.

Chapter 12, Business Activity Monitoring, shows how Business Activity Monitoring (BAM) can help an organization gain insight into business operations and outcomes in real time, thus enabling optimization, efficiency gain, and ongoing improvement to the business processes. This chapter defines the capabilities that a BAM platform should provide and the different types of insights that it delivers. It clarifies the difference between BAM and traditional Data Warehouse-based reporting solutions and describes how BAM integrates into SOA and BPM to monitor business processes and services in real time. It also presents a methodology and best practices to design and build BAM dashboards and the supporting data objects.

What you need for this book

The samples in this book are based on Oracle BPM Suite 12*c* and SOA Suite 12*c*. In order to develop the examples in this book, we need to install the integrated development environment and the process server environment in which the BPMN and BPEL processes, mediations, services, human tasks, and other service components will execute. For modeling and development purposes, we will use Oracle JDeveloper 12*c* 12.1.3. To execute these processes, we will use the Oracle BPM Suite and SOA Suite 12*c* 12.1.3.

The installation will consist of the following steps:

1. First, we need to download and install the Java Development Kit (JDK) and set the environment.
2. Second, we need to download and install the Oracle BPM Suite 12*c*, which includes the SOA Suite and JDeveloper.
3. Third, we need to create the default domain.

You can download the Java Development Kit from `http://www.oracle.com/technetwork/java/javase/downloads/index.html`.

You can download the Oracle BPM Suite 12*c* from `http://www.oracle.com/technetwork/middleware/bpm/downloads/`.

Detailed instructions on how to install the JDK and BPM Suite 12*c* with SOA Suite and JDeveloper and how to create the domain are provided at `http://docs.oracle.com/middleware/1213/core/SOAQS/index.html`.

Who this book is for

This book is intended for BPM and SOA architects, analysts, developers, and project managers who are responsible for, or involved in, business process development, modeling, monitoring, or implementation of composite, process-oriented applications. The principles are relevant for the design of on-premise and cloud solutions. This book is a design principles book, which provides principles and concepts behind designing sound process architectures for complex information systems. It requires basic familiarity with BPM and SOA, web services, XML, and general software engineering. This book uses Oracle BPM and SOA Suite 12*c* to demonstrate design principles and best practices in a real-world case study.

Conventions

In this book, you will find a number of text styles that distinguish between different kinds of information. Here are some examples of these styles and an explanation of their meaning.

Code words in text, database table names, folder names, filenames, file extensions, pathnames, dummy URLs, user input, and Twitter handles are shown as follows: "This file is to be found in the `soa-infra` MDS under `/soa/configuration`."

A block of code is set as follows:

```
<?xml version = '1.0' encoding = 'UTF-8'?>
<application xmlns:soa="http://www.oracle.com/soa/rest"
  xmlns:xsd="http://www.w3.org/2001/XMLSchema"
  xmlns:xsi="http://www.w3.org/2001/XMLSchema-instance"
  xmlns:weo="http://www.rylc.org/core/carrental"
  xmlns="http://wadl.dev.java.net/2009/02">
  <doc title="RequestVehicleRestSvce">RestService</doc>
...
...
...
</application>
```

New terms and **important words** are shown in bold. Words that you see on the screen, for example, in menus or dialog boxes, appear in the text like this: "Right-click on the **Vehicle Reservation & Allocation** chain step, and select **KPI**."

> Warnings or important notes appear in a box like this.

> Tips and tricks appear like this.

Reader feedback

Feedback from our readers is always welcome. Let us know what you think about this book—what you liked or disliked. Reader feedback is important for us as it helps us develop titles that you will really get the most out of.

To send us general feedback, simply e-mail `feedback@packtpub.com`, and mention the book's title in the subject of your message.

If there is a topic that you have expertise in and you are interested in either writing or contributing to a book, see our author guide at `www.packtpub.com/authors`.

Customer support

Now that you are the proud owner of a Packt book, we have a number of things to help you to get the most from your purchase.

Downloading the color images of this book

We also provide you with a PDF file that has color images of the screenshots/diagrams used in this book. The color images will help you better understand the changes in the output. You can download this file from: `https://www.packtpub.com/sites/default/files/downloads/9441EN_Graphics.pdf`.

Errata

Although we have taken every care to ensure the accuracy of our content, mistakes do happen. If you find a mistake in one of our books—maybe a mistake in the text or the code—we would be grateful if you could report this to us. By doing so, you can save other readers from frustration and help us improve subsequent versions of this book. If you find any errata, please report them by visiting `http://www.packtpub.com/submit-errata`, selecting your book, clicking on the **Errata Submission Form** link, and entering the details of your errata. Once your errata are verified, your submission will be accepted and the errata will be uploaded to our website or added to any list of existing errata under the Errata section of that title.

To view the previously submitted errata, go to `https://www.packtpub.com/books/content/support` and enter the name of the book in the search field. The required information will appear under the **Errata** section.

Piracy

Piracy of copyrighted material on the Internet is an ongoing problem across all media. At Packt, we take the protection of our copyright and licenses very seriously. If you come across any illegal copies of our works in any form on the Internet, please provide us with the location address or website name immediately so that we can pursue a remedy.

Please contact us at `copyright@packtpub.com` with a link to the suspected pirated material.

We appreciate your help in protecting our authors and our ability to bring you valuable content.

Questions

If you have a problem with any aspect of this book, you can contact us at `questions@packtpub.com`, and we will do our best to address the problem.

1

Business Process Management, Service-oriented Architecture, and Enterprise Architecture

The main objective of information technology is to provide support for business operations. Although in the past few years, the focus on composite application development, process applications, orchestration of services, and business process management (BPM) has improved the end-to-end business process support, flexibility, and insight into business operations, there is still a lot of room for improvement.

In this book, we will focus on design principles for process-driven architectures. We will look at how **service-oriented architecture** (**SOA**) can address the key challenges of BPM. **Business process management** (**BPM**) is a very important discipline, which is closely related to the operating efficiency, competitive position, and the ability of the company to grow. Business processes are also very closely connected with IT. One of the current challenges, which we address in this book, is how to provide support for knowledge-intensive processes. Such processes are usually complex and have many variants, and modeling them in the traditional way is inappropriate. Such knowledge-intensive processes are addressed with **adaptive case management** (**ACM**).

However, the key question is how to reduce the semantic gap between business processes and applications. **SOA** has emerged as a solution to these problems. In this book, we will show you how we can use SOA along with BPM. We will look at the complete life cycle, starting with business process modeling and ending with the application that implements such processes. We will see that SOA introduces new approaches with **Business Process Model and Notation** (**BPMN**), **Business Process Execution Language** (**BPEL**), **enterprise service bus** (**ESB**), services, human workflow, **business activity monitoring** (**BAM**), rule engines, API management, and others to fulfill the objectives. Since the early days, SOA has introduced business events and event processing, including the capability to identify complex event patterns, which has opened up new ways for loosely-coupled integration and emphasized the ability to integrate with the Internet of Things devices, which will play an important role in business processes in the future.

The **enterprise architecture** (**EA**) is the umbrella that ties together business processes, applications, data, IT infrastructure, and the strategy of a company or organization. Enterprise architecture is the master plan, which specifies how to relate and map the strategy to the business processes and business processes to the application, data, and IT infrastructure with the objective of a coherent, well-defined, and manageable system. An important part of the EA is the **business architecture** (**BA**), which provides a bridge from the business models and the whole strategy to the business processes.

In this chapter, we will look at business processes and their relevance to IT, application systems, enterprise architecture, reference models, and modeling principles. We will do the following in this chapter:

- Explain the importance of business processes
- Present different classifications of business processes
- Describe the business architecture and the enterprise architecture and their relation to business processes
- Dig into business process management and overview its life cycle
- Discuss process modeling and adaptive case management
- Summarize modeling principles and best practices
- Discuss process execution, monitoring, and analytics
- Explain process optimization
- Explain how SOA and BPM fit together and discuss new frontiers for SOA

The importance of business processes

A business process consists of a set of coordinated activities that accomplish a particular business goal. The order of these activities and the efficiency of those who perform the activities determine the overall performance of a business process.

> A business process is a set of coordinated activities that are performed either by humans or by tools with the objective to realize a certain business result.

In today's competitive market, the efficiency of a company is a key criterion for success because, in addition to innovation, operating efficiency is key to improving the company's competitive advantage in the market. Knowing and understanding the details of business processes is therefore highly important because this gives us the opportunity to identify the bottlenecks and optimize business processes. Having highly-optimized business processes is one of the most important priorities of companies.

> Optimized business processes are increasingly important for companies as they provide the company with a competitive advantage. With BPM/SOA, companies can optimize business processes easily, with less effort, and in a shorter time than with previous approaches.

However, it's not only the competitive advantage that matters; companies also need to react to changes in the global market, to new opportunities, and to threats from other companies. They react with modifications to their business processes.

Optimizing business processes is also related to information systems. Each change in the process requires changes in the related application systems.

BPM is not only about performance improvement and adaptability. It is also about change management. BPM can help to improve organizational procedures and rules and can adhere to industry standard compliance and legal compliance.

Modeling and optimizing business processes

We can get a complete understanding of a business process only when we look at the details. It's in these details that the complexity hides. We can model business processes in a variety of visual languages; the most widely used is BPMN. Until now, **event process chain** (EPC), **extended event process chain** (eEPC), UML activity diagrams, and others, such as flow charts, have been used. As we will see throughout this book, today's modeling tools, such as Oracle BPM Suite, provide comprehensive support for BPMN modeling. However, it is not enough to just model a process, it is also important to adhere to best practices, which we will explain in this book.

We use business process models to understand the processes. This gives us the opportunity to improve and optimize them. Business process optimization and re-engineering are very important, and it is up to our imagination to improve processes, integrate them to gain synergic benefits, and use other approaches to optimize them. Business process optimization is related to several important topics that should not be overlooked. We will mention just three here:

- Changing business processes requires changing the way people work. And people do not like change. Therefore, in order to be successful, we need to be careful about how we apply the changes to the real world and how we motivate the employees to change their way of working. Otherwise, even a theoretical process that is highly optimized will not work in the real world.
- Changing business processes does not mean changing only the behavior of the employees but requires changing the IT support and related application systems. This topic is of particular interest to us, and we will look at it in detail in the next section.
- Finally, changing the business processes only once is not the key to long-lasting success. If a company wants to have long-lasting success, it should develop an environment where business processes can be continuously optimized. This is a particularly difficult task because continuous change in business processes also requires continuous change in the way employees work and in the way IT supports the business.

Classifying business processes

Often, business processes are classified into internal or private business processes and public or global business processes. Internal business processes are related to a single company. Internal processes can be local to a single organizational unit, department, or line of business, or they can span multiple units, departments, or LOBs. Public business processes, on the other hand, connect two or more companies.

Business processes are often classified as **operational** processes, **management** processes, and **supporting** processes. Operational processes represent the core business and are, therefore, the most important. For example, a marketing company that manages advertisement boards relies on efficient processes that start with an order for advertising and end when the advertisement is published on boards throughout the country or abroad. The faster the company can realize the orders and the faster it can react to new requirements from customers, the better it is.

Management processes are responsible for managing and governing the enterprise. Supporting processes are those processes that support the core operational processes, such as support, accounting, and so on, and are usually found in the majority of companies.

Business processes, particularly operational and management processes, are always specific to a company. Companies, therefore, cannot buy IT support for these processes in the market but have to custom develop it to address their specific needs.

In some industries, **best practices** related to business processes have been gathered and published. In the telecommunication sector, a well-known business process framework is the **enhanced telecom operations map** (**eTOM**). eTOM defines the best process frameworks for different aspects related to telecommunication business, such as service configuration and activation, resource management and operations, resource provisioning, and so on. Other examples include the APQC **process classification framework** (**PCF**), 8 Omega, and so on.

Such **business process frameworks** can be used for various reasons, including:

- To standardize business processes in an industry
- To ease integration between different companies from the same industry/sector
- To use them as benchmarks to compare our own processes
- To follow and improve our processes

Some experts are of the opinion that best practices represent the average state in the industry. If our company is benefiting from such processes, it means that our processes are no better than average. Usually, companies that are above average keep their business processes confidential because they know that their business processes reflect their true competitive advantage.

The digital economy and knowledge-driven processes

Caring about business processes is not only about improving existing processes. It is also about creating new business processes that address new **digital channels** and business models enabled by the **digital economy**. Such processes can be directed towards consumers and facilitate digital channels, such as social networks. They can also be directed towards B2B integrations. Either way, often such processes rely heavily on services and their **application programming interfaces** (**APIs**) for integration. The **API management** and the **API economy** are therefore becoming increasingly important for modern process-driven architectures.

The second important aspect is knowledge-driven processes, which exist for several activities that do not follow an exact order or always the same order. Such processes cannot be easily modeled with traditional modeling languages, such as BPMN. Therefore, adaptive case management approaches have emerged, providing the opportunity for companies to address these knowledge-intensive processes as well in a structured manner. We will talk about ACM in *Chapter 9, Adaptive Case Management*, of this book.

Business architecture

Understanding the business is not only about individual business processes. It is also important to understand how business processes at different levels fit together and how they relate to the strategy, business model, products, services, and other aspects of an enterprise.

Business processes can be at different levels of decomposition. Top-level processes represent a high-level, bird's-eye view of an enterprise, business model, and strategy. On lower levels, business processes become more detailed.

> Therefore, it is important to understand that BPM is not about individual business processes only, but also about the overall business architecture.

Business processes can be structured into **levels**. Usually, we talk about four levels of decomposition:

- On the top level, we model process areas or business functions.
- On level two, we model process categories, which are often organized around value chains.

- On level three, we model business processes from the business perspective. As already mentioned, we often use BPMN for this step.
- On level four, we model processes for implementation. We talk about automated processes and decomposition of process elements. Here, we can use executable BPMN 2 or BPEL or a combination of both.

Business processes is, however, only a part of the business architecture. The other important parts are business information, governance structure, and the overall structure of the enterprise. According to the **Object Management Group** (**OMG**): the BA is *a blueprint of the enterprise that provides a common understanding of the organization and is used to align strategic objectives and tactical demands.*

The BA addresses organization, capabilities, information, and value chains. It also addresses products and services, stakeholders, vision, strategy and tactics, projects, decisions and rules, metrics, measures and key performance indicators, policies, and rules and regulations. The various aspects of the BA are shown in the following figure:

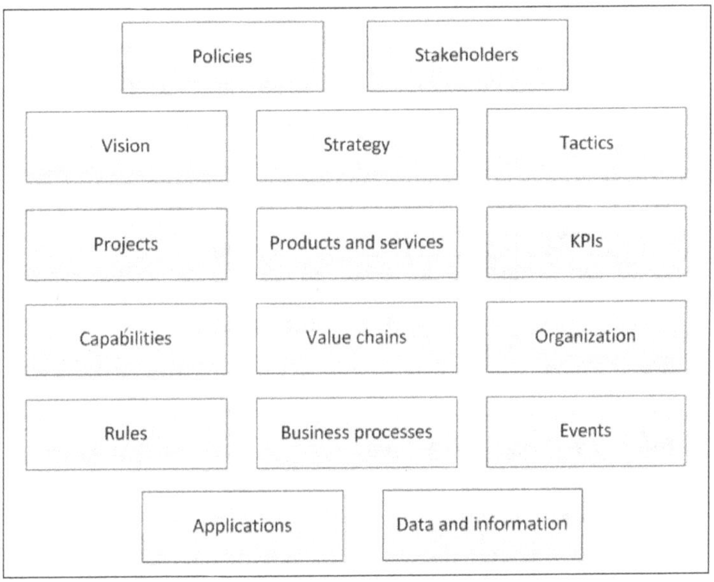

Figure 1: Business architecture aspects

Modeling the BA has traditionally not been integrated with business process modeling. However, in Oracle BPM Suite 12*c*, a lightweight BA modeling tool has been introduced. As modeling the BA is intended for business people, this tool is part of the web-based business process composer. It introduces the following:

- The **enterprise process map** is used for defining high-level business functions. This addresses the high-level decomposition, allows the identification business functions, and hierarchically orders them.
- The **value chain model** is used to decompose each business function into a value chain. A value chain can be further drilled down into child value chains or into concrete business processes represented by BPMN models.
- The **strategy model** is used for representing the relationship between BA artifacts. It encapsulates organization business goals, objectives, and metrics using strategy models.
- **Key performance indicators** can also be captured within BA and represent key success metrics.

We will talk more about BA modeling using BPM Suite in *Chapter 2, Modeling Business Processes for SOA – Methodology*. It is, however, important to stress that integrating BA modeling with business process modeling is very important for reducing the semantic gap.

Enterprise architecture

Business architecture is usually conducted as a part of the greater enterprise architecture. It is a common misperception that the EA is only about technological aspects.

Enterprise architecture is the high-level design of an organization, which includes the business architecture (business processes, organization, and people), application architecture (services, components, and applications), data architecture (data and information and data models), and IT infrastructure (software, hardware, network, and so on).

The EA applies architecture principles and sound practices to design business, information, process, and technology architectures necessary for companies to execute their strategies. The enterprise architecture is designed with these objectives: to improve manageability, effectiveness, efficiency, and agility of the business and their processes.

Today, it is believed that the enterprise architecture is the key to controlled improvement and the increased ability of organizations to change. These changes include the following:

- Improvement, integration, and standardization of business processes
- Innovation in the processes and organization
- Quality improvement and timeliness of business information

Several methodologies for the EA exist. The most popular are the following:

- **The Zachman Framework™** for enterprise architectures (`http://www.zachman.com/`)
- **The Open Group Architectural Framework** (TOGAF) (`http://www.opengroup.org/togaf/`)
- **Federal Enterprise Architecture (FEA)** (`http://www.whitehouse.gov/omb/e-gov/fea`)
- **The Gartner methodology** (`http://www.gartner.com/technology/consulting/enterprise-architecture.jsp`)

Enterprise architecture can help to choose the right architectural decisions for BPM (such as mapping to services, applications, using the right data models, and so on). It can enable reuse and make the delivery of new solutions quicker, more efficient, and better aligned with the organizational strategy. It can enable and foster governance.

In the future, the EA will tightly integrate with tools for modeling the BA and business processes and will become the top-layer modeling tool for each enterprise.

Business process management

Let's now look at the broader picture of business process management, which includes business process modeling. It is, however, much more than just modeling. It is about achieving the highest level of efficiency in terms of time and cost in performing any business activity. This has been the guiding principle of successful businesses for a long time. In 1911, Frederick Winslow Taylor, the father of scientific management, published the following four principles of scientific management:

- Replace rule-of-thumb work methods with methods based on a scientific study of the tasks
- Scientifically select, train, and develop each employee rather than leave them to train themselves

- Provide detailed instructions and supervise how each worker performs in his or her discrete task
- Divide work equally between managers and workers so that the managers apply scientific management principles to plan the work and the workers actually perform the tasks

Taylor defined ideas precisely about how to implement business processes efficiently. His belief was that this is possible only through enforced standardization of methods, adoption of best practices, working conditions, and cooperation.

Today, these thoughts are grouped under BPM, which is a method of aligning a business organization with the needs of its clients. BPM fosters business effectiveness and efficiency while striving for innovation, flexibility, and integration with technology. The major objective of BPM is to continuously improve the processes both within the company and with other companies (such as in supply chain management).

Business process life cycle

Until now, we saw that business processes are dynamic. To express the various stages of the business process, the business process life cycle has to be defined. A business process life cycle has to cover the following four phases:

1. Process modeling is related to the definition of the process model using the selected methodology and the notation.
2. Process implementation is related to the activities required to implement end-to-end IT support for the process.
3. Process execution and control is related to the actual running of the process, the supervisors controlling the process execution, and taking necessary corrective actions.
4. Process monitoring, analytics, and optimization is related to gathering data about the process execution. BPM provides the ability to gather real-time quantitative data using process monitoring or BAM tools. Optimization is responsible for interpreting these monitoring numbers and identifying optimization points.

The following figure shows how a process enters this circle and goes through various stages:

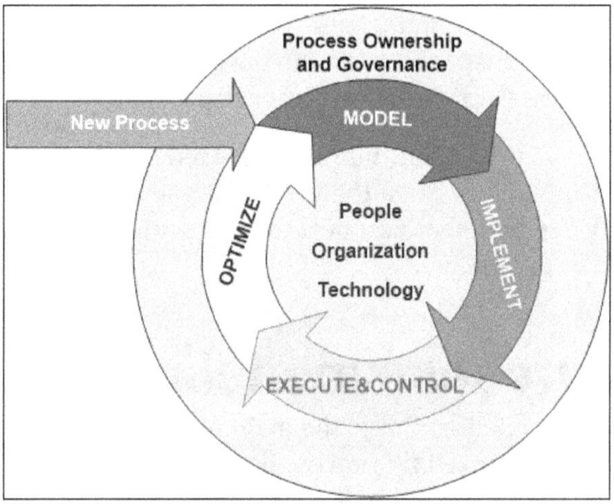

Figure 2: Business process life cycle

Process modeling is the phase where process analysts, together with process owners, analyze the business process and define the process model. They define the activity flow, information flow, roles, and business documents. They also define business policies and constraints, business rules, and performance measures. Performance measures are often called **key performance indicators** (**KPIs**). Examples of KPIs include activity turnaround time, activity cost, and so on.

Process implementation is the phase where the IT developers (SOA developers), together with process analysts, implement the business process with the objective of providing end-to-end support for the process using IT (applications). The process implementation phase using the SOA approach includes process implementation with executable BPMN, BPEL, decomposition in the services, identification of the service, implementation or reuse of services, and integration.

Process execution and control is the actual execution phase, where the process participants execute the various activities of the process. For end-to-end support in business processes, it is very important that IT drives the process and directs process participants to execute activities and not vice versa, where the actual process drivers are employees. An important part of this phase is process control, where process supervisors or process managers monitor whether the process is executing optimally. If delays occur, exceptions arise, resources are unavailable, or some other anomalies occur, process supervisors or managers can take corrective actions.

Process monitoring, analytics, and optimization is the final, and a very important, phase. In this phase, process owners monitor the KPIs of the process. Process analysts, process owners, process supervisors, and key users examine the process and analyze the process execution metrics. They also need to take into account the changing business conditions. They examine business issues and identify ways to improve business processes to eliminate these issues.

Once optimizations have been identified and selected, the process returns to the modeling phase to apply them. Then the process is re-implemented, and the whole life cycle is repeated. We talk about an iterative, incremental life cycle because the process is improved in each stage.

Business process modeling

In the business process modeling phase, the main objective is to develop the process model, which will define the existing process flow in detail. The transparency of the process flow is crucial as this gives the process owners, process analysts, and all others involved an insight into what is going on. An understanding of the AS-IS process flow also ensures that we can judge the efficiency and the quality of the process.

The main objective of process modeling is the definition of the **AS-IS** process flow. We will model the business process to satisfy the following objectives:

- To specify the exact result of the business process and to understand the business value of this result.
- To understand the activities of the business process. Knowing the exact tasks and activities that have to be performed is crucial to understanding the details of the process.
- To understand the order of activities. Activities can be performed in sequence or in parallel, which can help improve the overall time required to fulfill a business process. Activities can be short-running or long-running.
- To understand the responsibilities and identify (and later supervise) who is responsible for which activities and tasks.
- To understand the utilization of resources consumed in the business process. Knowing who uses which resource can help improve the utilization of resources as resource requirements can be planned and optimized.
- To understand the relationship between people involved in the processes and their communication. Knowing exactly who communicates with whom is important and can help to organize and optimize communications.

- To understand the document flow. Business processes produce and consume documents (regardless of whether they are paper or electronic documents). Understanding where the documents are going and where they are coming from is important. A good overview of the documents also gives us the opportunity to identify whether all the documents are really necessary.
- To identify potential bottlenecks and points for improvement, which can be used later in the process optimization phase.
- To introduce quality standards, such as ISO 9001, more successfully and to better pass certification.
- To improve the understandability of quality regulations that can be supplemented with process diagrams.
- To use business process models as work guidelines for new employees who can introduce themselves to the business processes faster and more efficiently.
- To understand business processes, which will enable us to understand and describe the company as a whole.

A good understanding of business processes is very important for developing IT support. Applications that provide end-to-end support for business processes can be developed efficiently only if we understand the business processes in detail.

Modeling method and notation

Efficient process modeling requires a modeling method that provides a structured and controlled approach to process modeling. Several modeling methods have been developed over the years. Examples include IDS Sheer's ARIS methodology, CSC's Catalyst, Business Genetics, SCOR and the extensions PCOR and VCOR, POEM, and so on.

Process modeling also requires a notation. Business Process Model and Notation 2 is the most comprehensive notation for process modeling thus far. It has been developed under the hood of Object Management Group. We will provide a detailed introduction to BPMN in *Chapter 3, BPMN for Business Process Modeling*.

With version 2, BPMN adds a crucial aspect—support for **executable processes**. Prior to BPMN 2, business processes were more or less diagrams. With version 2, BPMN has added the ability to execute BPMN process models on a process server. This way, BPMN process models have become even more valuable assets for each information system. The ability to execute BPMN models is nowadays supported by leading process servers, including Oracle BPM Suite. Support for executable processes has brought about another useful feature, that is, the ability to export BPMN process models into the interchangeable XML format, which means that, at least in theory, BPMN business processes are not dependent on a specific tool of the process server.

Adaptive case management

Until now, we have talked about strictly defined business processes. Such processes are common for scenarios where activities, the order of activities, roles, and other elements of the process are well defined and do not change often. Such processes are commonly used for scenarios where we want to standardize the work and make sure that all follow the same template.

Not all processes can be well defined in terms of strict process models. Business processes that require knowledge, work, and certain expertise usually cannot be modeled in terms of activities and transitions (such models would be too complex). Therefore, the alternative way of modeling such processes has been defined. It is called adaptive case management or advanced case management.

In contrast to traditional, rigid process modeling, in ACM, the activities within an adaptive process are identified. However, the transitions between the activities are not modeled. The transitions are either defined as rules, or it is up to the knowledge workers to identify the right order of activities for a certain case. However, the tools that support ACM should provide the ability to monitor, update, understand, and interpret every activity as it is processed. We will talk more about ACM in *Chapter 9, Adaptive Case Management*.

AS-IS process model diagram

The **AS-IS** process model for each business process consists of the top-level process model, which shows the high-level activities and the flow of these activities, along with the responsibilities of the roles involved in the process. It also includes detailed process maps for each high-level activity, with detailed representations of process activities. The detailed process map may have several decomposition levels depending on the complexity of each high-level activity.

Special attention should be placed on the exception-handling diagram. When modeling a business process, it is very important that we don't end up modeling only the optimal process flow (happy flow). We must not forget to identify the possible exceptions that might occur and specify how these exceptions are handled. An exception-handling diagram shows exactly this.

A well-designed process model should define at least:

- The process trigger, which tells us how the process is triggered to start the execution
- The necessary input information required in the process
- The process result or results
- Roles involved in the process or responsible for the process
- Responsibilities of the roles within the process, such as *responsible-for*, *executes*, *participates*, *supervises*, and so on
- Metrics used for measuring process efficiency
- Events that can interrupt the regular process flow and the compensation logic required to handle these interruption events
- Compliance with standards or reference processes
- The business goals a process contributes to

Exception handling

When designing the process, it is also particularly important that we identify not just the regular process flow but also the exception flow that each process has.

If an exception occurs, it should be handled. The exception-handling diagram shows how to handle these exceptions. We should specify how exceptions are handled, by whom, and where the process goes to after the exception has been handled.

Often, exceptions require that we compensate activities of the process flow that have already been completed successfully. We might also want to compensate activities if an event interrupts the process flow.

Modeling principles

When modeling business processes, our objective should be to develop sound process models. Soundness of the process models can be achieved if we follow a few basic principles:

- **Syntax**: Our model must have correct syntax as defined by the modeling notation. If we use BPMN, we should follow the BPMN syntax rules. Most tools can check the syntax.
- **Semantics**: Our model should also be semantically correct. This means that we have included all relevant activities, decisions, events, documents, and other elements. This also means that the process flow is correct and we have defined how to react to events, how to handle exceptions, and how to compensate if necessary. We should also use the correct names for all elements. Achieving semantic correctness is more difficult than achieving syntactical correctness.
- **Relevance**: We should model only those processes that are relevant to the problem domain. In modeling processes, we could easily get carried away because one process will typically relate to other processes. Sometimes, it is difficult to draw a line between what we should include and what we should not. The most basic principle is to include only those artifacts that are relevant from the perspective of the process and the problem domain we are focusing on. Too much modeling is a waste of time.
- **Cost versus benefit**: We model processes to achieve specific benefits. We should therefore weigh the amount of effort against the anticipated benefits. Usually, the 80/20 rule applies here as well. 80 percent of the benefit comes from 20 percent of the effort, and vice versa. Therefore, it is important to know the level of detail and when it is better to stop modeling. The required level of detail can differ. If we perform process modeling for quality assurance, a lower level of detail is required than if we perform process modeling for an SOA implementation.
- **Usability**: The model should be usable and understandable. Otherwise, the model is worth nothing. Business processes are complex. To achieve usability, we should decompose the model into various levels of detail. How we do the decomposition is important as the parts should be understandable. We usually prefer simple models over more complex ones.
- **Standards**: While modeling business processes, we should use and apply certain standards. First, we should use good practices and patterns. Second, we should use naming conventions. In some industries, standard or reference process models exist (such as eTom for telecom operators). We should look for compliance if it can add business value.

- **Integration**: We should integrate different models that look at the same or similar process domains from different perspectives. The integrated model will reveal all aspects of the process. We should also design a process map where all processes and relationships between them are listed.

Using these and a few other, more specific principles will help make our process models better and more usable over a longer period of time. We should, however, be aware that modeling processes is not easy although it might look easy at first sight. Therefore, in the next section, we will list common problems that we are likely to face.

Common problems in process modeling

When modeling business processes, we will face several challenges. We have identified some of these in the following paragraphs.

Modeling business processes should be aligned with the overall business strategy. If the objective of process modeling is not related to specific business goals, then it is a waste of time for all people involved. Therefore, it is crucial that we define, from the beginning, what the goals of process modeling are. The goal can be, for example, to provide end-to-end IT support for a specific process. The goal can also be to improve the efficiency of the process. It is, however, important that we do not stick to such high-level goals. We should precisely articulate the specific goals of the company. We should know the exact process for which we want to develop end-to-end support, where we want to improve the efficiency, and by how much. Without clearly defined goals with measurable outcomes, we should not start process modeling.

When we start process modeling, we should clearly define the responsibilities. In process modeling, people from different organizations participate. They must see value in participating, otherwise, they will not be willing to dedicate their time. Communicating the benefits of process modeling is, therefore, important. Even more important is to have support from the top management. Only the top management can order all employees to participate in the project.

We should define teams that will participate in the process modeling. Here is one possible structure of the team, which has proven to be efficient:

- Process owner
- Two persons, coming from the same department, to assist the process owner
- Process quality representative
- Business process analyst (or analysts)
- IT representative
- Optionally, an external consultant

We also have to define measurable goals to assess whether process management has been done the right way and what the benefits have been.

Publishing and communicating process models

An important part of business process modeling is communicating the models to all interested parties. This includes company management, unit management, supervisors, employees, quality assurance, and all other interested employees, all of whom can use the process model to better understand what is going on within the organization. They can also use the process model as work instructions.

Publishing the process model and communicating it to all interested employees is also important because, this way, we can gather feedback on the process and improve it even further. Publishing a process on the company's intranet is usually a good way to give visibility to process models.

Feedback on process models can improve quality and can be a good source of ideas for improving and optimizing the process. This is the first step in building continuous awareness about processes and their optimization among process owners and all others involved in the process.

Oracle BPM Suite 12*c* provides rich process reports that can be used not only for documentation and analysis, but also for communication. We will show how to use process reports later in this book.

Process execution, monitoring, and analytics

According to ancient wisdom, *if you can't measure it, you can't manage it*. This is particularly true for business processes. Measuring different aspects of a business process, such as activity duration, resource utilization, total execution time, average execution time, and so on, is crucial to understanding how the processes perform in the real world. We can only understand the process if we have numbers, and we can get numbers from measuring the process execution.

Business activity monitoring

One of the key elements of process control is BAM. The key objective of BAM is to provide a complete overview of business process execution within the company. The management and other people who are responsible for development and operations of the company use this data. The most important component of BAM is **time**. Time is crucial because BAM shows actual, near real-time information on process execution. This allows the company to react quickly and efficiently to the changes reflected through process execution.

> Business activity monitoring is real-time observation of key performance indicators.

`Whatis.com` defines BAM as follows:

> *"BAM, also called business activity management, is the use of technology to proactively define and analyze critical opportunities and risks in an enterprise to maximize profitability and optimize efficiency. The BAM paradigm can be used to evaluate external as well as internal factors.*
>
> *Three main steps compose effective implementation of BAM. First, relevant data is gathered in an efficient and timely manner and in sufficient quantities to provide meaningful results. Second, the data is processed to identify and categorize factors relevant to specific concerns. Finally, the data is analyzed and the results displayed in a clear, user-friendly interface so personnel can take appropriate actions."*

To provide information for decision making, BAM first has to gather data. This data is gathered from business processes and is related to process activities, resources utilized in these activities, such as employees, and so on. The more the data gathered, the better and the more statistically relevant the derived information. The BAM tools have to gather the data and calculate interesting information that can help in decision making. BAM can process the gathered data in different ways:

- Data can be processed immediately. In this way, the related KPIs will be calculated immediately and shown to the supervisors or sent to a decision-support application. Such KPIs can then be recalculated in near real time.

- Data can be used to notify supervisors and other people involved in the process that something important has happened. For example, if a KPI value is too high or too low, certain actions can be triggered. A supervisor can be alerted (by e-mail, SMS, or voice call), or an automatic action can be executed.
- BAM can also be used to identify patterns in the incoming data and notify or even react to them. Because BAM gathers data from different, independent business processes, BAM can identify certain patterns between the processes and can react to such patterns. This gives an additional level of control and flexibility to the information system.

BAM is not only a system that displays interesting information about processes; it consolidates data gathered from different, often independent, sources too. Connecting this data with past data enables BAM to identify critical situations in process execution or even automatically or semi-automatically solve some frequent critical solutions.

> The ultimate goal of each BAM user is to optimize the process execution, improve the process efficiency, and sense and react to important events.

Key performance indicators

Monitoring the processes closely is essential, and we use KPIs to specify what we wish to monitor. KPIs are financial and nonfinancial metrics used to help an organization define and measure process efficiency. Monitoring KPIs in real time is nothing but BAM. KPIs should be related to the strategy of a company.

Examples of a KPI are the average revenue per customer, average time for response to a customer call, average order amount, and so on. KPIs differ from company to company. Therefore, the first step in using KPIs is to identify them.

We identify KPIs for a selected business process, which has to be specified well. We must also have clear goals and performance requirements for that process. When we define KPIs, we should follow these SMART rules:

- **S**pecific
- **M**easurable
- **A**chievable
- **R**esult-oriented or **R**elevant
- **T**ime-bound

When identifying KPIs, we should apply considerable thought to them because, in practice, KPIs have a very long lifespan. After we have defined them, it is difficult to change them because, if we change them, we lose the comparisons to performance in the previous years or periods.

KPIs should also be defined in a way that will enable comparison with other similar companies. Therefore, KPIs should not be unduly confined to a company's internal specifics.

In the real world, measuring KPIs efficiently and accurately is a major challenge. SOA, together with BPM, offers huge advantages over previous IT architectures because most SOA platforms provide KPI measurements as a built-in function of process monitoring and control.

Process optimization

Process optimization offers huge opportunities for each company to distinguish itself from its competitors and focus more closely on customer wishes and requirements. Customers assess the whole shopping experience and not just the product or service. Therefore, it makes sense to optimize processes at all levels, from handling a sales inquiry to processing an order, product or service, production, delivery, and support.

> Process optimization can increase revenue and profits considerably if done the right way.

A systematic approach to process optimization, which should include all end-to-end processes, has multiple positive effects on a company. It can help increase the competitive advantage of a company in several ways. The following are some of the most important effects of process optimization:

- **Increased sales** of products or services through better service, better and faster production, increased flexibility, better customer experience, the ability to better sense customer requirements, and so on.
- **Cost savings** are the most obvious benefits and are directly related to optimizing activity execution times and people and resource utilization. Simplifying business processes also saves costs. Sometimes, process optimization helps in identifying processes or parts of processes that can be outsourced or shared.

- **Improved efficiency in business operations** is another important aspect. Process optimization is not only about minimizing process activity times. It is also about coordinating private processes (those processes that a company executes internally) with public processes (processes that involve business partners). Just-in-time delivery and manufacturing are just two examples of highly-coordinated business processes between several partners. Such processes save money and allow more efficient business operations.
- **Increased customer satisfaction** can be achieved through process optimization. Better support for customers, faster response times, and higher visibility into processes (for example, the ordering process where the customer can monitor online what happens with their order) are directly related to customer satisfaction. Integrating online customer support with a problem ticketing system is another example, and we could identify more.
- **Improved exception handling** can also be achieved. Exceptions are the most undesirable events in business processes because they interrupt or even stop the usual process execution. The fact is that when exceptions occur, they take up considerable time and resources. Optimizing and automating exception handling can be very useful.

From a technical perspective, process optimization is about developing optimized process models, which we will look at in the next section.

The TO-BE process model

Process optimization is the final phase in the BPM cycle. The objective of this phase is to develop the optimized process models called TO-BE models.

Developing the **TO-BE** process model is a challenging task because we must balance different factors. First, we have to define the objectives that we want to realize through process optimization. The most obvious objective can be that the process performs faster with less utilization of resources and people. The other objective can be to improve visibility into the process execution. Knowing the stage at which the process execution currently is can be helpful to the management as well as to the customers, who might even be able to track the process online. The objective of optimization can also result in improvements in the quality of products/services, better working conditions for employees, reduced impact on the environment, and so on.

Then, we have to identify where to start the optimization. To identify this, we use the data gathered in the process execution and control phases. The data gathered by BAM tools can be very helpful in identifying process bottlenecks in real time and in identifying activities or sets of activities that would be suitable for optimization.

Another way of identifying process optimization points is process simulation, which we mentioned earlier in this chapter. It is important to understand that BPM provides tools that propagate the data from BAM (process execution and control) into the process-modeling tool, where this real data can be used for process simulation. This is important because the tedious work of estimating process runtime parameters (activity execution, resource utilization, number of requests in a given period of time, and so on) is eliminated. At the same time, data gathered through BAM is much more accurate than estimates.

An important aspect of process optimization is new ideas. In closed organizational structures, the people involved in process optimization may be blinkered and may lack the ability to look at the process from a broader perspective. It would, therefore, be useful to recruit external consultants or other people from outside the organization, who can generate fresh ideas. Only in this way can we realize the full potential of process optimization.

However, when we gather new ideas, we should be careful to assess each new idea and find out whether it is realizable. We have to find a balance between new ideas and the level of changes a company's existing organizational structure can accommodate.

As employees do not like changes, we have to be careful in deciding how much change we want to introduce at one go. Ideally, we could change the process model considerably and try to implement changes in one large step. However, in many organizations, this has proved to be a failure because employees were unable to accommodate such changes overnight. If we do not invest enough time in communication with employees, they could start showing resistance to the changes. Therefore, it is often better to optimize in smaller steps and reach complete optimization over several stages.

On the other hand, we also have to be aware that process optimizations require modifications in the applications. Software modifications can be costly and they require time and resources. Therefore, from the IT perspective, it might be better to modify the applications at one go, that is, to optimize all at once.

Process optimizations often require changes in a company's organizational structure. We have to think about these changes too and obtain the necessary support from the top management. Otherwise, we will not be able to change the organizational structure.

Finally, we have to check whether the optimizations have been successful and whether we have achieved our goals. We do this by process simulation before it goes into production and after the process has been deployed to production through process control and monitoring.

Typical problems in process optimization

Process optimization is not an easy task. The following are some common problems that you might face during optimization:

- **Too little imagination**: When optimizing processes, we should not only improve bottlenecks in existing processes, but also include innovations and new approaches.
- **Noncritical experience consideration of other companies**: Although it is good to consider the experiences of other companies in process optimization, we have to be critical while comparing their experiences with ours and the facts related to our company. Therefore, before adopting them, we should assess whether these experiences are really best practices, and if they are, we should adapt them to our specifics.
- **Too much focus on IT**: When modeling or optimizing processes, we should not focus only on end-to-end support by IT. This may generate unrealistically high expectations. IT cannot solve all problems.
- **Praxis-relevance**: An optimized process model might seem perfect, but this does not guarantee that the process model will work perfectly in the real world. Therefore, we should put enough effort in process implementation; otherwise, we might end up with a failure.
- **Process metrics**: We should measure process-related metrics, such as KPIs, to be able to assess whether the process works efficiently. Without metrics, we will not be able to optimize processes because we will not be able to identify where the real problems are hiding.

With this, we have concluded our discussion on the BPM life cycle.

Oracle BPM Suite

In this book, we will use Oracle BPM Suite 12*c* to demonstrate the design principles for process-driven architectures. Oracle BPM Suite 12*c* provides comprehensive BPM tools, ranging from BA modeling, over business process modeling using BPMN, to BAM, analytics, and comprehensive integration with SOA, business rules, business events, and other aspects. For more technical information about Oracle BPM Suite 12*c*, please refer to `www.oracle.com/us/technologies/bpm/`.

In the next section, we will have a brief look at SOA.

How SOA and BPM fit together

To automate business processes, the challenge from the technical perspective converts to development of process applications, often referred to as composite applications. To be able to develop process/composite applications, that is, to compose business processes out of services, we need corresponding technologies.

SOA provides the technical architecture to develop end-to-end support for business processes. SOA achieves this objective by exposing an organization's IT assets as reusable business services that can be composed into processes on the one hand and can integrate and communicate more easily on the other hand.

SOA minimizes the semantic gap between process models and executable code. It achieves this objective by providing a common language to business analysts, IT architects, and developers. In this context, we should not forget the importance of **reuse**, which is the key to fast development of new solutions and minimized testing efforts (due to reuse of existing artifacts), as shown in the following figure:

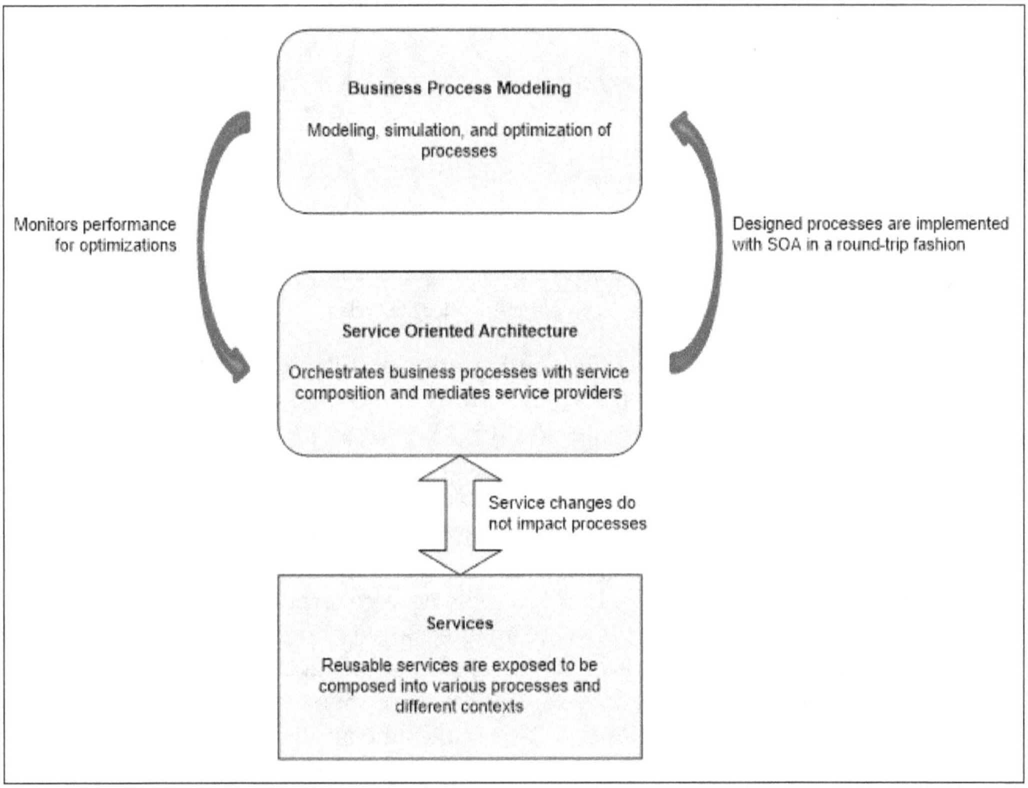

Figure 3: Relation between BPM and SOA

The service life cycle enables IT agility, while the process life cycle enables business agility. The following figure shows how the process and service life cycles match and how they interconnect:

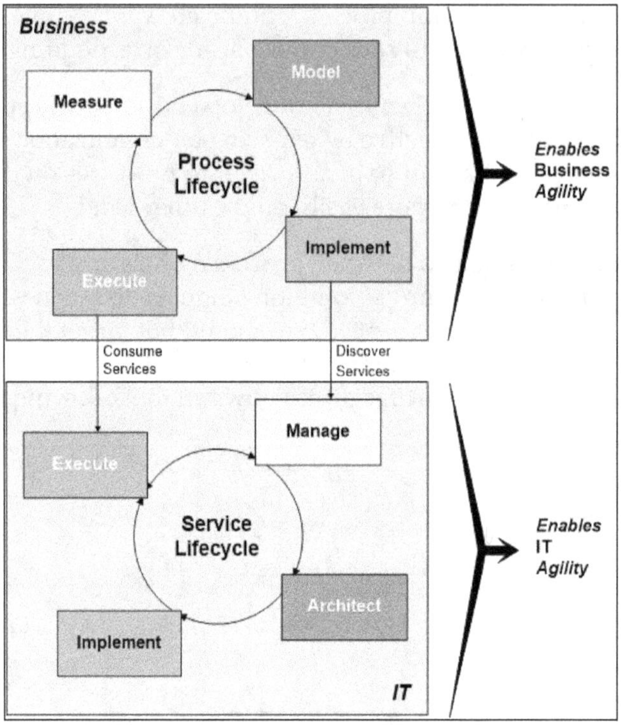

Figure 4: Process and service life cycle

From the bottom-up perspective, SOA is integration architecture. It provides technologies and approaches for the systematic integration of existing applications and the development of new solutions. With SOA, software architects develop a high-level integration architecture that uses common concepts to share data, information, and business logic between applications in a controlled, transactional manner using a service bus or other supporting technologies, such as rule engines, registries, and repositories. SOA is based on typed communication with messages that conform to common schemas. In SOA, in its new-generation avatar, business events have been introduced that provide an alternative approach to the realization of one of the most important goals of SOA—**loose coupling**. Loose coupling is an approach where different software services and components share the lowest common denominator of dependencies. This makes the application architecture more robust and resistant to changes. This will allow applications, components, and services to evolve and change with, or without, minimal effect on other applications, components, and services.

From this perspective, BPM and SOA are crucial to increasing the agility, improving time to market, and lowering the operational costs.

The following figure encapsulates this discussion:

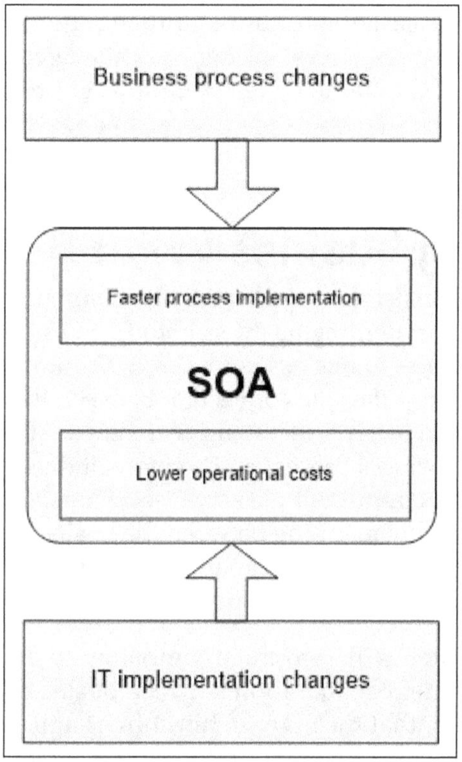

Figure 5: SOA for increased agility

Let's look at some of the benefits of this approach.

Agility

SOA can improve the agility of IT by enabling the development and adaption of business processes quickly and efficiently using the composition of business services, that is, through programming in the large. As business services are designed for reuse and integration, the design, development, and test efforts are considerably reduced. SOA promotes reuse, which leads to increased standardization and compliance at the enterprise level. SOA also minimizes the business-to-IT gap.

Resilience

SOA is concerned with the development of loosely-coupled information architectures, which shield business processes and services from changes and function independently of versions, locations, or technical details of applications systems. SOA also enables easier and less painful migration from legacy systems, consolidation of duplicated resources, master data management, multichannel access to applications, and the flexibility to develop variants of processes from the same base. Loose coupling enables IT assets to develop and evolve without the limitations imposed by interdependencies and point-to-point integrations.

Better aligning business with IT

SOA introduces a new dimension to application development with a major consequence—that of better aligning business with IT. SOA raises the level of abstraction from technologies to business services. SOA introduces business vocabulary to IT, which simplifies the connection between the IT and business people and enables them to better understand each other. Above all, SOA talks about applications in terms of business processes. Therefore, it does not require a complex mapping of requirements to represent the actual software. Further, SOA provides the ability to achieve two-way mapping between the business process model and the executable processes (and services). This guarantees better alignment between business and IT in the long run—even after several maintenance and upgrade cycles.

As SOA is related to BPM, it will encourage companies to think about business processes and achieve better collaboration between business analysts and IT. The business will discover that the SOA architecture is agile enough to adapt to requirements quickly, and IT will better understand the needs of the business. This will lead to business process optimizations and improvements and overall process excellence, which will have important impacts on the overall efficiency of the company.

New frontiers for SOA

SOA has been evolving over the years and expanded its reach beyond services, orchestrations, mediations, business rules, and human tasks. One of the major enhancements is business events, which are a part of **event-driven architecture (EDA)**. The EDA approach allows us to trigger services by events and not by explicitly invoking operations. This leads to even more loosely-coupled architectures, where a service component can trigger an event and several other components can subscribe to the event.

In addition to simple, event-based relations, events can also represent a means for integration with the **Internet of Things** (**IoT**) devices. In such cases, devices will generate large numbers of events, which need to be processed in real time or near real time. In such scenarios, we are not interested in individual events but often need to find patterns in event streams. This brings us to **complex event processing** (**CEP**).

The number of events and other data generated by business processes, composite applications, and services opens the opportunity for analysis of this data. This is where SOA connects to **big data**. Big data is particularly interesting for analyzing great amounts of data, which can be nonstructured or semistructured. Sometimes, this data needs to be analyzed in real or near real time, which brings us to **fast data**.

Furthermore, SOA has been designed around XML, web services, WSDL, and SOAP. Lately, another type of web service has emerged, **RESTful** services, or **REST** for short. REST services differ considerably from SOAP services. Instead of interface with operations, REST services use resources, which map URIs to specific actions. They also utilize HTTP methods. Although REST services can use XML format for payloads, it is more common that they use **JavaScript Object Notation** (**JSON**), which is simpler and easier to parse. Introducing REST to SOA has been a challenge lately and has been successfully solved on several SOA platforms, such as Oracle SOA Suite.

REST enablement is important for integration of BPM/SOA solutions with **mobile** devices and with modern **client-side web development** HTML5/JavaScript web pages, which are also known as one-page applications.

Mobile enablement is one of the key steps towards **multichannel** and **omnichannel** support. In contrast to multichannel support, where different channels for clients exists, possibly all leading to the same business logic in the backend, omnichannel support also provides true integration between channels on the backend, which means that a client can switch channels while retaining the session.

Although SOA is an integration architecture, new challenges have emerged to the integration with the **cloud**. As more applications use the **SaaS** model, integration with cloud applications and services needs careful consideration. Cloud integration can be solved with adapters or with **Integration Platform as a Service** (**IPaaS**). The cloud also provides new opportunities for integration and process support directly in the cloud.

The cloud is also related with the way applications are packaged and deployed. Traditionally, applications, even if designed and developed according to SOA, are packaged and deployed as single monolith archives (such as SAR, EAR, WAR, and JAR). Scaling such applications in the cloud is, however, not efficient. Therefore, modern applications are built following the **microservice** architecture that defines autonomous microservices as self-contained building blocks. Microservice architecture considerably improves flexibility and scalability and enables easier migration to new technologies and versions.

Finally, the emphasis on services and their interfaces has become even more important. As the number of APIs is growing, it is not only governance that matters, but the whole **API management** life cycle. Successful management of APIs is the key to the API economy and will become very important not only for Internet companies, but for all enterprises. The importance is denoted by the **API economy**.

Oracle SOA Suite

In this book, we will use Oracle SOA Suite 12*c*, which provides a comprehensive platform for SOA. Oracle SOA Suite provides full support for SOA and also addresses the new aspects of SOA. It provides Oracle Event Processing for EDA and CEP. It provides support for REST services, integration with the cloud, analytics integration, and even tools for API management. For more technical information on Oracle SOA Suite, please refer to `www.oracle.com/technetwork/middleware/soasuite/`.

Summary

In this chapter, we looked at the importance of business processes. We discussed why understanding business process is crucial for each organization. Modeling business processes is an important step towards understanding them. We have seen that business processes can be modeled at different levels of detail. Once modeled, such process models can be used for automation. Also, business processes should be optimized over time.

However, focusing on a single business process is not enough. Therefore, it is essential to design the business architecture, which provides the big-picture insight into an organizational structure. We have also seen that the business architecture should be considered as a part of the bigger enterprise architecture.

We gave you an overview of the BPM life cycle, which consists of business process design, process implementation, process execution and control, and process optimization. We focused on process design, where we explained the methodologies and notations. We mentioned adaptive case management. Further, we discussed business process modeling principles. We also discussed the process implementation, execution, and monitoring phases. We introduced BAM and KPIs and explained why it is useful for decision makers. We also identified some typical problems in process optimization.

We looked at the relation between SOA and BPM. SOA provides the technology platform for the implementation of the IT architecture based on business services, which is a foundation for business processes. SOA is an architecture that has introduced several important new concepts into application development. Lately, SOA has also introduced new building blocks, such as business events, EDA, CEP and integration with the IoT, big data and fast data, REST support and mobile enablement, omnichannel support, integration with the cloud, focus on microservice architecture, and API Management.

In the next chapter, we will look at the methodology for modeling business processes for SOA.

2

Modeling Business Processes for SOA – Methodology

This chapter describes the strategies and a methodology that can help us realize the benefits of BPM as a successful enterprise modernization strategy.

In this chapter, we will do the following:

- Provide the reader with a set of actions in the course of a complete methodology that they can incorporate in order to create the desired attractiveness towards broader application throughout the enterprise
- Describe organizational and cultural barriers to applying enterprise BPM and discuss ways to overcome them

The postmature birth of enterprise BPM

When enterprise architects discuss the future of the software landscape of their organization, they map the functional capabilities, such as customer relationship management and order management, to existing or new applications—some packaged and some custom. Then, they connect these applications by means of *middleware*. They typically use the notion of an integration middleware, such as an **enterprise service bus** (**ESB**), to depict the technical integration between these applications, exposing functionality as services, APIs, or, more trendy, "micro services".

These services are used by modern, more and more mobile frontends and B2B partners. For several years now, it has been hard to find a PowerPoint slide that discusses future enterprise middleware without the notion of a *BPM layer* that sits on top of the frontend and the SOA service layer. So, in most organizations, we find a slide deck that contains this visual box named *BPM*, signifying the aim to improve *process excellence* by automating business processes along the management discipline known as **business process management** (**BPM**).

Over the years, we have seen that the frontend layer often does materialize as a portal or through a modern mobile application development platform. The envisioned SOA services can be found living on an ESB or API gateway.

Yet, the component called *BPM* and the related practice of modeling executable processes has failed to finally incubate until now—at least in most organizations. BPM still waits for morphing from an abstract item on a PowerPoint slide and in a shelved analyst report to some automated business processes that are actually deployed to a business-critical production machine.

When we look closer—yes—there is a license for a BPM tool, and yes, some processes have even been automated, but those tend to be found rather in the less visible corners of the enterprise, seldom being of the concern for higher management and the *hot* project teams that work day and night on the next visible release. In short, BPM remains the hobby of some enterprise architects and the expensive consultants they pay.

Will BPM ever take the often proposed lead role in the middleware architect's tool box? Will it lead to a better, more efficient, and productive organization?

To be very honest, at the moment the answer to that question is rather *no* than *yes*. There is a good chance that BPM remains just one more of the silver bullets that fill some books and motivate some great presentations at conferences, yet do not have an impact on the average organization.

But there is still hope for enterprise BPM as opposed to a departmental approach to process optimization.

There is a good chance that BPM, next to other enabling technologies, will indeed be the driver for successful enterprise modernization. Large organizations all over the globe reengage with smaller and larger system integrators to tackle the process challenge. Maybe BPM as a practice needs more time than other items found in Gardner hype curves to mature before it's widely applied. This necessary level of higher maturity encompasses both the tools and the people using them.

Ultimately, this question of large-scale BPM adoption will be answered individually in each organization. Only when a substantive set of enterprises experience tangible benefits from BPM will they talk about it, thus growing a momentum that leads to the success of enterprise BPM as a whole. This positive marketing based on actual project and program success will be the primary way to establish a *force of attraction* towards BPM that will raise curiosity and interest in the minds of the bulk of the organizations that are still rather hesitant or ignorant about using BPM.

Oracle BPM Suite 12*c* – new business architecture features

New tools in Oracle BPM Suite 12*c* put BPM in the mold of **business architecture** (**BA**). This new version contains new BA model types and features that help companies to move out of the IT-based, rather technical view of business processes automation and into strategic process improvement. Thus, these new model types help us to embark on the journey towards enterprise BPM.

This is an interesting step in evolution of enterprise middleware—Oracle is the first vendor of a business process automation engine that moved up from concrete automated processes to strategic views on end-to-end processes, thus crossing the automation/strategic barrier.

BPM Suite 12*c* introduces cross-departmental business process views. Thereby, it allows us to approach an enterprise modeling exercise through top-down modeling. It has become an end-to-end value chain model that sits on top of processes. It chains separated business processes together into one coherent end-to-end view.

The value chain describes a bird's-eye view of the steps needed to achieve the most critical business goals of an organization. These steps comprise of business processes, of which some are automated in a BPMN engine and others actually run in packaged applications or are not automated at all. Also, BPM Suite 12*c* allows the capturing of the respective goals and provides the tools to measure them as KPIs and service-level agreements.

In order to understand the path towards these yet untackled areas, it is important to understand where we stand today with BPM and what this new field of *end-to-end process transparency* is all about. Yet, before we get there, we will leave enterprise IT for a moment and take a look at the nature of a game (any game) in order to prepare for a deeper understanding of the mechanisms and cultural impact that underpin the move from a departmental to an enterprise approach to BPM.

Football games – same basic rules, different methodology

Any game, be it a physical sport, such as football, or a mental sport, such as chess, is defined through a set of common rules. How the game is played will look very different depending on the level of the league it is played in. A Champions League football game is so much more refined than your local team playing at the nearby stadium, not to mention the neighboring kids kicking the ball in the dirt ground.

These kids will show creativity and pleasure in the game, yet the level of sophistication is a completely different ball game in the big stadium. You can marvel at the effort made to ensure that everybody plays their role in a well-trained symbiosis with their peers, all sharing a common set of collaboration rules and patterns. The team spent so many hours training the right combinations, establishing a deep trust. There is no time to discuss the meaning of an order shouted out by the trainer. They have worked on this common understanding of how to do things in various situations. They have established one language that they share. As an observer of a great match, you appreciate an elaborate art, not of one artist but of a coherent team.

No one would argue the prevalence of this continuum in the refinement and rising sophistication in rough physical sports. It is puzzling to know to which extent we, as players in the games of enterprise IT, often tend to neglect the needs and forces that are implied by such a continuum of rising sophistication.

The next sections will take a closer look at these BPM playgrounds and motivate you to take the necessary steps toward team excellence when moving from a small, departmental level BPM/SOA project to a program approach that is centered on a BPM and SOA paradigm.

Which BPM game do we play?

Game Silo BPM is the workflow or business process automation in organizational departments. It resembles the kids playing soccer on the neighborhood playground. After a few years of experience with automated processes, the maturity rises to resemble your local football team—yes, they play in a stadium, and it is often not elegant.

Game Silo BPM is a tactical game in which work gets done while management deals with reaching departmental goals. New feature requests lead to changed or new applications and the people involved know each other very well over many years under established leadership. Workflows are automated to optimize performance.

Game Enterprise BPM thrives for process excellence at Champions League. It is a strategic game in which higher management and business departments outline the future capability maps and cross-departmental business process models. In this game, players tend to regard the overall organization as a set of more or less efficient functional capabilities. One or a group of functional capabilities make up a department.

Game Silo BPM – departmental workflows

Today, most organizations use BPM-based process automation based on tools such as Oracle BPM Suite to improve the efficiency of the processes within departments. These processes often support the functional capability that this particular department owns by increasing its efficiency.

Increasing efficiency is to do more with less. It is about automating manual steps, removing bottlenecks, and making sure that the resources are optimally allocated across your process. The driving force is typically the team manager, who is measured by the productivity of his team. The key factor to reach this goal is the automation of redundant or unnecessary human/IT interactions. Through process automation, we gain insights into the performance of the process. This insight can be called *process transparency*, allowing for the constant identification of areas of improvement.

A typical example of the processes found in Game Silo BPM is an approval process that can be expressed as a clear path among process participants. Often, these processes work on documents, thus having a tight relationship with content management. We also find complex backend integration processes that involve human interaction only in the case of an exception.

The following figure depicts this siloed approach to process automation. Recognizing a given business unit as a silo indicates its closed and self-contained world.

A word of caution is needed: The term "silo" is often used in a negative connotation. It is important, though, to recognize that a closed and coherent team with no dependencies on other teams is a preferred working environment for many employees and managers. In more general terms, it reflects an archaic type of organization that we lean towards. It allows everybody in the team to indulge in what can be called *the siege mentality* we as humans gravitate to some coziness along the notion of a well-defined and manageable island of order.

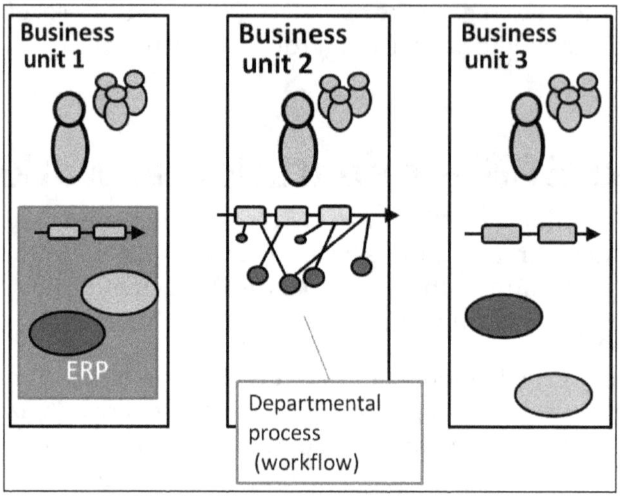

Figure 1: Workflow automation in departmental silos

As discussed in the introduction, there is a chance that BPM never leaves this departmental context in many organizations. If you are curious to find out where you stand today, it is easy to depict whether a business process is stuck in the silo or whether it's part of an enterprise BPM strategy. Just ask whether the process is aligned with corporate goals or whether it's solely associated with departmental goals and KPIs. Another sign is the lack of a methodology and of a link to cross-departmental governance that defines the mode of operation and the means to create consistent models that speak one common language.

To impose the enterprise architecture tools of Game Enterprise BPM on Game Silo BPM would be an overhead; you don't need them if your organization does not strive for cross-departmental process transparency.

Oracle BPM Suite 11*g* is made for playing Game Silo BPM

Oracle BPM Suite 11*g* provides all the tools and functionalities necessary to automate a departmental workflow. It is not sufficient to model business processes that span departmental barriers and require top-down process hierarchies.

The key components are the following:

- The BPMN process modeling tool and the respective execution engine
- The means to organize logical roles and depict them as swimlanes in BPMN process models
- The human-task component that involves human input in decision making
- The business rule for supporting automated decision making
- The technical means to call backend SOA services
- The wizards to create data mappings
- The process performance can be measured by means of **business activity monitoring (BAM)**

Oracle BPM Suite models processes in BPMN

Workflows are modeled on a pretty fine level of granularity using the standard BPMN 2.0 version (and later versions). BPMN is both business ready and technically detailed enough to allow model processes to be executed in a process engine. Oracle fittingly expresses the mechanism as *what you see is what you execute*.

Those workflows typically orchestrate human interaction through human tasks and functionality through SOA services. The next chapter discusses BPMN in greater detail.

In the next sections of this chapter, we will move our head out of the cocoon of the silo, looking higher and higher along the hierarchy of the enterprise until we reach the world of workshops and polished PowerPoint slides in which the strategy of the organization is defined.

Game Enterprise BPM

Enterprise BPM is a management discipline with a methodology typically found in **business architecture** (**BA**) and the respective **enterprise architecture** (**EA**) teams. Representatives of higher management and of business departments and EA teams meet management consultants in order to understand the current situation and the desired state of the overall organization.

Therefore, enterprise architects define *process maps*—a high-level view of the organization's business processes, both for the AS-IS and various TO-BE states. In the next step, they define the desired future state and depict strategies and means to reach it.

Business processes that generate value for the organization typically span several departments. The steps in these *end-to-end processes* can be mapped to the functional building blocks—the departments.

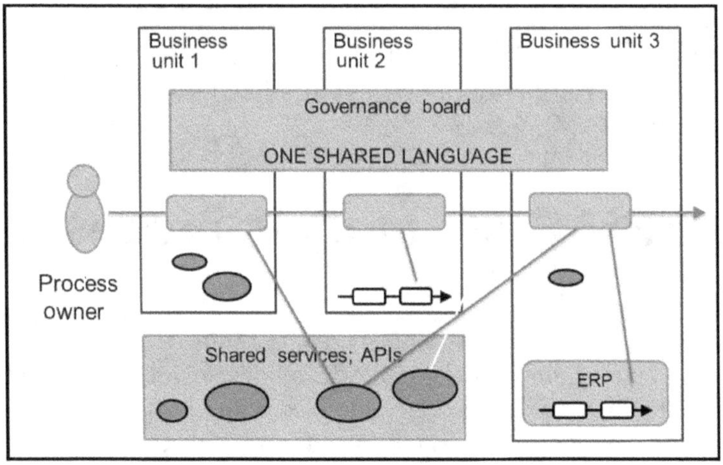

Figure 2: Cross-departmental business process needs an owner

The goal of Game Enterprise BPM is to manage enterprise business processes, making sure they realize the corporate strategy and meet the respective goals, which are ideally measured by key performance indicators, such as customer satisfaction, reduction of failure, and cost reduction.

It is a good practice to reflect on the cross-departmental efforts through the notion of a common or shared language that is spoken across departmental boundaries. A governance board is a great means to reach this capability in the overall organization.

Still wide open – the business/IT divide

Organizational change in the management structure is a prerequisite for the success of Game Enterprise BPM but is not a sufficient condition. Several business process management books describe the main challenge in enterprise BPM as the still-wide-open business/IT divide. There is still a gap between process understanding and ownership in Game Enterprise BPM and how automated process are modeled and perceived in departmental workflows of Game Silo BPM. Principles, goals, standards, and best practices defined in Game Enterprise BPM do not trickle down into everyday work in Game Silo BPM.

One of the biggest reasons for this divide is the fact that there is no direct link between the models and tools used in top management to depict the business strategy, IT strategy, and business architecture and the high-level value chain and between the process models and the models and artifacts used in enterprise architecture and from there, even software architecture.

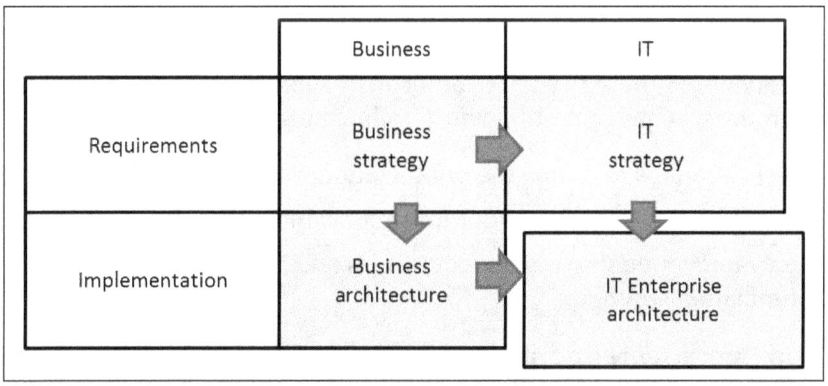

Figure 3: Gap between business architecture and IT enterprise architecture in strategic BPM

So, traditionally, organizations use specific business architecture or enterprise architecture tools in order to depict AS-IS and TO-BE high-level reflections of value chains, hierarchical business processes, and capability maps alongside application heat maps.

These models kind of *hang in the air*, they are not deeply grounded in real life. Business process models expressed in **event process chains** (**EPCs**), vision process models and other modeling types often don't really reflect the flows and collaboration structures of actual procedures of the office. This leads to the perception of business architecture departments as ivory towers with no, or weak, links to the realities of the organization.

On the other side, the tools and models of the IT enterprise architecture and software architecture speak a language not understood by the members of business departments. **Unified Modeling Language** (**UML**) is the most prominent set of model types that stuck in IT. However, while the UML class and activity diagrams promised to be valid to depict the nouns and stories of the business processes, their potential to allow a shared language and approach to depict joint vocabulary and views on requirements rarely materialized.

Until now, there has been no workflow tool vendor approaching these strategic enterprise-level models, bridging the business/IT gap.

Oracle BPM Suite 12*c* tackles Game Enterprise BPM

With BPM Suite 12*c*, Oracle is starting to engage in this domain. The approach Oracle took can be summarized as applying the *Pareto principle*: 80 percent of the needed features for strategic enterprise modeling can be found in just 20 percent of the functionality of those high-end, enterprise-level modeling tools. So, Oracle implemented these 20 percent of business architecture models:

- Enterprise maps to define the organizational and application context
- Value chains to establish a root for process hierarchies
- The strategy model to depict focus areas and assign technical capabilities and optimization strategies

The following figure represents the new features in Oracle BPM Suite 12*c* in the context of the Game Enterprise BPM methodology:

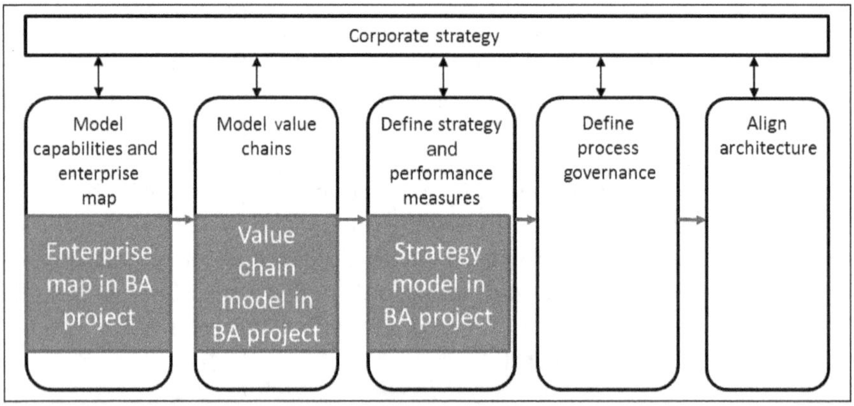

Figure 4: Oracle BPM Suite 12*c* new features in the context of the Game Enterprise BPM methodology

The preceding figure is based on the *BPTrends Process Change Methodology* introduced in the *Business Process Change* book by Paul Harmon.

These new features promise to create a link from higher-level process models and other strategic depictions into executable processes. This link could not be established until now since there are too many interface mismatches between enterprise tooling and workflow automation engines.

The new model types in Oracle BPM Suite 12*c* are, as discussed, a subset of all the features and model types in the EA tools. For this subset, these interface mismatches have been made obsolete: there is a clear trace with no tool disruption from the enterprise map to the value chain and associated KPIs down to the BPMN process that are automated. These features have been there in the EA and BPM tools before. What is new is this undisrupted trace.

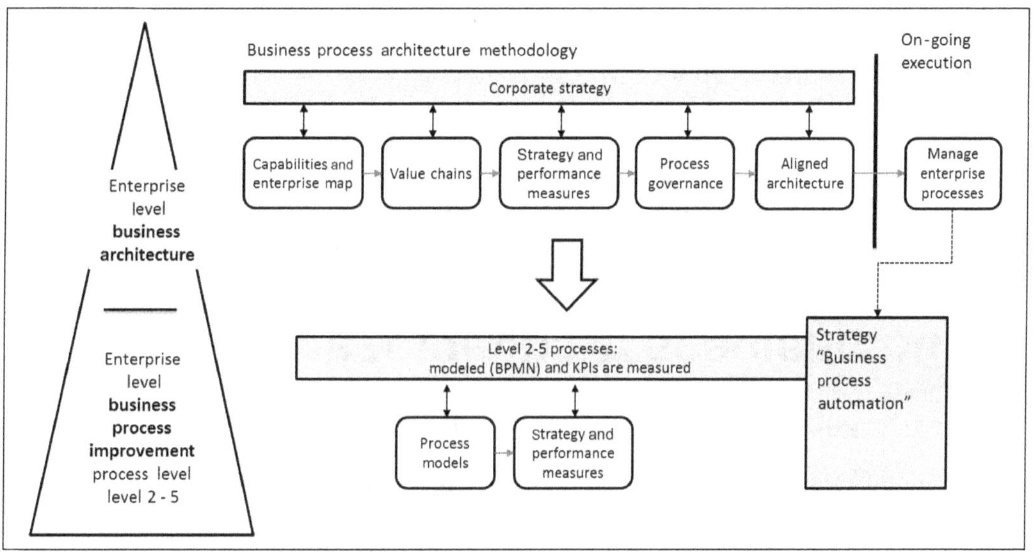

Figure 5: Undisrupted trace from the business architecture to executable processes

The preceding figure is based on the *BPTrends Process Change Methodology* introduced in the *Business Process Change* book by Paul Harmon.

This holistic set of tools that brings together aspects from modeling time, design time, and runtime makes it more likely to succeed in finally bridging the business/IT gap.

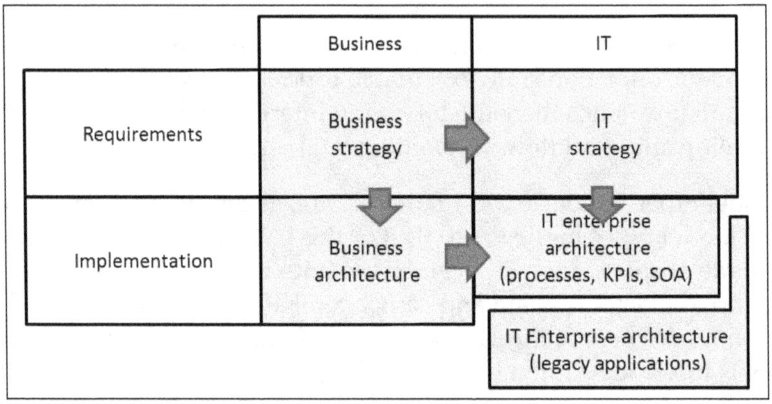

Figure 6: Tighter links from business and strategy to executable software and processes

Today, we do not live in a perfect world. To understand to which extent this gap is closed, it helps to look at how people work. If there is a tool to depict enterprise strategy, end-to-end business processes, business capabilities, and KPIs that are used in daily work and that have the means to navigate to lower-level models, then we have come quite far. The features of Oracle BPM Suite 12*c*, which are discussed below, are a step in this direction but are not the end of the journey.

Using business architect features

The process composer is a business user-friendly web application. From the login page, it guides the user in the spirit of a business architecture methodology.

All the models that we create are part of a "space". On its entry page, the main structure is divided into business architecture models in *BA projects*, which are described in this chapter, and the BPMN type of business process models in "BPM projects", which are described in the following chapter.

It is a good practice to start with an enterprise map that depicts the business capabilities of our organization. The rationale is that the functions the organization is made of tend to be more stable and less a matter of interpretation and perspective than any business process view.

Enterprise maps can be used to put those value chains and process models into the organizational and application landscape context.

Oracle suggests organizing the business capabilities into three segments. Thus, the default enterprise map model is prepopulated through three default lanes: core, management, and support. In many organizations, this structure is feasible as it is up to you to either use them or create your own lanes.

Then we can define within each lane the key business capabilities that make up the core business processes.

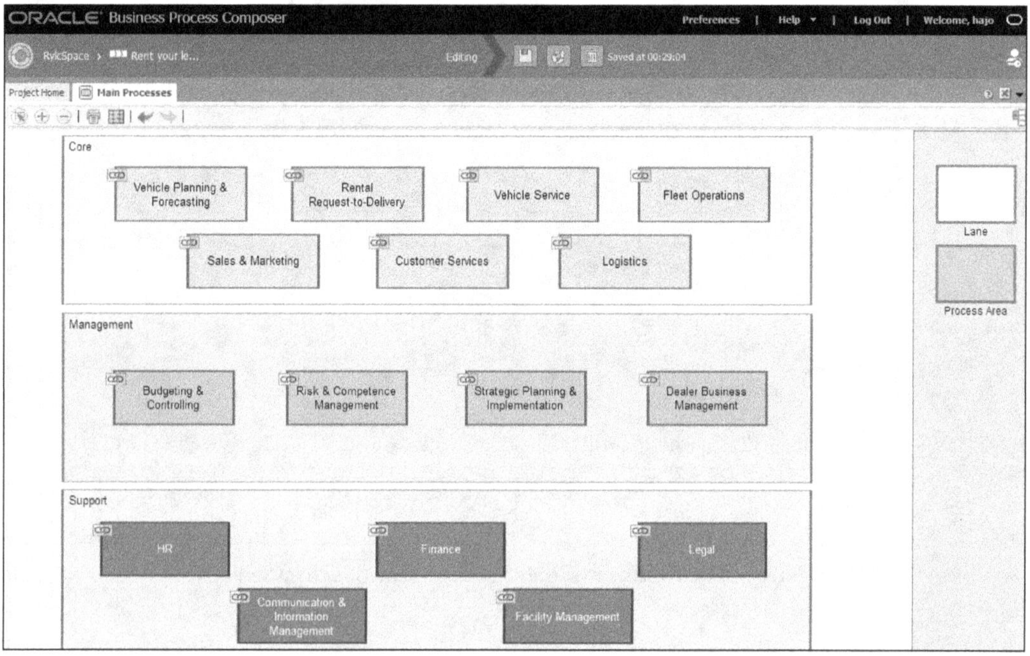

Figure 7: Enterprise map of RYLC depicting key business capabilities

Properties of BA models

Each element (goal, objective, strategy) within the model can be enriched with business properties, such as actual cost, actual time, proposed cost and proposed time. These properties are part of the impact analysis report that can be generated to analyze the BA project.

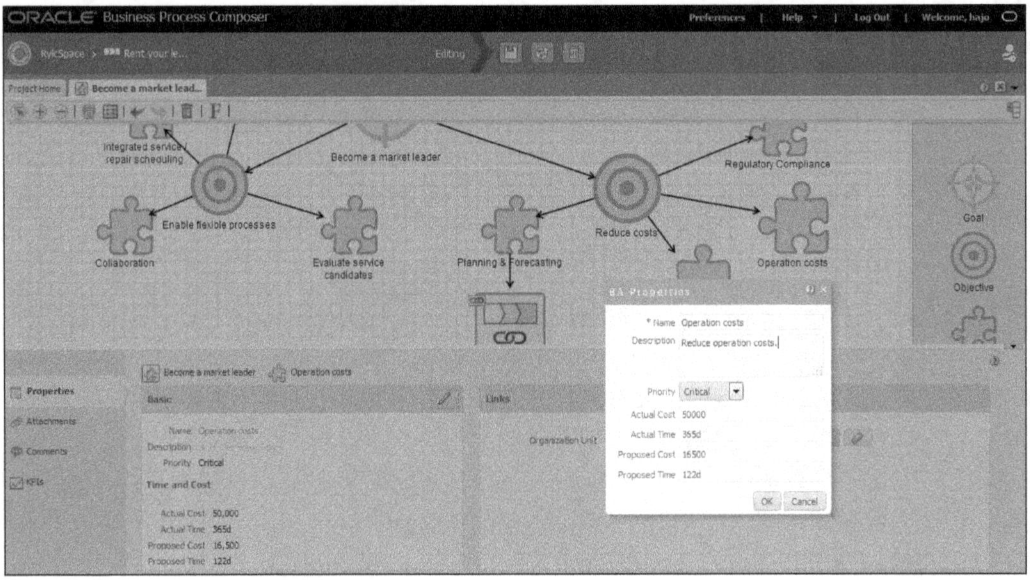

Figure 8: Use properties to specify SLAs and other BA characteristics

Depicting organizational units

Within RYLC as an organization, we now depict its departments as organizational units. We can adorn goals to each of the units, which depict its function and the role it plays in the concert of the overall ecosystem. This association of a unit to a goal is expressed via links to goals defined in the strategy model.

These goals will be used for the impact analysis reports that show the impact of changes on the organizational or procedural changes. It is possible to create several organization units as shown in the following screenshot:

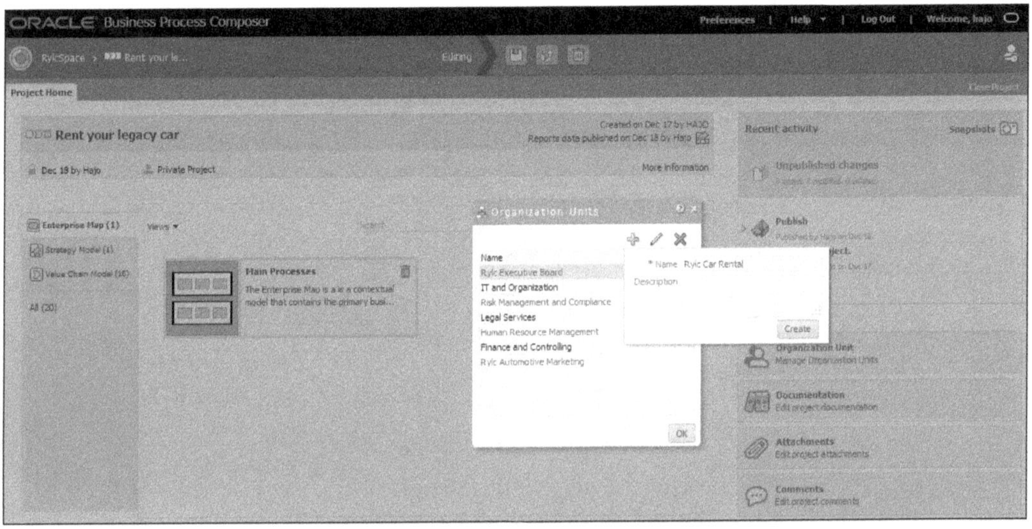

Figure 9: Define a set of organization units

Value chains

A value chain model forms the root of a process hierarchy. A value chain consists of one direct line of steps, no gateways, and no exceptions. The modeler in Oracle BPM Suite allows each step in the chain to depict associated business goals and **key performance indicators (KPIs)** that can be used to measure the organization's performance rather than the details of departmental performance.

The value chain model is a very simple one depicting the flow of the most basic business process steps. Each step is a business process in its own right. On the level of the chain, there is no decision making expressed. This resembles a business process expressed in BPMN that has only direct lines and no gateways.

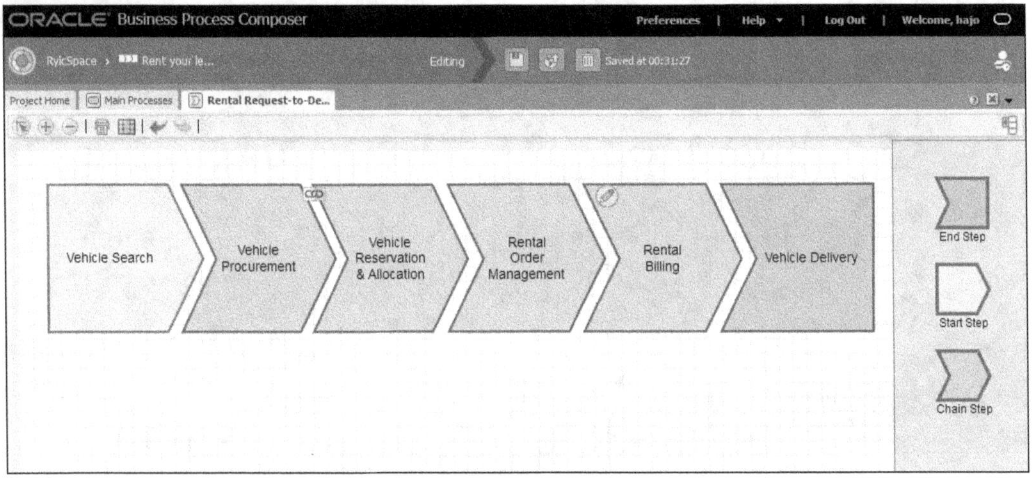

Figure 10: Creation of a new value chain model called "Rental Request-to-Delivery"

The value chain model type allows the structuring of your business processes into a hierarchy with a value chain forming the topmost level.

Strategy models

Strategy models that can be used to further motivate their KPIs are depicted at the value chain level.

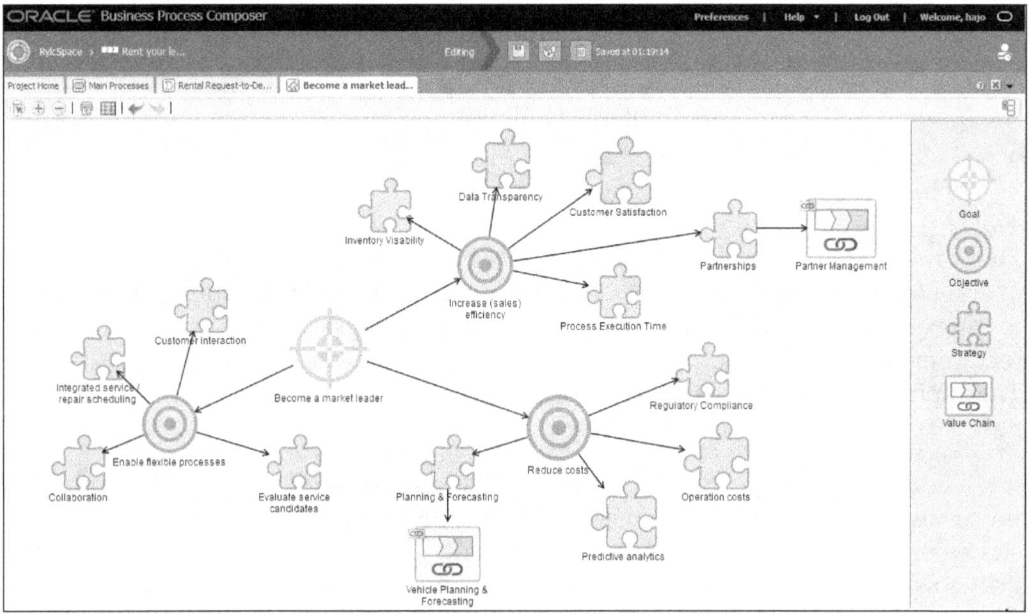

Figure 11: Building the strategy model for the strategy "Become a market leader"

These visual maps leverage existing process documentation and match it with current business trends and existing reference models. These models depict processes and associated organizational aspects encompassing cross-departmental views on higher levels and concrete processes down to level 3. From there, they prioritize distinct processes and decide on one of several modernization strategies—process automation being just one of several!

So, in the proposed methodology in the following diagram, in the **Define strategy and performance measures (KPIs)**, the team down-selects for each business process or even subprocess one or several means to improve process efficiency or transparency.

Typically, these means are defined as "supporting capabilities". These are a technique, a tool, or an approach that helps to modernize a business process. A few typical supporting capabilities are mentioned here:

- Explicit process automation (the topic of the next chapter)
- Implicit process handling and automation inside a packaged application, such as SAP ERP or Oracle Siebel
- Refactored COTS existing application
- Business process outsourcing
- Business process retirement

The way toward establishing these supporting capabilities is defined through a list of potential *modernization strategies*. Several of the modernization strategies relate to the existing applications that support a business process, such as refactoring, replacement, retirement, or re-interfacing of the respective supporting applications. The application modernization strategy that we are most interested in this and the next chapter is *establish explicit automated process*.

It is a best practice to create a high-level process map and define for each of the processes whether to leave it as it is or to depict one of several modernization strategies. When several modernization strategies are found for one process, we can drill down into the process through a hierarchy and stop at the level on which there is a disjunct modernization strategy.

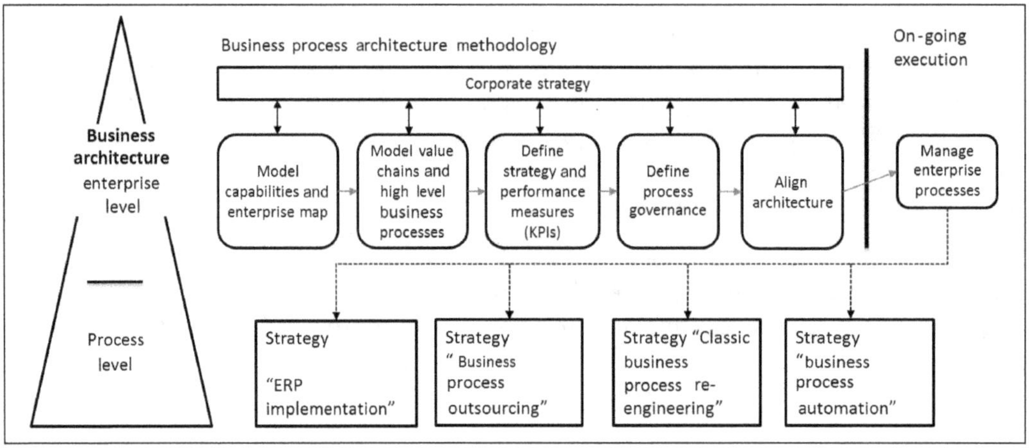

Figure 12: Business process automation as just one of several process optimization strategies

> The preceding figure is based on the *BPTrends Process Change Methodology* introduced in the *Business Process Change* book by Paul Harmon.

Again, just one of these technical capabilities in strategic BPM is the topic of this chapter and book: process automation. It is not feasible to suggest automating all the business processes of any organization.

Key performance indicators

Within a BA project (strategy and value chain models), there are three different types of KPIs that can be defined:

- Manual KPI: This allows us to enter a known value
- Rollup KPI: This evaluates an aggregate of the child KPIs
- External KPI: This provides a way to include KPI data from applications other than BPM Suite, such as SAP, E-Business Suite, PeopleSoft, and so on.

Additionally, KPIs can be defined on a BPMN process level, which is not covered in this chapter.

KPIs in the value chain step level

The following are the steps to configure the KPIs in the value chain step level:

1. Open the value chain model *Rental Request-to-Delivery*.
2. Right-click on the **Vehicle Reservation & Allocation** chain step, and select **KPI**.
3. Click on the + (plus) sign to create a manual KPI, as illustrated in the next screenshot.

The following image shows the configuration of the KPIs:

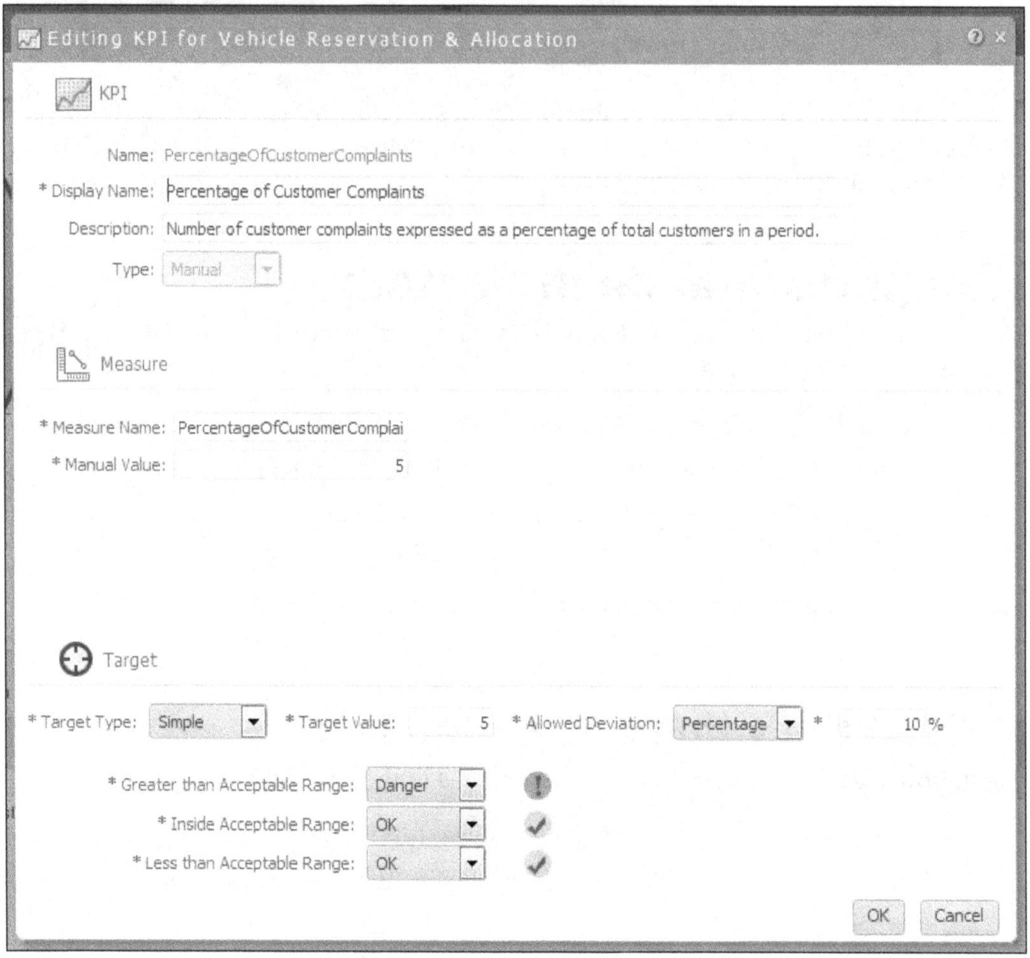

Figure 13: Configuring a KPI

Why we need a new methodology for Game Enterprise BPM

Now, Game Enterprise BPM needs to be played everywhere. This implies that Game Silo BPM needs to diminish, meaning it needs to be replaced, gradually, through *managed evolution*, league by league, aiming for excellence at Champions League.

We can't play Game Enterprise BPM with the same culture of ad hoc, joyful creativity, which we find in Game Silo BPM. We can't just approach our colleague; let's call him Ingo Maier, who we know has drawn the process model for a process we are interested in. We can't just walk over to the other desk to him, asking him about the meaning of an unclear section in the process. That is because in Game Enterprise BPM, Ingo Maier, as a person whom we know as part of our team Silo, does not exist anymore.

We deal with process models, with SOA services, with a language defined somewhere else, in another department. This is what makes it so hard to move up in BPM leagues.

Hiding behind the buzz term "agile" does not help. In order to raise BPM maturity up, when we move from Game Silo BPM to Game Enterprise BPM, the organization needs to establish a set of standards, guidelines, tools, and modes of operations that allow playing and succeeding at Champions League. Additionally, we have to define the modes of operations and the broad steps that lead to a desired state. This formalization of collaboration in teams should be described, agreed on, and lived as *our BPM methodology*. The methodology thrives for a team in which each player contributes to one coherent game along well-defined phases.

Political change through Game Enterprise BPM

The political problem with a cross-departmental process view becomes apparent if we look at the way organizations distribute political power in Game Silo BPM. The heads of departments form the most potent management layer while the end-to-end business process has no potent stakeholder.

Thus, it is critical for any Game Enterprise BPM to establish a good balance of de facto power with process owners acting as stakeholders for a cross-departmental process view. This fills the void in Game Silo BPM of end-to-end process owners. With Game Enterprise BPM, the focus shifts from departmental improvements to the KPIs and improvement of the core business processes.

Pair modeling the value chains and business processes

Value chains and process models down to a still very high-level layer, such as a layer 3, can be modeled by process experts without involving technically skilled people. They should omit all technical details.

To provide the foundation for automated processes, we need to add more details about domain knowledge and some technical details. Therefore, these domain process experts meet with BPM tool experts to jointly define the next level of detail in BPMN. In an analogy to the practice of *pair development* in agile methodologies, you could call this kind of collaboration *pair modeling*.

Ideally, the process expert(s) and the tool expert look at the same screen and discuss how to improve the flow of the process model, while the visual representation evolves into variances, exceptions, and better understanding of the involved business objects.

For many organizations that are used to a waterfall process, this is a fundamentally new way of requirement gathering that might be a challenge for some. The practice is an analogy of the *customer on site* practice in agile methodologies. This new way of close collaboration for process modeling is crucial for the success of BPM projects since it allows us to establish a deep and shared understanding in a very pragmatic and productive way.

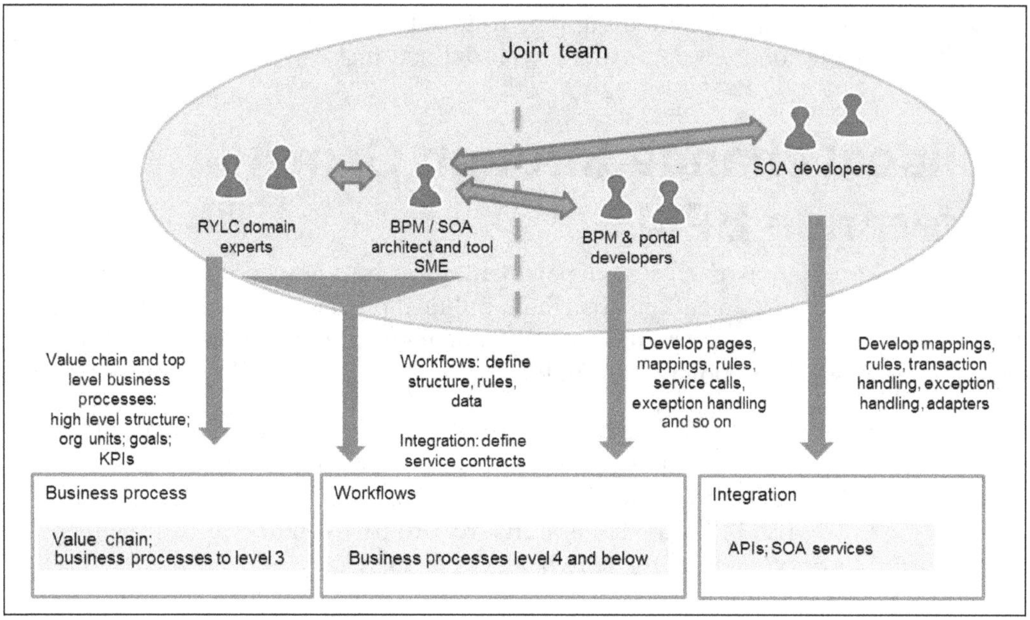

Figure 14: Roles and successful modes of collaboration

When the process is modeled in sufficient detail to clearly depict an algorithmic definition of the flow of the process and all its variances, the model can be handed over to BPM developers. They add all the technical bells and whistles, such as data mapping, decision rules, service calls, and exception handling.

Portal developers will work on their implementation of the use cases. SOA developers will use Oracle SOA Suite to integrate with backend systems, therefore implementing SOA services.

The discussed notion of a handover from higher-level business process models to development teams can also be used to depict the line at which it might make sense to outsource parts of the overall development.

Using guidelines and conventions to establish broad understanding

Departmental workflows that do not participate in an enterprise BPM program but are developed in isolation differ in one regard dramatically from enterprise BPM. They have been created in one small team. This implies that whenever somebody needs to understand certain aspects in the business process, they know its author and can approach him in informal ways via e-mail, telephone, or just walk up to his desk.

What happens if we apply the same type of modeling and collaboration to enterprise-level business process management?

Typically, we will spread that modeling work over different teams in a way that for a given moment in time, each team or group will work on one process model.

Inside each of these groups, a certain joint understanding establishes itself over time. Members will invest time and thinking in finding a way to express the complex aspects of the process using their own ways to structure it and name activities and data types inside their team. In other words, the group establishes their own language.

This is exactly the way departmental workflows have been developed in the past. The issue with this approach will become obvious when we think about what happens if members of group B, that is, from outside group A, attempt to understand the business process created by group A. In a way, this is similar to a Frenchman attempting to understand a sentence written in the German language. In order to grasp its meaning, he has no chance but to learn German. Therefore, the most important advice for any organization starting the journey on enterprise BPM is to tackle the void that is left when we do not know the author of a model or even a piece of code anymore. We have to find ways to establish models, vocabularies, and requirement documents that are self-explanatory.

For process models that work on complex structures, this can only be achieved by means of a consistent set of modeling guidelines and conventions.

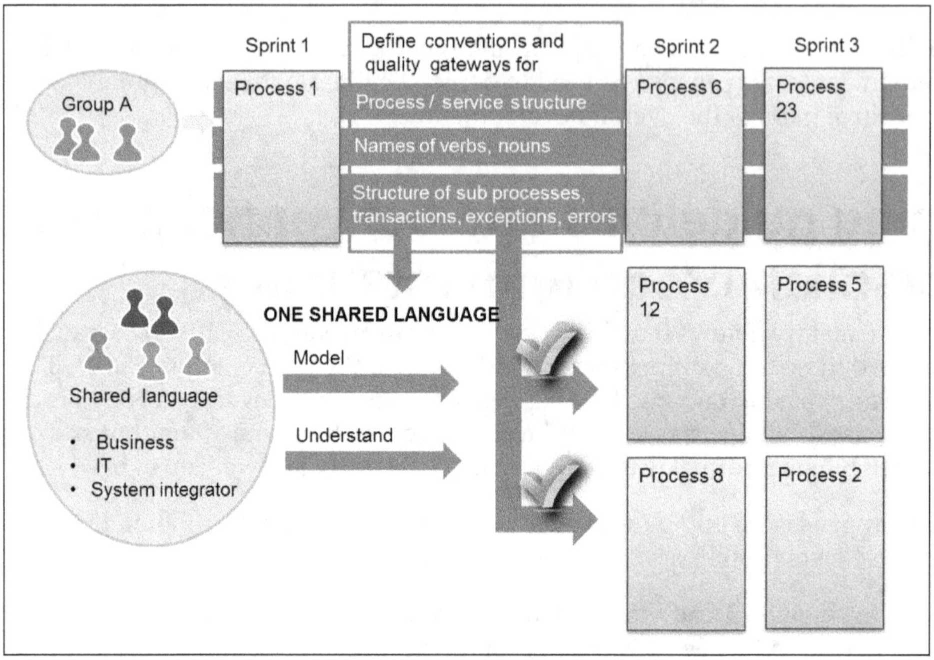

Figure 15: Standardization and homogenization of the solution benefit its success and acceptance

The governance model makes sure that each process model follows these conventions by passing through its quality gateway. This can be a set of critical conventions that need to be checked off by a dedicated process quality team. Establishing modeling standards that define structural and naming conventions is a prerequisite for standardized models that are consistently and easily understandable since they follow the same patterns.

Here are some examples of conventions:

- Names for roles in BPMN *pools* and *lanes*
- Names of verbs
- Names of nouns
- Version
- When exception, when variance
- When subprocess (inline and distinct)

BPM and SOA governance can help to ensure that these guidelines and conventions are consistently followed.

The BPM methodology introduced in the chapter is depicted in the following image. Its key feature is a well-defined relationship between activities on a strategic level, near the board of executives to steer the organization through times of change and on a local level, where actual people interact with systems and each other along the lines of a well-understood business process. In the strategy section on the enterprise level, BPM Suite 12*c* offers the first features to tackle the key activities that we discussed earlier. Here, we model the process hierarchy down and adorn the most fundamental KPI, based on which the organization wishes to measure its performance.

The *redesign* section of the methodology looks at concrete processes using concrete means that real people and services or systems are involved. Here, we analyze the AS-IS state, define the TO-BE state, and implement it as a executable BPMN process. There is an ongoing activity that looks at and manages all processes on a corporate level and decides, based on their performances, which of them should be run through the process redesign cycle again.

BPM Methodology for Oracle BPM Suite

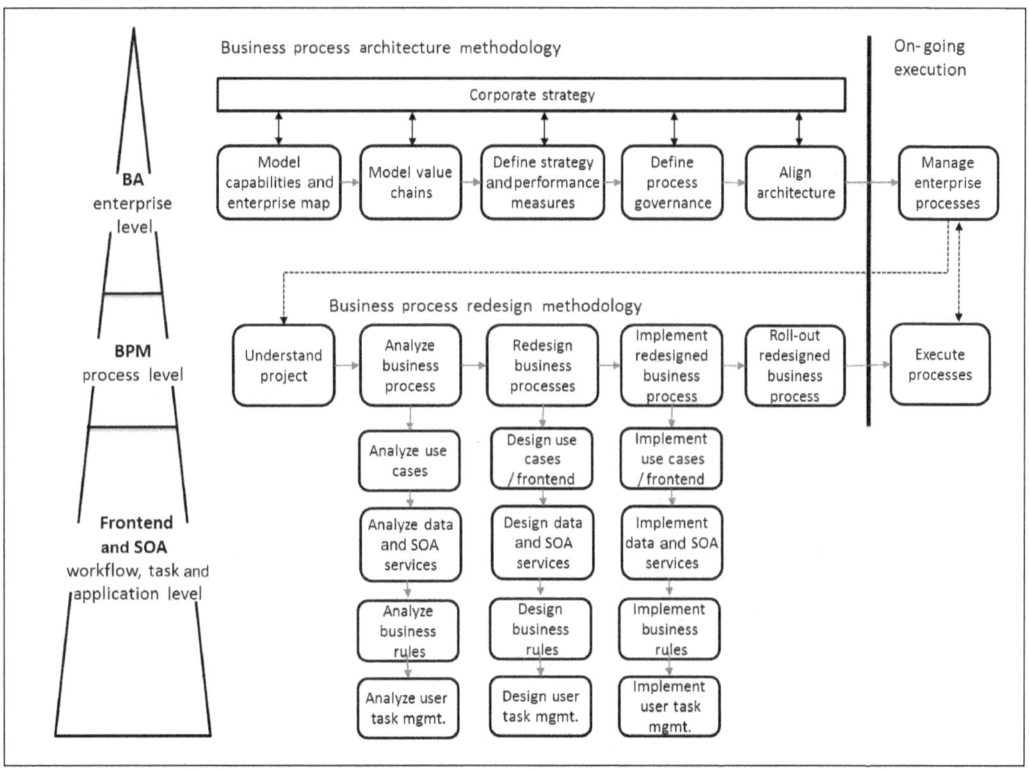

Figure 16: The enterprise BPM methodology covers the entire gamut from strategic to tactical

> The preceding figure is based on the *BPTrends Process Change Methodology* introduced in the *Business Process Change* book by Paul Harmon.

The key projects/activities in a BPM program are as follows:

- Establish new roles: workflow, owner, modeler, architect, designer, and quality governance
- Establish the workflow methodology and new modes of collaboration, from business models to executable
- Plan the first processes along APIs and services
- Define the means to measure KPIs in workflows
- Solidify tool selection through a prototype
- Create a reference implementation in tool selection
- Conduct the first workflow project (a model to test)
- Define conventions for models, names, user roles, versions, structure, design, deployment and testing
- Design event-collecting mechanisms through the notification engine and how workflows consume notifications from the engine
- Establish quality gateways, governance and training
- Establish operations model (plan early!)

Summary

In this chapter, we saw how BPM as an approach to model, automate, and optimize business process is typically applied rather on a departmental level. We saw how BPM Suite 12*c* introduced new features that allow us to cross the bridge towards the top-down, cross-departmental, enterprise-level BPM. We depicted the key characteristics of the enterprise BPM methodology, which aligns corporate or strategic activities with actual process automation projects.

We learned the importance of modeling standards and guidelines, which should be used to gain business process insight and understanding on broad levels throughout the enterprise. The goal is to establish a shared language to talk about the capabilities and processes of the overall organization and the services it provides to its customers.

The role of data in SOA that will support business processes was understood with a critical success factor being the definition of the business data model that, along with services, will form the connection between the process layer, user interface layer, and the services layer. We understood how important it is to separate application logic from service logic and process logic to ensure the benefits of a process-driven architecture are realized.

In the next chapter, we will get more concrete, showing how to actually design and implement automated business processes that guide people through a chain of steps in BPMN and how to define something more complex, such as a law service, which orchestrates a chain of service calls in BPEL. We will see how implementation details are added to the abstract services as composite applications. In subsequent chapters, we will see further benefits from separating our service architecture into layers and ensuring that presentation services (for use in human task user interfaces and mobile access to the services) and business services (for use in process execution) are built for a purpose and are ready to bring about a change in the life cycle that this usage dictates.

3

BPMN for Business Process Modeling

This chapter will introduce the foundations of business process modeling using a standard-based approach. In this chapter, we will discuss the concepts of using **Business Process Model and Notation 2 (BPMN2)**, a standard developed by the **Object Management Group (OMG)**. BPMN has become the de facto standard for modeling business processes. With version 2, it has gained the capability not only to model but also to execute processes—thus, it has become an executable language, which allows modeling business processes on different levels of decomposition, from strategy modeling all the way to modeling executable business processes.

Business process classification and BPMN

Business process modeling is aimed at capturing a range of information pertaining to how a business works and making this information available to a wide variety of stakeholders. This means that processes mapped in BPMN should easily be comprehensible across the organizational hierarchy. BPMN is therefore designed to cover a wide array of usages in its notation and allows the modeling of end-to-end business processes.

In general, BPMN can be used to model business processes, which are also called orchestrations. Furthermore, BPMN can be used to model choreographies and collaborations:

- Business processes (orchestrations) include:
    - Private business processes
      Private non-executable (internal) business processes
      Private executable (internal) business processes
    - Public business processes
- Choreographies
- Collaborations, which can include
    - Processes and/or
    - Choreographies

In most cases, as in this book, BPMN is used as a standard notation designed to model most kinds of processes used in an organization. Today, most organizations use BPMN to create a process repository for all of their processes. Hence, the range of processes mapped by BPMN can be categorized depending on the business usage, as described in the following sections.

Strategic or operational

Based on the level of a given business process, it could be categorized as strategic or operational. Typically, an organization will define high-level strategies, which will be decomposed to lower levels until a representation that can be implemented is reached.

As explained in the previous chapter, strategy modeling is supported in BPM Suite using strategy models. For example, gaining leadership status in online retail in the UK could be a strategic intent of an organization. These business strategies are further decomposed to a set of goals, which, if fulfilled, will help achieve the strategy. For example, reducing item delivery time can be one of the goals.

At the next level, we usually define the main business functions of an organization that are instrumental in the achievement of the goals. These business functions are typically represented using block diagrams. In BPM Suite, enterprise maps can be used. For example, to reduce item delivery time, the main business function to focus on would be the 'supply chain department', and other functions such as marketing and sales, which are part of the end-to-end order to cash process.

At this level, we can also have very high-level business process diagrams to provide an abstract view of the end-to-end operational process. Such processes will typically go through a series of decompositions before they reach an implementable stage.

These activities will again be further decomposed to add more details to the business process diagrams until we reach a stage where we can expose these business process diagrams to a BPM for implementation.

Process type

A business process can also be classified based on its type and the extent of the requirement for automation. In the BPM world, processes can be categorized as human-centric processes that mainly require human intervention for the process to move from one state to another. An example of such a process could be an underwriting process in insurance, where the underwriter needs to gather customer information before deciding on the insurance coverage and premiums. Similarly, there could be processes that are more automated, say a financial trading process, where the trade settlements between parties could be automated by integrating multiple systems to ensure minimal human intervention. Processes can also be categorized according to some other factors, such as how document-centric the process is or whether the process requires ad hoc case management. The categorization of the process in this manner is typically done during the initiation of a BPM project as the choice of the technology platform will depend on the process types (technology providers are still consolidating their offerings to cover all aspects of process automation).

Process scope

Typically, the business process scope could be limited to the organization. This is called a private business process. A business process could also be a collaboration process that involves interfacing with external parties, such as customers, suppliers, partners, and so on. This is called a public process.

In the case of private processes, the scope is to map out the operational processes for process improvement and implementation. Examples of private processes are the employee performance appraisal process, the ordering process, or the car rental process that we are using throughout this book. Private processes can be executable or non-executable.

In the case of public processes, where external parties interact with the organization process, the scope becomes larger, and this will require careful thinking about how the process choreography will happen across various external entities. In this case, all of them will have their own application infrastructure, which in turn, will pose its own interoperability challenges. In BPMN, a public process represents these interactions or sequence of activities as message flows and highlights the touch points between the entities involved. Typically, standards such as RosettaNet, ebXML, and so on would be mapped to a public process defined in BPMN.

Business process diagrams

In BPMN, there is a set of *core elements* that has been defined in a business process diagram, allowing users to start creating the essential gist of a process. These core elements can be further elaborated to take care of the complexities, while still maintaining the standard look and feel of the diagrams.

Core elements are subdivided into five categories, each of which contains a specific set of elements:

- Flow objects
    - Events
    - Activities
    - Gateways
- Connecting objects
    - Sequence flows
    - Message flows
    - Associations
    - Data associations
- Data
    - Data objects
    - Data inputs
    - Data outputs
    - Data stores
- Swimlanes
    - Pools
    - Lanes

- Artifacts
    - Groups
- Text annotations

Flow objects consist of the backbone elements in a business process diagram and are used to represent the basic behavior of any process. These elements are events, activities, and gateways.

Events	
Activities	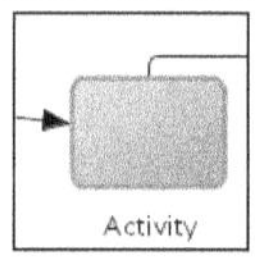
Gateways	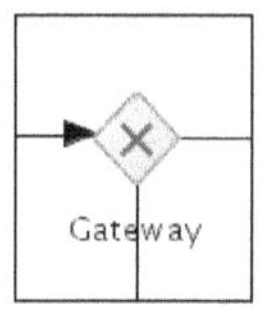

Figure 1: BPMN flow objects

Events represent the various states relevant for the business process, such as the start of the process, wait time in a process, termination of a process, and so on. Activities denote the work conducted as part of the business process. Gateways are used to represent the decision points where a split or join takes place in the flow of control.

Swimlanes represent the organizational relationships within a business process diagram. Pools usually represent the organizations that interact in a business process, while lanes denote the various departments within an organization.

For modelers who want to create an overview business process for their readers, use of the core elements of BPMN should be enough.

Deeper analysis of BPMN elements

Having looked at the core elements of BPMN from an understanding perspective, it is now essential to understand the various elements in detail and see what extensions BPMN provides to each of the elements to create truly illustrative and complete business process diagrams. Business analysts will realize that BPMN, apart from allowing easy process building, also provides sufficient detail and variety to allow a modeler to capture the complexities of real-life processes. It is also essential to understand how understanding these elements in detail will help the designers of business process and the respective IT teams later on to provide enough detail in a process to allow successful mapping from the process design to its execution in a BPM engine. Let's understand in some detail the main BPMN elements.

Events

Events play a vital role in modeling with BPMN. The comprehensive coverage of events makes BPMN more appropriate as a business modeling language than its counterparts. Events, as we have discussed, define how an organization will respond to a situation through its business processes. Events will usually trigger a flow or will generate a result. Events can trigger-start a particular process, for example, the *customer application form received* event starts the *opening a bank account* process. Alternatively, it could be an intermediate event used to delay the execution of the process, for example, an event of *wait five seconds* prior to the *send response to customer* activity. Finally, it could be an end event, say *account open complete*, which completes a given process. So, depending on where an event occurs in a process, we can divide them into three types:

- **Start:** This indicates the start of a process
- **Intermediate:** These are events that occur in between a process
- **End**: This is an event signifying the end of a process

Events come in two flavors—catching and throwing events:

- Events that catch a trigger are event consumers or event sinks. All start events and some intermediate events are catching events.
- Events that throw a result are event producers or event sources. All end events and some intermediate events are throwing events. Events that are thrown may be caught by another event that catches a trigger.

Furthermore, events can be interrupting or non-interrupting. An interrupting event will interrupt the activity which it is attached to, while a non-interrupting event will happen while the activity is still going on.

Events are further represented by types (none, message, timer, error, cancel, compensation, conditional, link, signal, multiple, and terminate).

Activities

Simply put, an activity denotes a unit of work that is performed. Activities act as the major components. A series of activities undertaken in order to achieve an objective with clear starting and stopping points is a process. From a process perspective, any activity can be categorized as atomic or compound. An activity would be an atomic activity or task if it cannot be further decomposed, and performs a single atomic action. On the other hand, *conduct interview* would be a compound activity or a subprocess if it involves several subactivities, for example, *analyze resume*, *ask questions*, *analyze answers*, *decide next steps*, and so on, to get the work done. In a process diagram, the representation of a process is hierarchical in nature, that is, a given process can have multiple subprocesses. This also allows the process modeler to organize complex business processes in a decomposed fashion, affording easy maintenance and navigation. Any given business process diagram can contain three types of activities: **process**, **subprocess**, and **task**. In BPMN, subprocess and task are represented as rounded rectangles. The activity notation changes with the type of activity and what happens within that particular activity.

Subprocess

In a parent process, a given subprocess will be represented with a plus sign inside the rectangle. This is also called the *collapsed process*, with a plus sign denoting that the given activity is further elaborated in a separate diagram. This can be seen in the following figure:

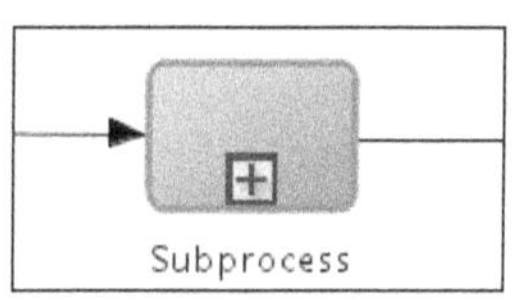

Figure 2: Subprocess

The collapsed process could be represented as an 'expanded process', which requires the details of the subprocess to be made available inside the given activity rectangle. Typically, depending on how a modeling tool implements this feature, it is either initiated by clicking on the plus sign or navigating to the subprocess. This can be used to flatten the process diagram to show the details for a process in a single diagram. This makes it easier to visualize the complete process. However, in some practical scenarios, a large diagram could be too cluttered if represented by expanding all subprocesses. The use of expanded subprocesses is also beneficial while visualizing exception flows and provides context to a set of activities inside a subprocess.

Further, a subprocess can have:

- **The collapsed subprocess**: This is represented with a plus sign. The collapsed subprocess marker can be used in conjunction with any of the four other markers.
- **The loop marker**: A subprocess with a loop is represented using a curled line with an arrowhead.
- **The multiple instance marker**: A subprocess with multiple instances is represented using two parallel lines. This marker cannot be used in conjunction with the loop marker.

A subprocess can also be divided into two types:

- **The dependent or embedded subprocess**: A subprocess is said to be embedded when the parent process spawns the subprocess. In this case, the subprocess is dependent on the parent process for initiation. The embedded subprocess will usually contain basic BPMN constructs, such as activities, flow control, and gateways.
- **The independent subprocess**: In this case, the subprocess is a complete business process in its own right. The called process is independent of the calling process and hence can be called by any process.

Task

A task is the atomic unit used to represent an activity. We use a task when we cannot break down a process activity into a lower level of detail. Typically, a task is a piece of work done by either an application or a user during execution of the process.

Based on the kind of work involved, a task can be further divided into various types. The task types are as shown in the following table:

Service: This is a task providing some kind of service; it could be a web service or an application.	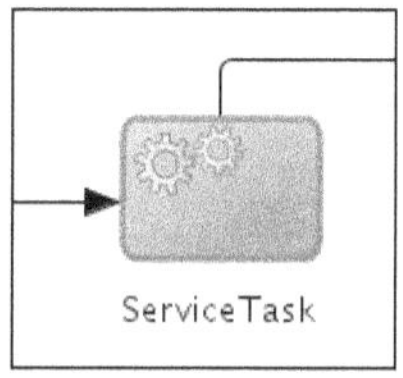
Receive: This is a task expecting to receive a message from an external participant in a process.	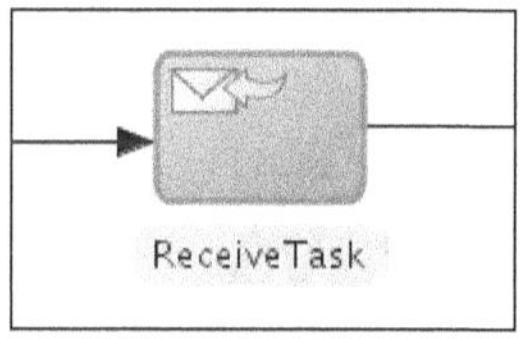
Send: This is a task that sends a message to an external participant.	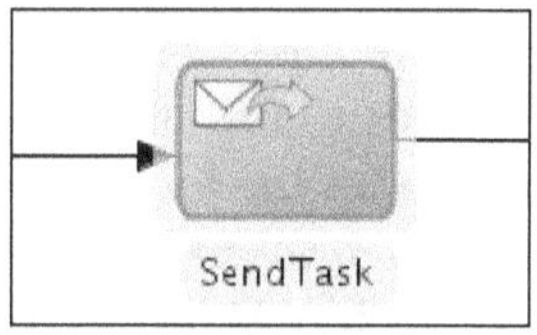
Business rule task: This is a business rule in a rule engine that helps to determine a decision in the process flow.	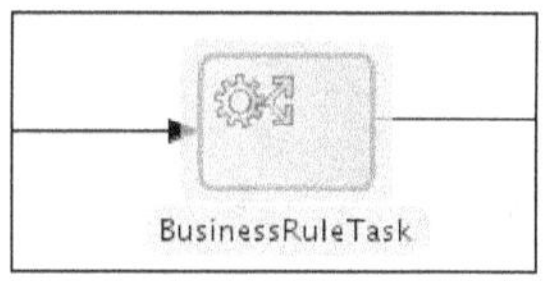
Script: This is meant to run a specific script by the execution engine. This kind of task will allow an implementer to specify a script to be run when the task is executed. The task is considered complete when the script has been run.	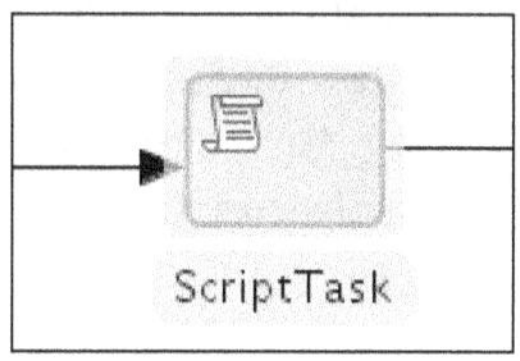 Figure 3: Tasks

User: This is a workflow-type task, where a user is supposed to perform an activity using an application. It can be also called a semiautomated task.	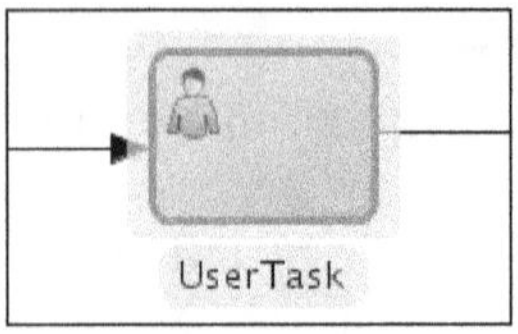
Manual: Typical manual activities, such as *agent shreds the document*. These tasks are performed without any help from an application or a BPM engine.	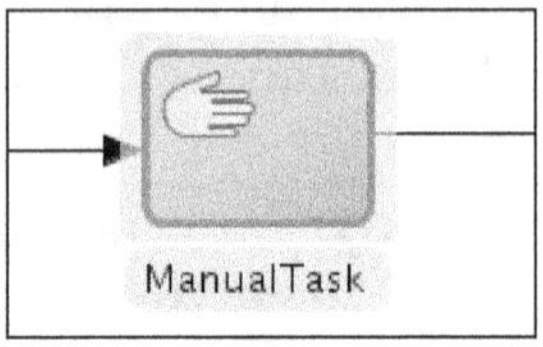 Figure 4: Tasks

In addition to standard BPMN tasks, BPM Suite provides some extra tasks, such as notification tasks to send notifications via e-mail, SMS, and so on. It also provides update tasks to update user (human) tasks.

Gateways

Gateways are used to control how flows interact as they converge and diverge within processes. In basic terms, gateways are like decision junctions where a particular flow decides to fork into multiple activities or join/merge back into an activity. Depending on the kind of behavior we want to control at a gateway, BPMN allows their representation as an open diamond with options to use markers to differentiate between various gateway types. Gateways can also be interpreted as *if-then* or *switch* constructs, which are typically used in programming control structures.

Sequence and message flows

The sequence flow represents the order in which activities are performed in a process. If you use a sequence flow to evaluate a condition before moving on to the next activity, then you use a conditional sequence flow. These are represented by a diamond at the start of the sequence flow, as can be seen in the following figure:

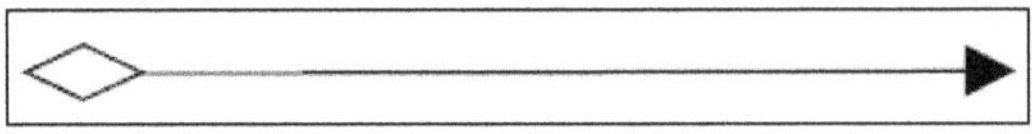

Figure 5: Conditional sequence flow

If you want to represent a default path among a set of options, especially in the case of decision gateways, a default sequence flow should be used. The marker used is a backslash at the beginning of the line, as follows:

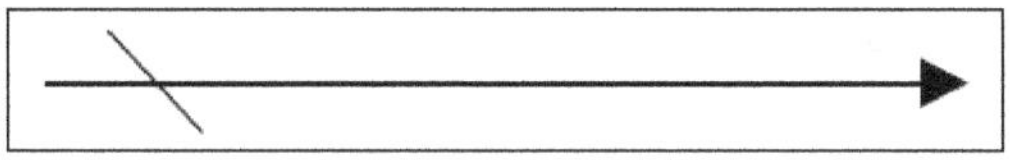

Figure 6: Default path

We represent message flows between two participants in a business process using a message flow element. In BPMN, two pools or swimlanes represent two participants involved in a process. For example, the finance department and the human resources department are participants in a process. Interaction between these departments would be depicted using message flows. A message flow must connect two pools or swimlanes or connect flow objects in one pool to flow objects in another. You cannot have a message flow connecting two objects in the same pool.

Message flow is denoted by a dashed line with an empty arrowhead and beginning with a small open circle, as follows:

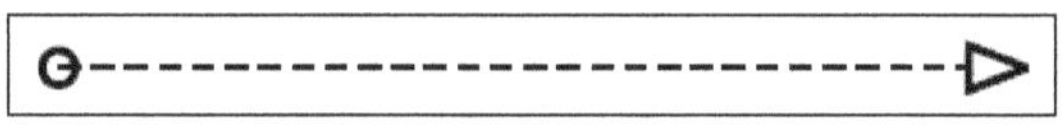

Figure 7: Message flow

A message flow can be from a flow object within one pool to a flow object in another pool. This is important mostly when depicting how the activities will send and receive messages from participants.

Pools and lanes

A pool depicts the participants in a given process. It allows the *swimlane* concept to be used in the diagram. The participants in an organization can be different internal departments. In a B2B process, they can be two organizations themselves, or from an SOA point of view, they can be different service providers or consumers. We will typically use a pool in our process diagrams to group various activities performed by different participants in a process.

In a given pool for a process, you may require demarcation of various activities, allowing further organization and categorization to provide greater clarity to the process users. A lane is used to do just that. It is used to subdivide a pool into multiple sections. For example, you might divide a pool representing a *loan department* into activities performed by the various roles within the department, such as customer service representative, underwriter, and so on. Or alternatively, if the pool represents a company in a collaboration process, lanes can be used to represent various departments within the company.

General guidelines for business process modeling

Before we move further, it's important to understand some of the rules that are helpful while modeling and designing our business processes. In this section, we will look into a few main modeling rules from the perspective of modeling a process and the instructions specified by BPMN.

Rule 1 – process models should provide aid in process understanding

A good process model should allow the overall process flow to be visible at one glance either from left to right or from top to bottom. To achieve that, a modeler can follow these basic rules:

- Aim for a minimum of four and a maximum of 15 tasks in a process diagram
- Aim for a maximum of three or four levels in a hierarchy

A good model gives you an intuitive and easy-to-understand overview of how a business process works as this is the main purpose of a graphic model. A model with a large number of tasks may be correct and unambiguous but becomes difficult to understand and, therefore, less useful. You can improve this diagrammatically by grouping tasks into a subprocess, that is, by creating a hierarchy of processes, subprocesses, and tasks. Depending on the complexity of the process, several levels of nested subprocesses are allowed. However, in terms of best practices, it's always better to keep the nesting to a maximum of four levels. This also ensures that the number of activities represented in a process is reduced to a maximum of 10 to 15, which can make the process more readable.

Rule 2 – match each split with a join

In the following figure, the process shows a common mistake with parallel tasks, where an AND split is not properly closed by an AND join:

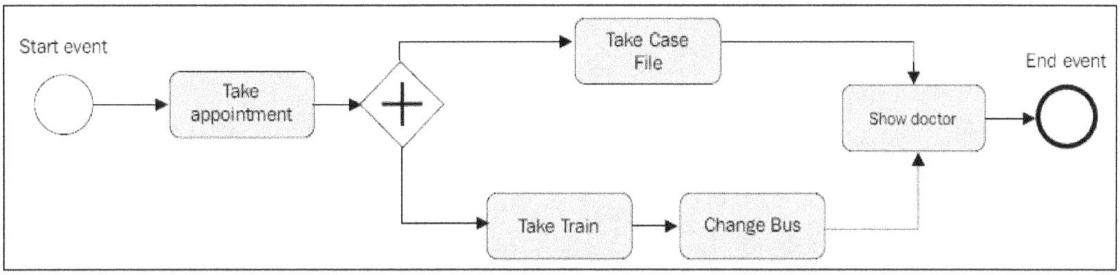

Figure 8: Process model without matching split and join

This mistake can cause a serious problem. Visually, if **Take Case File** is completed, then users might think that the process is ending, while it might be possible that the patient has still not reached the doctor. Therefore, it is wise to close the path by using an AND join to provide the process with a clear checkpoint. This will allow us to check whether all parallel tasks have been completed before the process can continue. The following figure is an example of using an AND join to ensure that the process can move forward with any further activities only after both the case file and patient arrive.

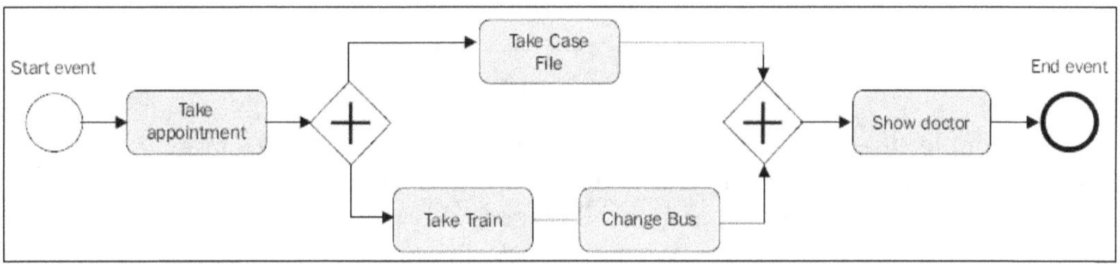

Figure 9: Process model with matching split and join

In addition, it is nice to use gateway symbols while modeling the process as this improves readability and understanding while reading or creating business process diagrams.

Another issue, especially with the use of the AND join, is the possibility of a deadlock situation in a process. Consider the following process:

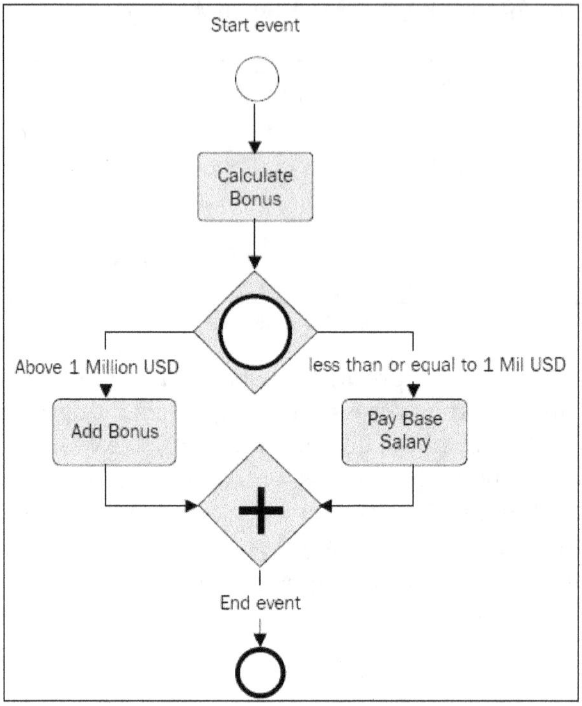

Figure 10: Process model with possible deadlock

In this example, an employee's bonus is calculated based on the sales targets achieved. The inclusive OR gateway ensures that only one option is taken. However, if you notice, the join gateway used is of the AND type and hence will wait for all parallel processes to complete. Now, we have a deadlock situation as the process will never take one of the paths. To avoid this situation, use an OR join instead of the AND join. The basic rule of thumb to avoid deadlocks is to ensure that every path in a process reaches the end state, especially when working with parallel or AND gateways.

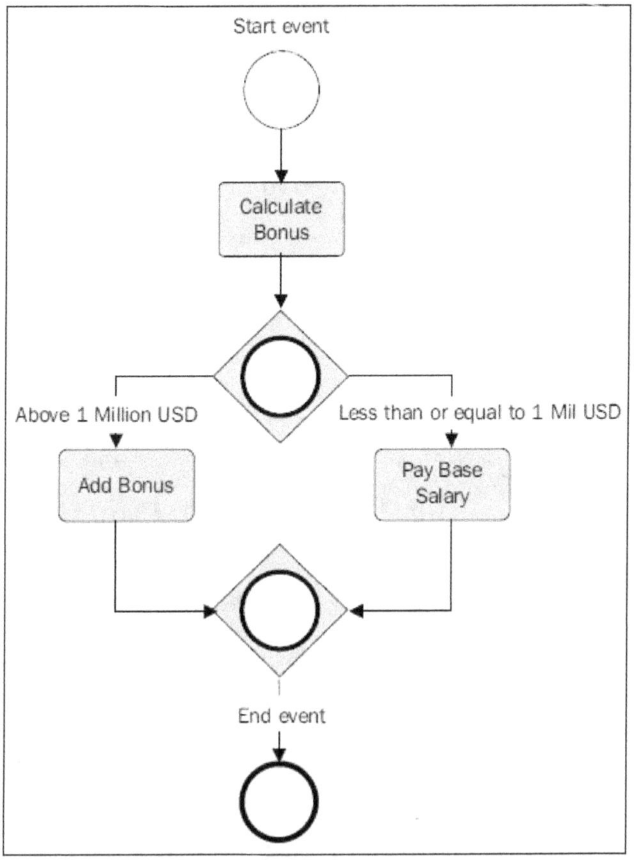

Figure 11: Process model without deadlock

Another technique to avoid a possible process deadlock is to always ensure there is at least one outgoing task for every possible condition at the gateway. Consider the following example:

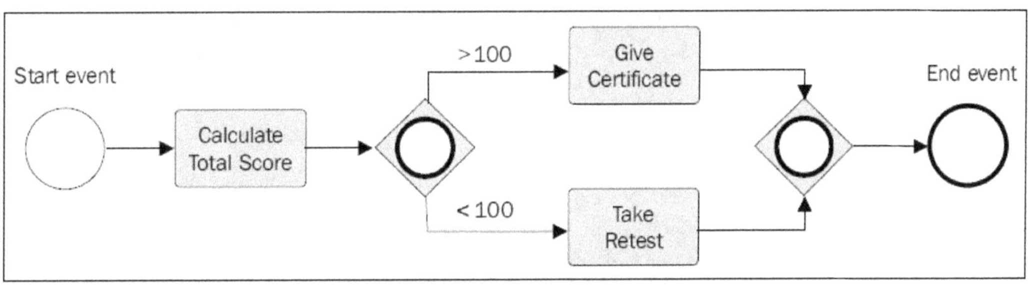

Figure 12: Process model with incomplete conditions

In this case, the conditions for both processes are either greater than or less than 100. Therefore, in a situation with an expression value of 100, there will be no output path. Hence, it could result in a deadlock. This is a simple example, and in some business scenarios, it may be overlooked by an analyst and can be misinterpreted as we go down the implementation route. To avoid this situation, it would be appropriate to use the default flow provided in BPMN or ensure that there is always at least one path out of the gateway.

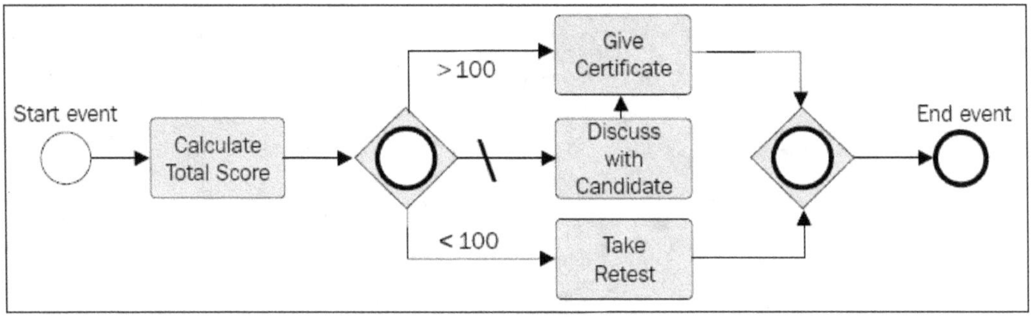

Figure 13: Process model with complete set of conditions

The notation used for the default flow in BPMN is a sequence flow with a tilde at its origin. In this case, if the candidate scores 100, they will be called in for a discussion before being given a certificate. This was just an example, but in normal process flows, care should be taken to provide default flows to prevent deadlocks.

Rule 3 – have well-defined start and end events

Though not mandatory, it's a good idea to start the process using the start event, and end the process using an end event. This keeps the process elegant and also gives motivation to designers to ensure that all paths are closed and linked from the start event or to the end event either directly or indirectly.

Rule 4 – look out for orphan tasks

Consider the following example:

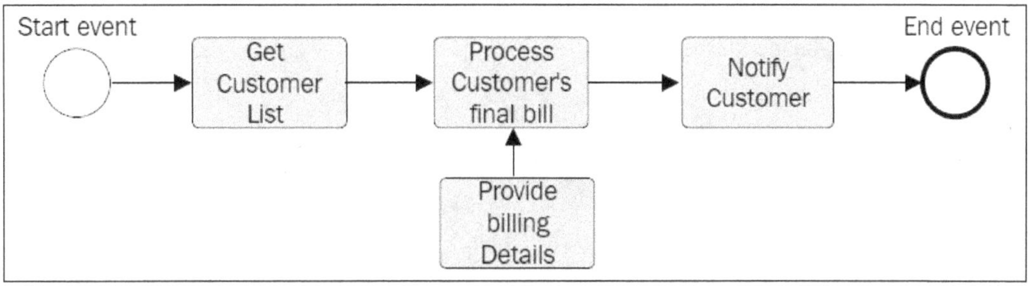

Figure 14: Process model with orphan task

The activity **Provide billing Details** will never be executed, as it does not have an input sequence flow to this task. As this is a simple process, it looks like an obvious mistake, but in a complex process, such a case can sometimes be overlooked. All efforts should be made to link every activity from the start event and have at least one incoming sequence flow to maintain consistency.

The BPMN standard also places a number of conditions on the representation of a process flow. The aim of this is to ensure consistency in diagram display and interpretation. These rules help in ensuring that BPMN maintains a degree of control over how a diagram is created, and at the same time, allows a bit of flexibility for a modeler and modeling tool vendors to work around the notation. Most of the modeling tool vendors are still maturing, and we will see further compliance with the standards and adherence to modeling rules as specified by BPMN.

Process modeling patterns and BPMN

While working on a process model, we will notice the use of several repeatable and reusable steps that are commonly used. These are referred to as business process patterns and are important for us to understand and keep in mind while developing a BPD using BPMN. These patterns began as developmental work by Wil van der Aalst, Arthur ter Hofstede, Bartek Kiepuszewski, and Alistair Barros, who together identified many workflow patterns that could be used to describe a process behavior and be considered for execution by a BPM system later on. We will be discussing some of the main business process patterns in subsequent sections of this chapter.

For ease of understanding, we can divide these patterns into the following categories:

- Basic control and sequence patterns
- Branching and synchronization patterns
- Iteration-based patterns
- Termination
- Multi instance
- State-based patterns

Basic control patterns

In this section, we will describe a few basic control patterns, which are needed while modeling business processes.

Simple sequence

This is a common pattern that a modeler and reader of the process model will notice. The following pattern represents a series of process steps executed one after another in sequence. In the following (figure), **Activity B** will start only after **Activity A** is completed:

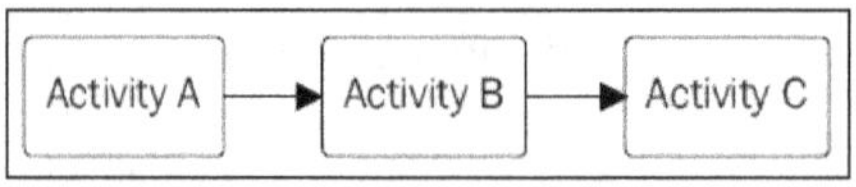

Figure 15: Simple sequence

This pattern can be better understood by examining a sample BPMN diagram. Notice the shaded area in the following diagram, which represents the use of a simple sequence pattern:

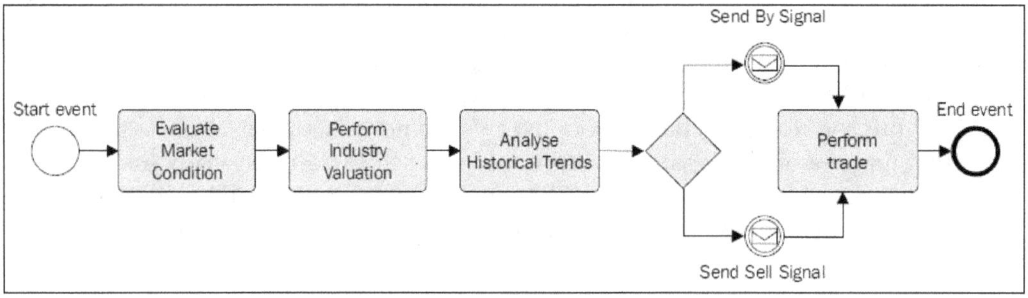

Figure 16: Example of simple sequence

In this example, as a simplification, we are assuming that a trader will go for industry valuation of the stock only after he has done a market evaluation of that sector. In other cases, it could be a parallel activity, but in this scenario, it's a sequence of steps that are dependent on the earlier activity ending.

Other examples of sequence patterns are:

- Printing of receipt after the purchase of groceries
- Elevator doors opening after the elevator buttons are pressed
- Creditworthiness checking after loan application forms are received

Parallel split sequence or forking

Type 1 – uncontrolled flow

This pattern is used where a process needs to be divided into multiple activities for the next steps to take place. This kind of flow is also called an uncontrolled flow as **Activity A** in the following diagram can fork out to both **Activity B** and **Activity C** without any conditions or dependencies. A fork in a process is initiated from either a task, subprocess, or start event.

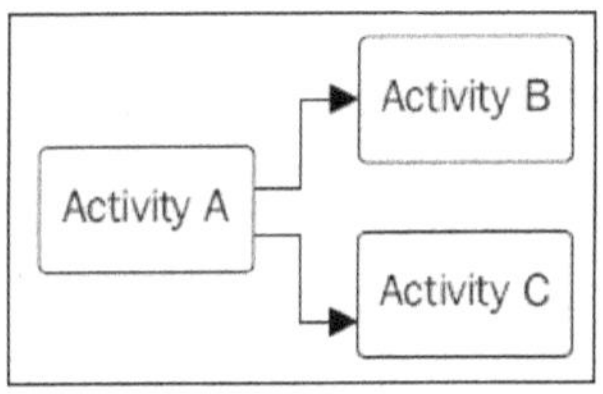

Figure 17: Uncontrolled flow

Type 2 – controlled flow

If you notice, in the previous fork pattern, the flow of a process was uncontrolled. A second mechanism, considered a *good practice*, is to use a parallel split or gateway between the sequence flows for control. Using the gateway, multiple threads will be executed in parallel, as shown here:

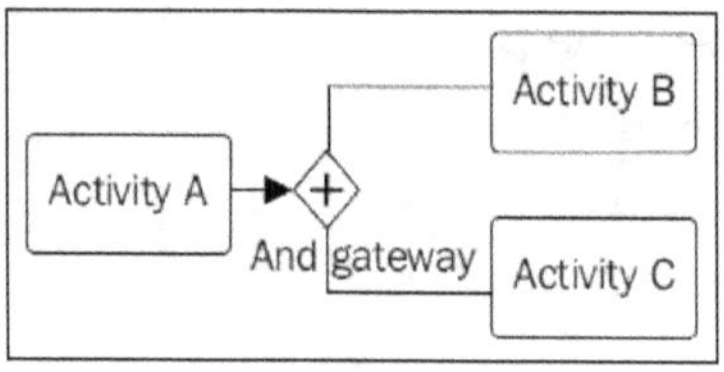

Figure 18: Controlled flow

Type 3 – parallel box

Another way of representing parallelism in BPMN is through the use of expanded subprocesses. In this method, a modeler can put the task elements inside a bigger process box to group the activities to be performed in parallel as shown in the following diagram. Again, this is an uncontrolled flow as Activity A will fork into Activity B and C with no dependencies or conditions. Typically, BPMN process diagrams should have start and end events. However, in this case, it's not necessary for the embedded subprocesses inside the main process box to have them.

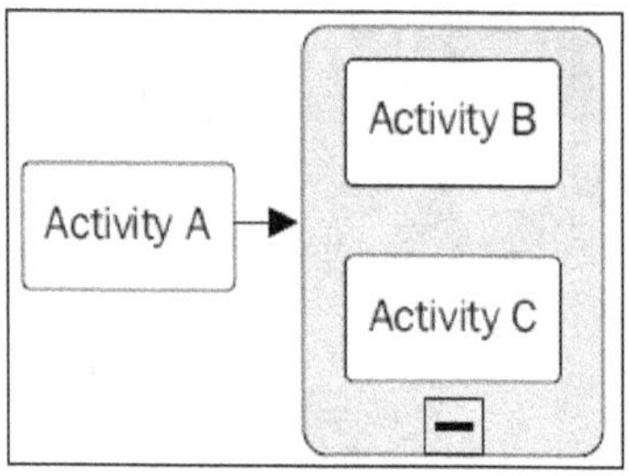

Figure 19: Parallel box

To demonstrate the parallel controlled flow, we can use the following example, where the highlighted portion is where a parallel gateway is used, signifying that both **Take Case File** and **Take Train** are activities to be performed concurrently.

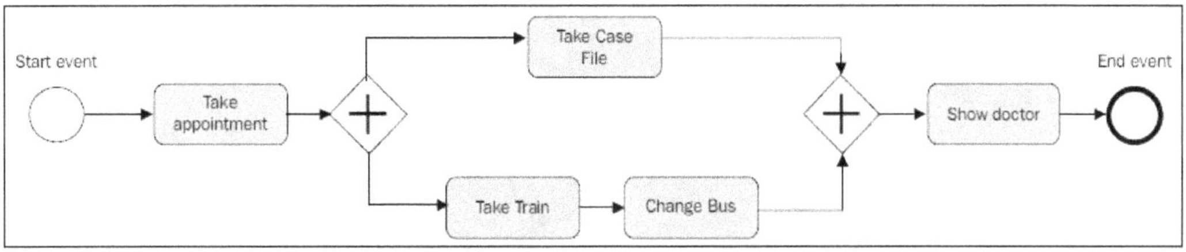

Figure 20: Parallel controlled flow example

Some other forking pattern examples are:

- When a customer query is received, send an acknowledgement mail and enter the details into the sales automation system
- On receipt of an online payment, provide a receipt mail to the customer and ship the goods

Synchronization or joining flow

This pattern would be used to model the join or convergence of one or more parallel flows into a single flow. If we look at it from a *token* terminology perspective, during the forking of a process flow, one token would be split into one or more tokens based on the number of flows that span out. During the joining of these flows, multiple tokens will converge and become one again before continuing forward.

Synchronization also has multiple ways of representation in BPMN:

Type 1 – use of the parallel (AND) gateway

The parallel, or AND, gateway is used to represent the convergence of two or more concurrent paths to produce a single output path. In the following diagram, **Activity A** and **Activity B** will converge using the AND gateway to create a single sequence flow to **Activity C**.

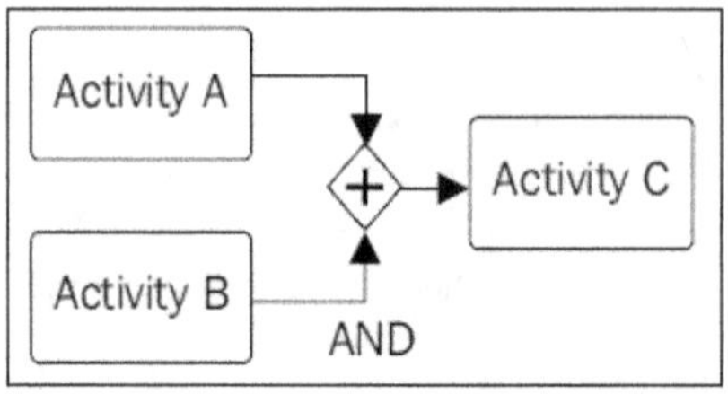

Figure 21: Parallel gateway for synchronization

Type 2 – subprocess completion

In this mechanism, synchronization is achieved by the completion of activities within a subprocess. As soon as all activities within the subprocess are completed, the subprocess will reach its end state, and control is given back to the higher-level process. This aspect of the subprocess makes it a convergence point. This is shown in the following diagram:

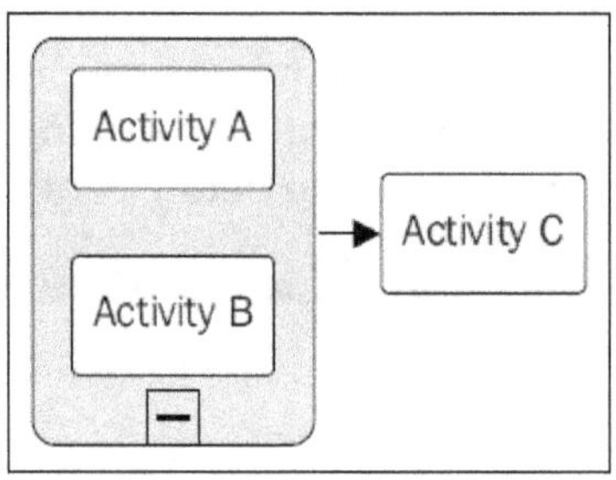

Figure 22: Subprocess completion

An example of using the synchronization pattern can be taken from the previous example of a visit to a doctor. In this case, **Take Case File** and **Change Bus** converge and cease to exist as separate paths. After that, one thread emerges, which is **Show doctor**. Another joining flow example scenarios **online tickets dispatched** after completion of the **address verification** and **credit card verification** processes:

Branching and synchronization patterns

In this section, we will describe more advanced branching and synchronization patterns, which we will need when modeling business processes.

Multichoice

Sometimes also referred to as conditional routing or OR switches, the multichoice pattern allows a particular thread of a process execution to be divided into multiple branches based on a selection criterion. This decision, to send the thread of execution to a particular branch or set of branches, is made during runtime. The choice can be based on a variety of factors, such as outcome, results from preceding tasks, value of data elements in the process, or output of a calculated expression.

In BPMN, multichoice can be implemented either through the use of an OR gateway or a complex gateway. It can also be implemented using conditional routing on the sequence flow. It is important to use a default path in a multichoice scenario as it can otherwise lead to a deadlock situation. There should always be at least one path that the process can take if no other condition is applicable

In the following example, once the customer's order is dispatched, the process involves sending some form of notification to the customer via mail, fax, or e-mail. So, the process based on the gateway could be to choose mail, fax, or e-mail, a combination of these choices, or all of them.

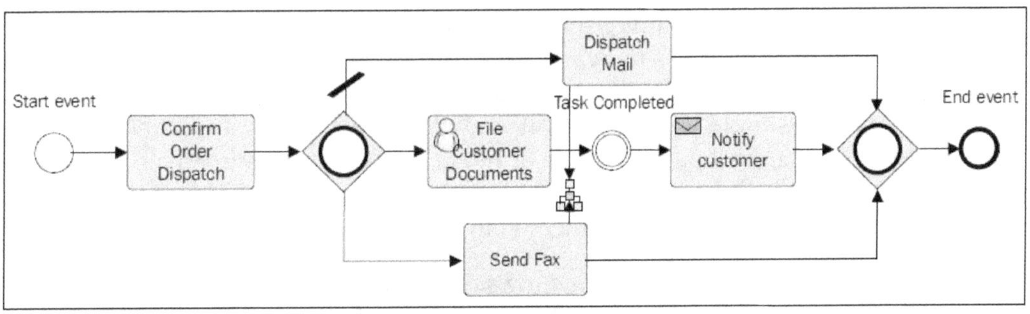

Figure 23: Multichoice example

Some other multichoice example scenarios are:

- Based on the nature of the issue, the helpdesk creates a severity ticket and sends a message to one or all of the network specialists, application management team and the data center management
- Depending on the product selection in the new account application form for a portfolio management service, send action tasks to one or all of the equity advisory, mutual fund, and insurance teams

Structured synchronizing merge

This pattern is used in conjunction with multiple choice constructs to merge all of the branches coming out of a multiple choice. The flow of control is passed forward to a single branch only when each incoming branch, which was created earlier by an OR gateway, is complete.

In BPMN, structured synchronizing merge is supported using an OR join gateway. We can use the same preceding example to show the join.

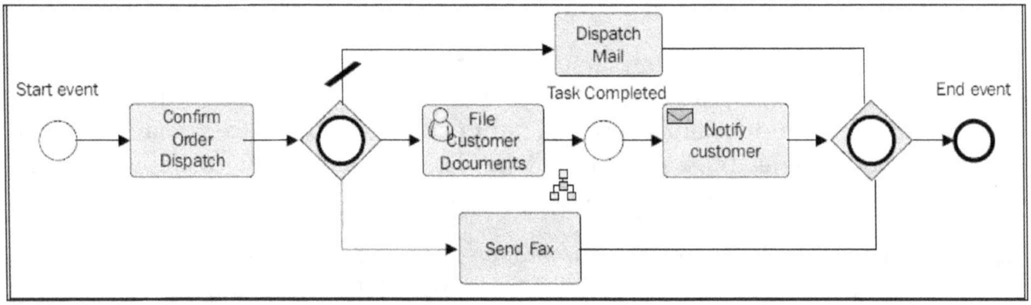

Figure 24: Structured synchronizing join

There is, however, one thing to note about this pattern, which can be a problem when modeling and understanding the process flow. As the OR join flow is waiting for the incoming threads, it has no way to decide how many threads are enabled by the OR split gateway. So, if a fax and a hardcopy mail have both been sent to the customer, what should the OR join gateway do once it knows about the fax? Should it wait for the mail path to arrive or move on to the next step? This is a classic example of where it's difficult to model the waiting time as it could be possible that the second thread never occurred, which would create a deadlock situation.

This problem can be solved on the modeling side by providing additional information on chosen scenarios and preferred wait times to reduce the chances of deadlocks, especially during implementation.

A few more examples for structured synchronizing merge scenarios are as follows:

- Based on the nature of a helpdesk ticket, the request is sent to both the hardware and application service groups; only after receiving feedback from both departments, can the **close ticket** activity start
- Depending on the product selection on the new account application form for portfolio management services, send action tasks to the equity advisory, mutual fund, and insurance teams; only on receiving input from each team can the response be sent to the customer

Multimerge

The multimerge pattern is used to represent the convergence of two or more branches of the process flow into a single ongoing branch so that each incoming branch flows without restriction to the continuing branch. This is different from a simple merge where, at the point of the merge, only one branch can be active. In the case of multimerge, it does not require such safety during merging and allows multiple branches to pass through at once. So, in BPMN, it's like an uncontrolled flow. Multimerge is generally used in the context of the multichoice pattern.

In the following example, any of the threads comings out of the OR split, such as **Dispatch Mail** or **Send Fax**, will immediately be sent for notification. This is actually asking for a customer response during each communication with the customer.

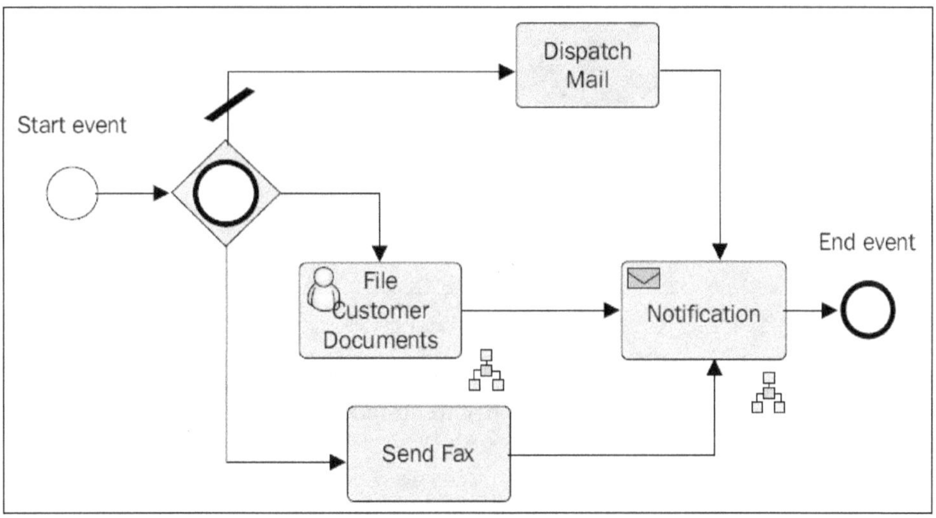

Figure 25: Multimerge example

A few more multimerge scenarios are as follows:

- **Send_Email** and **Send_Fax** can be parallel processes and different process branches. After each task is performed, it goes through a **Get_feedback** task from the customer.
- The **create_design_document**, **update_project_plan**, and **create_test_plan** tasks occur in parallel in different branches. After the completion of each task, they need to complete the **artefact_quality_check** before that particular branch of the process ends.

Iteration-based patterns

These sets of patterns are aimed at depicting repetitive behavior in a business process model.

Arbitrary cycles

This is a looping pattern that allows sections of a process to be repeated. This pattern allows looping that is either unstructured or is not block-structured. This means that it has the ability to represent loops in a process model that have more than one entry or exit point. It must also be possible for individual entry and exit points to be associated with distinct branches. The following diagram shows this:

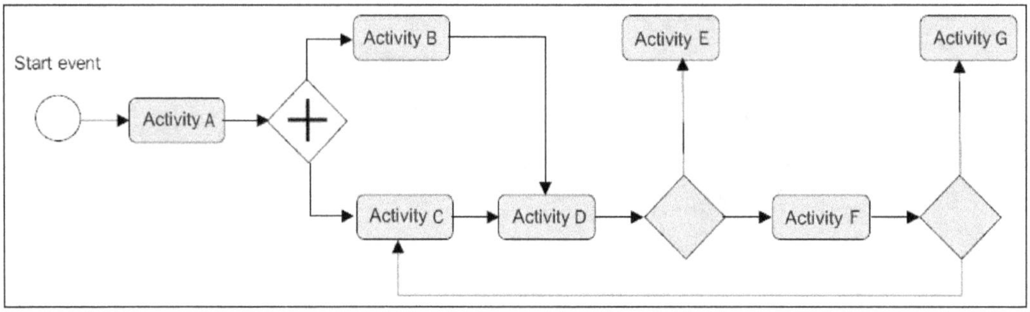

Figure 26: Arbitrary cycles

In BPMN, it is possible to create an arbitrary cycle pattern within a process diagram by connecting the sequence flow to any upstream activity.

Structured loop

This is a looping pattern used to depict repeatable tasks and subprocesses. The loop will have a pre-test or post-test condition that is evaluated either at the beginning or at the end of the loop, similar to the familiar *while-do* or *repeat-until* programming language constructs.

In a while-do construct, a pre-test condition is evaluated before the loop starts and allows repeated sequential execution of a specified task or subprocess zero or more times while the evaluated condition holds true. Once the pre-test condition evaluates to false, the thread of control passes to the task immediately following the loop.

In the case of the *repeat-until* loop, a post-test condition is evaluated after the first iteration of the loop, which then allows the execution of a task or subprocess one or more times, continuing with the execution as long as the condition is true. Once the post-test condition evaluates to false, the thread of control passes to the task immediately following the loop. The following diagram shows this:

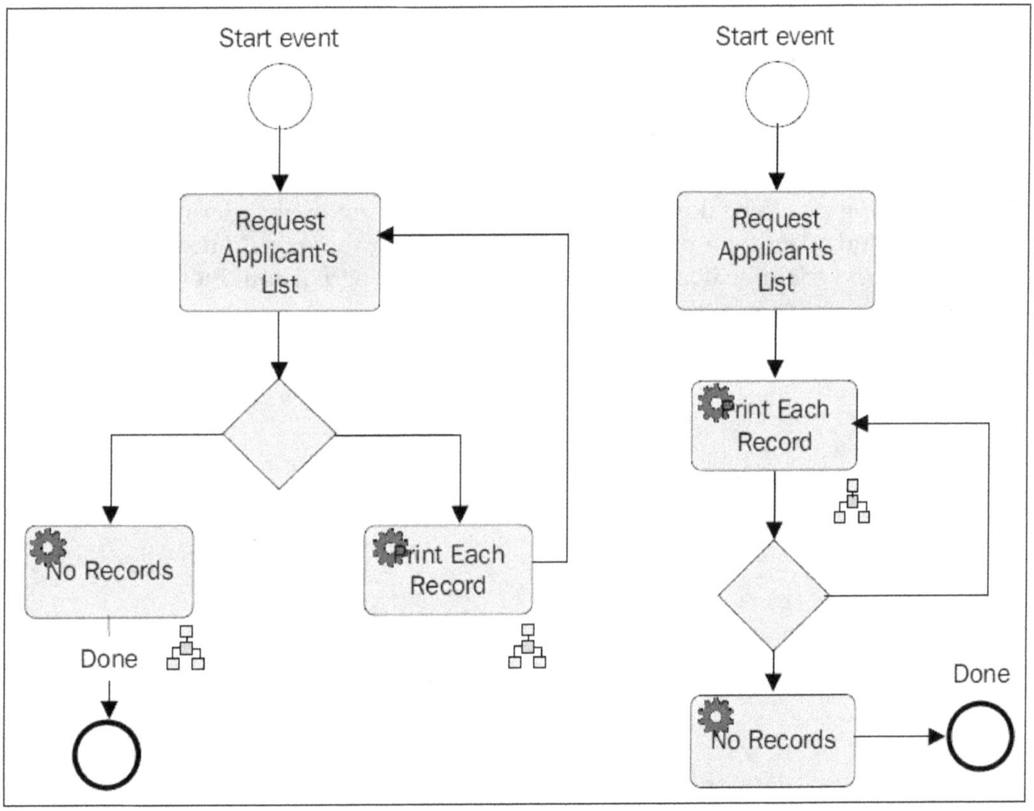

Figure 27: Structured loop

The preceding figure shows a structured loop using the *while-do* and *repeat-until* scenarios. This explains how each looping scenario can be represented. In the first case, the applicant list is printed based on the condition at the gateway. In the next case as well, the print loop is repeated until the conditions are satisfied.

BPMN also allows both pre-tested and post-tested loops to be captured through the loop task construct using a loop attribute for each activity. In the following figure, the loop conditions for the **Print Each Record** process are shown. In BPMN, there is no restriction on the expression language to define the conditions. So, we can use English or, as we go into detailed modeling, we can use exact mathematical expressions to facilitate ease of understanding during implementation.

There is also a recursion-based pattern suggested as a typical workflow scenario, allowing a recursive loop to be defined for a process.

Termination

These are patterns used to determine the completion of a process. They are typically divided into two types.

Implicit termination

Implicit termination provides a pattern of where a process should terminate when there is nothing else to be done. Mostly, in BPMN, we use explicit termination, where there is one end event for a process instance. However, there could be situations where a process could be in more than one state and where it could terminate. The following diagram shows this:

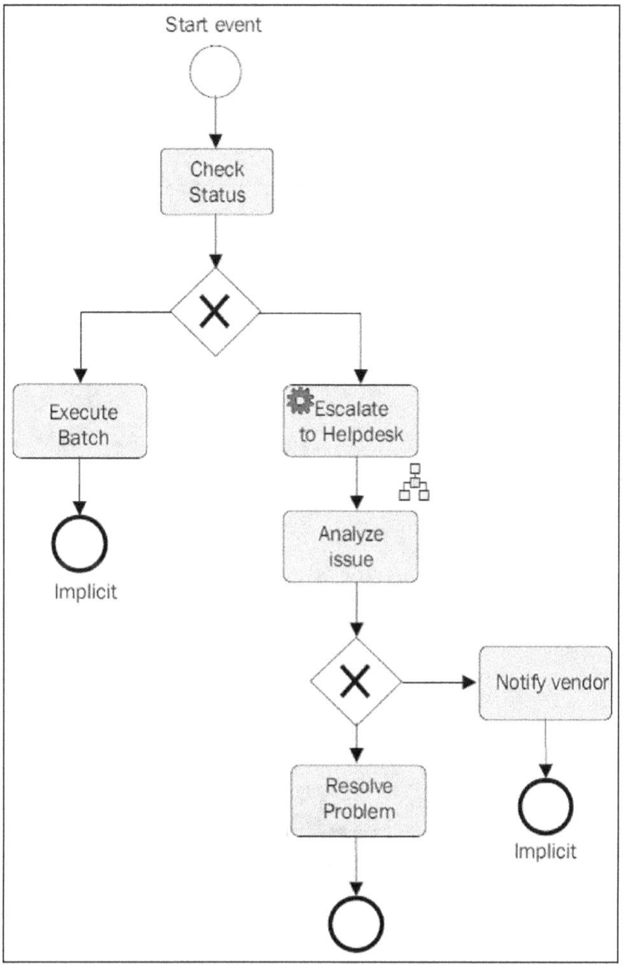

Figure 28: Implicit termination

To elaborate on the scenario after the **Check Status** activity, the gateway will route the flow based on the status of the error, and we can either directly execute the batch or escalate to the helpdesk department. The helpdesk can further notify the vendor as part of its action. In any of the three scenarios, it will reach its end, and the process will terminate as soon as the activity is complete. There is no other activity happening in parallel.

Explicit termination

In this case, there is an explicit end node, which, if reached by any branch in a process, will lead to the process being considered complete and any remaining tasks in the process being ignored and rendered cancelled.

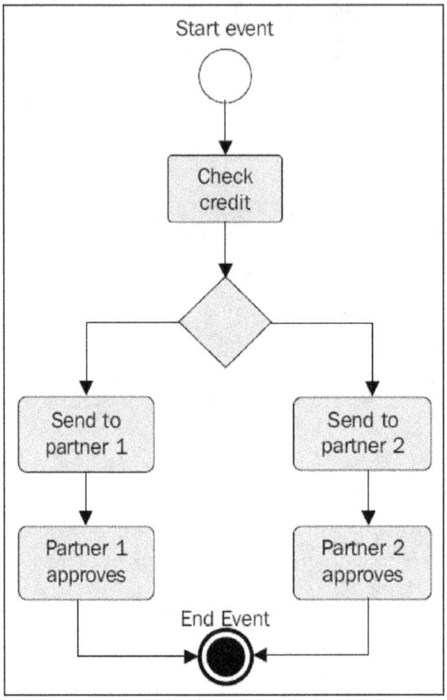

Figure 29: Explicit termination

To explain this scenario hypothetically, if **Check credit** is approved by any of the partners of a customer, the bank will ignore the input from the other partners and the process will terminate. The terminate end event is used in this case to implement the explicit pattern.

Multiple-instance pattern

Multiple instance patterns are used to define scenarios in which a given activity creates or instantiates multiple threads of execution. Typically, this scenario is seen where one activity, once triggered, creates multiple instances of itself.

Multiple instances without synchronization

In this scenario, for a given process, multiple instances of a task are triggered. For this specific pattern, the instances created are independent of each other and require no synchronization at the end of the process. In BPMN, this is achieved using a multi-instance task with the *loop flow condition* equal to *none*, signifying an uncontrolled flow. This means that all tokens created by the instances from this activity will move forward when completed. Oracle BPA does not depict the task with the multi-instance mark graphically, and the user will need to check the BPMN attributes for the subprocess or task to determine whether the process has the multi-instance parameter set.

Multiple instances with a priori design-time knowledge

In this case, multiple instances of a task can be created with a prior understanding of the number of instances required. The instances created run in concurrence and, post completion, will need to be synchronized before moving to the next activity.

Multiple instances with a priori runtime knowledge

In this case, similar to the design-time multiple-instance pattern, multiple instances of a task can be created for a given process. However, the number of these instances is not known to the modeler during design time. The number of instances can depend on various factors during runtime, but it is known before the task instance is set to be triggered. Similarly, post initiation, the instances run independent of each other, and, once initiated, these instances are independent of each other and run concurrently. It is also necessary to synchronize the instances before they move to subsequent activities. In this example, we would like to have the system perform some checks based on the type of tickets received and the list of errors generated based on unique error identifiers. Depending on the kind of ticket and the indication of the list of issues, the system can choose to perform a number of checks and controls.

State-based patterns

These patterns are used to model scenarios for processes that are affected by reasons outside the control of process engines. Most of these scenarios require process designers to consider the state of the process, which can be determined based on numerous considerations, including process-specific data used for process execution. BPMN is not well-suited to state-based modeling, but there are ways to implement some of these patterns using the specification. We will discuss the alternative *adaptive case management* in *Chapter 9, Adaptive Case Management*.

Deferred choice

As the name suggests, this pattern assumes that before a decision is made, all available branches are valid courses of action for the process. With this pattern, based on a decision, one of the branches will be chosen. Once the decision is made, all the alternate options are no longer available as options for this particular decision.

A diagram uses an exclusive data-based gateway to implement this pattern and makes the decision of which alternative path to take. This acts as the branching point and is followed by intermediate events linked to the sequence flows for each decision branch. When a token arrives at this gateway, it waits there for an event to occur, which usually is the receipt of a message. This event determines the next course of action and other alternatives are ignored. Instead of an intermediate event, a task of the *receive* type can also be used with similar results. The following diagram shows this:

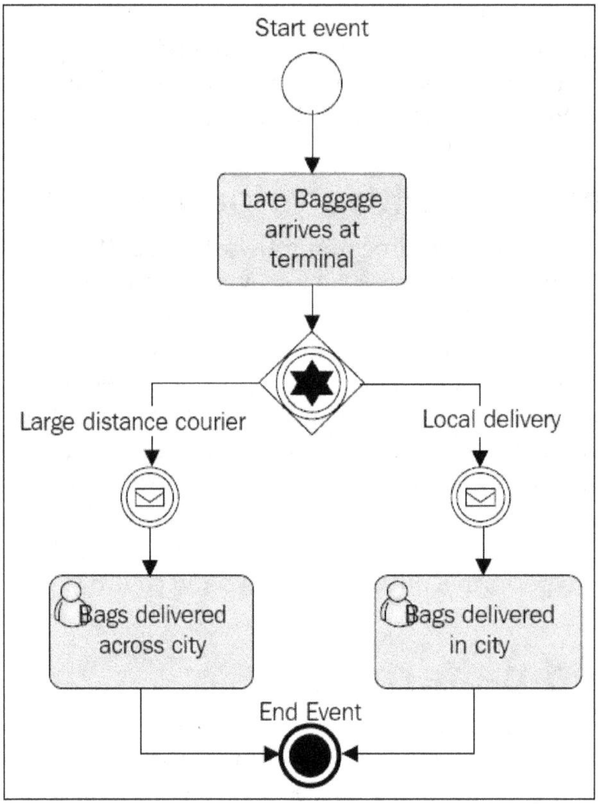

Figure 30: Deferred choice

In the scenario of late baggage arrival, as shown here, an airline has the option to use a long-distance courier company or local delivery companies depending on the distance of the customer from the airport. So, upon the arrival of the baggage at the terminal and the receipt of a message of the customer location, the bags can be sent by the appropriate means. Once the decision is made, only one route will be taken, and the other is ignored

Modeling an abstract BPMN process

Oracle BPM Suite 12*c* allows the initiation of the process-modeling exercise together with domain experts and representatives of business departments without forcing them into having to digest technical details by defining a so-called abstract process. Here, the flow becomes transparent, but we have not decided yet on the so-called activity type of each activity that defines how it's implemented. The following diagram shows this:

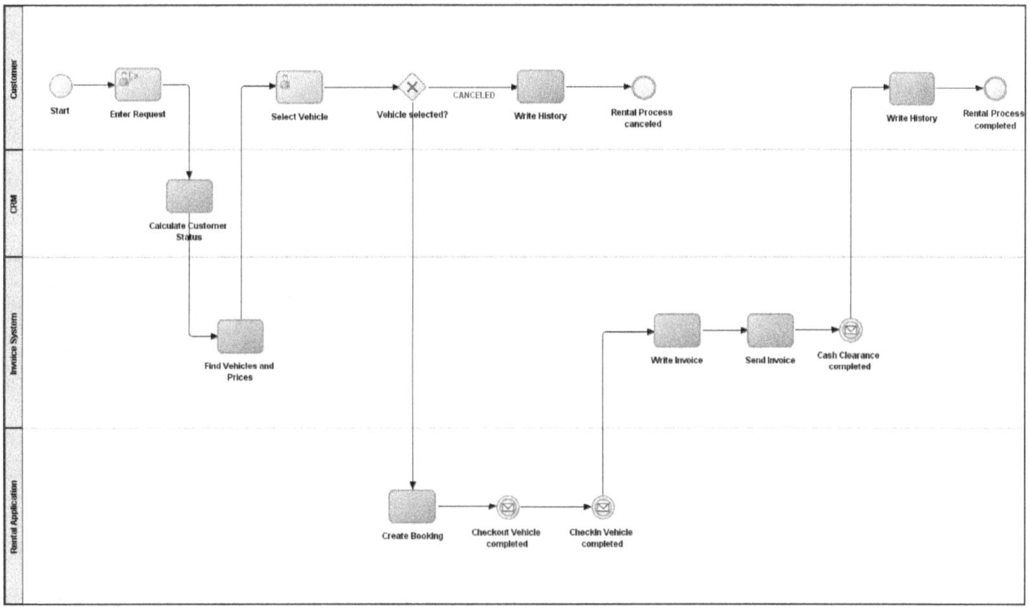

Figure 31: Abstract business process

Modeling an abstract business process is the first step towards the ultimate goal of defining an executable business process. Typically, a representative of a business department or a domain expert who knows the process in terms of its logical flow and the activities this flow ties together and a BPMN expert collaborate on defining the process model. Oracle Process Composer has quite a shallow learning curve, so it's not unrealistic to establish a practice in which these business departments are self-sufficiently creating abstract process models.

The process modeler starts by depicting the organizational units or logical roads by means of so-called swimlanes. The abstract process model of the RYLC booking process depicted earlier has roles such as customer and CRM, which depict a system. Then, the process modeler models the flow starting with a start event. It is a good practice to also think about the result of the business process and attempt to define it through one positive event that successfully reached the desired end result of this business process and, if necessary, a small set of business-relevant variants or faulted events.

Between the start and end events, we can depict the main activities along the notion of a clear flow. Ideally, this flow moves forward and we try to omit loopbacks since they raise complexity.

The ultimate goal of this type of abstract process model is to communicate relevant aspects of the flow of the business process not to depict any technical details. It focuses on what happens and not how it happens. When we look at a process model that is not easily understandable, we should attempt to refactor it. Reasons for the related clutter are too many variances or too many details of the process. The best practice, then, is to use hierarchical process decomposition. Then each screen has the same level of detail. On higher level processes, the details of each process step are hidden in the notion of subprocesses.

The result is a process hierarchy that starts with the value chain and stops at the level of very concrete activities that can be implemented as use cases or service calls.

For each of the process steps, we decide which level of abstraction to choose. The example process picture shows two types of activity: a human task indicating the interaction with a human and an abstract activity that is completely agnostic about how it's implemented.

Top-down modeling: where the value chain meets BPMN

Starting with a value chain means starting at the very top in the process hierarchy, often overarching functional domains and departmental silos. The next hierarchical layers can be used to depict strategies and the respective technical capabilities in order to optimize based on priorities set in strategy maps and KPIs in value chains.

At some point in the process hierarchy, we will find a level of granularity that is feasible to execute a BPMN-based process engine. Ideally, the executable process is based on the same model that is also used to depict the relevant aspects of the business. The IT model becomes a refinement of the business model. Another way to look at it is through the notion of a filter, so ideally, we have a business filter and an IT filter on the same process model. In real life, very often we maintain two distinct models, which impose the need to keep them in line if we want to maintain the notion of the business model documenting the executable model. This relationship is discussed in the next section.

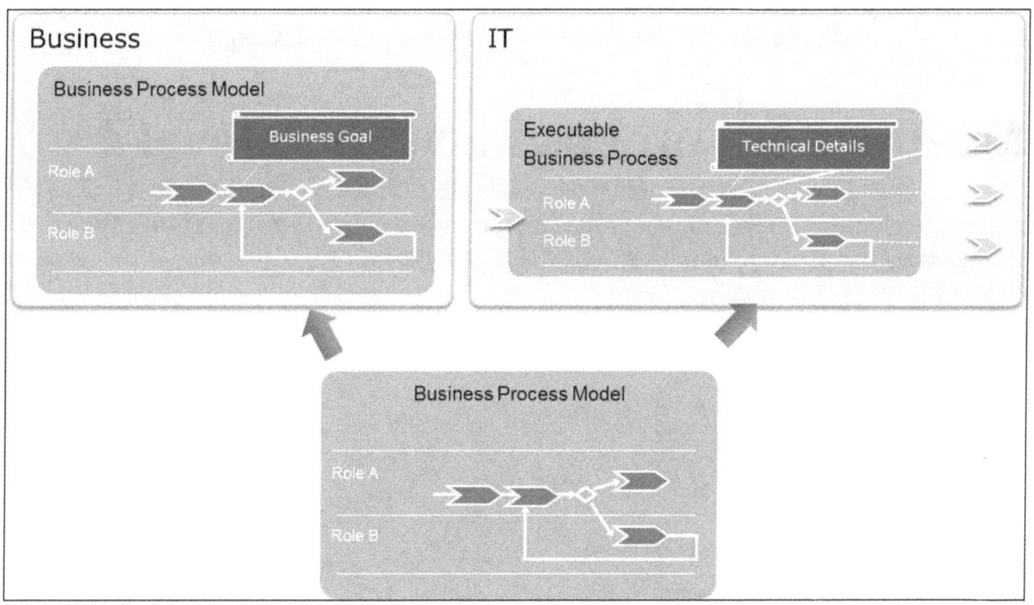

Figure 32: Relationship of business aspects and IT aspects

The business processes and subprocesses that have been chosen to automate are typically modeled in the first attempt by process experts at a level of detail that is almost algorithmic. In most cases, these models are a few steps away from being scripted in the level of detail that is sufficient to be the basis of process automation. Specifically, they lack the necessary details for algorithmic descriptions of variances and exception paths. BPMN expert Bruce Silver depicts this type of process models as business models (he calls them *level 1* models, while calling automated processes *level 3* models).

The goal is to establish a graphical representation of the process that is easily understandable by business representatives and management.

This is important as the primary goal of strategic BPM is to gain process transparency: enabling the organization as a whole, from high management through all the layers down to IT management, architects, and designers in order to speak the same process language and understand the core business processes in order to make strategic decisions on improvement and get as broad a buy-in as possible.

Process models that express too many details and demand too much technical expertise for everybody to understand them prohibit this kind of broad understanding and, thus, prevent the reaching of the ultimate goal of process transparency.

Moving from process level 3 to level 4

There is a need for process models to be executable. The suggested approach is to maintain a loose but recognizable relationship between the finest levels of processes modeled by business stakeholders and the highest level of the automated processes or workflows.

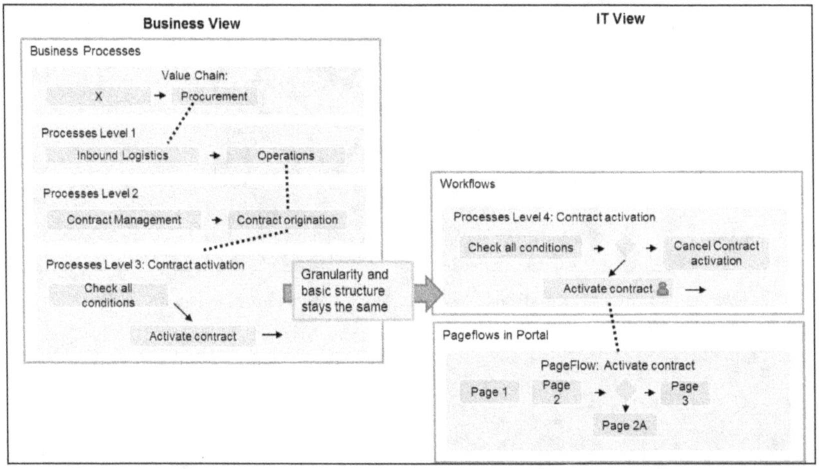

Figure 33: How to get from process models (L3) to executable processes (L4) through well-defined collaboration

Note that processes at level 4 are on the *same hierarchical layer in the process hierarchy* as level 3, but provide *additional technical details* needed to make the process automated.

As discussed earlier, BPM Suite 12*c* allow us to gradually move from an abstract viewer to a more concrete view. The key mechanism is providing an activity type called extract activity, which leaves the decision on how this activity is implemented, for example, either by a human task or an SOA service to a later stage.

Differentiating automated process/workflows and page flows

Business architects, enterprise architects, and business departments often model business processes without considering the architectural layers they are positioned in. Many modeling tools further support this approach. For example, it is possible to use **Event Process Chains** (**EPC**), the very prominent modeling language right below value chains, down to use cases, and here, detailing out toward last-minute details of user interactions. When we attempt to automate processes, there is an important architectural barrier depicted earlier as page flows. Other feasible terms are *UI flows*, *sequence of forms*, steps in *user stories*, or *use cases*.

The demarcation line can be drawn at the notion of human tasks entered in process models. When a user logs in to a role that is recognized by the process engine since it is configured as a lane in the model, the automatic process enters a task for the user or his role. This task is presented as an item in a task list. When the user clicks on this task, a use case starts, such as *review and approve order*.

We saw EPC-based process models that would start at this human interaction level of the process hierarchy and delve into up to 14 levels down, acting more like a detailed business rule than a business process.

While this was perfectly fine with EPC's, BPMN 2.X is not the right notation for executing the user–system interaction that is triggered by a human task! On the Oracle platform, you can use ADF task flows to model and execute this level of detail. Use case steps can be associated with screens or forms and modeled in a flow that depicts their order and even decisions that indicate one of several potential next pages or forms.

Summary

In this chapter, we took a deeper look at BPMN 2, a representation of structured business processes that has both a visual representation that is comprehensible by business stakeholders and a runtime dimension, in which the flow is executed in a BPMN engine. Oracle phrased these two sides of the same coin, *what you see is what you execute*.

This chapter focuses on the visual language BPMN itself and how to best use to it create models that communicate best with a broad set of readers—both technical and business. While developers often assume they still need to code, with BPMN in Oracle BPM Suite, it is best to attempt to code as little as possible, relying as much as possible on the wizards and configuration the tool provides. Also, it is key that business stakeholders grasp the flow of business processes. This chapter provides key mechanisms to structure processes in a way that best deals with complexity by breaking down the structure through hierarchical decomposition. Further, do not use BPMN for all process types. BPMN is best used for highly standardized, structured processes with a comprehensible set of variances. Processes in which control is owned by end users benefit from alternatives such as document driven or adaptive case management. Furthermore, if you have a BPM practice in place, focus on a proven mechanism that helps to delve into BPMN from existing higher-level business process models along the notion of a process hierarchy. Besides, have at least one person in the team who deeply understands the building blocks of BPMN and how to use them correctly. This expert should coach the rest of the team and should participate in joint modeling sessions.

In the next chapter, we will take a deep look into the design aspects of SOA services that complement BPMN in the BPM/SOA paradigm. It discusses the services that are called from BPMN and frontends to make a decision, store data, integrate with a backend or calculate a business rule.

4
Process-driven Service Design

Service-oriented architecture (**SOA**) is a fundamental building block of a successful business process-driven architecture. To build agility and business alignment into our processes, we must ensure that the functionality that the processes implement is also designed in an agile, modular, and business-aligned fashion.

The IT architectures of many organizations have grown in an organic way through the adoption of new packaged applications (both commodity applications and industry-specific applications), custom-built applications in areas of differentiation, and hosted partner or cloud services. Integration of these systems becomes an increasing challenge with the divergence of the definition of business terms, technical protocols, and location of the systems. Whether these systems provide key engagement with customers, partners, and employees or are just a system of record, they are still required to interact with the organization's business processes. To give the business the control over the process that they require, the functions as well as the processes themselves can no longer be embedded within the systems. This becomes increasingly important as processes cross boundaries of ownership, for example, across organizational silos, partner organizations, and devices (mobile, tablet, desktop, and so on).

To ensure that business processes are not constrained by the IT architecture that supports them, a further layer of business functions must be provided for the business processes to interact with—one that speaks the business language, can interact in a consistent way with all the organizations or partner IT systems, and can provide information, actions, and functions across multiple devices. This is the role of the SOA layer. In this role, SOA is more than just a set of standards to allow systems to interoperate; it is a design approach that, if implemented correctly, will be a key enabler to a process-driven architecture. The design of the service layer must ensure that the change in IT systems has limited impact on the process layer and that business change can be facilitated by the IT systems with similar limited impact. One of the key drivers of BPM is to accelerate business change without too much IT involvement; this is only possible with the correct service architecture and approach in place.

> If business process change requires constant IT refactoring of the services and functions that implement the process, then it will never truly deliver the business agility desired.

This chapter will outline an approach and a set of guidelines to design your services in such a way that they facilitate usage by the business process layer. We will do the following:

- Describe the role of a service in a process-driven architecture
- Explain the importance of service design in the context of business processes
- Set out a series of guidelines that should be adhered to in designing services
- Discuss the role of data in a service-oriented architecture
- Outline the impact of the lack of design of the service layer
- Discuss what should come first: the business process design, service design, or data design

Service design guidelines

As you roll out business processes to your organization, it will become increasingly important that a good set of service design guidelines are defined, communicated, and governed against. The definition of a service in your organization and the contract between the consumer and the provider will enable the separation of concerns between the two parties. It will allow the consumer, that is, the business process, to concentrate on delivering the outcomes they are responsible for without being concerned with the functions and activities over which they do not have control—which is now the responsibility of the service provider.

> A business service is a contract between the provider and multiple consumers. It provides a guaranteed and repeatable behavior that allows the consumer to concentrate on the usage of the service rather than the details within the service.

Benefits of service design for BPM

BPM promises a fast rollout of processes that align closely with business needs. However, this cannot be achieved by process modeling alone. Implementing a good phase of service design within a BPM initiative will give the following benefits:

- **Response to business change**: A well-designed SOA will allow business processes to respond to changing business conditions in a fast, flexible manner, thanks to the ease with which services can be revised and reused. If application functionality is bound directly to the business process, then this can allow the first process to be implemented very quickly, but any change in that process will be constrained and delayed, and inconsistency will be introduced as new business requirements are responded to.
- **Adaptability in process execution**: With a good service architecture supporting the business processes, there will be more confidence in supporting variations in processes. Very often, changes to rules, parameters, or additional data being presented to the user may be implemented solely within the service layer, minimizing the impact of change of the process layer. In addition, if the service is designed for multiple usage scenarios, then changes in the process behavior could be implemented by just changing the inputs to the service layer. Customization of the process should result in minimal or no change at the service layer if the services are designed correctly.
- **Consistency in data**: SOA allows the enterprise to share data, information, and knowledge more readily through open standards and common protocols. SOA supports more effective communication both within an enterprise and between an organization and its supply chain since communications are not hampered by incompatible systems. This helps us to implement processes that cut across data domains and organizational boundaries.

- **Simplification of the process layer**: SOA simplifies the development, maintenance, and integration of enterprise applications through standard, reusable components. This building block approach means that an enterprise can add, remove, and swap out components without the pain that typically results from reprogramming large applications. Since applications can be reconfigured without rewriting the underlying code, changes can be made to any function by simply plugging in a new component. This allows new processes to leverage coarse-grained business functions as new systems are implemented, cloud applications are adopted, and partner providers are enrolled.
- **Secure business processes**: SOA supports security-enhanced environment and identity management. SOA allows administrators to define security policies for legacy, web, or cloud applications as well as for an entire organization. That way, employees gain access only to the data they're allowed to see, and any policy changes take effect almost immediately across the entire enterprise, preventing the business process from being concerned directly with the securing of functions or the trusting of identities.
- **Support and maintenance**: A good service design will reduce the overhead in supporting and maintaining business processes. It allows the business process to track the steps the business is performing and reporting on and does not dilute that layer with technical and functional details. With a more direct integration approach, it becomes difficult to trace the downstream impact of process steps, issues take longer to resolve, and they involve more teams, thus becoming a costly task.

Key service design principles

In Thomas Erl's book *Service-Oriented Architecture: Concepts, Technology, and Design*, he outlined a set of service-oriented principles that should be adhered to in building a service-oriented architecture. These principles give the service architect a good checklist to ensure that the services are working towards a solid service architecture that will satisfy the strategic goals of the enterprise. These principles are very relevant for service design that supports a process-driven architecture:

- **Service contracts**: A fundamental component of service-oriented architecture is a service's contract. Every service must have an accompanying contract. The service expresses its purpose and capabilities via this service contract. It is the contract that informs potential consumers of that service and about what they can expect from it (and hence forms the basis for enabling service reuse—a key goal of SOA). This includes both what functionality it implements and what *nonfunctional* service levels it will meet. The latter includes how secure it is, what response times and throughputs it can achieve, and what level of availability it will guarantee.

A service should be defined based on its external value and not its internal implementation. This is why services suit BPM so well—the business process can concentrate on the outcomes of the service rather than its implementation.

The service contract does not just define the interchange of data, but also its runtime behavior, activities, and outcomes. A service contract expresses how interface and data types are defined, and any policies and quality-of-service factors are attached to the service, but the contract also must communicate the outcomes expected when invoking these services. That is why a WSDL itself is often not enough to define the behavioral contract of a service—this is where a specification of the services and associated service tests come to the fore. Service tests are a crucial part of a well-defined service architecture and build up the trust that is required when reuse is promoted. A process analyst will be more inclined to leverage and reuse existing services if they can run simple service tests to validate that a service will give the outcomes required in the process they are defining.

The focus within the service design stage of any process implementation is to ensure that the service contracts are optimized at the correct level of granularity for the business processes and standardized to ensure services are consistent, reliable, and governable.

- **Loose coupling**: Coupling refers to a connection or relationship between two items. Within SOA, there will always be many interactions between services. When designing these interactions, it is essential that we make the linkage as generic and as *loose* as possible. This is to ensure that the services are shareable between different consumers or solutions, while also being easy to change without impacting any of the consumers of the service.

  Where practical, we wrap the service with a virtual service (or proxy). There are two drivers for this. Firstly, we want to virtualize the endpoint—we don't want to hardcode into our service that we are calling service X on server Y. This would mean that every time X is moved to a different server, we would need to change the process. Similarly, if we replaced X with a new service, our service would need to be modified. It is imperative that the business process does not need to know about where the service implementation is running. Secondly, we want to exchange messages in a generic format—we do not want our service to handle messages (data) in formats that have been defined outside our canonical or business data model. If we pass data to/from service X in X's own format and then we later upgrade or replace X, then our service will need to be changed—even if the change affects a data item that we have no interest in.

  This technique will promote loose coupling between services. This is an essential principle of designing solutions for change.

- **Abstraction**: Through abstraction, we are able to protect the consumer from the details of the underlying service implementation. This is done by abstracting logic into more generic services that can be reused independently and mapped closer to business terms than IT terms. This is an important principle in ensuring that the services satisfy the requirements of the business process but are also designed to offer wider capabilities for the business and are not tied to a service implementation that is just specific to one given process step.

  All business services should deliver a high level of abstraction and should not be dependent on a specific implementation. This provides maximum reuse by allowing access through multiple types of interfaces. It also provides greater versatility in how they are deployed. Business services should only contain essential information in terms that can be understood by all consumers without containing any implementation-specific detail or being tied to any particular underlying technology, delivery channel, or physical location. Changes to the business service implementation should have minimal impact on the service consumer, and there should be no dependency within the implementation on the identity of the consumer that invokes it.

- **Reusability**: Reusability can be seen as one of the key principles and drivers behind SOA. Service reusability focuses on ensuring that services can be reused across the organization without the need to recreate the business logic each time. If reusability is not considered during design, the reuse potential of services would be minimized. What is more worrying for a process-driven architecture is that inconsistency in the behavior of functionality will be introduced where similar services may diverge over time, providing unintentionally different outcomes.

  There is an important handoff between the process designers and the service governance team through the design of services within a process-driven architecture. Each service requirement that a process introduces must be cross-referenced against the existence of an additional planned or implemented capability in the service catalog.

- **Composition**: SOA-based solutions are built by *wiring together* discrete services in such a way that data (or messages) flows between them in order to achieve the desired business objectives. From a solution designer's perspective, SOA is like designing for previous generations of technology—the problem domain needs to be divided into a hierarchy of *modules*. SOA differs from previous efforts due to its near-universal support; the modules you wire together can be implemented in a multitude of differing technologies—both modern and legacy.

The prevalence of SOA and standardized APIs also means that designers no longer reinvent everything from scratch. The first step now is always to try to find existing chunks of functionality that can be composed to meet new requirements. However, the state of the existing implementation will need to be verified to ensure that it meets quality criteria, and that it is in a technology that is not currently scheduled for retirement.

- **Autonomy**: The ability of a service to exercise control and governance over its execution environment is the key for it to provide reliable runtime performance. If a business process is reliant on a set of services that may be owned by different domains, it is essential that their execution is predictable.

  All services must have independence from outside influences with a clear functional boundary and little or no overlap between services. This is essential for their reuse in the BPM layer; otherwise, the business process would need to know about dependencies to facilitate the execution.

- **Discoverability**: A key consideration during design and governance of solutions is how to discover what assets currently exist. It is important to understand the need to identify where opportunities arise for potential reuse. This could be at a high level for the reuse of a business service across multiple business processes or at a lower level for reuse of individual artifacts within the service architecture. The business catalog within Oracle BPM will be populated as services are made available for use in the process layer. To ensure that an enterprise-wide view of the service architecture is given, the services created must be visible to other consumers. Then, services will not be built just to satisfy one business process step but will be able to be discovered and reused in the design of other business processes.

  All services used externally to a given SOA domain are published and consumed via a service catalog, such as Oracle API Catalog. The SOA governance board will ensure that new candidate services adhere to the service governance life cycle, which will be implemented in Oracle Enterprise Repository.

- **Statelessness**: The management of excessive state information can compromise the availability of a service and undermine its scalability potential. Services are, therefore, ideally designed to remain stateful only when required.

  The business process should store any state required to link steps in the process together but no more. Business services should be designed to be short running, where possible, and repeatable. Any long waits should be controlled by the process layer to allow the provision of human interruption, escalations, and reporting.

- **Encapsulation**: Each *module* that we need to set up in our hierarchy must be treated like a *black box*. We do not want to know what goes on inside it—just what effect it achieves. In other words, each service must provide a clearly defined set of operations passing clearly defined data in and out, with all external dependencies (for example, database tables accessed, flat files read/written, and other services invoked) noted.

  It is imperative that we document the capability of a service in a standalone manner for every service—without this, reuse of these services in future business processes will be severely hampered, and changes to these original business processes will be lengthened as the process designers try to understand the actual implementation of the service to verify what capability it serves. Service unit tests should be designed to demonstrate the capability of the service, focusing on what the service delivers rather than how, to allow full encapsulation of the functionality.

Service granularity

Services can be either coarse-grained or fine-grained. A coarse-grained service performs a *big* task. To achieve the same outcome, the alternative would be multiple fine-grained services (with a thin layer of logic to link these invocations together). The first factor that drives the choice of granularity is why that service is being made available. If the service is being made available to remote consumers (trading partners or one of your international data centers), then a coarser granularity will reduce the time spent on network latency and hence improve overall performance. If the service is for local consumption, then finer-grained services are more preferable. By splitting a service into smaller subservices, you increase the likelihood of services being reused. Also, you reduce coupling (the consumer doesn't have to deal with parameters that aren't needed in the one bit of the service it wants to use). This can also improve performance since the consumer may already have some of the data that the service needs; thus, it can skip the service that would have reread that data and go straight to the service that uses it.

It is, of course, perfectly acceptable to expose both the inner workings as subservices and then provide one big service that remote consumers can avail of to execute the whole—getting the best of both worlds. There is always a tradeoff within a service architecture between reusability of fine-grained services and the management overhead added, so the right balance is needed. But within a process-driven architecture, the granularity that is exposed to the business process should be defined by the granularity of the business task at hand. The process should not need to call more than one service for the one business outcome that it requires.

Service categories

As your service architecture evolves and matures, the designers will build up a catalog of services, with each fulfilling a different purpose and each having different life cycles. Some will be shared externally with partners, some used directly within the enterprise business processes, and some intended to be used internally within one project only. As services get built and published beyond one team, a design hierarchy of service layers is required, and it is important that each service is categorized within that hierarchy. A layered architecture helps to assist with meeting the key SOA goals, such as loose coupling, improved reusability, abstraction, and improved agility. The layering is a design pattern that will lead to successful SOA implementations, especially with the introduction of BPM. However, it should not be mandatory to use all layers in all cases. Breaking a service down into smaller components adds flexibility if done correctly but also adds an overhead (at design, development, and runtime), and so must be challenged on each occasion to ensure that each component adds the right value. If a layer is in place that is serving no purpose, then it should be removed.

Implementing a reference service architecture and classifying the services into categories, each with differing roles and rules surrounding their usage, will ensure consistency throughout your design, development, and operations of the SOA environment. It will also allow multiple teams to contribute to the service architecture, allowing teams who know and understand the existing applications to provide services to teams who know and understand the business processes or user interface layer.

Without a governed reference service architecture and classification method, your architecture will deviate away from the structure that allows the benefits of SOA to be realized. An entangled, unstructured set of services would ensue, resulting in an architecture where the impact of change is wide and reuse is minimal. The maintenance of such an architecture will become more difficult than when using point-to-point integrations, and the business process layer will become tightly coupled to a chain of services, losing the clarity and simplicity that it would have if it were built on a well-defined and governed SOA.

> Never mix application logic with business logic in a service; they change at different rates with different stakeholders. Keeping their life cycles separate minimizes the impact of change and increases reuse and agility.

Different organizations will choose different ways to categorize their services. If an organization is heavily reliant on packaged applications, such as **Oracle Cloud Applications** or **Oracle Fusion Applications**, for their core master entities, such as customers, products, and invoices, this may lead to the adoption of a service architecture model and classification closely aligned with that. It is the **application integration architecture** (**AIA**), in Oracle's case, which is built on top of the **trading community architecture** (**TCA**) business data model.

An organization that works predominately to offer out services to partners and wants to closely integrate its business processes with its partners will focus its service categorization on public-facing services and design for multiple protocols with a data definition that can be easily understood by their partners (in an industry-specific vocabulary).

In this book, we will present a service classification model that will allow services to have a well-defined business entry point that allows a catalog of services to be produced and consumed by the BPMN business process. Within these classifications, there will be other metadata that will define the further characteristics of a service, such as whether the service externalizes business logic as rules to allow easy change. This includes whether the service is data-centric or function-centric so that the consumer can understand the downstream impact of invoking the service.

The following reference service architecture model shows one way to categorize your service to ensure there is clarity and governance as to which services should be used in the business process and by its supporting user interface. This model takes into account the requirements of various service consumers. This allows services to be exposed in different protocols with different levels of security as boundaries to consumer change and with variants of data being shared (perhaps based on consumers privileges). The model also presents a series of cross-cutting concerns that must be applied across all service layers to enforce consistency and ensure guidelines are followed in the design and creation of services.

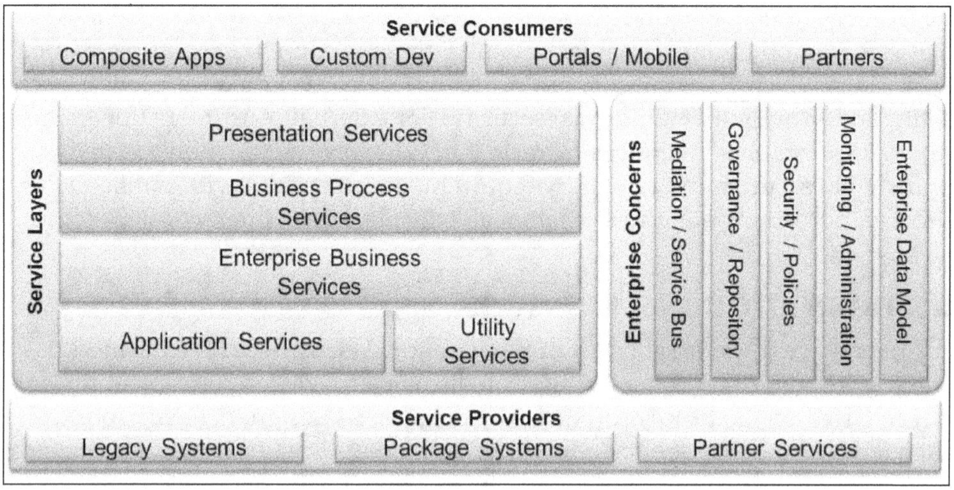

Presentation services

This service layer is responsible for ensuring that the user of the service can consume it in their own preferred way from the operations, data, and protocol perspectives. For instance, a presentation service can publish a REST interface for usage by a partner who wants to visualize data or present functionality via a mobile device. It can present an event interface for consumers who want to decouple their application from the producer's services. It may present a well-secured SOAP interface for a consumer who requires to access sensitive data or functionality. Presentation services should not contain any business logic themselves; they should just facilitate access to business process services or business services to different consumers.

Presentation services enable specific service functionality to be grouped together to provide ease and efficiency for consumers. The purpose could be to minimize calls from a portal's browser to the middleware, to minimize the volume of data returned when providing an interface for a mobile device, or to provide specific naming, structuring, and protocol translation to ease the integration of your service into a partner's environment. It is important that these services are named for public consumers to understand and that the message structure is simplified from the canonical form. For example, the complex types referenced in a set of public-facing presentation services should be flattened into one schema definition file, the consumer should not be responsible for checking whether multiple schema definitions are imported into their projects, and it should be made as simple as possible to consume the presentation service.

For use across domains within an organization (for example, within a business process layer or other departmental systems), these services will be implemented on a service bus, which gives specific protocol support, ease of data translation, caching benefits, and provision of additional security. For external consumers (for example, partner APIs or mobile interfaces), Oracle API Gateway will be used to satisfy the nonfunctional security and reliability requirements associated with public-facing services, supporting system-to-system, web UI, and mobile interaction protocols.

Business process services

A business process service consists of the functional elements of the business processes, with no technical or application-specific knowledge residing at this layer. It will be based on the process models that the process designers have produced written in BPMN. These services should be written in the language of the business. The steps in the business process should mirror how the business sees that process, wherever possible, with the responsibility for the technical details of how that is made possible passed to the business service layer. The business process service should also manage the interaction between automated steps and manual or off-system tasks. The business process service should be aware of the input and output from the off-system tasks and any dependencies between automated steps and the off-system task.

An organization arranges business processes in a hierarchy to manage their complexity, so the business process service should be reusable itself where appropriate. A business process service is typically long-running with multiple participants (defined in swimlanes) and will generally include user interaction and workflow functionality to facilitate the inclusion of manual tasks within the business process.

In order to achieve the loose coupling and flexibility that BPM promises, it is critical when designing the business process service that you focus on what a process does and the steps required to reach the desired business outcome are, rather than how it does it. The *how* will be covered in the implementation of the process steps, which will be delivered via other services within the model. If the distinction between the business process services and the implementation of the functionality in the other services is kept strict, then the business process should only change when the business model changes or when process improvement is carried out. Likewise, any changes to the services that implement the business process should have no impact on the services until there are new features that the business want to leverage.

Enterprise business services

One of the primary aims of SOA, especially in the context of a process-driven architecture, is to abstract functionality away from the underlying IT systems and surface it in a layer more closely aligned with the business. Enterprise business services are a key component in delivering against that aim. They will act as the service façade to a more complex implementation of the functionality exposed. There can be different types of enterprise business services, but all should provide a set of business functionality to deliver business outcomes that can play a part in the business process architecture and communicate in a common business dialect. Enterprise business services will be shared on the service bus and made public across different SOA domains. The interface of an enterprise business service needs to be motivated by the customer's perception from a functional and data perspective—there should be no technical or implementation-specific details exposed. These services should always be designed contract-first, with the implementation added to meet the contract requirements. Therefore, if the implementation changes, such as routing to a new application provider for the service, the interface for the public consumers can remain stable.

These types of services will form the business catalog that a process analyst will utilize in building the BPM process and give a business abstraction of more granular services that deal with the logic and that produce the results that the process layer requires. Their responsibility is to route requests to the correct service that will give the functionality required within the process and will simplify the process analyst's interaction with SOA. They can be further classified into the following types:

- **Business activity services** provide business logic to control the steps to reach a business outcome. BPEL is often used to deliver these services as an orchestration of subservices. Business activity services are normally defined by a noun operating on a verb, such as `issueInvoice` or `checkCreditHistory`.
- **Business entity services** wrap entities from master data sources for a consistent view and maintenance of key business entities. These services should be defined against a business definition of the entity (customer, product, and so on), and it is important to distinguish whether the entity is within the context of a department, a business domain, the enterprise as a whole, or even wider than that, such as leveraging an industry standard canonical model and including partner concerns within the entity.

- **Business decision services** encapsulate frequently changing business rules that should be maintained by specialists within the business department, such as underwriting rules, price determination, customer classification, and so on. A business decision service should still have clear input and output that will form the facts for the decision, but the rules that determine the results should be stored and maintained separately from the service itself as part of Oracle Business Rules.
- **Human task services** present information to users to link off-system tasks or allow users to participate in the business process with knowledge-based decisions. Human tasks can be embedded in the business process if their usage is entirely for that one step of the business process. However, if there is scope for the tasks to be incorporated into other business processes, they should be created as reusable services. If more data in addition to that already used in the business process is required to complete the task, then the retrieval of this data should be included in the human task service.

> Enterprise business services form the basis of Oracle BPM Business Catalog and so should be named with the business stakeholders in mind. If the name and description do not make sense to that audience, then maybe they are not true enterprise business services—a further level of business abstraction is needed for them to make sense in that context.

Application services

Application services play a crucial role in ensuring that the logic held within the business process and enterprise business services is not polluted by logic specific to an application. These services will change only as the applications they connect to change their interfaces or when the business services want to leverage more functionality from the services. These services are responsible for the translation of data between the application's data representation and the business schemas used by the process architecture. Application services will have the name of the application within their name to denote that they are tightly coupled with the applications interface. If the business functionality is migrated to another application, then the application services should be replaced too.

Utility services

Utility services are commodity infrastructure services that provide functionality that is not tied to any business entities, project-specific logic, or applications. These will include services for error reporting, auditing/logging, PDF generation, and so on. These should be standardized across business processes and will be used by multiple business services.

Service design – an enterprise concern

As a service architect, meeting the requirements of the initial design use case is only one of the concerns. It is essential that the wider SOA landscape is considered when producing the blueprints for a set of services within a project or process implementation. We could build up a micro service landscape with each service just meeting the need of the immediate requirement from a project. However, very soon, we will build up services that overlap functionality and that will lead to data quality issues, consistency problems, ownership debates, and ultimately a high cost of refactoring the architecture. If services are not layered correctly, it may seem simpler in the short term, but there will be a large management overhead for the services.

Security should also be the concern of the SOA framework. It is imperative that secure content can be included in the business process, but it should not be the process designer's job to implement the security. Security policies are required that can be attached at the services layer, hiding the complexity of working with these policies from the process designer.

To reap the benefits of an SOA in supporting your BPM initiate, you will need to get your monitoring in place early and at the right level. There is IT operational monitoring that needs to be considered as well as business monitoring. IT monitoring will assist in keeping the BPM execution running smoothly, ensuring that dependent services are responding correctly. Get the SOA monitoring right and the business process monitoring can concentrate on the KPIs and leading indicators that will enhance business operations rather than monitoring IT variations and faults.

One other, very important enterprise concern is the enterprise data model that, from a BPM perspective, should be synonymous with the business terms that support your business architecture. Get this defined right in a collaboration between the BPM designers and the SOA architects, and the processes and services will be built on consistent foundations.

> The more fine grained the services are, the bigger the chance of overlap and increased management overhead. The coarser-grained they are, the more the impact of change. A balance is needed between the two, and service governance is required to maintain the balance that is right for your organization. This governance is of equal importance as you strive for a process-centric view of your service architecture.

Data in the context of SOA

The success of a service-oriented architecture is often in its logical data design. There are subtle differences between modeling a physical data store and a logical model to support the usage of data in services. Physical design concentrates on the system of record, optimizing the storage of data and access to that data in the most efficient way. On the other hand, services and processes deal with the usage and communication of data in the form of messages. This data should be structured in a way that the consumer will understand and include metadata about the message itself (such as the message sent time or source system) rather than about the physical storage of the data (such as last update details).

> Physical data models focus on the storage of data to ensure consistent use across the enterprise, ensuring attributes are stored in one and only one place. Logical service data models focus on the usage of data, ensuring the meaning of the data is included in the service contract and that the consumer is abstracted away from being required to understand the physical model.

The logical data model for SOA is often referred to as a canonical model. The role of a canonical model is to give an abstraction from the physical data model and allow the consumer of services to concentrate on the business definitions of entities without being required to understand the details of data that is proprietary to a specific application.

In building a canonical model, a general model, such as the OASIS canonical model or a more industry-specific model can be utilized. If you have a large application footprint predominately from one vendor, then it is common to base the canonical model on theirs, such as Oracle's **trading community architecture** (**TCA**) model. Organizations can also build their own canonical model that is closely aligned with their business model—this facilitates the use of a common language when multiple business domains are crossed by a business process.

Objects will be used in service design to model the structure of messages that will be passed around the service infrastructure. They represent the organization of the messages that will facilitate the service-oriented architecture. These are hierarchical in nature and shouldn't be tied to a physical data model. Messages will be used to define the data passed between the services and processes—these messages will reference complex types that are grouped together in the object definitions. Both objects and messages will be defined in the form of **XML schema documents** (**XSDs**), so it important to distinguish between them with naming conventions. It is also normal to distinguish between an object/message that is tied to the data structures of a specific application and those that relate to the canonical or business model.

- **Enterprise business objects (EBOs)** give a business representation of an entity. These objects represent the business catalog of data that should be used referenced by business services and processes.
- **Application business objects (ABOs)** give the structure of an application entity that will only make sense within the context of that application.
- **Enterprise business messages (EBMs)** are instances of data that will be transmitted between services and processes. These will reference common elements defined in the EBO. These messages will form part of the service contract for public services and processes.
- **Application business messages (ABMs)** are application-specific data representations that will be mapped to the enterprise data structures via application services.

XSLT and XQuery will be the primary tools used to map messages from one service request to another. XLST is very good at transforming one XML representation into another representation. It has techniques such as templates, allowing the reuse of logic across multiple nodes in the XML document. It is very suitable for data mapping of one structure to another and is very common in integration scenarios. XQuery's strength lies in extracting sets of nodes, performing processing actions on those nodes, and building up the new document based on the results of these actions. Many of the concepts of XQuery will be familiar to an SQL developer, such as querying hierarchical and tabular datasets, restricting and manipulating these to form result sets, and so on. If your requirement suits the method of stepping through each node while mapping the data to a new structure, then XSLT is likely to be the simplest. If the mapping requirement requires more processing on specific parts of the document, then XQuery is likely to be more suitable. Within SOA Suite 12*c*, both tools are available in BPEL and the service bus, so a mixture can be used for their best purpose.

When designing the service interfaces for process-driven services, the language represented by messages is crucial. You must ensure that the messages are understandable to the layer that is consuming the service. Business services should ensure that the process designer has all the data required to populate the input message of a service and returns all the data required for subsequent steps.

> Remember that all data items included in the interface message exposed by a business service in the business process catalog are to be populated by the BPM developer as a part of the composition of the business process, so make sure they are structured suitably and in a dialect that the process designer can understand with limited scope for variance in interpretation.

Service virtualization

SOA promotes loose coupling of components in an attempt to break the dependency and impact of change. Therefore, we should apply this principle of loose coupling within the service design of our process architecture. Services and components of services should not be bound directly to each other. All services should be virtualized to allow routing to the physical service to be changed at runtime. Any service endpoint changes should only result in a small configuration change for its consumer rather than any disruptive redeployment. All public services should be deployed to the service bus to facilitate the mediation of messages between the consumer and the provider. The service bus can also allow the same service to support diverse protocols that a consumer service may require. This virtualization should never incorporate any business logic but should have knowledge of the different versions of services that can satisfy the requests. It can also perform the role of caching or throttling data to protect more complex business service from undesired load.

For routing requests between services within a service domain or between components in a composite service, the mediator can be used. However, if the service is used by service domain boundaries or by different teams, then the service bus should be used. All services should be versioned to ensure backward compatibility of functionality, that audit trails of previous versions should be stored while the new service is transitioned, and consumers are allowed more scope to move to new services at their pace rather than the producer's pace. Services should be versioned with a **major.minor.build** structure:

- **Major** changes denote that the service contract has changed. These are disruptive and effort is required by the consumer to work with the new version of the service. Previous versions are normally kept operational in parallel until all consumers have moved across to the next major version.

- **Minor** changes denote that the functionality or contract structure has changed but that the interface and outcomes are backward compatible with the previous minor version of the service—allowing consumers to pick up the latest minor version without change. As a service consumer, it is important that automated tests are in place to verify that minor changes have not broken the usage scenarios that the consumer relies on the service for.
- **Build** versions are internal iterations of the services and may not be publically deployed and distributed.

Major changes will affect the service contract and require that the consumers rebind to the service to take advantage of the new version. It is crucial that the service deployed on the service bus supports multiple major versions of the service to allow consumers to use upgraded major versions at the stage in their delivery cycle that is appropriate for them. However, there is a tradeoff between being customer focused and offering wide choice and independence to the consumers versus the maintenance overhead that multiple service versions introduce (regression testing as well as the resources that each deployed service may consume). Therefore, a clear and published service decommissioning strategy is required, whereby the consumer knows how long superseded versions of a service will be supported and at what stage they would be required to upgrade.

Service decommissioning strategies often relate to the number of versions of the service deployed (for example, version n-2 always gets retired when version n of the service gets deployed). This is acceptable for services within a domain, but when a service is offered to another domain of ownership or external party, then more planning is needed for the consumer to upgrade to any new version of the service. In this case, the strategy should focus on supporting previous versions of a service for a period of time after a new major version is deployed, where the timeline is agreed with consumers upfront and included in the service contract. The period is intended to give enough time to allow the consumer to make the changes required bind to the new version and have confidence that the new version is stable. Typically, with this approach, public consumers are given 6–12 months before old major versions of services are no longer supported.

Ensuring that the correct version is invoked should be the role of the service bus. The service designer should decide whether service invocations should be routed to the latest major service (with the consumer not specifying any version), a specific minor version, or the highest minor version of a service for which the consumer specifies the major version. This can then be managed operationally at runtime with consumers given the flexibility of which version of the service they utilize.

Service design methodology

There are multiple approaches to defining the portfolio of services that will be delivered as part of an SOA. There is no one-size-fits-all for an approach to identify the right services needed to support current and future requirements. Service should be cataloged into service domains that will define the ownership, funding, usage rights, and categorization of the services.

Service domains are often driven by projects—to understand the ownership of services and how they can facilitate cross-organization business processes, these need to be realigned with business domains. However, business domains get restructured, so these domains should not be confused with an organizational model, which is normally a management structure to facilitate the people organization within departments of a company. SOA domains should be based on people, processes, and outcomes that are required to meet the organization's goals. With this in mind, the collection of services into domains should only change as the operating model of the organization changes and evolves.

Top-down portfolio-driven service design

This approach decomposes the business operating model and supporting business architecture into domains and identifies services to satisfy the functions within these domains. All services are defined upfront, with services implemented as they are required. A central authority is required to govern consistency across service domains, and any new request for services must be ratified from the top-down perspective to ensure it meets requirements set out in the operating model. This method of service design often produces services that map entities and functions to organizational structures, which should be avoided. It is important that the domains, functions, and entities map to the business model and that ownership is defined separately to the organizational silos.

Bottom-up application-driven service design

Often driven by integration projects or package implementations, this approach builds up a catalog of services from how the applications are designed, with the services composed together for usage in different contexts. It is very easy for this approach to produce a *wild west* SOA with a proliferation of services that make sense in one context, but do not support reuse and do not map to the business processes of the organization. It is acceptable to identify what services are available when a new application is implemented, but these services should be classified as application services and treated as such rather than forming part of the business service design.

Use case-driven service design

This approach arises when project requirements dictate the service design. Each use case in a project is considered to produce service requirements, and services are built directly to satisfy the project. In a mature service-oriented organization, this approach can work well, but normally the governance aspects of SOA, that is, ensuring that reuse ensues and that design is consistent across projects, are compromised for project deadlines. This can often result in a *not built here* attitude to the trust of services delivered by other projects and lead to projects repeating work and diluting the link between the service architecture and the business model and processes.

Process-driven service design

This is the preferred approach to build a service portfolio that supports a process-driven architecture, with the business process design dictating the requirements of the service architecture. This approach draws in features of the other design approaches, with services being cataloged into domains and checked against existing services as process requirements arise. They will also utilize application services via the service categorization model (abstracting the application integration away from the business process). Services will still be defined as use cases but within the context of the processes that require the functionality.

Service design should start at the abstract business process, identifying the capabilities required to satisfy each process step and the contract that should be agreed with the service provider to deliver that capability. This contract provides a demarcation between the process definition and the service implementation. There may already be a service defined in the service catalog that will satisfy, fully or partially, the capability required. There may also be an existing application that delivers a functionality that can satisfy the implementation requirements. The following diagram outlines the steps to follow when defining services to support process definitions:

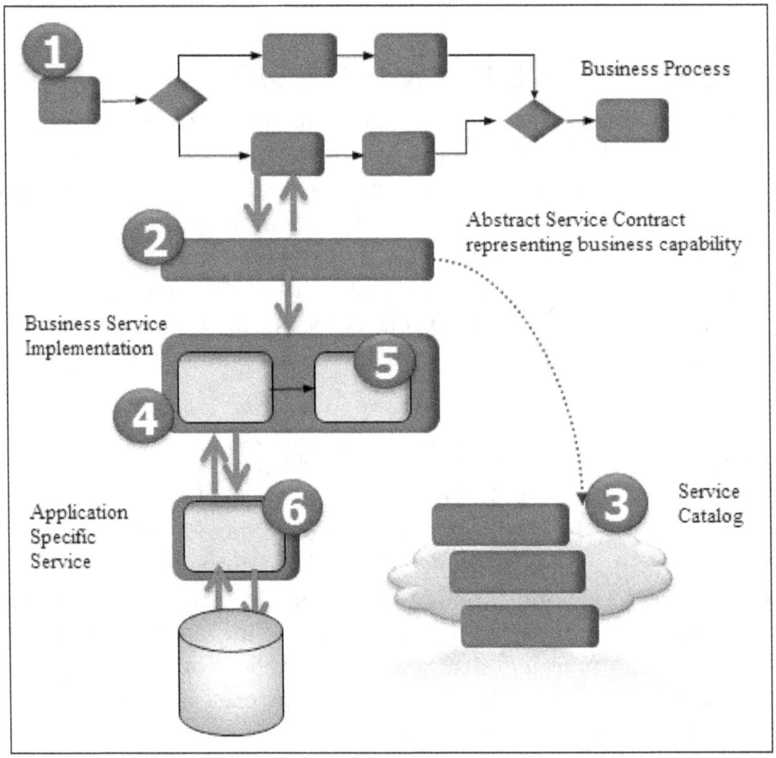

1. **Design abstract business process**: No system terms should be included in this process service, each step should map to an activity to be completed, and the implementation of the step should be of no concern at this level.
2. **Identify abstract services**: Define the contract of the service operation first before any implementation details are considered. Operations, style (asynchronous/synchronous/one-way/event-initiated), business outcome required, data input and output (as business messages), nonfunctional requirements, and service domain/owner.

3. **Refine based on the SOA portfolio**: Group the service operations into service contracts that can be packaged together. Operations will be grouped if they operate on the same objects, perform related activities, or are a part of the same change life cycle. Review the service contract definition and requirements against the current and planned services. Identify change requests to already implemented services that have been initiated by other projects. Submit a request for the new service if there is no existing or proposed contract that satisfies the business process step requirements. If an existing service satisfies the requirement or comes close to the requirements, then initiate tests against the service and identify gaps for which a change request can be raised and the impact assessed. Finally, submit any new service contract or change it from an existing service contract to the catalog for review and reuse within other processes.
4. **Identify implementation details** to define the business logic, application integrations, and mappings required to satisfy the use case and add physical details to service.
5. **Apply service principles** to ensure the SOA reference architecture layering standards are adhered to and identify the composite service required. Classify these as being within the service categories. Break down the service functionality into these layers to ensure that the impact of change is minimized and reuse is maximized.
6. **Identify the use of application services** and map to the application portfolio, defining which application services should be grouped together. Wherever possible, application services should satisfy one outcome, and if multiple calls are required to the application to meet one outcome, these should be combined as a BPEL composite service. If APIs are available for applications, then keep extensions to these at a minimum within the application. If you are building the application service implementation in the source application, then ensure that the service principles are adhered to and that each implementation maps to a specific business outcome in the application, thus minimizing the number of calls into this application.

Applying service design to RYLC

The first task of a service architect within a process-driven architecture is to review the business process design to ensure that the design meets the principles laid out for process services. There should be no implementation details in the process. The process steps should be written in the business dialect, and there should be no splitting of the granularity of business steps due to the process designer's assumption of what services are available. This review of the process model is useful in bringing together the process analyst and the service designer to focus on one common architectural goal. The initial review of the business process that will be executed and the set of business services that will support that execution should be a collaborative process.

Rationalizing the RYLC process into abstract services

In the RYLC example, the service architect walks through the process looking at each step and considering these as abstract services, questioning whether multiple steps in the process could actually be satisfied by one business step, whether a step in the process includes a reference to IT applications that shouldn't be assumed, and whether there are individual steps that are providing multiple business outcomes that you may not always want to be tied together as the process is implemented.

The service designer should pay particular attention for a common process anti-pattern, whereby consecutive steps that do not handoff the process flow to different roles or between manual/automated tasks and determine if there is a business reason for this split. For instance, within an initial RYLC process that the service architect was presented with, the first two steps in the BPMN model performed by the customer relationship manager do not have any true message flow between them and stay within one swimlane. As service architects, we must determine whether these should be implemented as one abstract service or two. The following diagram contains a model that shows an example of this:

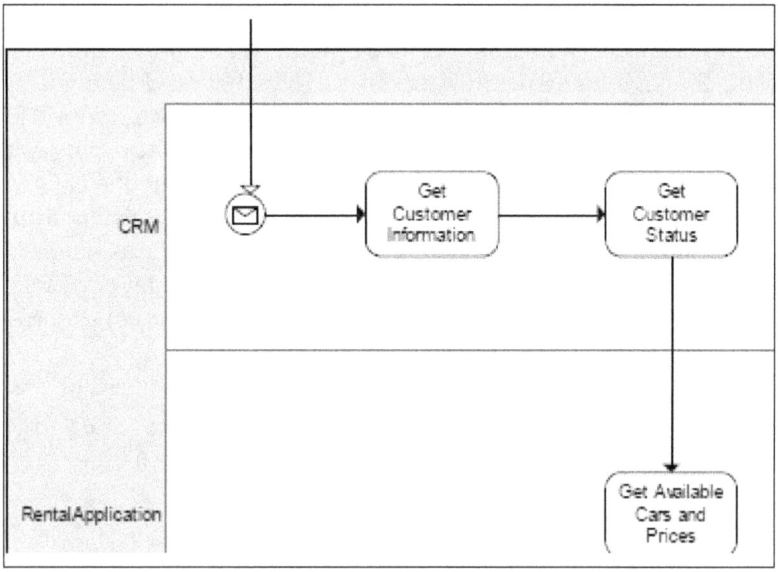

The two steps for **Get customer information** and **Get customer status** are implemented for the same business outcome in this case—to determine the history of rentals from the customer, the classification of the customer from a reward perspective, which will be used when pricing offers, and some general details that will be used when communicating with the customer. The process designer may have split these two steps as they know that traditionally, different systems master the customer contact information, history, and rewards.

However, in the definition of services to support the business process, there should be no application knowledge involved, so granularity of the business service should just be determined based on the process requirements. So, you would only split these steps into two services if the business wanted to report on one step in isolation of the other, if the business wanted to reuse one of the steps multiple times in the process with different input and output, or if the business specified that one of these steps may be owned by a different role in the future.

None of these are applicable here, so the service would create the `CalculateCustomerStatus` abstract service operation that may be part of a composite `CustomerManagementEBS` service, which would take in a `CustomerIdentificationEBM` message and return the `CustomerDetails`, `CustomerHistory`, and `CustomerStatus` complex types—all adhering to the `CustomerEBO` model. This business service can then orchestrate the calls to the customer relationship management and the customer benefits system applications to retrieve the customer information and customer rewards status before returning control back to the process. The following diagram shows the layer of services to be implemented as part of the **Rent a Car (calculate customer status)** process step:

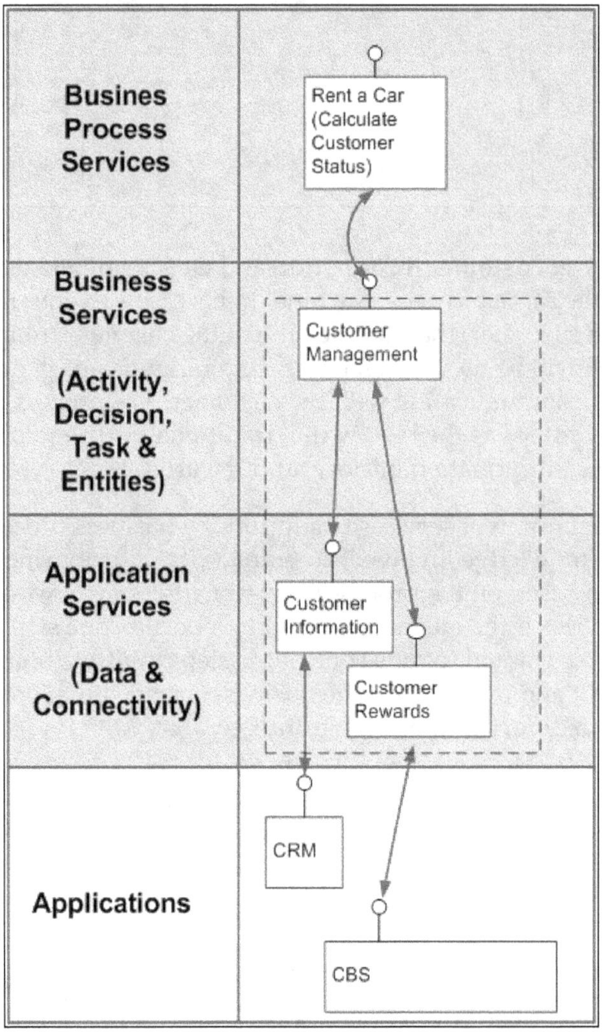

With this design, the multiple steps of accessing this information from different application systems is abstracted away from the business process to keep it easy to understand and simple to change. As application services change, the service contract for the business process should be kept stable. Only changes that result in additional functionality that the RYLC business process would like to leverage (such as a Twitter handle added to customer details) should result in a change to the business service contract.

This approach of contract-first development of business services is accelerated by the service bus that allows the creation of abstract services prior to concrete details being added as the composite service is built to support the functionality. This allows the creation of service catalog entries and tests for those services to be created in advance of the service implementations. The Rent A Car service has a key role as it will be published publically for use in a mobile and web user interface. Therefore, this is implemented with two service interfaces, SOAP and REST. This is achieved by creating a service bus pipeline that will expose the interface through two proxy services, `RequestVehiclePS` and `RequestVehicleRestPS`.

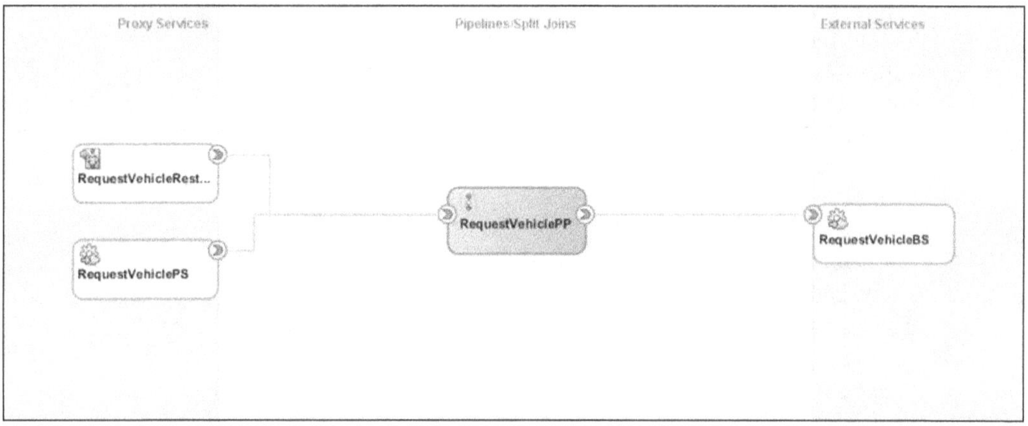

The SOAP interface will be represented by a shared WSDL and XSD. The following code shows this:

```
<?xml version="1.0" encoding="UTF-8" ?>
<definitions targetNamespace="urn:RentACarBPS"
  xmlns="http://schemas.xmlsoap.org/wsdl/"
  xmlns:tns="urn:RentACarBPS"
  xmlns:soap12="http://schemas.xmlsoap.org/wsdl/soap12/"
    xmlns:mime="http://schemas.xmlsoap.org/wsdl/mime/"
  xmlns:xsd="http://www.w3.org/2001/XMLSchema"
    xmlns:soap="http://schemas.xmlsoap.org/wsdl/soap/"
  xmlns:weo="http://www.rylc.org/core/carrental">
  <types>
```

```
      <xsd:schema>
      <xsd:import schemaLocation="../Schemas/requestVehicle.xsd"
        namespace="http://www.rylc.org/core/carrental"/>
      </xsd:schema>
    </types>
    <message name="requestVehicleInput">
      <part name="parameters" element="weo:RequestVehicleInput"/>
    </message>
    <message name="requestVehicleOutput">
      <part name="parameters" element="weo:RequestVehicleOutput"/>
    </message>
    <portType name="RequestVehiclePort">
      <operation name="RequestVehicle">
       <input message="tns:requestVehicleInput"/>
       <output message="tns:requestVehicleOutput"/>
      </operation>
    </portType>
    <binding name="RequestVehiclePortSOAPBinding"
      type="tns:RequestVehiclePort">
      <soap:binding style="document"
        transport="http://schemas.xmlsoap.org/soap/http"/>
      <operation name="RequestVehicle">
        <soap:operation style="document"
          soapAction="urn:RentACarBPS/RequestVehicle"/>
        <input>
          <soap:body use="literal" parts="parameters"/>
        </input>
        <output>
          <soap:body use="literal" parts="parameters"/>
        </output>
      </operation>
    </binding>
  </definitions>
```

The XSD structure is kept as simple as possible for the outward facing consumption, with all complex types defined inline in the schema. This is a simplified version of the vehicle rental structure that will be used within the business process itself:

```
  <?xml version="1.0" encoding="windows-1252" ?>
  <xsd:schema xmlns:xsd="http://www.w3.org/2001/XMLSchema"
    xmlns="http://www.rylc.org/core/carrental"
    targetNamespace="http://www.rylc.org/core/carrental"
    elementFormDefault="qualified">
    <xsd:complexType name="tRequestVehicleInput">
      <xsd:sequence>
```

```
      <xsd:element name="VehicleType" type="xsd:string"/>
      <xsd:element name="CustomerName" type="xsd:string"/>
      <xsd:element name="StartDate" type="xsd:date"/>
      <xsd:element name="EndDate" type="xsd:date"/>
      <xsd:element name="Location" type="xsd:string"/>
    </xsd:sequence>
  </xsd:complexType>
  <xsd:element name="RequestVehicleInput"
   type="tRequestVehicleInput"/>
  <xsd:element name="RequestVehicleOutput"
    type="tRequestVehicleOutput"/>
  <xsd:complexType name="tRequestVehicleOutput">
    <xsd:sequence>
      <xsd:element name="requestResult" type="xsd:string"/>
    </xsd:sequence>
  </xsd:complexType>
  <xsd:element name="RequestVehicleError"
    type="tRequestVehicleError"/>
  <xsd:complexType name="tRequestVehicleError">
    <xsd:sequence>
      <xsd:element name="ErrorMessage" type="xsd:string"/>
    </xsd:sequence>
   </xsd:complexType>
</xsd:schema>
```

The REST version of the service still uses the same data structure and offers the same operation, but its specification is shared in the WADL format, as follows:

```
<?xml version = '1.0' encoding = 'UTF-8'?>
<application xmlns:soa="http://www.oracle.com/soa/rest"
  xmlns:xsd="http://www.w3.org/2001/XMLSchema"
  xmlns:xsi="http://www.w3.org/2001/XMLSchema-instance"
  xmlns:weo="http://www.rylc.org/core/carrental"
  xmlns="http://wadl.dev.java.net/2009/02">
  <doc title="RequestVehicleRestSvce">RestService</doc>
  <grammars>
    <xsd:schema xmlns:tns="urn:RentACarBPS"
      xmlns:soap12="http://schemas.xmlsoap.org/wsdl/soap12/"
      xmlns:mime="http://schemas.xmlsoap.org/wsdl/mime/"
      xmlns:xsd="http://www.w3.org/2001/XMLSchema"
      xmlns:soap="http://schemas.xmlsoap.org/wsdl/soap/"
      xmlns:weo="http://www.rylc.org/core/carrental">
      <xsd:import schemaLocation="../XSDs/requestVehicle.xsd"
        namespace="http://www.rylc.org/core/carrental"/>
    </xsd:schema>
  </grammars>
```

```
    <resources>
      <resource path="/requestVehicle">
      <method name="POST" soa:wsdlOperation="RequestVehicle">
        <request>
          <representation mediaType="application/xml"
            element="cns:RequestVehicleInput"
            xmlns:cns="http://www.rylc.org/core/carrental"/>
        </request>
        <response status="200">
          <representation mediaType="application/xml"
            element="cns:RequestVehicleOutput"
            xmlns:cns="http://www.rylc.org/core/carrental"/>
        </response>
       </method>
      </resource>
    </resources>
  </application>
```

The two service interfaces exposed rely on the same service implementation that will be implemented as a composite of other services from the service catalog.

Building the RYLC service catalog

RYLC wants to ensure that the services that are created to meet the business processes are aligned with their business model and have the correct ownership and change is managed by the business areas responsible for the functions. Therefore, they define a set of service domains with representatives from the business engaged as domain owners. At the start of their journey towards a service-oriented architecture, the involvement of the domain owners is low; they will review the structure of the initial services and ensure that the role of the services that their domain offers to the process architecture is complete.

As the architecture evolves, the domain owner's role will become a key part of business governance over SOA, managing change to the services, assisting reuse of the services, and reviewing the usage and SLAs of the services. They will work closely with the process owners to ensure the correct value is being obtained from the business service layer.

The following are the service domains and responsibilities of RYLC:

Business segment	SOA domain	Responsibility
Core	Car rental	This is responsible for the customer-facing rental services, including all customer channels, which are the branch front office, Internet, mobile and call center. A customer experience representative is appointed to ensure that the processes and services that back the user interfaces lead to a joined-up experience for the customer.
Core	Product and marketing	This contains all the services that facilitate or result from campaigns, promotions, and prospect or customer segmentation and targeting. All decision services relating to pricing a rental package will be included in this domain. A representative from the marketing department has been selected to become an SOA stakeholder and review the marketing capabilities that are surfaced to the process layer and how these will interact with the marketing, car rental, and customer relationship management business processes.
Core	Customer management	Customer experience is paramount within this process and will be focused on all services that produce an outcome for the customer and not just the user interface elements. A representative from the customer account management team will ensure all CRM services meet the need to manage the customer experience effectively and will review the processes to ensure that the end-to-end customer experience is satisfied, suggesting new services or refinements where gaps are found.
Core	Fleet management	The fleet team is responsible for the logistics of ensuring that the vehicles are in the right place for each rental, adding to the stock, and monitoring the use of the vehicles for replacement. They will need to make sure they get the information they require on the return of the vehicle to keep the fleet management efficient and work towards the KPIs and goals set out for fleet management in the business architecture.
Core	Repair	This is responsible for the condition evaluation, repair, and valeting of the returned vehicles. It will be essential that a stakeholder from the repair team understands the effect of the outcomes and SLAs of the repair services on the *new business* processes such as the Rent A Car process.

Business segment	SOA domain	Responsibility
Support	Handling and financials	The role of the finance domain owner of SOA is to ensure that the Rent A Car process utilizes the financial services in the correct way to expedite any invoice processing and to ensure accuracy and minimize faults in the financial processes. Very often, invoice errors will be down to data issues in the upstream process, so it is imperative that there is a finance input into the RYLC Rent A Car process and services.

We will package the business services together into the web services listed in the following table. However, we will leave the application services finer-grained as the rate of change of these services is dictated by the source legacy systems that they operate on, where JCA adapters or APIs from these source systems will be encapsulated in a service that will be invoked from the more coarse-grained business services.

Taking fleet management as one of the key business services and expanding the hierarchy of services within it, we can define the following service catalog. The business service contract should be base-lined early with the SOA developer and SOA testers, so it is imperative that a collaborative review of these definitions is done with the team. However, the more granular layers of the service will be expanded by the SOA developer, and you are likely to see extra services and components added purely for implementation reasons, such as error and compensation handlers, delegators and audit components. These services should not appear within the business catalog and, therefore, would be invisible to the process designer as they extend existing processes or make use of the business services in new processes.

The following table represents an extract from service catalog for fleet management:

Catalog SOA domain	Service operation	Service category	Service description	WSDL
Fleet management	`requestVehicle`	Human task service	This requests a rental on the entered vehicle and date criteria	`RentACarBPS.wsdl`
Fleet management	`findAvailableVehicleTypes`	Human task service	This returns a list of available vehicle models	`FleetManagementEBS.wsdl`
Fleet management	`findAvailableVehiclesAndPrices`	Business decision service	This retrieves a list of vehicles and calculates the rental price for each based on the terms of input given to the service	`FleetManagementEBS.wsdl`

Catalog SOA domain	Service operation	Service category	Service description	WSDL
Fleet management	`bookVehicle`	Business activity service	This registers a rental period for an existing customer	`FleetManagementEBS.wsdl`
Fleet management	`undoBookVehicle`	Business activity service	This cancels a rental period for an existing customer	`FleetManagementEBS.wsdl`
Fleet management	`checkoutVehicle`	Business activity service	This gives a notification that the vehicle has been handed out to the customer	`FleetManagementEBS.wsdl`
Fleet management	`checkinVehicle`	Business activity service	This gives a notification that the vehicle has been returned from the customer	`FleetManagementEBS.wsdl`
Fleet management	`releaseVehicleForRental`	Business activity service	This makes the vehicle available as part of the pool of rentals	`FleetManagementEBS.wsdl`
Fleet management	`evaluateVehicleCondition`	Business decision service	This is a rule-based service to evaluate the vehicle condition	`FleetManagementEBS.wsdl`
Fleet management	`bookVehicleCBS`	Application service	This books and unbooks the vehicle into the CBS booking system	`BookingInformationCbsReqABCS.wsdl`
Fleet management	`updateFleetData`	Application service	This updates the fleet information in the CRS fleet management system	`updateFleetData.wsdl`

The service identification process would continue to observe each step in the abstract business process, allocate it to the correct SOA domain, and discuss the purpose of the service with the owner of that domain to make sure the service reflects the business capability required and not just the immediate use case instance of that service. This role is often fulfilled by the SOA architect as the organization's SOA matures, but even in these early stages, involvement should be sought from the relevant business stakeholders in the definition of the enterprise business services and their allocation to domains. Once the service architecture is defined and each business service has its operations, types, and messages defined, these can be exposed in the business catalog and added as implementation details to the process. The specification of these business services and the supporting application services can then be passed over to the SOA developers for implementing.

Service architecture for the Rent A Car process

The following diagram represents a service architecture map for the Rent A Car process with the process, business, and application services identified and allocated to their owning SOA domains. This diagram, along with a service specification, normally including a service definition, use case, and test scenarios, will be passed on to the SOA development team.

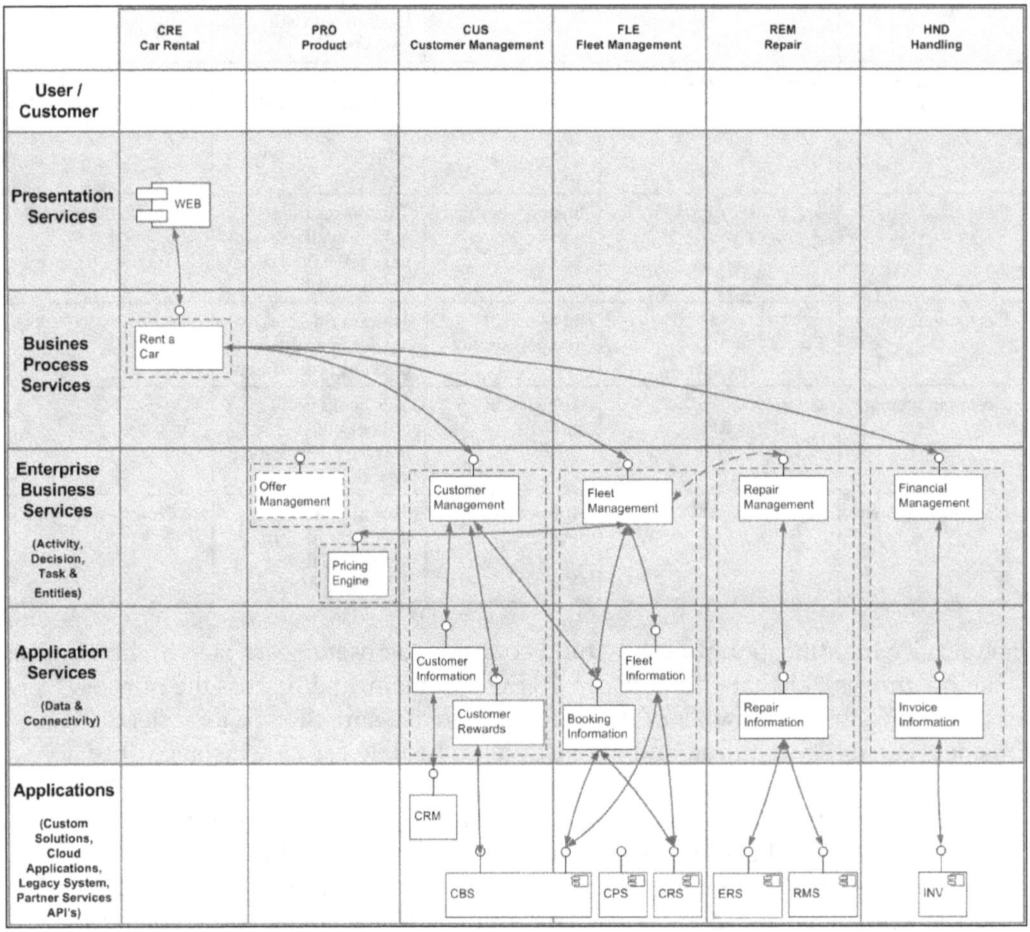

Summary

In this chapter, we introduced the importance of defining your services based on the business architecture as abstract services and adding the implementation details in a layer of services subsequently. The role of data in an SOA that will support business processes has been understood with a critical success factor being the definition of the business data model that, along with services, will form the connection between the process layer, user interface layer, and the service layer. We have understood how important it is to separate application logic from service logic and process logic to ensure that the benefits of a process-driven architecture are realized.

There are a number of key takeaways from this chapter, the first among them being to ensure that the design of the services is considered in the business context to ensure that the service layer does not become a one-to-one mapping of each process step. Then, public services should be designed with the customers in mind, ensuring that the service granularity, protocols, data structures, and naming approach are simple and intuitive to consume. Finally, a service versioning strategy should be defined and communicated with service consumers, with minor service changes not impacting the public service interface and major service changes adhering to a clear rollout and decommissioning strategy.

A service catalog that publishes a list of services with a defined capability in business terms is critical to the success of a consistent process-driven architecture.

5
Composite Applications

In this chapter, you will learn key ways to architect and design the backend services that comprise the composite application based on the example of a new car rental system for our example company RYLC that runs throughout this book. The composite application will be built using Oracle SOA Suite 12*c*. You will meet many of the technologies that form a rich toolset allowing us to tackle various tasks, such as integration to backend systems, complex orchestrations, data validations, and calculations. You will be able to put SOA Suite 12*c* into the broader picture of the modern enterprise toolkit that is Oracle Fusion Middleware. We will shed some light on new features, such as Templates, that help to create a successful solution that follows consistent architecture and design standards.

SOA + applications = composite applications

RYLC has undergone an evaluation of its strategy by looking at the business processes and core capabilities. Now, the board has made an important decision. RYLC aims to take a place among the top three players in the car rental industry. Therefore, a management consulting company has been hired to assess the application landscape and recommend strategies and focus areas that promise the highest impact on increasing RYLC's market share.

Now RYLC's main client-facing application, its rental website, comes under close scrutiny. It has aged. Its rigid design will not support the flexibility needed to support new channels and is not ready to take on an active role as a part of RYLC's emerging automated business processes.

RYLC customers have often complained about the lack of accuracy and responsiveness. In 2014, they don't tolerate having to wait for a confirmation e-mail; they want an immediate and reliable *yes* or a well-explained *no*. The current solution is not built for such obliging online interactions with the customer. It is built in a way that does not even prevent data—that is presented to customers—from being out of sync with the backend data stores.

The reasons for these calamities spawn from its fundamental architecture that is depicted in the following figure. Frontend and business logic are tightly coupled to the data structures in a local database. The data from transactions is sent to the owning applications via nightly batches.

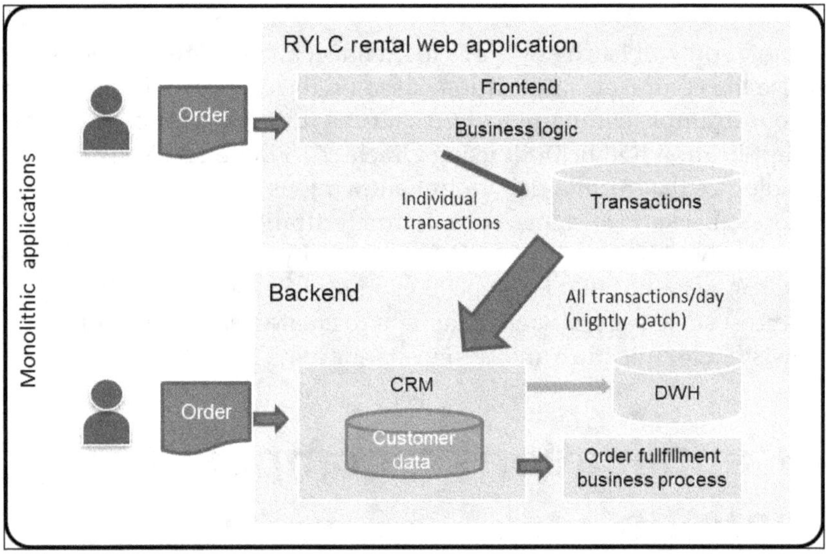

Figure 1: AS-IS - Monolithic application design of RYLC's rental system

This is a classical application design that we find often in transactional systems of the 1990s and recent years, following the model view control pattern with the model, that is, the database, acting as a preliminary data store that needs to be synced with central CRM systems and ultimately the data warehouse.

If we gather all the applications in any large organization in an application landscape map, such intermingled monolithic applications that speak to each other directly via messaging queues, files, batches, and stored procedures are probably still the norm.

SOA is backed up by user requirements

It is worth noting that the needs of a real-time interface, also known as a bunch of SOA services, stems not from SOA-minded ivory towers depicted as the enterprise architecture department inside the organization but from concrete customer requirements of the existing rental application. They request a unified experience and access to the same set of data regardless of the channel they used to interact with RYLC. One of the harshest complaints stemmed from the behavior in the case of an exception in the backend system. If they get a confirmation, they rely on its accuracy and do not tolerate notifications of problems that would arise hours later. In an SOA world, this is an issue since sometimes problems with transactions are caught minutes or hours after the data has been entered by the user.

Always link new architecture styles back to highly prioritized business requirements

The SOA enthusiasts in RYLC's IT teams happily embrace the implicated change away from nightly batches toward SOA-based communication between the applications.

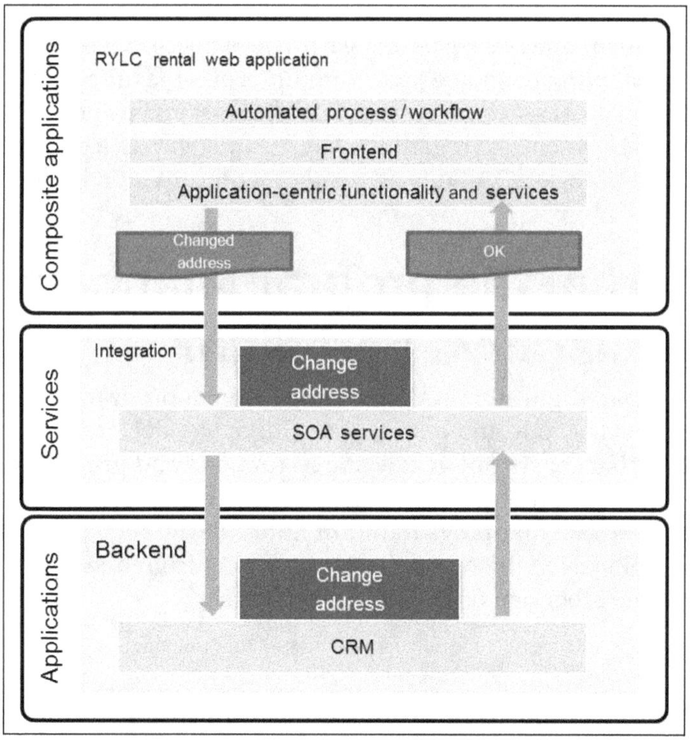

Figure 2: TO-BE - How services help to reuse functionality and integrate with the backend

What are composite applications?

The SOA service's job is to provide pluggable functionality as reusable building blocks by abstracting existing applications and data stores. Still, most of the time, these SOA services are too abstract or generic to be placed into concrete use cases as they are. Approaching the last mile, they leave you on your own at places where something concrete happens and where a user interacts with a system to solve a concrete business problem, such as *booking a rental*.

Composite applications form a set of best practices and technologies that support the positioning of our SOA services into the context of concrete use cases. These best practices ensure the pluggability of reusable services into concrete frontends. This kind of functionality, which is local to a concrete use case, a channel, or a scenario, is depicted in the preceding architectural figure as **Application-centric Functionality and Services**.

Composite applications can be seen as the latest step in the evolution of fundamental software decomposition concepts. This journey began in the 1990s with CORBA, which laid the foundation for the concept of isolating the complex aspects of the technological challenges of a distributed component model into an early version of middleware. CORBA was also an early adoption of the emerging object-oriented paradigm of software development. The late 1990s and early 2000s injected these concepts into the Internet programming language Java, with **Enterprise JavaBeans** (**EJBs**) offering remoteable functionality as scripts (Session Beans) and core business objects (Entity Beans). It makes perfect sense to regard the key technologies in a modern SOA middleware such as Oracle SOA Suite as yet another incarnation in this journey.

Moving from the programmatic paradigm to the declarative paradigm

The fundamental paradigm shift is a move away from a programmatic (code) solution that consists of code and annotations (EJBs) to a declarative (models and wizards) solution that consists of visual representations and graphical editors. Thus, the scripts in Session Beans become orchestrated services in the composition language *BPEL*. The data mappings found in Entity Beans become wizard-driven, visual *XSLT* mappings, in which you draw a mapping from one attribute on the left-hand side to the other one on the right-hand side.

The Oracle SOA Suite journey

By nature, this journey towards the declarative approach to software engineering was sometimes bumpy, and early adopters remember the frustration tolerance needed to deal with creating complex BPEL processes around 2009. Cryptic exceptions resembled the experience of early J2EE development in the late 1990s. Meanwhile, Oracle spent a lot of time and effort in making the development experience as smooth as possible. We can see how history repeats itself. The 12*c* versions show a plateau of development maturity that is similar to the J2EE development experience of the early 2000's application servers that was based on well-understood design patterns and robust design-time and runtime behaviors.

To which degree all the statements that have been made on the adoption of recent SOA/BPM middleware remain mere marketing statements remains to be seen. Yet, it will be measurable. While currently most skills are still available on large programming languages, it will be very interesting to see how the *Oracle SOA Suite developer* becomes a mainstream skill. Through consolidation of skills, large system integrators tend to build Oracle teams and look out for the respective skill sets.

Beyond 12*c* – the trend of the zero code

The longer term trend is clearly a *zero-code* approach to software development. On the Oracle platform, we can develop enterprise software, such as automated business processes, visual depictions of page flows, using natural language for business rules, and using the expressiveness of visual orchestration of services in BPEL, that is code free to a large degree.

How to get on board?

It is still important to recognize the dominance of existing development cultures. It is a daunting change management task to move the mindset of a whole existing in-house development team that heavily identifies itself with programming languages or open source to such a declarative visual approach. This indeed implies a fundamental mental shift, and existing skillsets that individuals are proud to have gathered over many years are in danger of becoming obsolete.

SCA as the next generation of containers

Services are positioned to coexist and collaborate with building blocks that bridge the gap between the business and the IT domains. **Service Composite Architecture** (**SCA**) composites are becoming commonplace as simple services that are combined and orchestrated into more sophisticated composite services, designed to ensure business agility and flexibility and to guarantee high elasticity, scalability, and availability.

SCA is becoming the next-generation runtime container. Composite applications built on Oracle Fusion Middleware rely on SCA as the technical umbrella. BPMN-based business processes, BPEL-based integration processes, business rules, and data mappings all reside in the common playground of SCA composites.

This notion of *container* was the key benefit that EJBs brought into the Java world. It allowed abstracting away complex transactional and exception handling logic and providing a convenient frame in which to develop heterogeneous types of solutions.

The difference between SCA and EJBs is that what sits in a container can be code but is not restricted to programs in one programming language (Java). Instead, what runs inside a composite can be chosen from an emerging array of building blocks to structure business software, such as business rules, programmatic procedures, data access, access to message queues, and access to serialized objects, containing different types of functionality, such as agent, aspect, service, process, event, use case model, and composition.

This reflects that SOA services expose functionality that potentially leverages many different implementation technologies for business logic and data access logic. These technologies range from mainframe CICS web services and Java EJBs to BPEL and rule engines.

Thus, SCA is becoming the standard that many vendors embark on to create composites. SCA aims to provide a model to create service components and a model to assemble service components into business solutions.

How does SCA composite behave from the outside?

From an architectural point of view, SCA allows a **component-based development** (**CBD**) approach. CBD follows the key SOA principles, such as reusability through encapsulation with an external service contract and an assembly model to deploy and maintain the internally used artifacts as one complete module.

To make the service-oriented approach usable on each architectural level, the main SCA design concept is the independence from the transport protocol and implementation technology. To achieve this, the external communication protocol is bound separately to the composite. This means that SCA services internally don't have any primary dependency on **Simple Object Access Protocol** (**SOAP**), which is one of the protocols that the SCA composite offers for communication to the outside world! Thus, the description and representation of an SCA composite's exposed service interfaces is technology neutral. Hence, the SCA container implementation can accommodate possible data format conversions, such as WSDL to Java and Java to C++. SCA allows provision of the same interface to different transport mechanisms, such as SOAP over HTTP, JSON over HTTP, SOAP over JMS, and others.

The many colors of SCA's internals

Service composition and application design can encompass all architectural layers. SCA composites aren't restricted to integration aspects. It's possible to create an SCA composite that embeds BPMN-based business processes, BPEL-based integration processes, Java-based application logic, rule engine-based rule logic, and even database access logic.

Whether it is good designing is another matter, yet it is possible to mix and merge such heterogeneous technologies under the umbrella of one SCA composite. And they can share one transaction context, thus providing a seamless set of collaborative technical team players.

Impacts of SCA on the architecture and design guidelines

Architects need to understand this openness of SCA and provide clear guidance for the developers. They need to stick to the *separation of concerns* principle. This can lead to design guidelines that forbid mixing integration logic with database access logic in the same SCA composite.

SCA provides a language-neutral syntax using XML to configure and wire disparate and distributed service components together to create business-aware composites. One SCA composite can comprise several components that are wired together to provide coherent functionality.

An SCA composite is typically designed in a graphical editor. We can configure the operations and channels of the service that the composite exposes to its consumers as well as the references that provide the bindings to external resources that the composite depends upon, such as deeper-level services and adapters. This means that implementation can use other providers' services hosted elsewhere. As an example, an SCA composite that is categorized as a task service can call several SCA composites that are categorized as entity services and utility services. We can use an ESB as an intermediary to establish further decoupling. Through the SCA visual framework, we can wire together the components needed for each operation, such as the BPEL process and a few supporting Java Spring Beans.

An implementation can also have one or more configurable properties. We can configure a property, and this activity affects the business function of the implementation. The SCA assembly layer captures the configuration of components and their dependencies on other components' services that have been created based on the SCA programming model. SCA comes with a proven mechanism to build coarse-grained components as assemblies of fine-grained components.

Templates in SOA Suite 12*c* for consistent designs

To define a reference design for certain types of services is one thing. To ensure that all developers always adhere to this design is a completely different task. For example, an architect mandates to use BPEL for an *orchestration* of services, which is a series of calls to underlying web services. What we see very often in projects is that a developer who is not familiar with BPEL uses the SCA feature of embedding Java and uses a programmatic solution for calling those services. If there is no governance that indicates such derivations from the mandatory design, the result is a heterogeneous solution architecture.

In SOA, this is very problematic since it results in an overall solution that is much harder to understand, document, and maintain. Often, the corresponding issues won't be recognized until the development team changes. Then, very often, the complexity of the solution is understood to be high enough to motivate a complete rewrite.

Oracle SOA Suite 12*c* introduces a feature that helps to ensure a higher degree of consistent, homogenous design. Architects or chief developers are able to create a template for each service category that can be used as a starting point for the development of individual composites. An example is a *business activity service* (or *task service* in the taxonomy of author Thomas Erl) that contains BPEL and for each endpoint, a mediator. A *business entity service* can be defined to access a database and another one to access a message queue.

This new Template feature thus greatly enhances middleware development maturity because it allows a broad range of developers to design and implement high-quality solution components.

A template is typically not a complete, fully coded, piece of functionality, but a skeleton that can be used for the following:

- To suggest a specific design for certain types of services
- As a starting point for different service types
- As a BPEL scope, which deals with repetitive functionality, such as exception handling

The deployment model for SCA

SCA offers a mechanism to package and deploy sets of closely related components that are developed and deployed together as a unit. It decouples service implementation and assembly from the details of infrastructure capabilities. Thus, SCA relieves programmers from the drudgery of traditional middleware programming by abstracting it from business logic. It allows developers to focus solely on writing business logic.

The building blocks of a composite architecture

Now that we have understood the underlying component model, SCA, we will look at the technologies that make up a composite application. While in this chapter, the attempt is to cover all these technologies and put that into the perspective of a clearly layered complete architecture, the remaining chapters will take a deeper look into several of these.

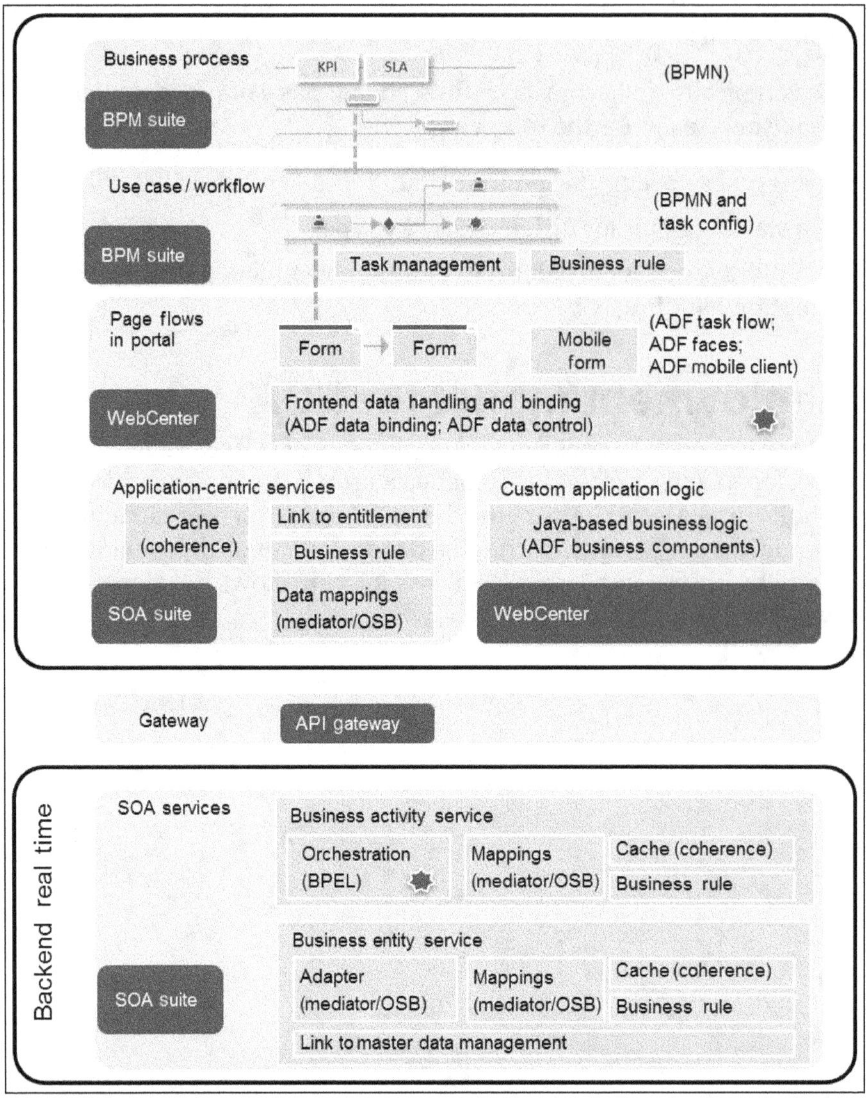

Figure 3: Putting a composite application in the context of a complete enterprise solution

An end-to-end walkthrough – from processes to use cases

To address the issues with RYLC's rental application, major aspects of its design are changed following the notion of a composite application. The goal is to enable the company to inform both customers and employees about important events and certain actions they need to take. Therefore, they get tasks assigned to them depicted by a certain state in the end-to-end *order to cash* business process. We will go through one scenario that is a part of this process.

Here's what has happened until now. The customer has entered a rental request. The rental system recognized that all cars are already booked for the requested period. It offers the user that they be on a waiting list and to inform them when a car becomes available. This conditional behavior has been implemented as a condition in an ADF task flow in WebCenter Portal.

Now, an event has been created through real-time event processing in Oracle BI that indicates that for this particular timeframe, the desired car type becomes available. This event triggers a distinct subprocess of the order to cash process—*waiting list - product available*. Therefore, we use OSB to create a BPMN process start event (notification). This process has been modeled and designed in the BPMN notation and runs in the BPMN process engine in BPM Suite 12*c*.

Thanks to the new features, it is possible to align this detailed subprocess and the events it generates to the *increase the count of renters per customer contact by 20 percent* KPI. This KPI has been defined on a step in the value chain in the new BPM Suite feature, *value chain map*.

The process *waiting list - product available* now enters a task in the customer's task list. Since we cannot assume that the customer regularly checks for the tasks that RYLC assigns to them, this task is implemented as an actionable e-mail. This e-mail contains a URL that points to a prepopulated proposal for a rental based on the conditions the customer expressed interest in before.

Designing read services – a shift from WSDL to REST

Another ADF task flow guides us through the activities of the respective use case *decide on available car*. Each of the forms in this use case retrieves its data via APIs that use JSON as the exchange format. Please note that we do not use WSDL-based services here. Instead, we use a lightweight mechanism in an SCA composite in Oracle SOA Suite: The OSB accesses this data from a prepopulated set of cached data, and it exposes it in the JSON format. The cache can be implemented using the coherence cache, which comes out of the box with the OSB *business service* using the data format **plain object format** (**POF**) to store data in the most efficient way. The mediator uses the binding features in SCA to retrieve this data.

The solution design neglects some of the more rigid SOA best practices that impose a more heavyweight approach using XML schemas in WSDLs for each service instead of JSON. Such a pragmatic approach to SOA is justified by the need to provide access to cached data in the most time- and memory-efficient way. Additionally, JSON and REST are becoming increasingly the default approach to read data. This change to REST and JSON stems from mobile applications since here, they form the most used transport mechanisms.

This shift towards REST for the reading functionality implies a shift in terms of governance. SOAP- and WSDL-based services are governed at the level of the data type definition from the exchanged data—XML schemas (XSDs). In the REST style, the quality of the data in the data source, which, here, is the data in the cache, becomes the focal point of governance.

Designing writing services – WSDL and SOAP still reign

At the end of the use case, all rental-relevant data has been gathered. Now, we need to store this rental in the backend systems. This is a business-critical functionality in which we need to be able to track successes, all kind of failures, performances, and timestamps. Therefore, the laxness proposed in the read functionality earlier is permitted for important transactional behavior. Now, all rigid and strict SOA principles and design patterns apply. We use the WSDL-based operation *confirm rental*. This operation consists of a rental type that contains the customer type and product type, or it is expressed in all detail through XML schemas (XSDs) that jointly make the payload part of the service interface.

The ADF task flow, therefore, calls an application-specific version of the confirmed rental service. It is here that we apply application-specific checks on user roles and rights, determining whether the user, in the role he is assigned to, is allowed to make the attempt to make changes. These checks are not implemented right here but are consolidated in the business rules of the entitlement component. This isolation of the user roles and rights functionality above the "public service layer" is critical to the success of the overall solution since it enables a high level of reuse on the level of business activity services that are available domain-wide. All business logic that deals with actually confirming the rental is not positioned in this application-specific service type; in this regard, it acts as a mere façade.

From composite applications to domain services

Until now, we have not left the boundaries of the composite application part of the overall architecture. The application-specific service now calls its domain-wide available public service counterpart, the *confirm rental BAS*, where **BAS** is short for **business activity service**.

The notion of a context-specific functionality that should reside outside of reusable services as motivated here is controversial. Many SOA architects would argue that all functionality, including entitlement aspects and local data mapping, should reside in a central service catalogue. Thus, it is an architectural decision that each organization needs to address and follow consistently. The fundamental advice is to set up a governance model in place that ensures that decisions on ownership are followed consistently.

Now, we need to ensure reliable entry of all data in the consistence of the *confirm rental BAS*. Therefore, this service uses BPEL to call more atomic services. To secure the transaction, we can use either implicit transaction monitoring mechanisms if they are supported by all backend systems that we integrate with, or we have to use the notion of compensating operations just in case something goes wrong. BPEL is well positioned to deal with both solution types.

Then, we must find a way to access backend systems. It is a good practice not to position such integration logic in a business activity service. It is better to isolate the various formats and data mappings into an open category depicted as **Business entity service** in the preceding image. The architectural relationship of these service categories is described in the preceding image.

Now that we have been through the overall application, we will spend a bit of time on each layer and discuss the functionality, technologies, and the Oracle middleware tools.

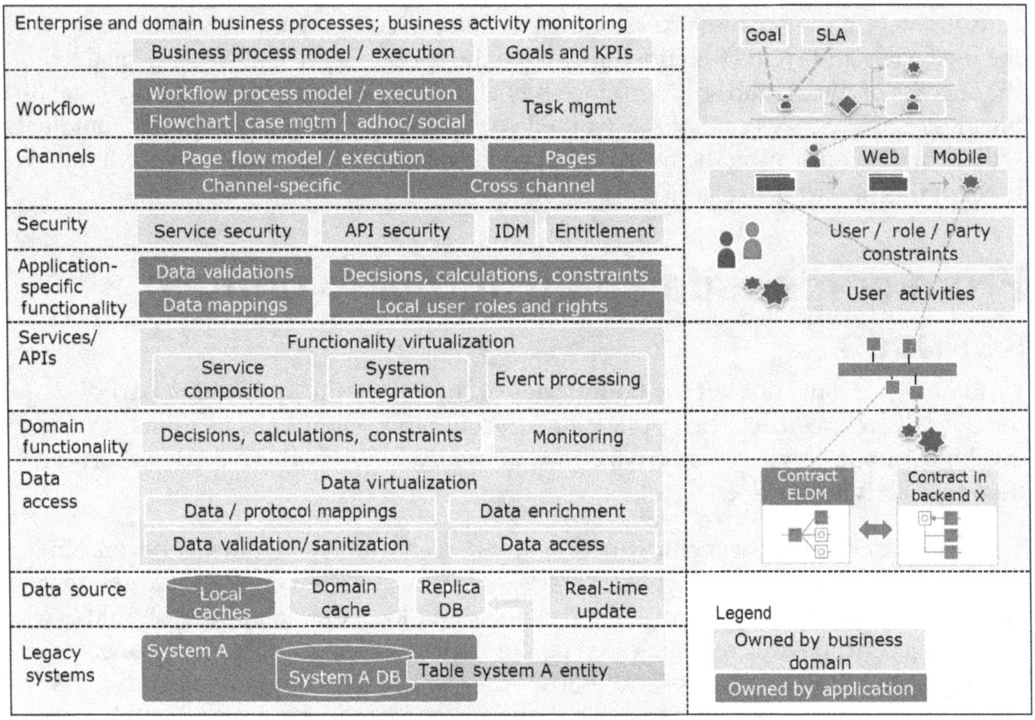

Figure 4: Functionality and position of architecture layers

Linking domain processes to local workflows

It is important to recognize that many composite applications will continue to not be aligned with domain- or enterprise-level automated processes. To reflect such a reality, the highest layer, *enterprise BPM*, will exist in isolation or be weakly linked to composite applications in many organizations for several years. The future will show whether the approach of aligning and linking departmental workflows with such business domain- or enterprise-level processes, that cross-departmental silo barriers will indeed emerge. The good news is that Oracle BPM Suite 12*c* allows such a link between enterprise and business architecture down to composite applications and their business processes.

Components of the process layer

The functional building blocks of the process layer, the supporting standards and technologies, and the respective Oracle tools are put into perspective in the following figure:

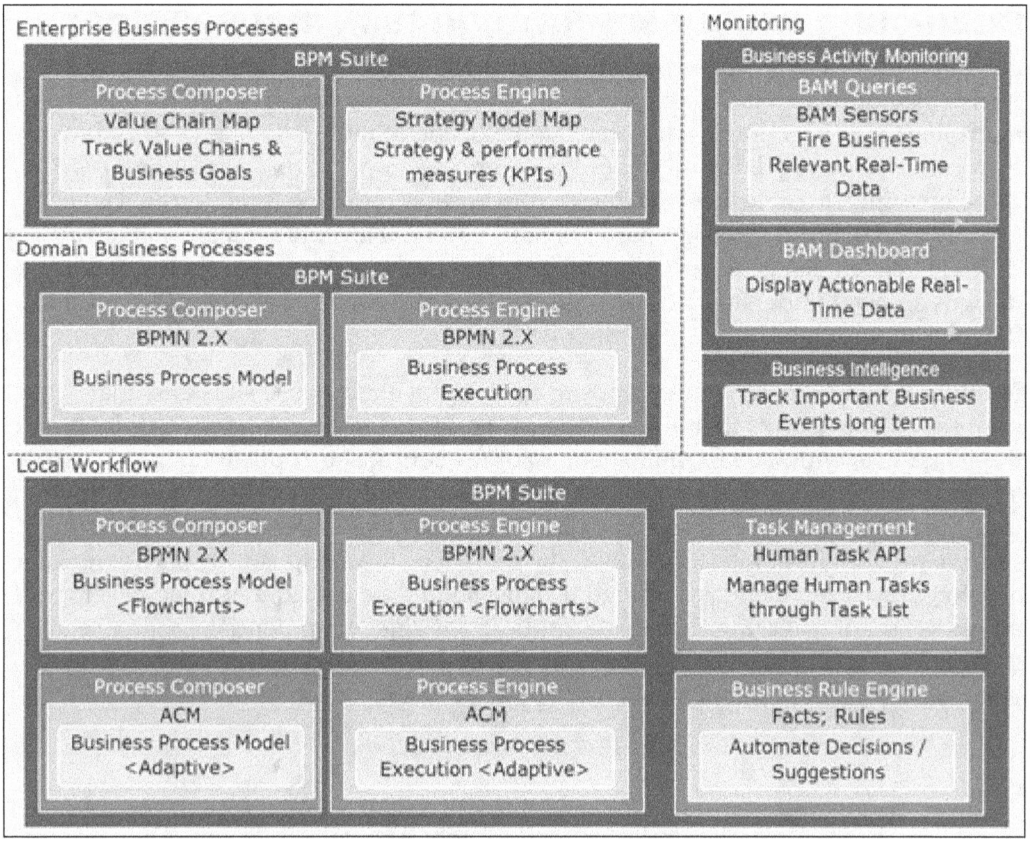

Figure 5: BPM - Functionalities, technologies/standards, and Oracle tools

Automated processes are the new kid in town

When we look at RYLC's car rental system and how it was developed in the first place several years back, we can see that in the past, there were discussions on putting a process automation layer on top of the application. It just has never materialized. This is very typical of the level of adoption of BPM. We can see many organizations realize that now is the time to reconsider process automation since the need for process transparency and adapting to the customer's needs for tracking and understanding the status of interactions becomes paramount.

The lesson learned here is that it's important to start introducing automated processes as part of composite applications only when a strong business case outperforms the forces of fear that go with introducing a very new, potentially disruptive technology.

Interacting with users through task management

An automated business process sometimes needs decisions or data from humans. It uses the notion of a task to obtain it. Most applications that exist do not have task management as part of the solution design. So, one of the challenges of introducing a process automation layer on top of the composite applications' user interfaces is to come up with a feasible solution design for process/human interactions via *human tasks*. Fortunately, such design patterns have emerged around Oracle's stable *Task API*. The real challenge is not technical but rather making sure that such solution designs are well understood among the business stakeholders and developers since it's such an unfamiliar concept for many.

If you find that users of your composite application already use a task list that imposes and structures their daily work, you might want to consider consolidating these task lists with the task management of the composite application into a *unified human task component*. It is a good practice to isolate the creation of such a component into a micro project in itself since it potentially invokes a distinct budget that you want to prevent from interfering with the budget of the composite application. Such a technology component as a unified task list should be considered to be developed across the set of emerging composite applications since it's potentially valuable at the domain level or even at the enterprise level. It is best to apply service-oriented principles to the creation of such cross-application components.

Notifying through business activity monitoring

With the introduction of an automated business process comes process transparency. Now, you probably do not want to look at individual process instances each time you want to find out how your *rental* process performs. To obtain an aggregated view of what's going on right now and what's gone on in the immediate past, business activity monitoring is the tool to use. Oracle worked hard on migrating its BAM tool into the infrastructure of the fusion middleware, and it is becoming well integrated with the enterprise and business architecture features in BPM Suite 12*c*. The line that divides BAM from classical BI is best understood by noting the time window they are concerned with. While BAM gathers a huge amount of data, which needs only to live typically for one week, BI stores all relevant business events much longer, up to 10 years for regulatory reasons.

The following figure puts these aspects into the perspective of a *decision dashboard* that uses **adaptive case management** (**ACM**) features to suggest the following actions and supports decision making. In the future, complex event processing, making real-time decisions, and aggregated big data will further enhance such applications that support decision making.

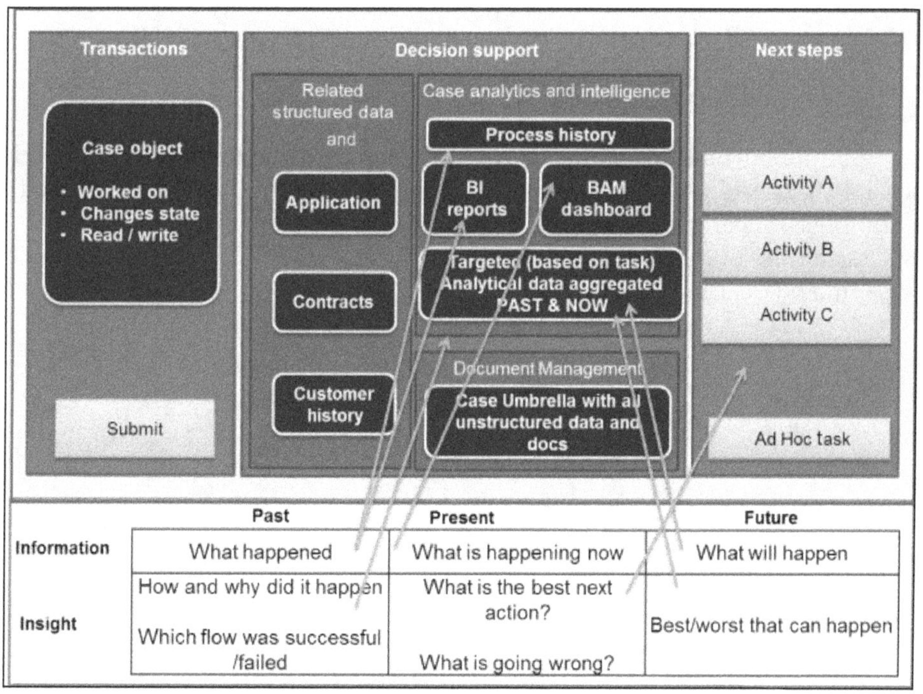

Figure 6: BAM and BI in the context of a "decision-making cockpit"

When to use a business rule for decision making in the process

A process model is made of activities after which one or several activities follow. In the simplest scenario, the relationship is expressed through a direct line. If we have to make a decision on the next activity, we use a BPMN *gateway* in the process model to express that decision. It is good practice not to use a set of gateways in order to express the algorithm of decision making in the process model. Instead, use a rule service that calculates the potential next steps, and use a gateway that retrieves the calculating data and decide on the flow.

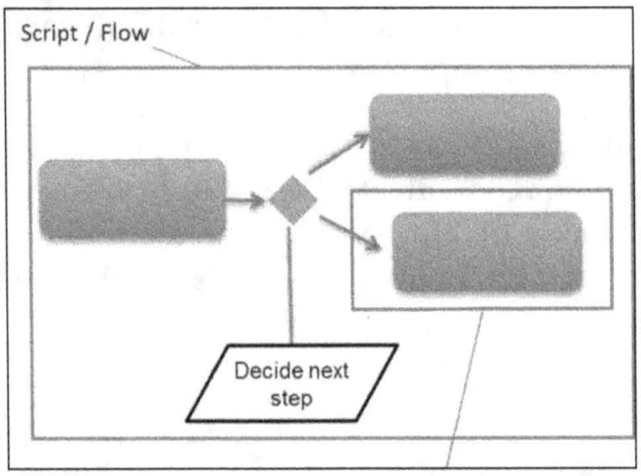

Figure 7: Business rules in processes - deciding followup activities

For very simple calculations that just work on process variables that exist already, it is feasible to use a lightweight XPath expression. When the decision rule is either more complex or changes independently of the design of the process, it is better to use Oracle Rule Engine, which is part of the license of BPM Suite to isolate the business rule on decision making.

Components of the multichannel application layer

It is crucial to depict the goals of your individual instances of a composite application. For example, it might be necessary to isolate user interfaces, while maintaining the desired reuse for the flow of a use case and the look and feel across channels.

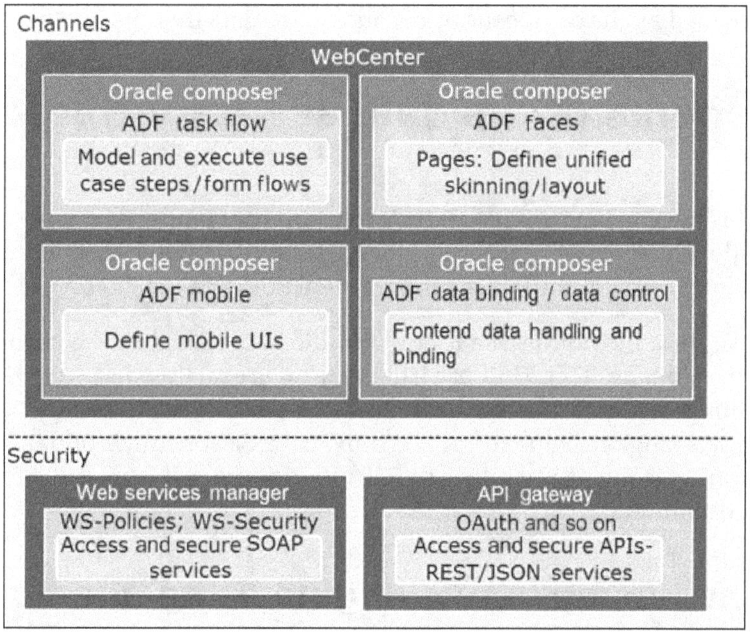

Figure 8: Channels and security – the functionality, standards/technologies, and Oracle tools

The security features in the *web service manager* and the *API gateway* sit on top of the services provided by SOA Suite.

Current application frameworks have a tendency to create a deep dependency on architectural layers, such as business logic and database access, that should not concern frontends anymore. To design a maintainable solution, it is crucial to understand these dependencies and process them in regard to broader architectural goals. The trend in composite applications is that each architectural layer is independent of the others. Then, it is easy to exchange one layer's technology without affecting the other ones. It is always wise to question your solution design, *How much of an effect would the exchange of the used application frameworks have on the overall solution?*

Establishing the notion of a clear service/API layer prevents such undesired dependencies from being created. The preceding figure shows this as a distinct gateway to SOAP-based services and another one to APIs that work on JSON in the REST style.

Components of the functionality virtualization layer

Now, finally, we've come to the heart of integration logic. The goal is to provide a flexible set of tools to read, write, and update data in a database that is located in an application owned by the composite application or in data that sits in other applications.

Components of the data access virtualization layer

Currently, it is hard to summarize all the tools and the standards and technologies that potentially collaborate in order to achieve access to local and remote data into one tool category, such as *ESB* or the more recent *API gateway*.

Instead, we suggest the notion of a logical bundle of tools under the umbrella term *data access virtualization*. This kind of virtualization is exactly what we strive for. It must be completely transparent to the user of a piece of functionality, where the data that it's working on stems from. The only aspect a consumer of data access should care about is this: "What does the service do for me?" This is the essence of SOA-based thinking.

Using the business rule engine as an alternative to classical integration tools

Business rule services encapsulate decisions in a decision tree, such as *if good customer, then...*, as well as validations that are often used as preconditions for a function. Validations ensure that the data is in the correct state and is context-specific when required, such as *customer data is correct*.

The solution matrix for data access virtualization might be surprising for some, where the usage of the business rules engine is suggested. This reflects a subtle but strong move away from more classical approaches to all kinds of logic, to which integration logic belongs, towards using the business rule engine. Illustrated in the following figure is how the notion of decisions on what happens next is at the core of many architectural components of an enterprise software solution:

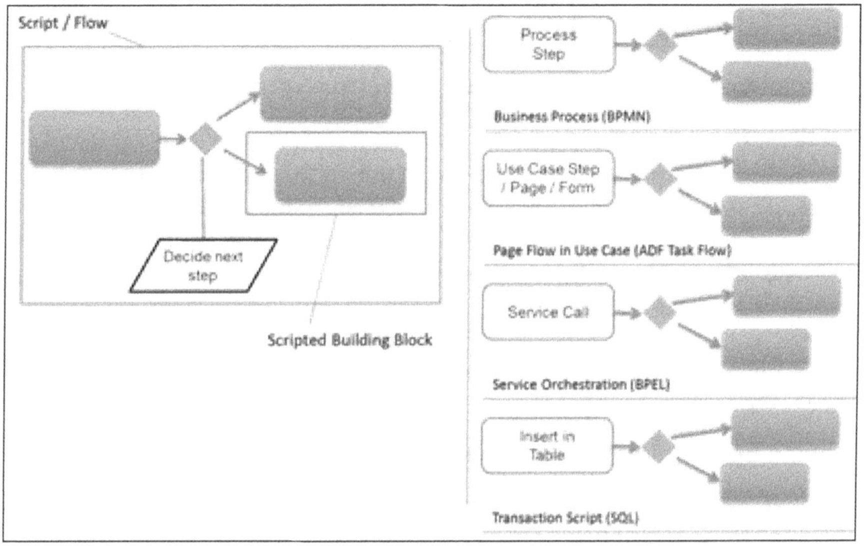

Figure 9: Decision rules found all over enterprise software

The following forces can well indicate the usage of a business rule in a rule engine, over a more classical approach:

- The logic is of business relevance
- The logic changes more often than the script/flow that uses it: note that requirements change often in early phases and soon stabilize, so the question is, how often the rules in a well-introduced environment need to be changed
- The logic is too complex to be used through a middleware wizard (XSLT mapping, SQL query creation)
- If the code is expected to be maintained over time, especially if a flexible sourcing strategy with exchanged teams is desired, migrating the logic to a rule engine will be beneficial

Other types of integration logic that motivate a business rule engine

Too often, developers motivate a fallback to well-understood programmatic solutions when faced with a challenge where the wizards of Oracle Fusion Middleware are too simplistic. A good example is the mapping of complex business objects, for example, a contract that contains a customer and several products. Very often, the better alternative to Java or other programming languages is the usage of a business rule engine.

The solution matrix for data access virtualization suggests the usage of a rule engine in the following scenarios:

- **Create SQL query**: Complex query aggregating data from several tables
- **Data format mappings**: Complex data mappings (compound entity) instead of XSLT/XQuery
- **Validate/sanitize data**: Complex validation rules instead of XML schema checks and Schematron
- **Entitlement**: Define roles and rights - configure rights per role in relation to data entities and their attributes

We see that the business rule engine becomes a potent player on many design challenges that can help to achieve the goal of *zero code*, while improving the collaboration between business and IT, as well as managing time to market for changed algorithms.

So, there is a major trend toward using the rule engine instead of programmatic solutions; the figure indicates where its use should be considered.

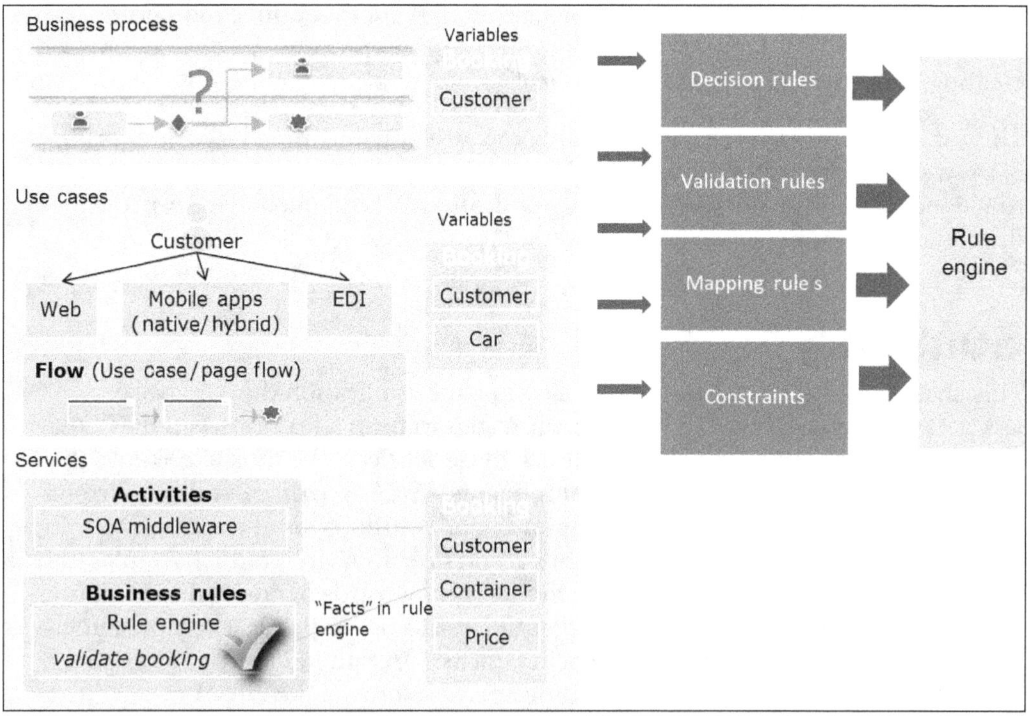

Figure 10: The rule engine as an alternative for most kinds of business logic

Still, there are functionalities that cannot be realized with the means of a rule engine although we predict that these *no-go zones* for business rules will shrink with the evolution of business rule engines.

Maybe the easiest way to depict whether a business rule engine makes sense is to try to formulate the requirement through a business rule using business language by following the formulas:

- *IF .. THEN .. ELSE .. THEN*
- *CASE 1 .. CASE 2 .. CASE 3 ..*

If this is not easily possible, consider not to use a rule engine.

Okay, now that we have a composite application, do we automatically have an SOA?

The business need for the new *change address* service originated in the project that built the refactored web-based rental application. If another application needs the same functionality or something similar, then nothing prevents its developers from creating their own change address service!

Thus, if we really want to make the move towards organizational—or enterprise—SOA, we need a shared service team. This team recognizes all the needs for a similar functionality and is responsible for the application of fundamental SOA principles throughout all projects.

Summary

This chapter introduced the notion of a composite application that can be seen as a set of design best practices and technologies to form a link between the SOA services and concrete applications that use those services. We took a look into the standard for creating such reusable components—SCA. We discussed the current trend towards moving away from programmatic solutions to typical programming tasks, such as integration or business rules, and how they are gradually replaced by a declarative approach in which we use models and wizards to create these solutions. In a brief walkthrough, we touched upon the key technologies that comprise these composites and saw how new features in Oracle SOA Suite 12*c*, such as *Templates*, allow more consistent architecture and design.

We looked at emerging ways of virtualizing the access to data and functionality through tools such as the API gateway.

A key focus of this chapter is on architecting and designing the respective composite applications and their building blocks and discussing proven practices and guidelines.

In the next chapter, we get more concrete, showing how to actually design and implement automated business processes that guide people through a chain of steps in BPMN and how to define a more complex law service that orchestrates a chain of service calls in BPEL.

6
Process Execution with BPMN and BPEL

An important success factor for enterprises is their adaptability to the changing market conditions. The increasing transparency of the market and increased customer requirements require an efficient organization of business processes. Both past and present are, however, predominantly coined from rigid application monoliths, which support these technical process cycles only insufficiently. This prevents one-time, near-market adjustments since the IT cannot adapt itself fast and flexibly enough to changed processes. In this context, we frequently hear about the "business's execution gap"—the gap between the ever rapidly changing business requirements and the supporting information systems.

In order to become agile in a constantly changing market environment, many enterprises feel compelled to restructure the existing IT systems. While conventional application architectures are rather technically aligned, the approach of **service-oriented architectures** (**SOAs**) places the technical aspects in the foreground. The flexible and rapid adaptation of IT to the dynamic business objectives of the organization is to be assured through the tight integration of technical processes with technical services. However, technical processes have specific requirements that cannot be converted to identical figures at the technical level. Thus, how can IT be connected with the business strategy in order to be able to obtain an increase in value with SOA?

A holistic business process management makes a crucial contribution here. This must extend over the entire life cycle, that is, the modeling, simulation, analysis, automation, implementation, execution, monitoring, and optimization of the enterprise processes are to be considered.

In the previous chapters, we clarified how enterprise processes are ideally modelled. Thereupon, we showed how to design the functional building blocks of our architecture and how to create a composite application from that. This chapter will outline an approach, a set of guidelines to actually implement your processes, and the associated services based on the concepts we saw earlier. We will do the following in this chapter:

- Describe how to define an implementation roadmap
- Explain how to implement the **Service Facade** and **Delegation** patterns in BPEL
- Discuss how BPM Suite helps to find the right level of variances
- Highlight the degrees of coupling between technical components
- Set out a series of best practices, for example, naming conventions for composite partitions

Implementation roadmap

The main goal of this chapter is the implementation of the rental process that has been defined and modeled in *Chapter 3, BPMN for Business Process Modeling*.

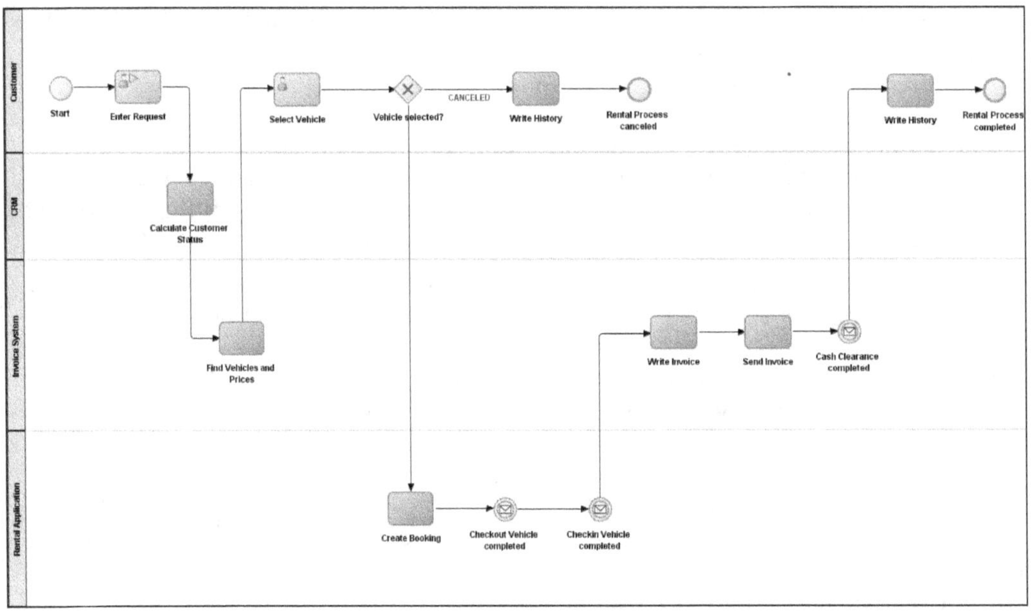

Figure 1: Abstract rental process as defined in Chapter 3, BPMN for Business Process Modeling

From process requirements to design

In order to create a process that can be executed on a runtime engine, it is important to understand the process requirements that determine the technology choices used in implementation and thus its design. For this, it is recommended that you go step by step through each process activity.

> In Oracle BPM Suite 12*c*, it is possible to define the so-called "business properties" (for example, organizational unit, application system, and costs) directly in the BPM composer. They can be used to further describe models and activities. The information documented therein is also part of the process reports that can also be generated from the BPM composer.

The following summary briefly describes all activities of the rental process as illustrated in *Figure 1*.

- **Enter Request**:
    - **Description**: This allows a customer to initiate the rental process via a form in a human task
    - **Organizational unit**: Customer
    - **Implemented as**: Human task
- **Calculate Customer Status**:
    - **Description**: This is a system task to get the status of the appropriate customer
    - **Application system**: Customer management
    - **Implemented as**: This is implemented as a service, with a focus on integration
- **Find Vehicles and Prices**:
    - **Description**: This is a system task to find available vehicles and their prices
    - **Application system**: Fleet management
    - **Implemented as**: This is implemented as a service, with a focus on integration
- **Select Vehicle**:
    - **Description**: This is a manual task to make a selection from the list of available vehicles
    - **Organizational unit**: Customer
    - **Implemented as**: Human task

- **Create Booking**:
    - **Description**: This is a system task that writes the booking into the rental system, updates the CRM, and returns the booking ID
    - **Application system**: Fleet management
    - **Implemented as**: This is implemented as a service, with a focus on integration using BPEL for complex stateful integration along a chain of service calls to backend systems
- **Checkout Vehicle completed**:
    - **Description**: This is an intermediate event that waits until the appropriate vehicle is delivered to the customer
    - **Application system**: Fleet management
    - **Implemented as**: Event-based communication
- **Checkin Vehicle completed**:
    - **Description**: This is an intermediate event that waits until the vehicle is returned
    - **Application system**: Fleet management
    - **Implemented as**: Event-based communication
- **Write Invoice**:
    - **Description**: This is a system task to create an invoice
    - **Application system**: Financial management
    - **Implemented as**: This is implemented as a service, with a focus on integration
- **Send Invoice**:
    - **Description**: This is a system task to send the invoice to the customer
    - **Application system**: Communication management
    - **Implemented as**: Notification
- **Cash Clearance completed**:
    - **Description**: This is an intermediate event that waits until the invoice is paid
    - **Application system**: Financial management
    - **Implemented as**: Event-based communication

- **Write History**:
    - **Description**: This is a system task that adds details to the customer's history
    - **Application system**: Customer management
    - **Implemented as**: This is implemented as a service, with a focus on integration

Evaluating the associated components

Now, it is time to look at the associated components that should provide the actual data and functions for each process activity. Here, the aforementioned analysis helps to prequalify the areas that need to be investigated. In this case, we need to look at components within **Customer Management**, **Fleet Management**, **Financial Management**, and **Communication Management**.

> An application landscape, as the one in *Figure 2*, provides a good overview of the dependencies between the process and its associated components. It also helps to identify missing components and redundancies.

The questions that need to be answered as part of the component analysis are:

- Which components and services exist and who is responsible for each of them?
- Are the required capabilities supported by the available components? Do they provide the relevant data and functions? Is their use strategic?
- How is the change management of those components handled? What impact does an update have on existing service consumers?
- Which interfaces and protocols are supported? Which message exchange patterns are used?
- Which flaws exist in today's components that could affect the process critically?

For this chapter, the main focus is on the following components (also highlighted in red in *Figure 2*): the **Rent a Car Process, Fleet Management**, and **Customer Management**.

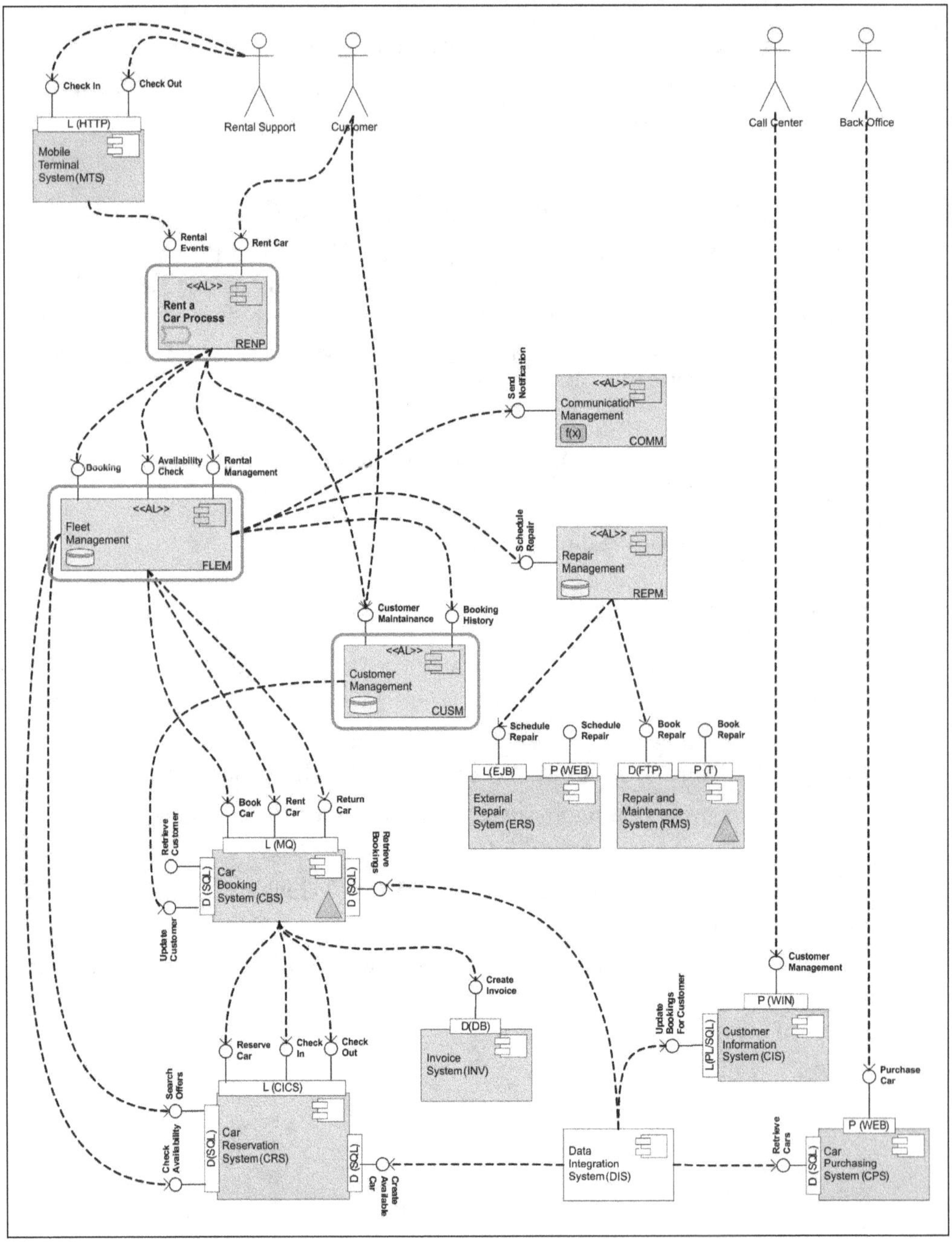

Figure 2: Rental process and associated components

Defining the implementation steps

The two previous steps help to get a clear understanding of the type of development that is needed to satisfy the requirements for the implementation of the rental process and to achieve the desired TO-BE architecture. The different development types that should be considered while defining an implementation roadmap are:

- **Update**: The AS-IS and TO-BE components are identical; only small updates on the data level and configurations are needed
- **Migration**: The AS-IS component requires interface and/or infrastructure changes
- **Enrichment**: Besides potential interface and/or infrastructure changes, the AS-IS component also requires functional enrichments
- **New Development**: A new TO-BE component will be developed that is aligned with the defined infrastructure and integration architecture

With the information on what the process needs and what is actually available, we are able to specify the implementation roadmap. For all the missing parts that have been identified during the AS-IS analysis, we evaluate which of the available development types can be used to satisfy the requirements. We prioritize them and assign them to one of the iterations within the development cycle. *Figure 3* shows an example of an implementation roadmap. Here the pre-analysis shows that a new fleet management is necessary. It is a key component of the rental process that has to be integrated with the reservation system as well as the booking system. The implementation and the appropriate design patterns are described later in this chapter. Additionally, we'll explain the implementation of **Rental Process (RENP)**, which is part of step 2 within **New Development—Iteration 1**. Please note that the roadmap also contains implementation steps marked with a gray background color. Even though they are important for the overall solution, they are not covered in this chapter.

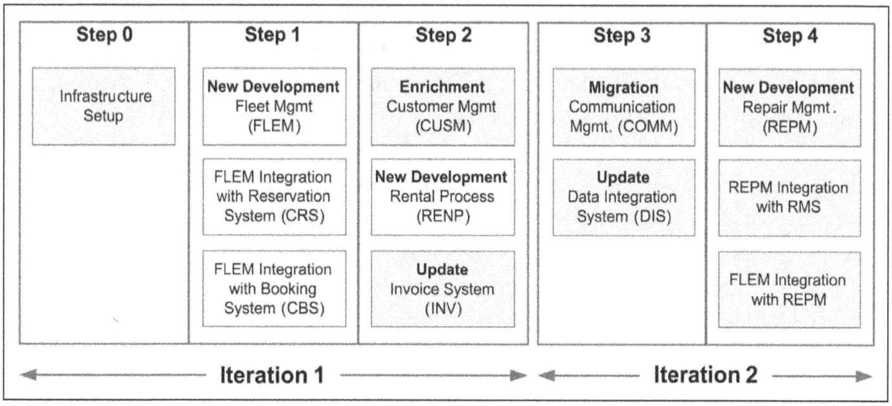

Figure 3: Implementation roadmap

Deciding where to use BPMN and where BPEL

Chapter 2, Modeling Business Processes for SOA – Methodology, discussed a BPM methodology. This is the base to understand and decide where to use BPMN and where BPEL (see *Figure 4*). It is important to mention here that there is no hard-and-fast rule that defines which notation should be used when. Both have their strengths and weaknesses in Oracle BPM Suite 12*c*. Nevertheless, it is important to define consistent guidelines about their usage.

When we deal with a business process that crosses functional units or roads, when we can depict the flow of activities in a rhythmic way without capturing it with too many variances, and when this process involves human interactions, we call this an automated business process best implemented in BPMN. In addition, we recommend considering BPMN in the following scenarios:

- Use BPMN for the implementation of top-level business process services (see *Chapter 4, Process-driven Service Design*, for more details about this service category).
- Leverage the tools that Oracle BPM Suite 12*c* provides for BPMN (only) to bridge the gap between the business and IT. This includes, for example, the BPM composer to model business processes in the web browser, a wide range of process documentation capabilities, simulation and testing functionalities for rapid prototyping, and many out-of-the-box process analytics especially for human-centric processes.
- Existing BPMN process models that have been modeled in Visio or other tools can be imported into the BPM composer so that you don't have to remodel everything.
- Grab and alter flow to stop a process at any time and move to another point in the process.

Do not confuse the business process with a lot of technical activities (for example, script tasks and logging activities). Implement these technical details on a lower architecture level. Also, limit the mix of different technologies (for example, BPEL, Spring, adapters, EJB, and web services) in a BPMN composite to keep it readable for business users. On the top architecture layer, we always try to stick with web services, human tasks, and business rules only. This also increases the maintainability of your composites. The main difference between BPEL and BPMN is that BPEL is not as user-role-centric as BPMN.

We use BPEL to implement stateful integration processes that do not require a lot of loopbacks and do not have many human interactions between different user roles. In the past years, there has been a significant investment in Oracle BPM Suite to make BPMN as powerful as BPEL, and it would be reasonable to assume that this will continue. However, we consider using BPEL in the following scenarios:

- Use BPEL for system-oriented processes that implement the logic and orchestrate services for the BPMN activities. This approach helps to keep the *business view* in the top-level process.
- Take advantage of the extended transactional support in BPEL. It provides powerful compensation capabilities to roll back business transactions in error situations.
- BPEL offers a wide range of properties to optimize the runtime behavior of a process in high throughput scenarios.
- Leverage many options, such as sensor actions, assertions, subprocesses, and templates, to reduce technical boilerplate code.

It is important, though, not to confuse SOA services in Oracle Fusion Middleware with having to use BPEL! There are many services that merely act as a facade to backend systems or databases and do not impose the need for complex orchestration. For those services, we can use the Mediator component or **Oracle Service Bus** (OSB).

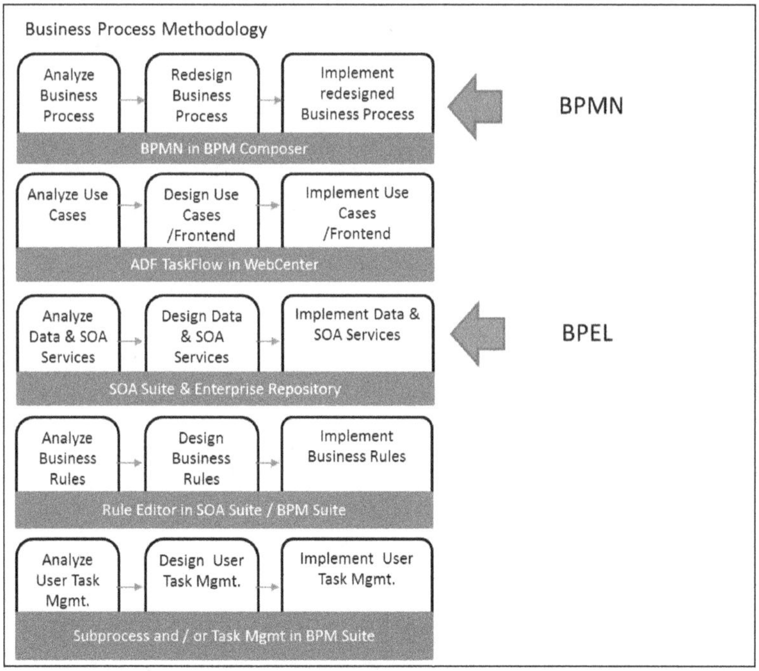

Figure 4: Deciding on BPMN or BPEL based on activities in the business process methodology

Using BPEL to implement fleet management

The following section describes the concepts and patterns that have been chosen to implement the new fleet management.

Solution concepts

The fleet management component is categorized as a business activity service (also see *Chapter 4, Process-driven Service Design*, for more details about service categorization). It integrates several backend systems, for example, the reservation system, booking system, and customer management. The component offers a wide range of operations that cover different aspects of the rental process, such as the booking of vehicles, availability check, and rental management. Since some of those operations are asynchronous and stateful, it has been decided that fleet management should be implemented as a BPEL composite.

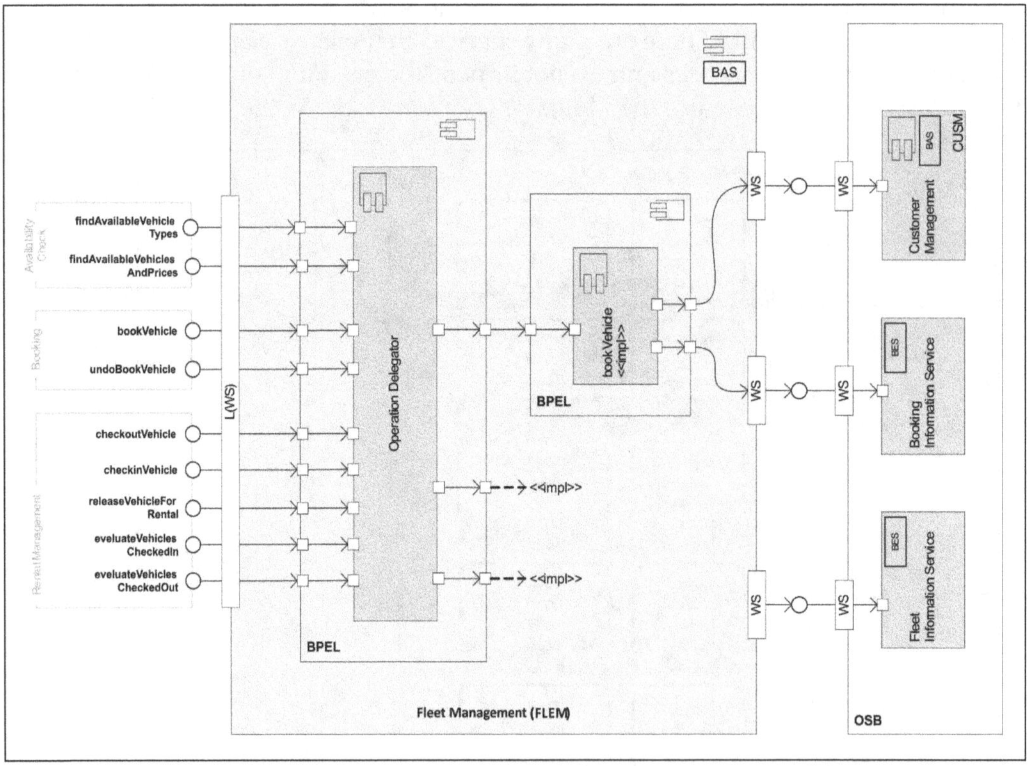

Figure 5: Fleet management component view

As illustrated in *Figure 5*, the composite consists of **Operation Delegator** implemented in BPEL that routes between the different operations provided by the service facade. An incoming request is delegated to the appropriate component that contains the logic for the operation, for example, `bookVehicle`. These subcomponents are private within the composite. They usually interact with other external systems and services, orchestrate single working steps, and take care of complex data transformations.

Service facade and contract-first composite design

One of the main functions of fleet management is that it has to fulfill the role of a service facade to decouple the consumers from the reservation as well as from the booking system. Any changes on these systems should not have a direct impact on the consumers. The number of consumers also might increase over time. Before we start implementing, we first define how the service facade should look. For this, the important questions are the following: which operations are needed? What is the input data and what is the output data? Which message exchange patterns are suitable?

From there, we develop the service contract of the facade and publish it. After that, we can start implementing the composite by performing the following steps:

1. Open Oracle JDeveloper 12 and create a new SOA project `FleetManagement` within a `RentalServices` application. Then, click on **Next**. This is shown in the following screenshot:

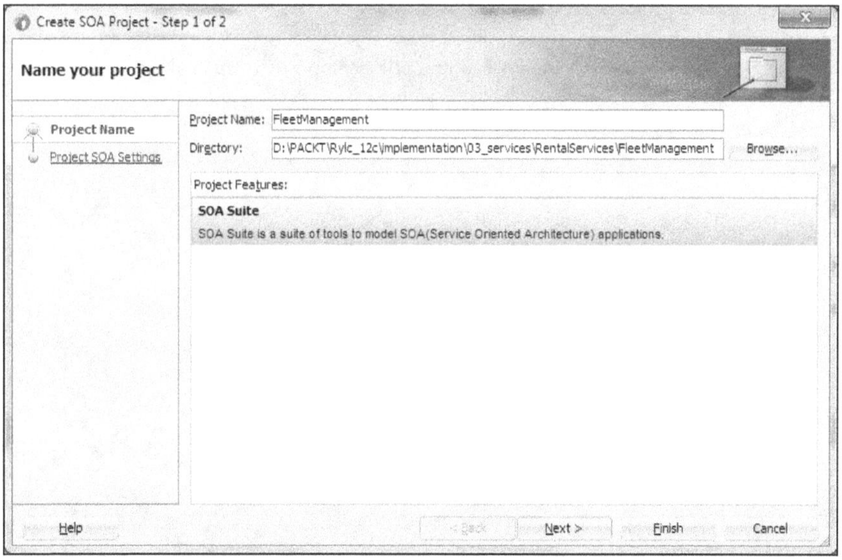

Figure 6: Create a contract-first composite (step 1)

2. Enter a composite name, select **Standard Composite**, click on **Empty Composite** within the following list, and click on **Finish**. This is shown in the following screenshot:

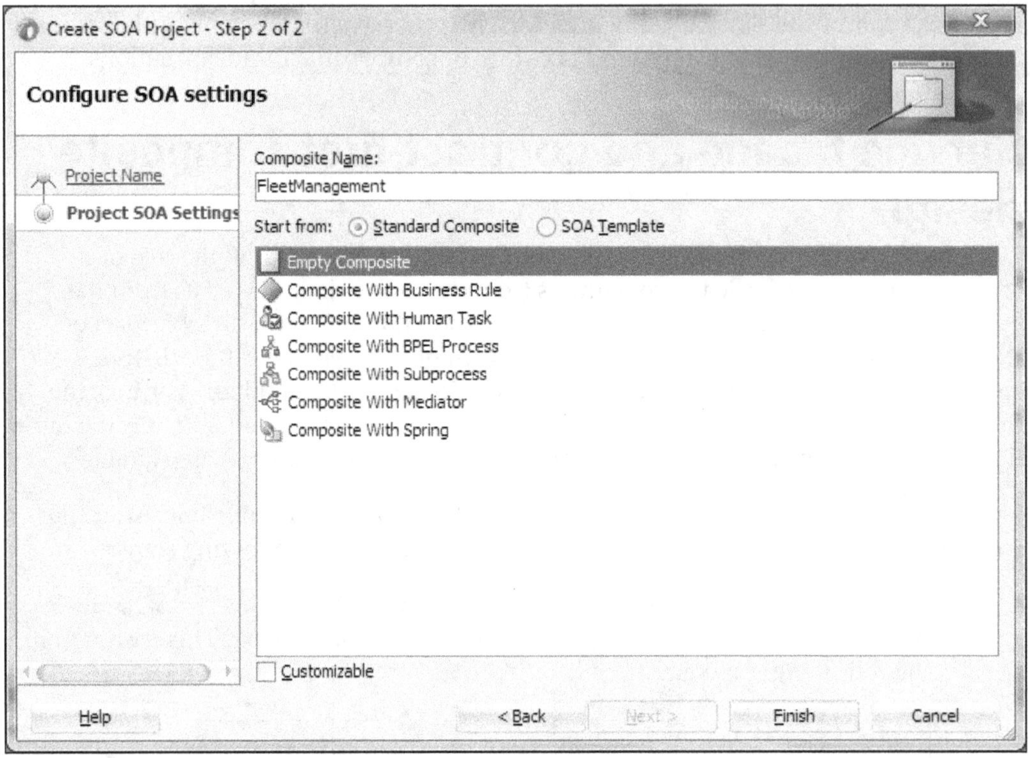

Figure 7: Create a contract-first composite (step 2)

3. Drag and drop a SOAP service component into the **Exposed Services** area. The **Create Web Service** wizard opens. Enter the name `FleetManagementService` and click on **Find existing WSDLs**. Navigate to the existing service contract `FleetManagement.wsdl` within the MDS. Confirm two times with clicks on **OK**.

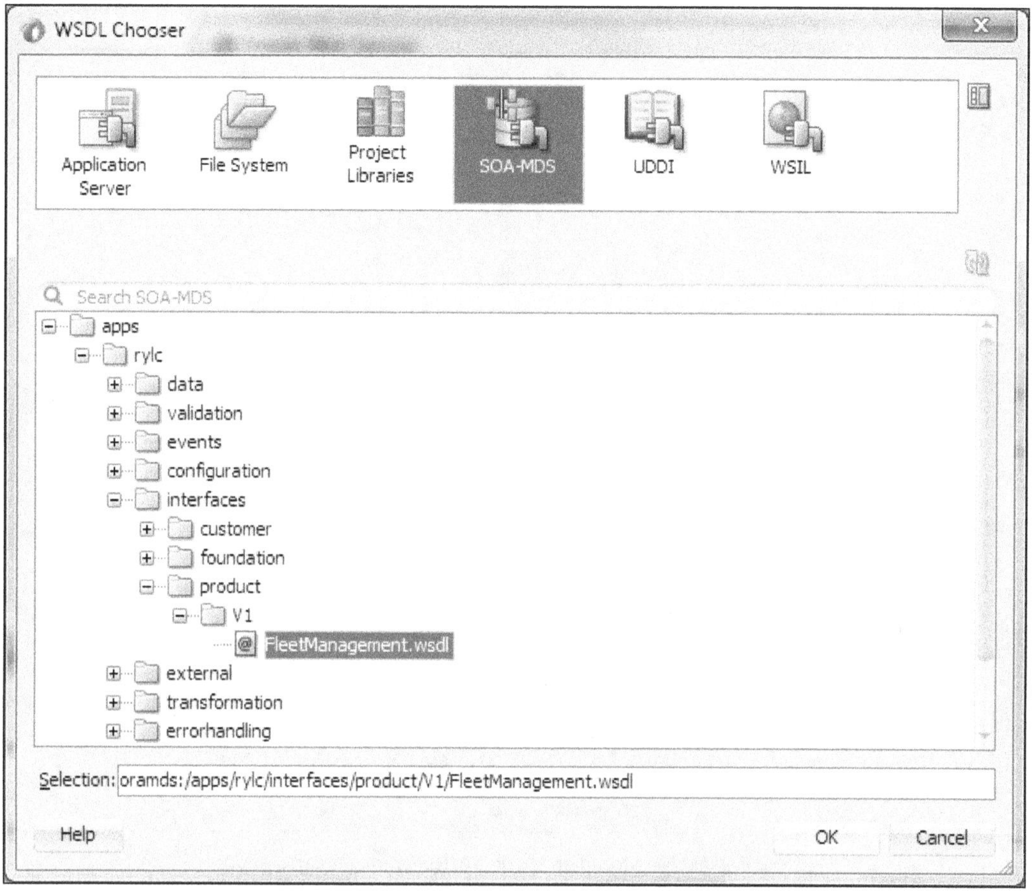

Figure 8: Browse for the service contract in MDS

4. The fleet management composite now provides the requested service interface with the appropriate operations. This is the base to act as a service facade for the corresponding backend systems. The next step would be to implement the service operations so that a call of the service facade triggers the right actions in the underlying systems.

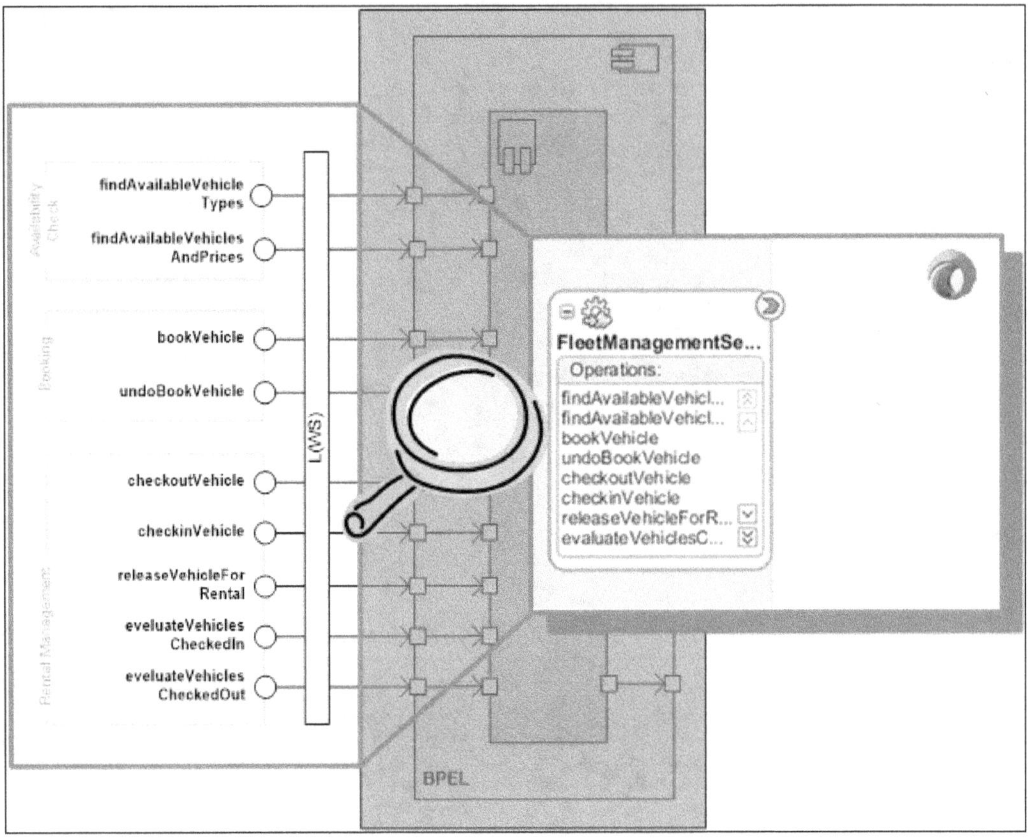

Figure 9: Exposed service interface of the fleet management composite

Delegation pattern

With the current setup, our fleet management composite already provides a set of operations. They will be used to trigger different actions within the context of the rental process. In order to route between different operation calls, we will add **Operation Delegator** to the composite as shown in *Figure 5*. The function of this component is delegating responsibility to one or more associated components depending on the requested operation. In software engineering, especially in object-oriented programming, it is a common approach to keep the source code clean and understandable.

Implementing the OperationDelegator

Within a composite, the delegation pattern can either be implemented in BPEL or with a Mediator. We decided to implement the pattern in BPEL. The reason for this is that a few of the operations to be implemented are asynchronous with multiple callbacks. Here, the BPEL component has some advantages compared with the Mediator. The following table provides an overview of the criteria, which are of particular interest:

Criteria	**Mediator**	**BPEL**
Implementation effort	Low.	Medium
Synchronous messaging	Supported.	Supported
Asynchronous messaging	Limited supported. It cannot consume multiple asynchronous callbacks. Within a routing rule, just one callback operation can be selected. That makes fault handling in asynchronous communication quite hard.	Supported
Options to control the audit and the dehydration behavior on a component level (`bpel.config.auditLevel` and `completionPersistPolicy`)	Not supported.	Supported
Usage of component properties (`bpel.preference`)	Not supported.	Supported

The following steps describe how to implement `OperationDelegator` as part of the fleet management composite:

1. Drag and drop a BPEL component to the fleet management composite. Enter the name `OperationDelegator`, define a namespace, and select the **Define Service Later** template, as illustrated in *Figure 10*:

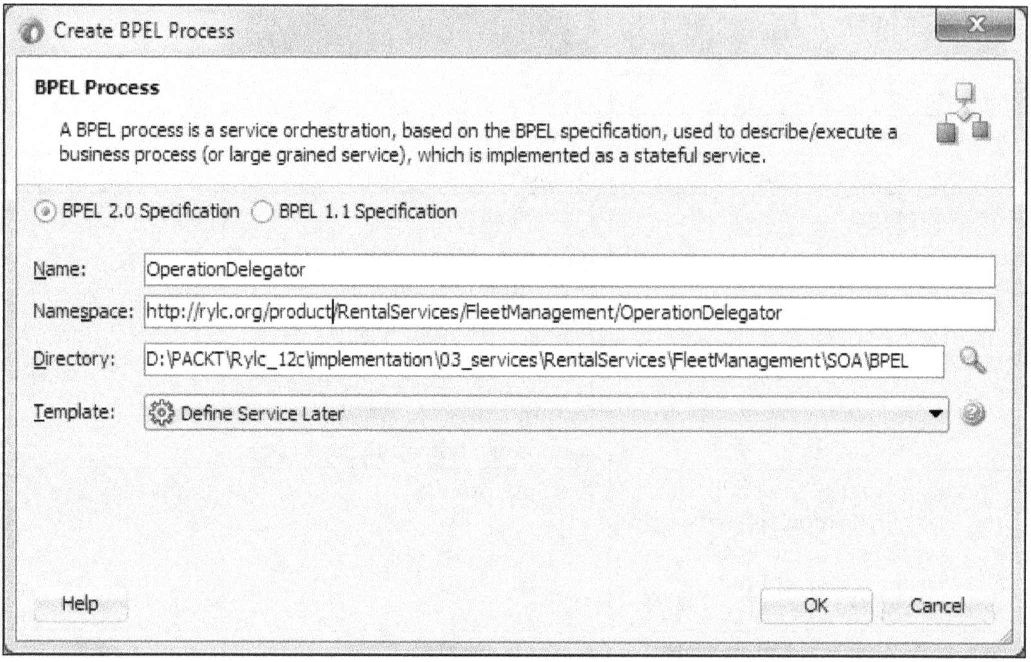

Figure 10: Create OperationDelegator

2. Create a connection between the exposed `FleetManagementService` and `OperationDelegator`:

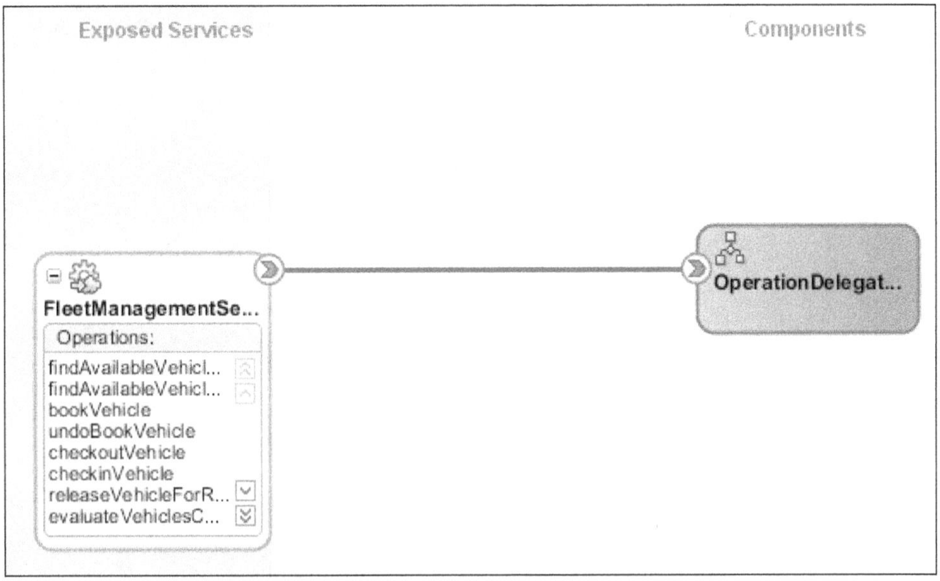

Figure 11: Connect the service facade and OperationDelegator

3. Open the `OperationDelegator` component and add a `Pick` activity to the empty process. Double-click on the `Pick` activity and activate the **Create Instance** checkbox. We use the `Pick` activity here because `OperationDelegator` has multiple incoming operations (for example, `findAvailableVehicleTypes`, `findAvailableVehiclesAndPrices`, `bookVehicle`, and so on).

4. Double-click on the initial `OnMessage` branch and choose the **Partner Link** as `FleetManagementService`. As shown in *Figure 12*, select the **findAvailableVehicleTypes** operation from the dropdown list and autocreate a variable. Then click on **OK**. This is shown in the following screenshot:

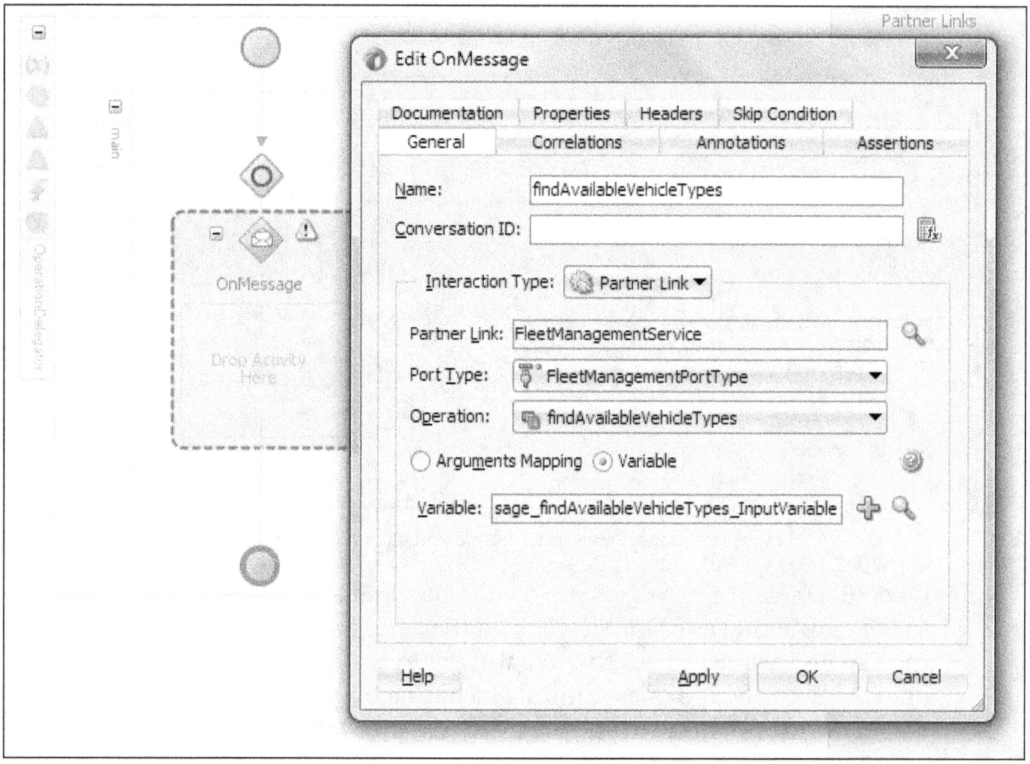

Figure 12: Create an OnMessage branch for each operation

5. As described in the previous step, create additional `OnMessage` branches for the other operations of the service facade (for example, `findAvailableVehicleTypes`, `findAvailableVehiclesAndPrices`, `bookVehicle`, and so on).

Implementing service operations

The next step is to implement the different service operations of the fleet management composite. Here, we are still following the delegation pattern because the operations are implemented as separate private BPEL components. Let's have a look, for example, to the `findAvailableVehiclesAndPrices` operation. It gets a list of the vehicles that are currently available from the vehicle reservation system. After that, `PricingEngine` needs to be called to calculate the prices. As illustrated in *Figure 13*, such an orchestration can be easily implemented in BPEL. The subprocess that implements the operation is called by `OperationDelegator`. In order to perform the call from there, an `Invoke` activity with pre- and post-data associations has been added to the appropriate `OnMessage` branch. This is shown in the following image:

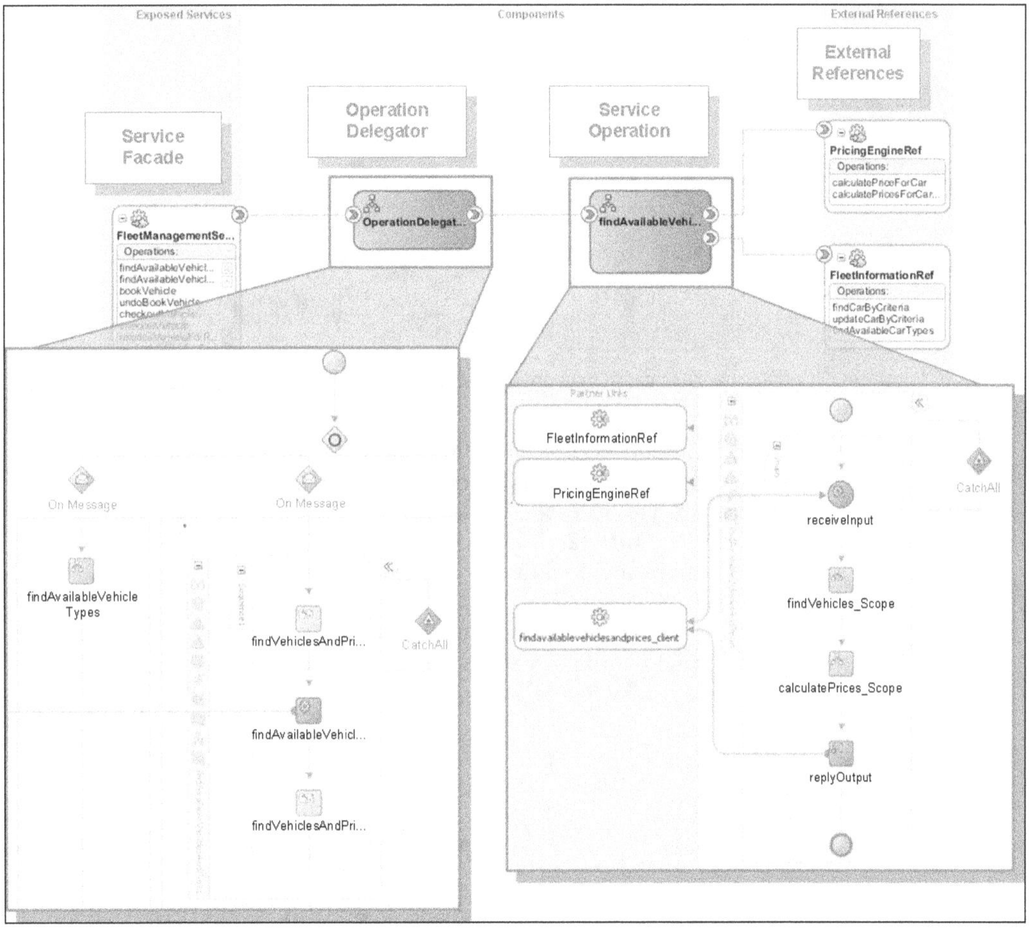

Figure 13: Implementation of findAvailableVehiclesAndPrices in BPEL

The other operations of the composite are implemented by following the same approach. If it is just a single call of an external component, and no orchestration or complex pre- and post-processing is required. We usually implement the call directly from the delegator rather than adding another process layer (for example, for `checkoutVehicle` and `checkinVehicle`). *Figure 14* shows the final implementation of the fleet management composite.

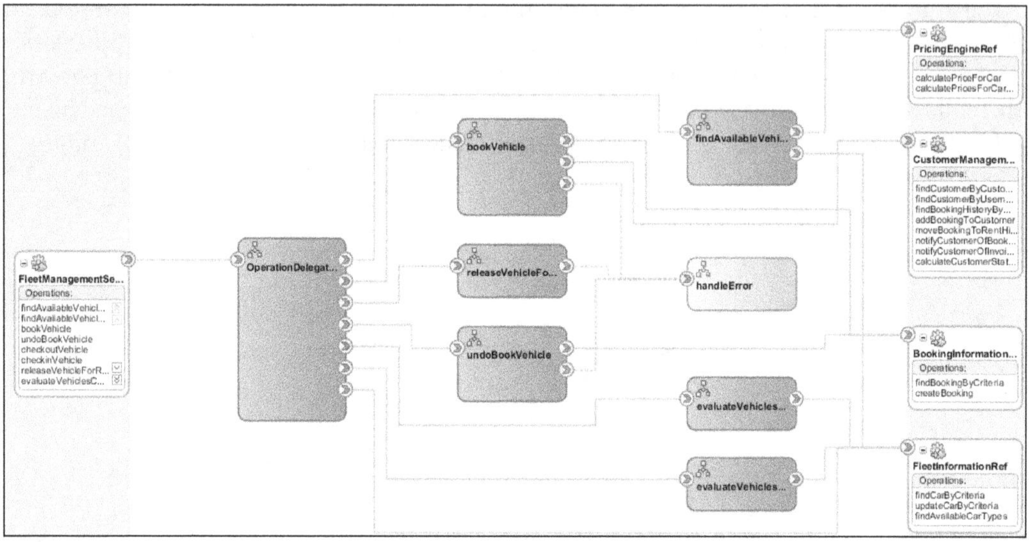

Figure 14: The fleet management composite with all operations

> You might have noticed that the composite in *Figure 14* contains an additional component, `handleError`, which is called by several BPEL processes. This is a so-called BPEL subprocess—a new feature of BPM and SOA Suite 12*c*. It allows the implementation of reusable content that can be invoked from many BPEL processes. The *Oracle® Fusion Middleware, Developing SOA Applications with Oracle SOA Suite 12c (12.1.3)*, contains a detailed overview about reusable subprocesses and templates within *Chapter 39, Oracle SOA Suite Templates and Reusable Subprocesses*.

Using BPMN to implement the rental process

Chapter 3, BPMN for Business Process Modeling, explains the concepts of business process modeling with BPMN. Most likely, the first version of a BPMN model concentrates on the logical flow of activities. Aspects such as exception handling, data mapping, or the decision between synchronous and asynchronous system calls, are very often not part of the abstract model that the developer gets from the business analyst. In order to make the model executable, we need to concretize it step by step.

Finding the right level of variance paths

An executable business process needs to deal with all the variances that can happen in real life. Abstract business process models focus on communication with business departments. It is thus feasible to omit some of the more obscure variances. The art of concretizing the business process model that we get from the business department and refining it towards being concrete is difficult since it's important to find the right balance between expressing all the variances that we anticipate to happen, while still maintaining the notion of a recognizable flow. It is not a good idea to model everything until the last of the thinkable variances that might never happen in real life.

Instead, it may be a good idea to allow a variance to occur as a fault and by observation over time understand which variances really happened.

The ultimate goal is to express the bulk of the variances that are meaningful and contribute to the understanding of the process, while treating most obscure variances that would clutter the process model as exceptions that are dealt with individually. When we observe that such an exception happens many times, we can find the process model to glorify that variance as a part of the overall process flow.

Bridging the gap between the business and IT

As discussed in *Chapter 2, Modeling Business Processes for SOA – Methodology*, and *Chapter 3, BPMN for Business Process Modeling*, the gap between the business and IT is wide, and it's a daunting and delicate task to bridge it. A business process model that is cluttered with technical details is not understandable by business departments. Thus, it is best practice to avoid starting to model the process with too many technical details.

Following the separation-of-concern principle, technical details, such as data mapping from one format to another, do not belong in a business process model in the first place!

Concretizing the process

The abstract business process contains a rather logical depiction of each activity in the business process. We now have to concretize these elements. This includes, for example, the start and end events with their incoming and outgoing messages. We also have to decide whether an activity is executed by a human or by a system. In *Figure 15*, the **Calculate Customer Status** activity in the business process is defined abstractly so that it could be implemented by a human task, service call, notification, or any other activity type that BPMN provides.

It is even possible that one activity in the abstract process model ends up being implemented through a manual task—an activity that is not controlled by the process engine. A good example is a manual task that reminds you to "water the flowers".

Now, as part of the implementation phase that morphs the abstract process into an executable process, we need to change each abstract activity into proper and executable activity types. The next sections provide best practices and guidelines that describe how to achieve this using Oracle BPM Studio 12*c*.

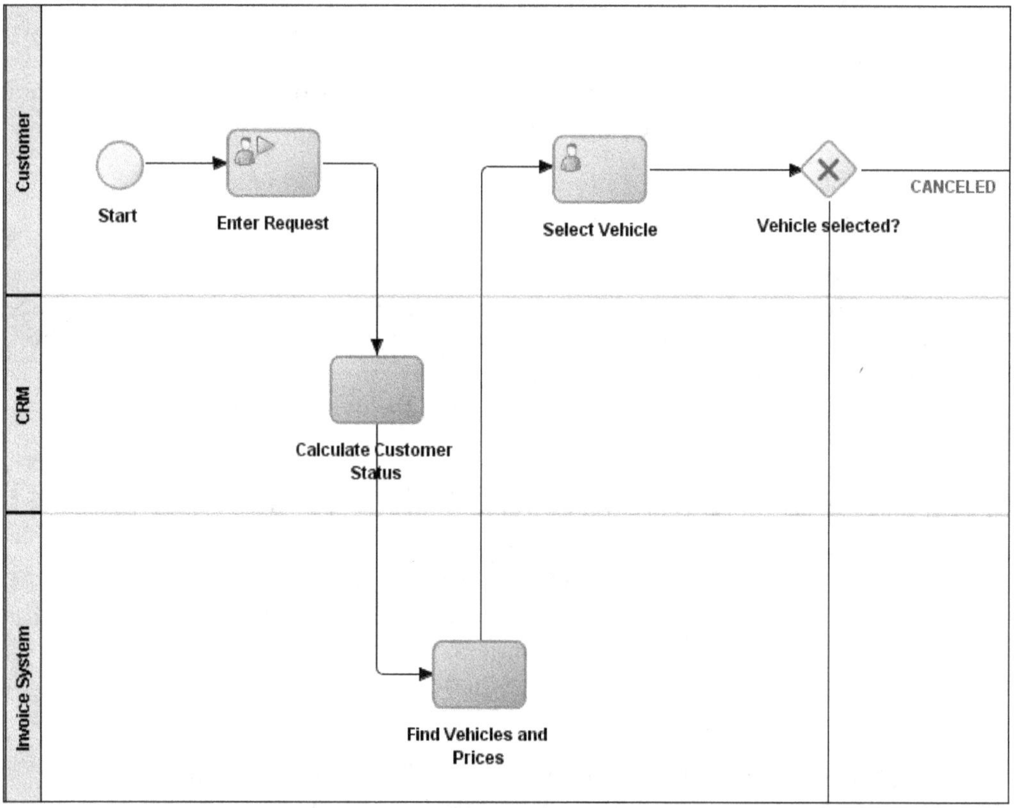

Figure 15: An abstract process model does not yet decide on activity types

Deciding on the coupling levels per activity

For each of the activities, we need to decide on the level of coupling that ties the BPMN process model to the actual implementation. As discussed in *Chapter 2, Modeling Business Processes for SOA – Methodology*, very often BPMN is used to optimize a departmental workflow. This is a very controlled environment, in which it is absolutely clear how to implement each activity. There's no doubt as to which role is assigned to a human task or which application is integrated beyond the service facade. In such a scenario, we can decide the activity type for each activity through the means of a tight-coupling model. This means that for each activity, there is no decoupling of a logical depiction from *what* the process step does and *how* it does it. To be very concrete, each activity is typed according to the activity types that BPMN provides, such as a human task or service call.

On the other side of the spectrum, there is a need to decouple the logical name of an activity with its implementation. This can be motivated through local variances, such as variances in regional governmental requirements. In one country, the *check creditworthiness* process step in a bank might involve a lengthy human-centric subprocess in which an employee needs to assess the worth essence of the customer by physically visiting him. In another country, this check may be completely automated by means of calling internal applications and an external web service. These differences might be motivated through local factors, such as labor cost and availability of established packaged applications.

In such scenarios, we desire a loose coupling of describing the activity and its outcome, such as *check creditworthiness* and its implementation. A good way to achieve such a decoupling is by transforming such an abstract activity into a subprocess. Then, we can use this subprocess to depict the implementation type.

Such a subprocess is also a great place to detail out exception handling and variances, thus freeing the overall business process model from clutter.

If we need to even further abstract implementation from the logical flow, we can define the activity type as a service. Then, we can use a Mediator or even Oracle Service Bus to apply content-based routing. This would allow the activity to check in which country it's running and route dynamically to the appropriate implementation for this particular country.

Defining the activity type per activity

For each abstract activity, ultimately we need to define the concrete BPMN activity type. We can do this either in Oracle BPM Studio or the BPM composer. *Figure 16* shows the refined rental process, where all the abstract activities have been changed into a concrete activity type.

The first activity is **Enter Request**. If you compare *Figure 2* and *Figure 16*, you will see that this activity has already been defined as a human task in the abstract process. Nevertheless, during the implementation phase, we need to further describe the technical details of the activity. In Oracle BPM, this includes the definition of a human task pattern to describe whether it is an initiator task that starts the process, a simple task, a group vote, or an informal notification task. Additionally, the associated input and output data as well as the assignees need to be defined. You can find more details on human tasks in *Chapter 7, Human Interaction with Business Processes*.

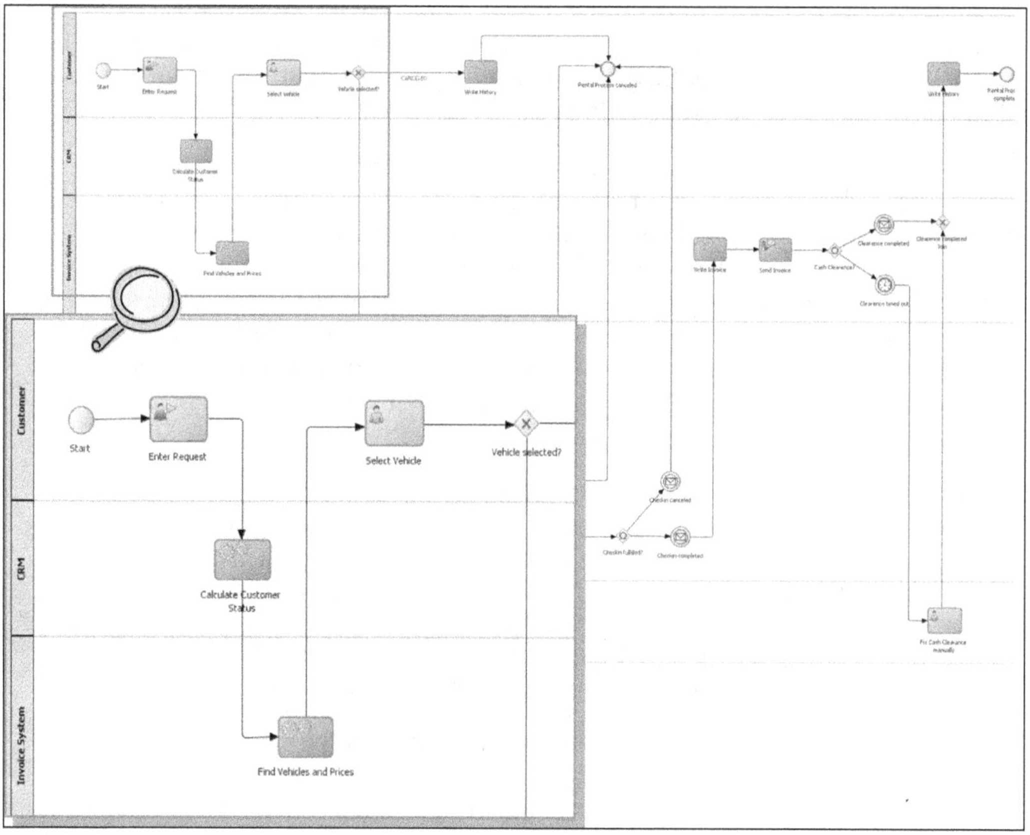

Figure 16: Rental process with concretized activity types

The next activities that we have to transform from abstract to concrete representations are **Calculate Customer Status** and **Find Vehicles and Prices**. From the earlier sections in this chapter, we know that both activities are automated system tasks. In order to get the relevant data into the process, we have to call functions provided by the **Customer Management** system and the **Fleet Management** system. In the rental process example, these functions are exposed as web services. In order to concretize the activity to call the appropriate web service, we have to open the **Properties** window for that activity. Therein, the implementation type should be changed from **Activity** to **Service task** as shown in *Figure 17*. After that, the service and its operation need to be selected. For the remaining activities, a similar approach is necessary.

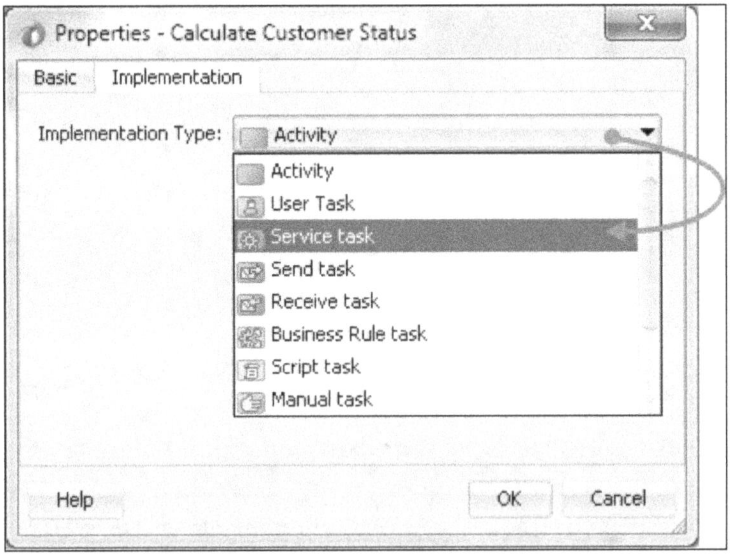

Figure 17: Changing the Implementation Type value per activity

Designing the referenced services

Now, we need to define the implementation technologies for each service called by the business process or a use case that implements an activity of the business process.

Here, we need to decide which types of logic belong together on the level of services, which determines which tool to use—either SCA in SOA Suite or OSB. Inside the SCA composite or OSB-based service, we need to select the technical components that belong together. Driving factors for these design choices should be desired levels of coherence, reuse, and separation of concern.

Deciding on message exchange patterns

Business processes will need to invoke services and other processes running under the control of another application. When you invoke another service or process, you can call it synchronously or asynchronously.

For synchronous calls, the calling process waits until the called service or process completes. In the rental process example, we have a couple of synchronous service calls, for example **Calculate Customer Status**, **Find Vehicles and Prices**, and **Write History**.

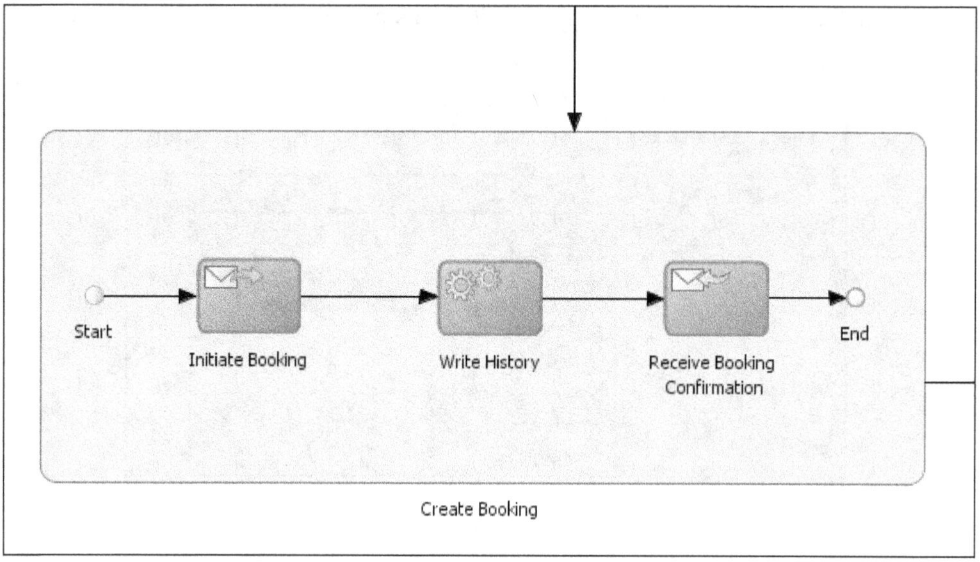

Figure 18: Asynchronous message exchange pattern with send/receive tasks

For asynchronous communication, the calling process uses **Send task** or **Message throw event** to start a service and then continues its own work in parallel. Later in the process, **Receive task** or **Message catch event** waits for the callback from the called service. The example in *Figure 18* is using **Send task** to initiate a booking. The booking service is asynchronous because several systems are involved in the booking process. Many requests can occur in parallel, so this might take some time. It is important that each request is visible in the history. For this reason, the synchronous service task, **Write History**, is called immediately after the initiation. After that, in **Receive Booking Confirmation**, the process waits until the appropriate callback message is received.

> There is no hard-and-fast rule in BPMN that defines when to use **Send task** as against **Message throw event** and when to use **Receive task** as opposed to **Message catch event**. More or less, it is a question of taste. Some people prefer to use tasks because the process model seems to be more readable—especially when you have a lot of asynchronous service calls. Others prefer intermediate events to describe and implement the same behavior.
>
> Another benefit of using tasks instead of intermediate events is the capability of attaching boundary events. We always try to stick with the principle that we use send/receive tasks for asynchronous service communication and throw/catch events for asynchronous, event-based communication.

Adding exception handling

BPM is about process transparency. One of the keys to achieve this is making sure that for each error or exception, it must be crystal clear as to which part of the business process it has occurred and which subsequent actions should be triggered. In order to achieve this, Oracle BPM Suite offers a wide range of options to handle exceptions. We recommend using a combination of the configurable fault management framework, subprocesses, and process-internal fault handling. Especially for the latter, a distinction between synchronous and asynchronous calls is necessary. Exceptions coming from synchronous requests can be caught via boundary events. In asynchronous scenarios, the process receives different callback messages.

Figure 19 shows how the abstract model is different from the concretized executable process. The abstract model contains an intermediate event to describe that the process has to wait for the cash clearance. However, for an executable process, this might not be enough. What should happen if the cash clearance message is not sent in a certain timeframe or if somebody or something canceled it? Since the cash clearance is asynchronous, we added an event-based gateway that decides between a timeout and different callback messages.

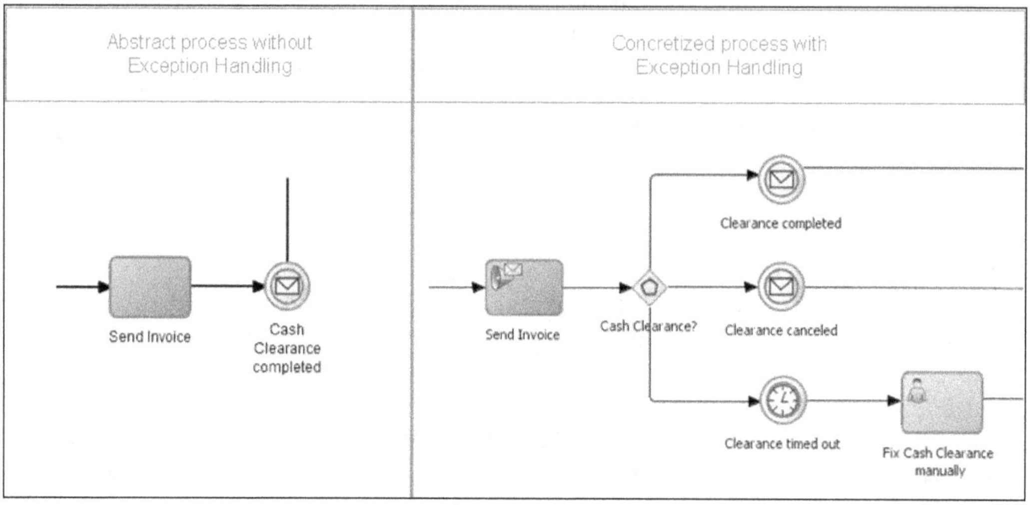

Figure 19: Exception handling in the rental process

Defining the correlation of events to processes

An event that references a specific process instance must be able to affect a specific running process instance through correlation. Examples in the rental process are checkout and checkin car that can be identified by a car identifier and its associated booking number. Again, this is a technical detail, which most likely is not covered in the abstract process model, but it is very relevant in order to execute the process.

Figure 20 shows the checkin/checkout part of the rental process. After the booking confirmation has been received, the process waits until the checkout is fulfilled. As soon as the car is handed over to the customer, the **Checkout completed** event is published. In Oracle BPM, we can use the **event delivery network** (**EDN**) to publish events to one or more subscribers.

In order to correlate between the event and the subscribing process instance, it is necessary that the rental process initiates **Correlation set** using the unique identifiers of the car and the booking. Once the checkout event occurs, the BPM engine evaluates which process instance belongs to that event by comparing the values in **Correlation set** with the details of the event.

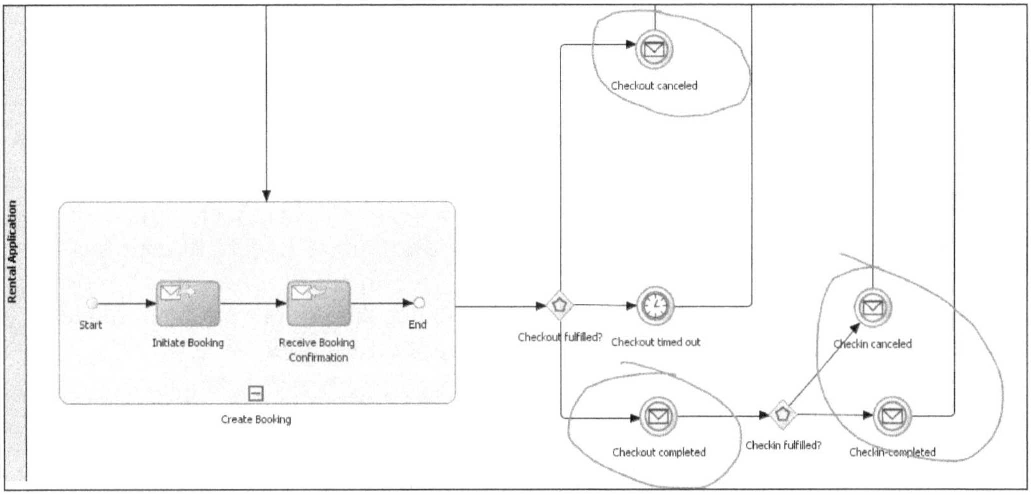

Figure 20: Intermediate (catch) events in BPMN with correlation

It might be possible that an event affects multiple processes, for example, as soon as the car is returned, the invoice should be created, the car should be checked for damages, and it should be cleaned for the next customer. The EDN then performs a fan-out to identify the affected processes.

Decoupling business data from process instance data

When you implement a BPMN process in Oracle BPM Suite 12*c*, you have to deal with different data objects. This includes the input and the output parameters of the process itself, several input and output variables per activity, and potential transport variables, which move data values through the process. These variables are based on XML schemas. During runtime, the values of these process variables are stored in the underlying database of the BPM engine (SOAINFRA schema).

Now, let's assume that we've defined the `bookingRequestVar` transport variable, which transports all booking details in one data object through the process. After the request has been received, this variable becomes initialized with the general request data. The next process steps are **Calculate Customer Status** and **Find Vehicles and Prices**. Each activity has an input and an output data association. The input data association defines the field mapping from `bookingRequestVar` to the input parameters of the activity. The output data association maps the output of the activity back to `bookingRequestVar`. For the remaining process activities, the same approach is used.

The problem here is that the business data and the technical process instance are tightly coupled, which makes maintenance and versioning quite hard. If someone changes the data structure of `bookingRequestVar`, many data associations within the process need to be modified. From an operations perspective, tight coupling is also very critical because it can make the patching of an environment much more complicated. Also, the cleaning up of the old instance data might not be possible because it means that we can lose business-relevant information.

These are the main reasons why we recommend the decoupling of business data from the technical process instance data. That means that we always try to avoid the transport of large data objects through the whole process. Instead of that, we reduce our data objects so that only the following values are considered:

- Attributes, which are needed to control the process flow
- Identifiers, which are required to call for additional data (at the point of time needed and without redundancy)

Best practices

This section contains additional best practices that should be considered while implementing composite applications in Oracle BPM / SOA Suite 12*c*.

Degrees of coupling between technical components

Let's assume that a BPMN process contains complex decisions that will be implemented in a rule engine. Now, we need to decide whether the rule sits in the same composite as the BPMN process or not. Here, the key decision is whether this rule will be reused in other contexts.

The degrees of coupling between the technical components are defined on the enterprise level. They determine which technical components play together in which typical scenarios. A good example is a strict separation of business process logic, integration logic, and user interaction logic.

On the other hand, in departmental attempts at workflow automation, it might be feasible to disregard all architectural sophistication and throw all the components that make up the business process together in one composite. This should only be considered a valid design when the result is rather of a disposable nature, which sometimes can be the case.

The best practices based on the degree of coupling are:

- Loosely coupled services and components should not share access to the same database table
- Decoupled services and components will communicate in asynchronous communication style, which are as follows:
    - Message based communication
    - Event-oriented communication
    - Batch processing
    - Caching and replication
- Loosely coupled components and services ideally do not share a transaction
- Loosely coupled components and services that participate in transactions will provide compensating operations to undo a state

Organizing the MDS structure

As part of the deployment, a BPM composite is automatically stored in the metadata service (repository)—in short, the MDS. A common best practice is to use it also for artifacts that should be shared across many composites, for example, fault policies, **data objects (XSDs)**, **web service interfaces (WSDLs)**, and **domain value maps (DVMs)**. *Figure 21* contains an example structure that we use to organize our MDS content:

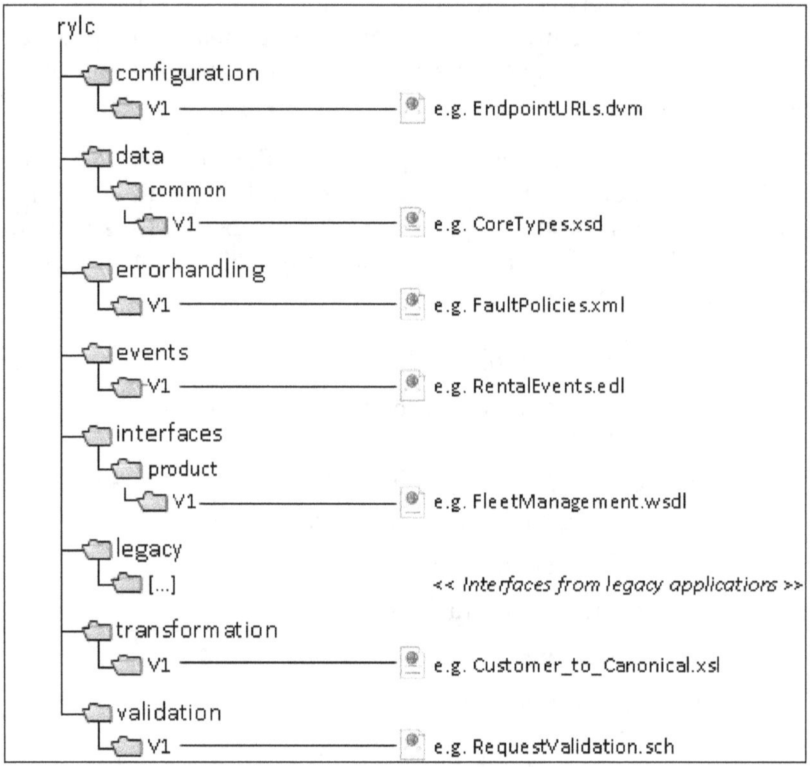

Figure 21: MDS folder structure (example)

Distinguishing between public and private interfaces

Earlier in this chapter, we explained how we can implement a composite based on a web service interface (WSDL) that is stored in the MDS. We often call this the contract-first approach. Other composites might use the same interface as a reference to call that composite. Hence, the WSDL files in the MDS can be seen as public interfaces used by one or many composites.

As described in the *Implementing service operations* section, a composite can have multiple components (see *Figure 22*). Each of those components needs to provide its own interface. But how should this private interface look? Should we just reuse the public interface?

Let's assume that we used the same public interface in **OperationDelegator** as well as in the local BPELs that implement the **findAvailableVehiclesAndPrices** and **bookVehicle** operations. During the implementation, we recognize that **OperationDelegator** should pass some extra parameters to one of the local BPELs (for example, for exception handling). How could we achieve that if the appropriate parameters are not contained in the public interface? Should we update the public interface each time we have specific requirements for local components? What happens if we change the public WSDL? Overall, this doesn't seem to be a good option because it will affect all the components that are using the same interface.

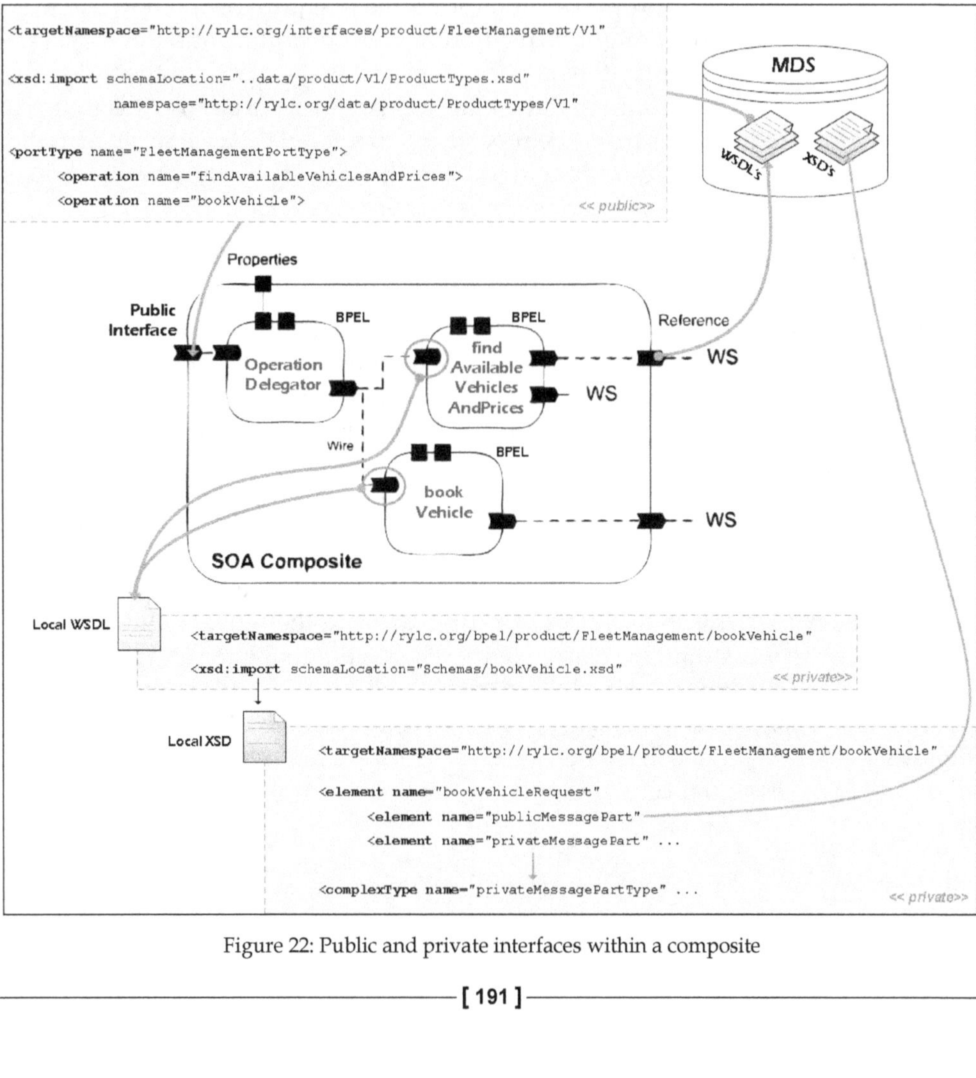

Figure 22: Public and private interfaces within a composite

For maintenance and versioning reasons, we recommend that you distinguish between private and public interfaces from the beginning. Use public interfaces for exposed services and references. Local components without an exposed interface should have their own WSDL with an independent namespace, private operations, and local message types. These message types should have a public part and a private part. The public message part can be used to import public data types from the MDS to avoid duplication. The private message part can be used for local enrichments. The delegation component handles the message transformation from a public request to a local component and vice versa.

Archiving and monitoring with BPEL sensors

A common requirement is the traceability of business processes. Oracle BPM / SOA Suite 12*c* provide detailed views to drill down into process instances and faults. However, very often, the appropriate monitoring tools require deep knowledge about the platform, and they might be focused on administrators and developers. These tools can also just display the data that is currently available in the BPM repository. In order to make sure that the platform performs properly, it is important to purge completed instances from the repository on a regular basis. After that, these instances cannot be used for further analysis. For this reason, a frequent question is: *How can we provide long-term monitoring of our process transactions?*

One option would be to use **Business Activity Monitoring** (**BAM**). It provides powerful dashboards for detailed process analytics. However, sometimes a couple of simple logging tables in the database seem to be sufficient. In order to fill these tables, we don't want to enrich our processes with a lot of logging-related activities. A much better choice for this is the so-called sensors. They can be used to track key execution points within a process. Basically, there are two types of sensors available—BPEL sensors and Composite sensors. In this chapter, we are concentrating on BPEL sensors. They can be categorized into variable sensors, activity sensors, and fault sensors.

Sensors are associated with sensor actions. These actions can publish the sensor value in a database (dehydration store), or they can send the sensor value to a JMS queue/topic or to a custom Java class. This is where you define to send the sensor data into the logging tables. Typically, you add or edit BPEL sensors and their actions during design time in Oracle JDeveloper. Note that you have to change to the monitor view for this. We believe that BPEL sensors are a convenient tool to restrict the process to the essential activities.

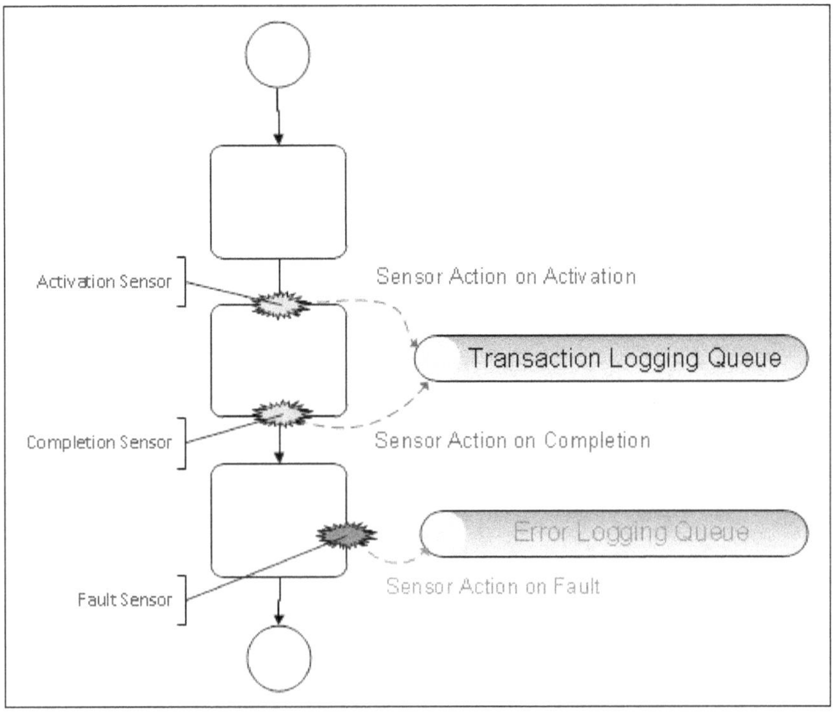

Figure 23: Sensor values published by JMS sensor actions

Keeping processes clean using assertions

Another way to keep processes clean and easier to read is via assertion conditions. They act like pre- and post-conditions upon `invoke` activities, `receive` activities, `reply` activities, `scope` activities, and `onMessage` branches. In addition, there is also a standalone `assert` activity available.

Let's assume the following for our car rental example. If fleet management isn't able to find an available vehicle, there is no need to perform an additional call to the pricing engine. Without assertion conditions, we would probably add an `If` or `Switch` activity in order to react on the different return values from **findAvailableVehicles**. The result would be that the process becomes more and more difficult to read, especially if similar measures are necessary for additional activities.

With assertion conditions, we just have to define a post assert on the invoke activity of **findAvailableVehicles**. As part of this, we need to define an XPath expression, which causes a BPEL fault to be thrown as soon as it is evaluated to false. *Figure 24* shows the wizard to create assertions. If the number of returned cars is less than or equal to zero, then `assertFailure` will be thrown. Of course, this exception needs to be handled.

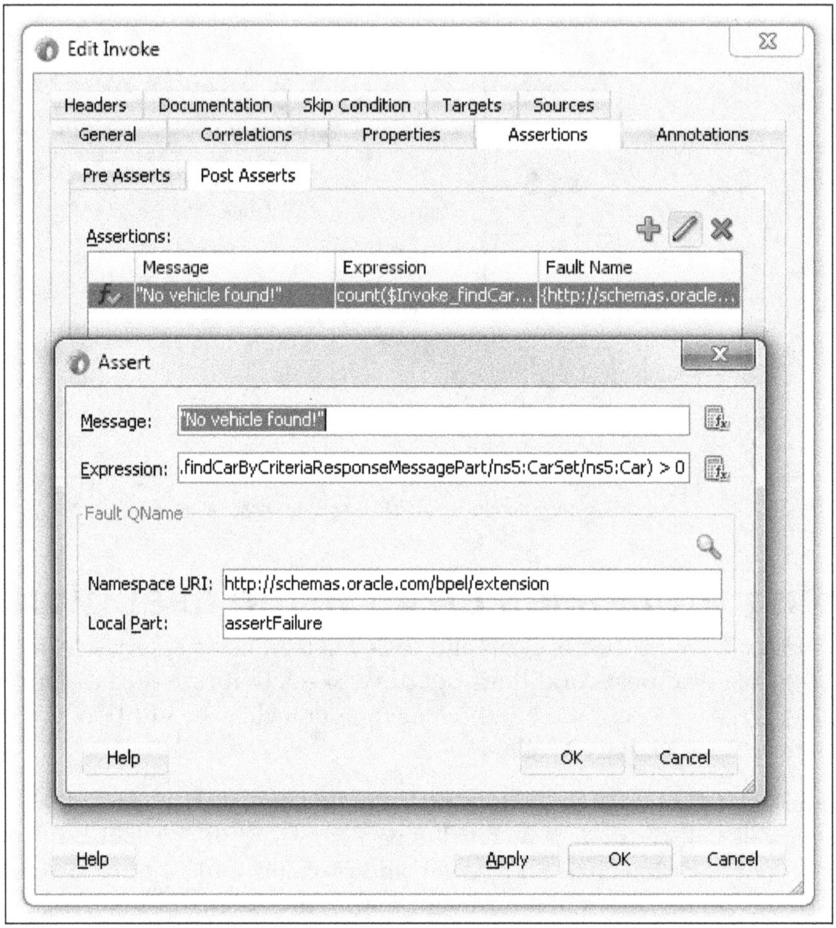

Figure 24: Wizard to create assertion conditions in BPEL

Naming criteria for composite partitions

Partitions permit the grouping of SCA composites at runtime. The principle is comparable with the tray of files in a folder structure. However, partitions cannot be organized in a hierarchy. The structuring of partitions can, for example, be based on a functional level or be application oriented. Partitions are administered via Enterprise Manager, ANT, or WLST. Storing the partition data takes place in the MDS within `folders.xml`. This file is to be found in the `soa-infra` MDS under `/soa/configuration`. Within Oracle Enterprise Manager, the following activities are available on a partition level:

- Activation or deactivation of composites
- Deployment or undeployment of composites

Enterprise Manager behaves with the partitions as it does with the definition of the structure for applications and projects. Different approaches to group composites also exist here. It essentially concerns the following aspects:

- **Togetherness and/or separation from components**
    - How can the composites be grouped from a business perspective (for example, individual project components, departments, domains, and/or subdomains)?
    - Which service categories and/or architecture components exist?
- **Number and fluctuation of the contained composites**
    - How many composites are expected in the long run (extremely complex partitions are unclear)?
    - How frequently are new composite versions made available? Does this affect existing deployments?
    - How many versions of one composite are to be operated in parallel?
    - Are composites called explicitly in their respective version or is the default revision always used (per partition, only one default revision of a composite is possible)?
- **Runtime behavior and operation aspects**
    - Are composite instances long running (asynchronous), short running (synchronous), or event based?
    - For which composites would we like to execute the same administration activity simultaneously (starting, stopping, and deletion)?

 - Is there a fixed release cycle or does the deployment take place individually?
 - How does the supply of coherent composites/releases take place (always complete or only individual components)?

We recommend making the designation of the partitions consistent with the defined project structure. In the following list, several naming patterns with their pros and cons are listed:

- **<Domain/Subdomain>**: This is suitable if the containing composites can be grouped into business-related domains or logical components, for example, car rental, fleet management, and customer management. The advantage is a business-oriented structuring of the composites. Unfavorably, the number of composites can increase during a longer period because this way of structuring is quite coarse-grained.
- **<Domain/Subdomain>_<VERSION>**: Large enterprises often have fixed release cycles for entire application packages instead of individual deployments of a single composite. We could, for example, have a requirement that all the composites within the CarRental partition should always be deployed and maintained together as a package. A new major version of one composite within CarRental would also mean that the corresponding composites within the same partition should be deployed with a new version as well. If we do so within the same partition, then the number of composites can increase very quickly. With each release, it becomes more and more difficult to maintain the composites. For this reason, we recommend that you extend the partition name with a version identifier, for example, CarRental_V1.
- **<CATEGORY>**: In *Chapter 4, Process-driven Service Design*, a set of different service categories has been introduced. This naming pattern uses the category identifier to group the composites, for example, into **business process services** (**BPS**), **business activity services** (**BAS**), and so on. However, this grouping is suitable only in environments of small complexity since clarity and handling in the Enterprise Manager for categories with many composites decrease strongly. For maintenance reasons, we recommend that you use abbreviations with coherent capital letters. If needed, this naming pattern can also be combined with the major version, as shown earlier.

- **<CATEGORY>_<Domain/Subdomain>**: In relation to the first naming pattern, this variant has the advantage that the coarse-grained domain identifier is further divided into the service categories, for example, BPS_CarRental. The approach is in particular suitable for scenarios where the number of composites within a domain is medium or large or where a significant increase is expected in the future. With few composites (for example, only one composite per partition), this way of structuring might be a bit confusing and redundant. The two components of the partition name are connected with one "_". If needed, this naming pattern can also be combined with the major version as shown earlier.

> You can follow similar criteria to find names for your Oracle BPM Studio applications and projects.

Summary

In this chapter, we concentrated on various topics around process execution with BPEL and BPMN. First of all, we started with the definition of an implementation roadmap. As part of this, we analyzed the different systems that are involved in the car rental process, and we specified which type of development is needed for each component in order to satisfy the requirements. After that, we briefly explained where to use BPEL and where to use BPMN.

In the implementation roadmap, fleet management and rental process were defined as new TO-BE components that should be developed from scratch. Fleet management is a key component for the rental process. It integrates with the reservation system as well as the booking system—sometimes in an asynchronous and stateful manner. For this reason, we explained how to implement it as a BPEL composite. In this context, we described the concept of a service facade combined with a contract-first approach. In detail, we explained how to implement a delegation pattern with BPEL.

Afterwards, the chapter covered important aspects that need to be considered for the implementation of executable BPMN processes. The basic concepts of BPMN were already discussed in *Chapter 3, BPMN for Business Process Modeling*, but from a pure modeling perspective. Here, we concentrated on the transformation from an abstract process model that describes the logical flow of activities into a technical process that can be executed on a BPM engine.

In the end, we listed a couple of best practices about naming criteria, coupling levels, the separation between public and private interfaces, and some tips to avoid BPEL processes with a lot of boilerplate code.

This chapter has a number of key takeaways. First, an application landscape map provides a good overview about the dependencies between the process and its associated components. It also helps to identify missing components or redundancies. Then, you learned that the main difference between BPEL and BPMN is that BPEL is not as user-role-centric as BPMN. We use BPEL to implement stateful integration processes that do not require a lot of loopbacks and do not have many human interactions. Further, in asynchronous scenarios, BPEL has some advantages compared with the Mediator, especially when you use it as a delegation component. Furthermore, the selected message exchange pattern (synchronous/asynchronous) affects the design of the process as well as the exception handling. Moreover, in order to keep the composites maintainable, it is important to decouple private components (components without an exposed service interface) from public interfaces. Finally, with BPEL features such as sensor actions and assertions, you are able to focus on the essential aspects of a process. Boilerplate code is hidden, which keeps the code as well as the audit trail clean and easy to read.

The next chapter will focus on human interactions with business processes. It will introduce the Oracle Human Workflow components and a couple of important concepts, such as user interface design and user experience. In addition to these conceptual topics, the next chapter will explain the possibilities that Oracle BPM 12*c* provides to incorporate human interactions with automated business process flows. As part of this, the chapter will describe several best practices from numerous BPM implementations. This includes the general process design, a few modeling techniques, and different approaches to implement a custom inbox application.

7

Human Interaction with Business Processes

Business process automation is essential for companies to guarantee their business agility and to increase process transparency, which, as a consequence, leads to operational excellence. As explained in the previous chapters, a holistic business process management (BPM) defines the way to achieve these goals and to ensure the structured automation of companies' end-to-end processes along the delivery chain. One important aspect to gain the most benefit from process automation is to avoid media breaks. Usually, a full automation of business processes is not possible because on dedicated points, a business process needs input from an external human participant. Classic examples for that are approval scenarios. The challenge here is to seamlessly integrate automated business processes and human actors.

This challenge is not new, and in the meanwhile, specifications dealing with the standardization of human integration with the IT system, that is, automated business processes (Read more about **WS Human Task (WS-HT)** at `http://docs.oasis-open.org/bpel4people/ws-humantask-1.1-spec-cs-01.html`) are available. Today, every BPM platform supports human integration out of the box, which is also due to the fact that BPMN 2.0 defines a user task activity.

How business process modeling and automation could be done using Oracle BPM Suite 12*c* was showed in the previous chapter. We have explained how to compose a BPM application by combining BPEL and BPMN components to depict the RYLC car rental process. In this chapter, we will introduce the human task service component architecture (SCA) component, which is used to involve human actors from within a BPEL or BPMN component. We will do the following:

- Introduce basic concepts of UI design and guidelines about user experience (UX)
- Introduce concepts of the Oracle Human Workflow components

- Discuss implementation and architectural aspects regarding the definition of task-based UIs
- Show how human interaction can be incorporated with automated business processes
- Discuss best practices approaches when defining human interactions

User experience guidelines

The design and implementation of user interfaces has changed significantly over the decades. The chosen technology evolves from host-based forms of a mainframe application into fat-client applications that are implemented, for example, using Java Swing. It can also evolve into thin-client web applications, **Rich Internet Application** (**RIA**), and finally, multichannel applications that must support diverse platforms. There is no end in sight as regards this evolution. Hand-in-hand with this technological evolvement, the expectations of business units and thus of the end users are also changing. Enterprise applications are expected to generate business value today.

> **User interface** (**UI**) intensive applications must enable end users to handle their daily work as efficiently as possible. That means a paradigm shift for application developers—end users and their desires become the focus.

To allow good and structured UI design, standards on how UI can be defined effectively and efficiently have been established. An example is the ISO 9241 standard. The main objective is to provide a good overall **user experience** (**UX**). Enterprise applications that show a great UX are characterized by the following:

- **Effectiveness** in the processing of tasks can be evaluated based on the number of processed tasks per user
- **Efficiency** of system handling; one indicator for that may be the time a user needs to complete a task in the context of a business process
- **Intuitiveness** with reference to the complexity of the user interface may be characterized by the memorability, which means how long a user needs to re-establish if not using an application for a while
- **Flexibility** in the way tasks can be completed; may be determined by checking the number of different ways that can be adopted to achieve the same goal within the application

- **Consistency** in application behavior and design

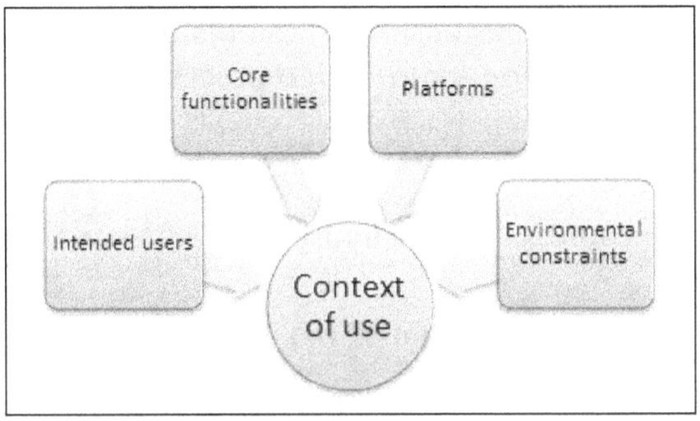

Figure 1

A good UX with reference to the UIs usually satisfies the end user's needs and thus is the key to user acceptance of enterprise applications.

Before implementing an enterprise application, it is important to analyze the corresponding context of use. As the preceding figure shows, the context of use depends on different factors and so is individual for every project. To know what the users of an application are, their use cases, and also their IT affinity, it is essential to create applications that meet the user's expectations. Consequently, it is important to know about the core functionalities an application should provide because these depict the daily business of the end users and so are most relevant for user acceptance. Another crucial point is to figure out whether an application should support different platforms. This is essential because today we have a variety of different devices, for example, mobile devices running Android, iOS operating systems, and desktop Windows systems. Due to the rapid technological evolvement, further constraints have to be considered, such as offline application usage in the case of mobile devices and associated security requirements in the direction of data integrity.

Obviously, building usable user interfaces is not straightforward. From a technical perspective, the evolution of interactive applications is resulting in new challenges, making application development more complex. Application developers are confronted with having to consider a new dimension in addition to usual business requirements when building highly interactive enterprise applications—the user's psychology and physiology. End users and their needs are positioned in the middle of the considerations; business needs are fading into the background. Complying with those requirements is difficult but necessary to ensure user acceptance of new applications, which is essential for the generation of business value.

User experience is an important factor to be considered. Large software vendors have their own user experience guidelines, which are basic to implementing applications in a consistent and intuitive manner to provide the best user experience to end users.

Oracle, for example, shares its UX best practices with the community (`http://www.oracle.com/webfolder/ux/applications/uxd/index.html`). Here, a collection of design patterns, guidelines, checklists, and templates are provided. In addition, a corresponding three-step, user-centered design process (`http://www.oracle.com/webfolder/ux/applications/uxd/design.html`) is described. The high-level steps are as follows:

- Discovering the context of use: identifying the users, their needs, and how they work
- Designing the UIs: addressing user needs and providing a sufficient solution
- Deploying the application: being confident about the user acceptance

Every high-level step is further divided as the following figure shows. Using the steps and activities provided by the design process as a checklist helps developers to consider UX requirements consistently along the development process.

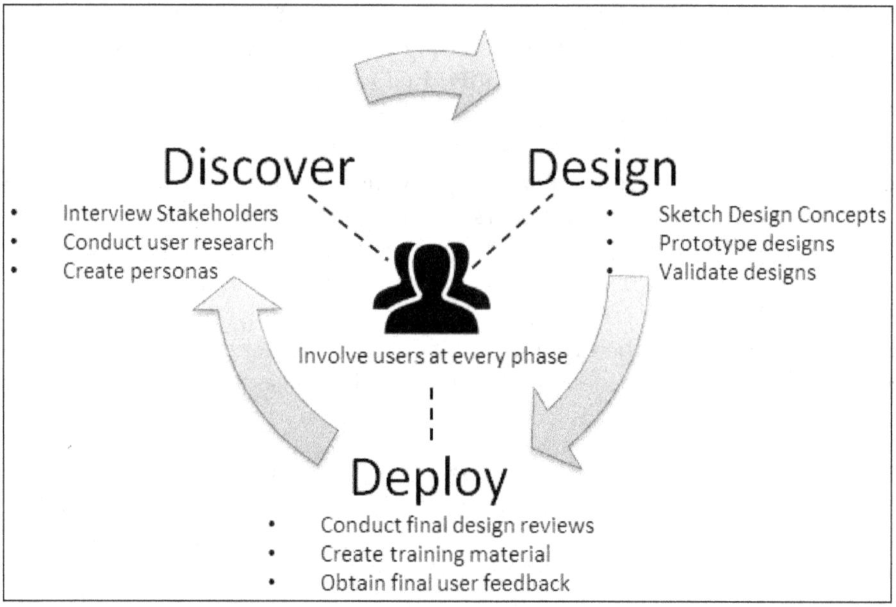

Figure 2

> The involvement of users in every step of the process is essential to ensure that users' needs are addressed adequately. Early and constant user feedback is necessary to achieve a good UX. Choosing an agile development approach will additionally support early feedback during implementation.

User personas and user journeys within a business process

Knowing the users of an application and their needs, wants, and limitations are the key to user acceptance, as was shown in the following section. Business processes and thus the corresponding applications usually have different types of users, with different interests and responsibilities. The design and implementation team should have a common understanding about the intended users, including their responsibilities.

According to Oracle's design process, these are tasks from the discovery step. As a part of this, the creation of personas to gather and prepare information from interviews with real users is suggested. Personas are fictional characters used to describe a specific group of users that work within the area an application should be built for. The description is done in the form of a so-called user persona description or a user profile, which should be centrally accessible to every team member. In its methodology, Oracle provides an example that can be used as a template to create persona descriptions (`http://www.oracle.com/webfolder/ux/applications/uxd/assets/templates/user-persona-template.pdf`).

Once the potential users have been identified, the next step is to identify the primary tasks of the intended users. These could usually be derived from the persona description. The documentation of these core functionalities may be done in the form of user journeys. Basically, a user journey is one path users could take through an application. It might be realized as one simple page or even a complex sequence of pages. It always has a specific goal, for example, with reference to the car rental example, the completion of choosing and booking a rental car. A user journey is usually broken down into different steps. For the car booking example, the valid steps may be login and choose a car or choose payment information. Defined user journeys, consisting of multiple steps, are measureable. So, it is, for example, possible to monitor the end-to-end performance. This enables the opportunity to set up specific monitoring per user journey, which can be used to further optimize the user experience during a journey. A possible problem that may be found out by monitoring end-to-end user journey performance is a bad navigation design. This means that the form design as such is good, but the navigation concept is not. Without predefined user journeys, such kind of analysis and problem identification would not be possible because only single page performance measurements are feasible.

The communication between automated processes and human actors happens using so-called tasks. A task is a data object that holds custom information with respect to the current business context as well as information about priorities, deadlines, and responsibilities. In the case of Oracle BPM Suite 12*c*, the Human Task service engine cares about task life cycle management.

Within a running business process instance, a task could have different stakeholders with different responsibilities regarding the task and so may directly influence the further progress of the process instance. In Oracle BPM Suite 12*c*, different task stakeholders are predefined, which have to be mapped to the existing organizational structure of the corresponding business domain to depict the responsibilities regarding a process, and its tasks can be defined as follows:

- The **owner** is a business administrator who can act on a task on its own or on behalf of another user. It can change assignments and the outcome of a task.
- The **initiator** of a business process can review the task's status and can provide additional information for other process participants.
- The **approver** represents a single user responsible for processing a specific task that is directly assigned to the approver.
- The **potential approver** can take over the responsibility of processing a task. Usually, there is a group of potential approvers sharing the responsibility of a group of tasks. A single user may claim a task and so become the exclusive approver. Afterwards, the task can be approved or released so that another potential approver can claim it.
- The **reviewer** can view the status of tasks and can add comments as well as attachments.
- The **administrator** can view and act on all tasks in an administrative way. It cannot perform business actions such as completing a task like an approver to continue the business processing.
- The **error assignee** becomes automatically responsible for tasks that are in an error state, when, for instance, a task should be assigned to a non-existing user.

The stakeholder and responsibility definitions provided by Oracle BPM Suite 12*c* could be taken as a basis for structuring the intended users of a BPM application, identified and characterized by persona descriptions, into groups. So, it can be ensured that real users have the intended responsibilities within the business process at runtime.

As process-to-user interaction happens based on tasks, BPM client applications are usually provided in the form of an inbox application. Just as with an email application, such as Microsoft Outlook, the users can choose between different tasks and work on it. An example for such a task-based application is Oracle BPM Workspace, which is shipped with BPM Suite 12*c*. The following screenshot shows this:

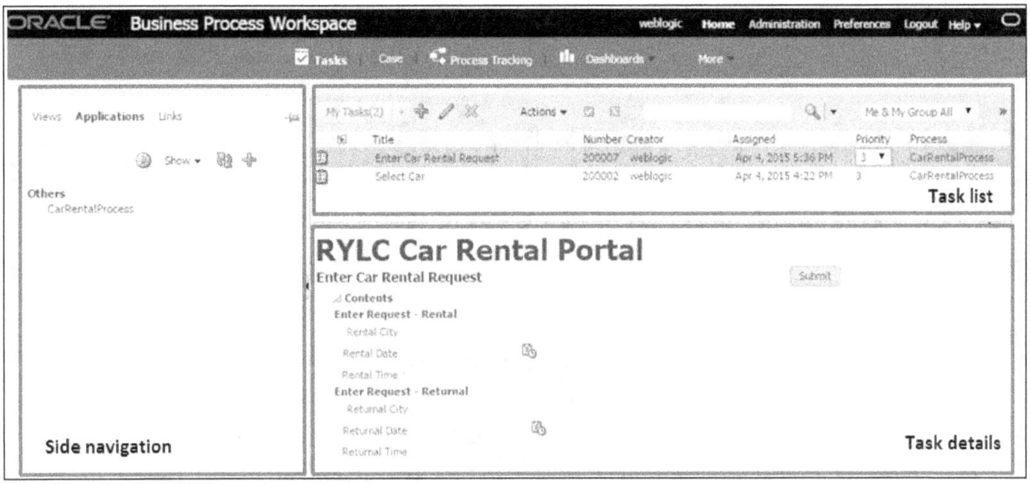

Figure 3

The central element for such applications is a task list where all tasks, and the current user or one of its groups, are displayed. In the task list, the users can see diverse nonbusiness-related task information, such as priority, description, or assignee. By choosing a task from the list, the task details containing business-related data could be accessed. Tasks may be filtered, ordered, and processed if the permissions allow this.

From the corresponding functionalities described earlier, the following basic and commonly needed functionalities regarding task processing can be identified:

- Search
- Review
- Complete
- Claim
- Release
- Reassign

Based on these essential functionalities, general user journeys can be defined that can be used as an abstract basis to derive concrete user journeys for a specific business domain. An example user journey for the search task functionality can be the following:

A user logs into the inbox application. After successful login, the user applies filter criteria to a specific open task that should be processed. The search results are displayed and the user chooses the desired task. This user journey is usually implemented as a one-step page flow.

Designing the user interface – wireframes, task-driven, process insight

A consistent and intuitive UI design is essential for good UX. In this context, wireframes are used to define and coordinate a user-centered and basic form design used throughout the whole application. The wireframes are defined in different levels of detail. In addition, interaction models are used to describe how the interaction with an application happens.

> Wireframes and their corresponding interaction models can be understood as guidelines for UI implementation. Therefore, these are basic for a good UX and important for user acceptance.

With respect to the interaction models, it is important to notice that end users often internalize a special kind of interaction model. So, when a long-term, established interaction model is changed significantly, users may become dissatisfied with the new solution. This has to be considered, especially when building task-driven BPM applications.

In traditional applications, where the business logic is tightly integrated with the UI logic, the communication between frontend and backend components is usually done using a synchronous request-response message exchange pattern. Service calls return immediately after the call so that client processing can continue. The process flow logic is depicted by the page flow logic in this case.

For BPM applications, this traditional approach is no longer applicable. The business flow logic moves from the frontend over to the backend controlled by the automated business processes. The communication in the backend usually happens asynchronously, especially when long-running operations are invoked. From a business process perspective, a human invocation is a long-running operation. For client developers, this means a paradigm shift. The challenge is that human actors incorporated into the business processes should not notice that the interaction model should remain as is. Let's have a look at an example that describes what happens if we change the interaction model to an asynchronous, inbox-oriented approach.

A customer who wants to rent a car initiates a corresponding process instance in the background. After two automated steps performed by RYLC backend systems, the process comes back to the user to select a car. For this reason, a task is created in the background on which the user has to act to step forward in the process. When following the introduced inbox-based approach, the customer has to login to the inbox, search, and complete the corresponding task by selecting a car. This is confusing and very unsatisfactory for the customer. It would be no wonder if the customer chooses another car rental company the next time.

The example might be a little artificial, but it shows two major issues of the inbox-oriented approach because the user is forced to do the following:

- Switch between applications proactively, for example, between the inbox application and the current business application the user works with
- Identify the right task for the current business context

With respect to a real-world business scenario where users may have a great number of tasks in their inboxes, this approach does not support the users' work efficiently. In addition, application switching is quite uncomfortable and leads to user dissatisfaction in consequence. Obviously, another approach is needed that ensures efficient work support, and which is able to guarantee the familiar synchronous interaction model. In addition, the duplication of the business process flow logic in the frontend application must be avoided.

The challenges described earlier are subject to the **UI mediator** pattern introduced by Thomas Erl (`http://soapatterns.org/design_patterns/ui_mediator`). It describes the problem and provides a solution at a highly abstract layer. As a more concrete variant of the UI mediator pattern, the Masons of SOA, an inter-company network founded by architects, introduced **Service Human Interaction Layer (SHIL)**.

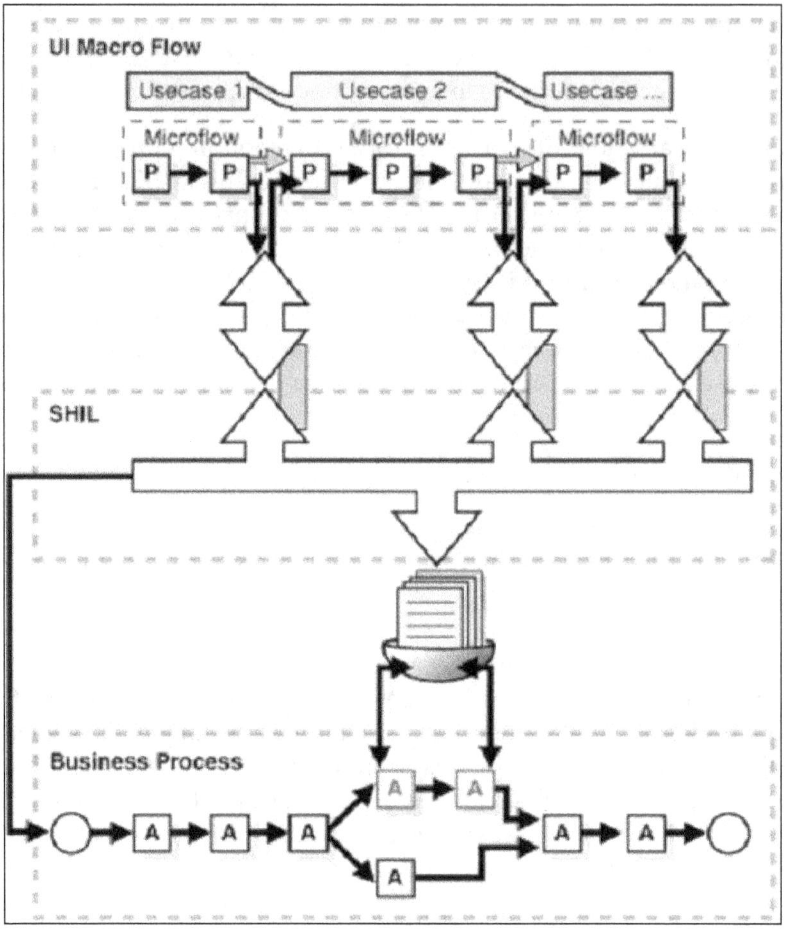

Figure 4

Basically, SHIL defines an abstraction layer between the business process backend and the frontend application. The SHIL layer fulfills the requirement to simulate synchronicity in the frontend, while the backend works highly asynchronously from a technical perspective. The receding picture shows the inbox approach, including the implemented SHIL on top.

The essential implementation components for SHIL are a pair of micro and macro flow controllers. The **micro flow controller** is a frontend controller, such as Faces Servlet in Java EE applications, which implements and controls the UI page flows. A specific flow could be started using a unique flow identifier. The **macro flow controller** resides between the processes and the frontend. It controls the interaction between the UI and the process without implementing any page flow logic. If a UI-based use case is needed, the process triggers the macro flow controller, which informs the micro flow controller in an event-based manner. The micro flow controller receives a corresponding flow identifier for the current use case, resolves it, and is able to display the correct UI for the current use case. Implementing this pattern leads to a clear separation of page flow and process flow logic, where no duplicate logic implementation is contained. In addition, it helps ensure UX because the interaction model is close to the familiar behavior of the traditional applications, so the users can nearly work as usual without serious implications. This is important to ensure end user satisfaction, and in consequence, the acceptance of task-driven BPM applications.

Task identification and patterns

Tasks are the essential objective to enable information exchange between automated processes and their participants. The invocation of human actors happens explicitly at defined points within the business process flow. The invocated actors are required to provide relevant information to the business process flow so that it can continue.

To ensure task processing, tasks will be allocated to responsible process participants or groups of participants, which can be defined in the corresponding task configuration at design time. The assignable participants and groups are obtained from an identity directory, such as a company's LDAP system. Often, it is necessary to define authorizations in a fine, granular manner at the application level. Usually, application authorizations are not mapped in an enterprise identity store because sooner or later, this approach would end up in a mess of application-specific roles and users. Consequently, this would lead to an increased administrative overhead. Oracle BPM Suite 12*c* introduces the concept of **application roles** to address this challenge. Conceptually, this allows the definition of application-specific authorizations irrespective of any enterprise identity store. Creating an application role can be done in the BPM Workspace application. Users and groups obtained from an enterprise identity store as well as other, already existing application roles can be associated to it.

The participant assignment to tasks at runtime could be done in astatic, dynamic, or even rule-based way (there is a more detailed explanation at `http://docs.oracle.com/middleware/1213/soasuite/develop-soa/soa-bpm-workflow-intro.htm#SOASE20423`), as shown in the following list:

- **Static task assignments** mean that a task is always assigned to the same configured list of participants and to the same single approver.
- **Dynamic task assignments** could be done realized through a predefined **assignment pattern** with specific XPath expressions or by a combination of both approaches. Task assignment to a user happens automatically based on the specified pattern or expressions provided. The available assignment patterns for dynamic assignments are: least busy, round robin, and most productive. The Human Workflow engine considers a specified pattern during the task assignment procedure and optimizes the assignment of tasks with respect to the throughput of processed tasks, workload balance for users, or the average processing time. Alternatively, when defining no assignment pattern, the potential approvers have to explicitly claim tasks manually.
- **Rule-based task assignments** use a ruleset described in the form of a rule component, where complex task-routing decisions can be defined. Rule-based assignments may also be combined with the predefined assignment patterns.

Real-world business decisions, which have to be performed by human actors, are complex and multilevel. A single-approver scenario is often not applicable in such cases. Oracle BPM Suite 12*c* offers prebuilt task-routing scenarios, described in the following list.

- A **single approver** is the simple case, when the defined task participant maps to a single user, group, or application role.
- A **parallel** is used to map group-voting scenarios, where a task is assigned to a group of participants that each has to give their vote regarding the business case. A voting percentage defines when the task is completed.
- A **serial** is used to define a set of users that have to work in sequence. With this pattern, management chains and corresponding escalations or a four-eye principle assignment flow could be realized.
- **For your interest** (**FYI**) maps to a single user, group, or application role, such as the single approver. This generates a notification task and does not wait for a participant's response. Such participants could not directly influence the task outcome. If permitted, they only can add comments or attachments to support the task approvers.

In addition, the Oracle Human Workflow component provides the opportunity to model more complex scenarios by combining the prebuilt task-routing scenarios. The organization of the single approval levels is done using so-called approval stages. Within an approval stage, one or more participant types can be combined. The whole routing and assignment flow is called the routing slip, in which different stages can be combined to allow complex routing and assignment modeling for human tasks. The processing of the routing slip may stop at any point within the routing slip, which could be achieved by defining corresponding conditions that are based on the outcome of a specific stage.

The processing time of business processes is a **key performance indicator** (**KPI**) when rating the business efficiency. Optimizing processing times may be one goal of a BPM initiative. In some scenarios, legal restrictions define time limits to fulfill a complete business request. The maximum expected processing times are often specified within **service level agreements** (**SLAs**). To ensure compliance with the given SLAs, it is necessary to ensure that human tasks within a business process are completed within a sufficient timeframe. The Human Workflow component within Oracle BPM Suite 12*c* provides different deadline mechanisms, which could be used to ensure the specified SLAs of a business process flow are achieved. By default, a task has no deadline, so it will never expire. To avoid unlimited task processing times, expirations after a specific period of time can be defined. The action on task expiry can be defined within the business process flow or directly in the human task, for example, by defining an e-mail notification. Furthermore, an escalation strategy can be defined for a task that can be used to ensure task processing in time. In escalation scenarios, a task expires after a specified period of time and then is escalated, that is, to the line manager of the current task assignee.

When using one of the described mechanisms to ensure task processing times, it is usually not intended that the corresponding task expiry or escalation occurs outside the core business time. Expirations on weekends or labor days should be avoided. To control this, BPM Suite 12*c* provides a business calendar functionality, where the core business times can be specified. Furthermore, a list of holidays can be associated with a configured business calendar, where labor days or annual closings can be defined. A business calendar in turn could be associated with a human task definition. When a concrete task instance is created, the information from the specified business calendar is considered by the Human Workflow engine when calculating a tasks expiration date.

Invoking human tasks from BPMN and BPEL

Until now, we have discussed what a task-driven approach means from a user's perspective. The consequences for the business process are not considered yet. So, in this section, we will focus on the process side and on what will happen from a business process execution perspective when a human task activity is reached. Therefore, an overview on the high-level architecture of Oracle Human Workflow, in conjunction with business process modeling, should be given, and afterwards, we will demonstrate how to incorporate the RYLC car rental process with human actors by introducing a human workflow component.

Human Workflow architecture

Oracle BPM Suite 12*c* has a modular architecture consisting of different service engines. This ensures separation of concerns and provides the needed flexibility to application developers to build scalable as well as adaptable business applications. As mentioned earlier, there is also a separate service engine that cares about the lifecycle management of tasks—the Oracle Human Workflow engine. The WS-HT specification, for example, recommends this way of architecture due to a clear separation of business process execution and task lifecycle management.

The following figure gives a high-level overview of how human interactions are working from an architectural perspective when using a process notation such as BPMN in connection with human tasks. At design time, a human task is declared in the form of a separate component within a composite. In the task definition, details about the routing slip, the business data, deadlines, and so on can be specified.

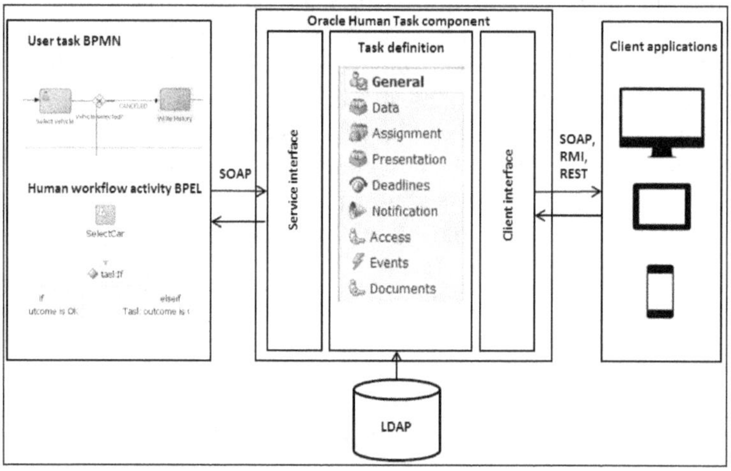

Figure 4

The example figure shows the integration of a Human Workflow component with a BPMN component. Within a BPMN process standard, user task activity is used to implement the interaction with a human task component. The integration of a BPEL process with a Human Workflow component works similarly. Here a BPEL extension activity is used, which underneath uses standard BPEL constructs, such as assign or invoke activities, to perform the Human Workflow invocation. As we can see, the invocation of a Human Workflow component is irrespective of the chosen process implementation language.

From a process's perspective, involving a human actor is the same as invoking an asynchronous service. The process instance executes a service call to the Human Workflow engine, which initiates a task based on the specific task configuration. Using a corresponding client API, the communication between the Human Workflow engine and different devices could be realized. The client API is exposed using different technologies and protocols (see `http://docs.oracle.com/middleware/1213/bpm/workflow-api-ref/toc.htm` for more detailed information). An inbox application can use the provided client API to query and process the available tasks.

Although the provided API methods are using a synchronous interaction pattern, the background processing happens asynchronously. The Human Workflow engine marks the task as completed and calls back the triggering process instance, which waits for the corresponding task to be completed, with the information about the task outcome. The process instance receives the response from the Human Workflow engine and continues the process execution. So, the subsequent process execution highly depends on the decision made by the human actors. Due to this, a decision activity, such as a BPMN gateway, could often be found after a user task activity that controls the further process execution.

Authenticating users on the basis of an identity directory ensures security aspects in human interaction scenarios, such as authenticity and authority. By default, Oracle WebLogic's internal LDAP is used. The use of an already existing LDAP is also possible. A custom identity directory has to be configured in the WebLogic server that provides the users and groups from the identity directory to Oracle BPM Suite using **Oracle Platform Security Services** (**OPSS**), which is the common WebLogic security layer. The advantage of OPSS is also that other applications can use the credentials coming from a configured LDAP by utilizing the provided WebLogic APIs. So, a consistent handling of users and groups coming from a single identity directory is possible.

Example: Adding human interaction to a business process

In the RYLC car rental process, human intervention is mandatory. A customer starts a concrete instance of the process by entering a corresponding rental request. In the following step, the customer has to select the car that they want to rent. To realize these requirement, the RYLC process developer have to enhance the existing process by adding Human Workflow components to the composite application.

First, the process developer decides to draw some wireframes, which have to be discussed with RYLC sales and marketing, before implementing the task forms. During a subsequent beta phase, where the forms will be implemented as depicted in the wireframes, the UIs will be further enhanced with reference to the corresponding user feedback. The following figure shows this:

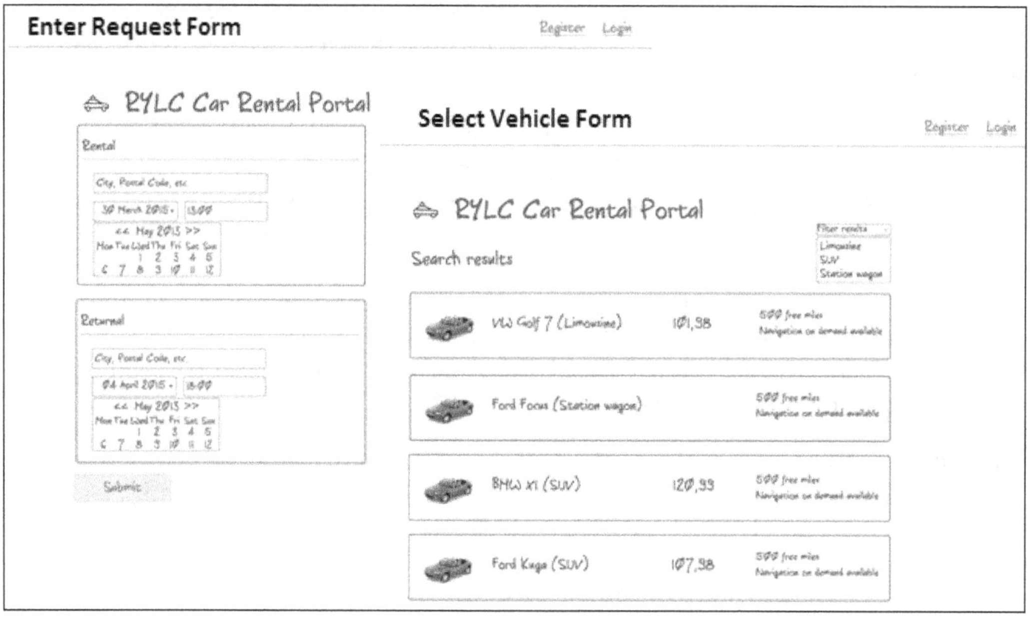

Figure 6

After the discussion with the business side, the process developer starts with defining the Human Workflow components that are used as concrete implementations for the BPMN user tasks. The following figure shows this:

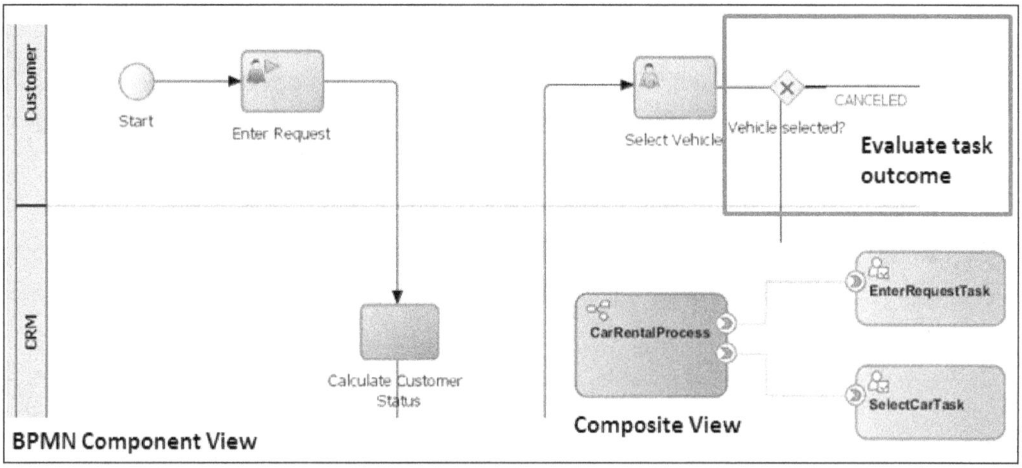

Figure 6

Implementing the Human Workflow components is straightforward because for the car rental process, simple single-approver scenarios have to be implemented, where the approver is the customer. So, for the most part, the default configurations are sufficient to implement a beta version. For the **Select Vehicle** user task activity, the process developer has to ensure that they return the expected task outcomes from the Human Workflow component so that the process flow continues correctly. The BPMN process evaluates the task outcome at the **Vehicle selected?** gateway. The task outcomes can be configured in the human task configuration. The developer adapts the corresponding configurations and associates the user task activities with the added Human Workflow implementations. The following screenshot shows this:

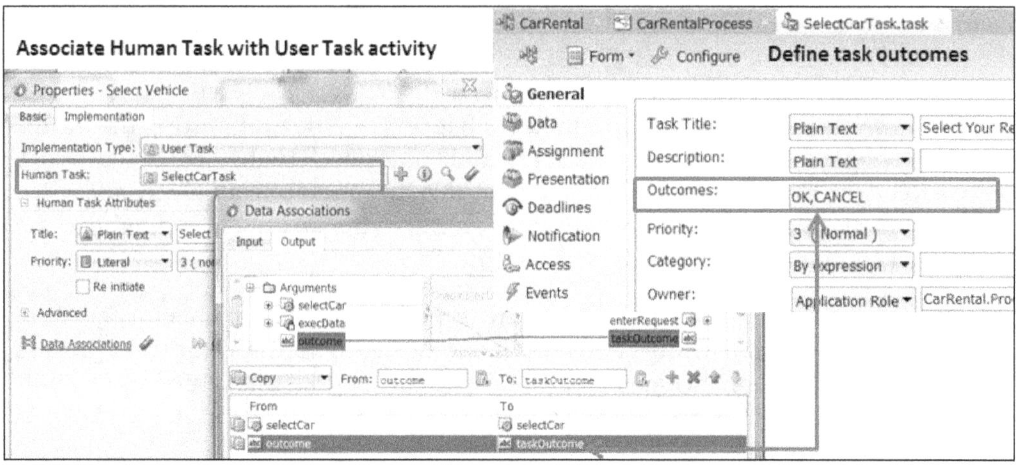

Figure 8

After the changes have been applied to the car rental process successfully, the developer creates the corresponding task detail forms. To ensure maximum flexibility and integration with Oracle BPM Workspace, the developer chooses ADF to implement the UI. In this first phase, RYLC decides to use the default BPM Workspace application as a process portal due to time and monetary reasons. The following screenshot shows this:

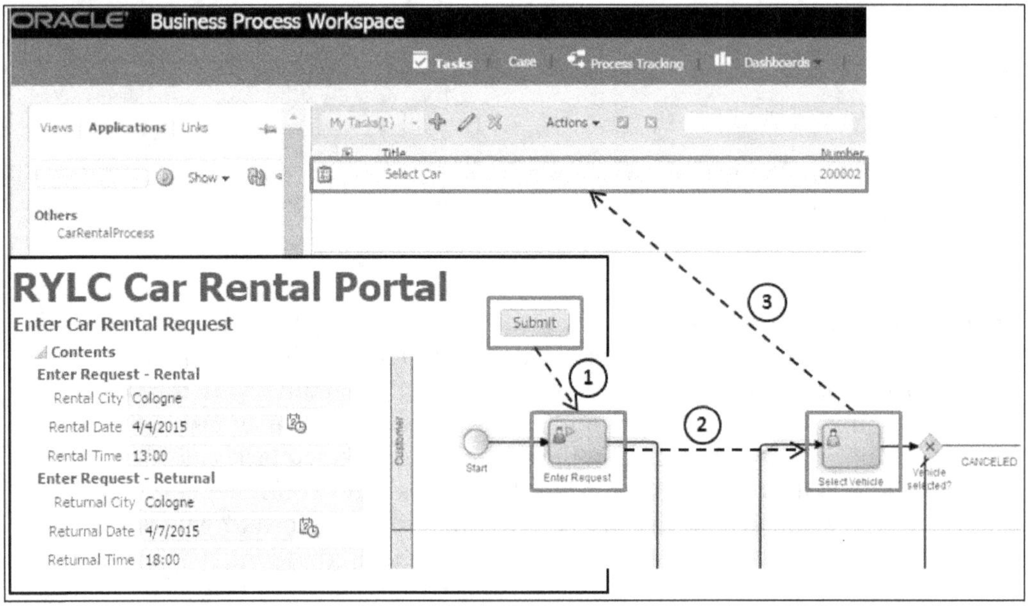

Figure 9

To first do developer testing, the RYLC process developer deploys the BPM composite application, including the UI project, into its local development environment and initiates a car rental process using BPM Workspace by entering a first car rental request using the specified ADF form (1). After submitting the form, the BPMN engine processes the request (2), and comes back to the user when a car has to be selected. The BPMN engine does this by generating a **SelectCarTask** (3). Using the task and its corresponding task form, a car can be selected, which afterwards continues the business process flow.

These initial results are promising and address the RYLC requirements for the first beta version. The human actors have been incorporated with the automated process successfully. Further enhancements of the UI structure or the interaction model will be made in subsequent project phases.

Building task-driven user interfaces – workspace, web forms, ADF, .Net

As already indicated throughout this chapter, BPM applications are highly interactive and so need a good UI design to support users effectively in their daily work. It must be ensured that all relevant and contextual information of the current business context are made available to the users in a clear, comprehensible, and easy-to-understand manner. The information provided is important to guarantee the quality of a business decision made by human actors. In a specific detailed view of a task, this information is displayed to users. The detailed view can consist of a simple one-page flow or even a complex sequence of pages depending on the corresponding business case.

Implementing task-driven UIs for BPM applications with Oracle BPM Suite 12*c* is generally possible using any technology. The recommended way to do the implementation is using Oracle's standard technologies. To implement the task UIs, Oracle ADF is recommended, which allows seamless integration with BPM Workspace as an inbox application because it is also implemented using ADF. So, developing a custom inbox solution is not necessary unless the inbox-oriented approach is not sufficient.

Nevertheless, in a few cases, following the recommendations is not applicable due to the following:

- Missing ADF knowhow within the user company
- Limited customizability of BPM Workspace (only the logo and CSS are customizable)
- Existing corporate guidelines that define other strategic UI technologies, for example, .NET
- Existing portal solution where the BPM application should be integrated
- Insufficiency of the inbox approach

In the following subsections, different approaches to implement task-driven UIs will be presented, discussing advantages, disadvantages, and scenarios.

ADF

As already mentioned, one approach to define task-driven UIs is using Oracle ADF, which is the recommended approach. Basically, there are two approaches as to how this can be done:

- Auto-generating the UI based on the defined task data
- Implementing the task UIs manually from scratch

When auto-generating the task UIs, a separate ADF web application per human task definition is created, which has to be deployed along with the BPM application. The autogeneration approach is useful when doing proof-of-concept implementations for BPM because development can be done fast and easily. Generally, the autogeneration approach does not presuppose deep ADF or JEE knowledge. However, for real-world scenarios, we do not recommend that you use this approach because of less flexibility and difficulties regarding the maintenance, especially when applications are evolving. The generated task forms are static due to the fact that generation is based on the underlying task definition and the configured task data. Usually, only a minimal set of data is available in the context of a business process instance and thus only this data is available for a human task because it is populated from the current business process context. The pattern to carry only a minimal set of data through a business process ensures platform performance on the one hand and guarantees that the data within a process instance's context does not become outdated. So, task forms need the ability to obtain relevant business data from external data stores. From a maintenance and operational perspective, the autogeneration approach is also difficult to handle because generating a separate ADF web project per human task will sooner or later end up in a bunch of different projects, which is confusing. It is not necessary to have a separate project per human task detailed view and, therefore, should be avoided.

Amore flexible approach is to build task forms manually from scratch. A developer has full control of the layout of the task forms, the displayed data that could be fetched from different data stores, and the structure as well as the architecture of the web application. Although this approach requires expert knowledge about ADF and JEE to implement the task forms. So, either the process developers have this knowledge, which is often not the norm, or an additional resource is needed for building the necessary user interfaces. This results in more effort but guarantees a maximum adaptive and customizable approach.

Web forms

Besides using ADF, Oracle BPM Suite 12*c* provides an alternative approach to building human task UIs using so-called web forms. Web forms are based upon standard technologies, such as XHTML, CSS, and JavaScript, and can be created using BPM Composer directly while implementing the business process and the user tasks. Intentionally, this way of implementing human task forms should address business analysts. Nevertheless, a basic understanding of the aforementioned technologies is useful.

Building web forms is basically done in a drag-and-drop style, where the so-called form controls, such as text fields, radio buttons, checkboxes, and so on, are arranged on a canvas to depict the necessary information for the business scenario. The behavior of a web form and the corresponding web form controls can be defined using form rules, which are pieces of JavaScript code edited in the form rules editor of Business Process Composer. The forms are based on an underlying data structure described in XSD, which corresponds to the business data description of the associated human task configuration.

Generally, there are two approaches to developing web forms. The first one is the data-first approach, where the human task form is developed after the business data definition has been created. The second way is the form-first approach, where the web form is created first and afterwards, Oracle BPM generates the corresponding XSD on the basis of the form controls added to the web form. When a so-created form is associated with a human task, the generated data structure is used for the definition of the business data payload. Relative to the form-first approach, the advantage of the data-first approach is that the defined data structures might be reused to build further web forms.

> From an SOA perspective, where reusability is a key concept, the data-first approach would be the preferable one when working with web forms.

Web forms are a lightweight alternative in contrast to building heavyweight ADF-based human task forms. The key features are a great compatibility with all common browsers, a nearly zero-coding development approach, except the definition of the behavior of the form and the controls, as well as a business user-friendly development environment. Like ADF forms, web forms are also tightly integrated with the Oracle Human Workflow infrastructure and can be used seamlessly within Oracle BPM Workspace. The restriction on web forms is that they can only be edited in BPM Composer. There is no support for building web form-based UIs in JDeveloper.

Our recommendation regarding web forms is to use it in simple, human task scenarios without complex task flows that have a sequence of task forms. Use cases for web forms can be administrative scenarios that are using a simple form, for example, when applying for a passport.

.NET

As an alternative to nearly every aforementioned Oracle-based solution approach, it is also possible to use other technologies to build task-based UIs. Integrating .NET-based forms with Oracle BPM Workspace, for example, is also possible. In this case, the implementation approach is that the UIs will be implemented in the external development environment, for example, Visual Studio. Afterwards, the resulting UI application must be provided in an appropriate server environment, such as Microsoft's **Internet Information Services** (**IIS**).

The connection between a Human Workflow component defined within the BPM application that is incorporated with a specific business process and the corresponding UI application that is developed in .NET can be defined using the enterprise manager console after deploying the composite application.

In the composite view of the deployed BPM composite, the appropriate Human Workflow component has to be selected from the list of components contained in the currently displayed composite. In the administration tab of the specific Human Workflow component, the URI information for the task form has to be defined. After applying the changes, the integration between the .NET application and the BPM application is defined properly. At runtime, when the specified human task is activated, the corresponding .NET task form will be displayed within BPM Workspace when selecting a task from the task list. The following screenshot shows this:

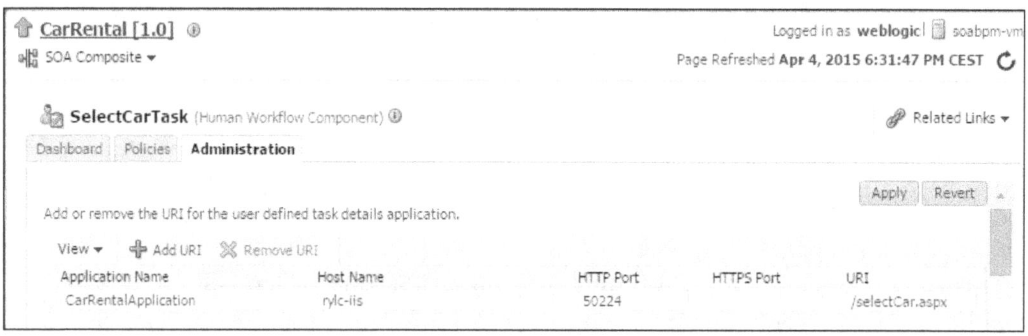

Figure 10

As illustrated, using non-Oracle technologies to define task UIs is possible. The approach is similarly flexible to the manual ADF approach. The integration with BPM Workspace is possible but less seamlessly than with ADF. From this perspective, we would rather recommend that you think about implementing a holistic approach using the preferred technology, including an inbox application.

Implementing a holistic custom solution, including an inbox application and the corresponding task forms, regardless of the client technology, is possible on the basis of the Human Workflow API provided by Oracle BPM Suite 12*c*. Oracle BPM Workspace also uses this API to depict the corresponding functionalities to work with the task.

When deciding on the holistic approach, the development of inbox application and human task forms are straight forward and independent from the business process and the human workflow definition. The implemented .NET client application simply uses the provided API for authentication, querying, and completion of tasks. Using this approach provides the highest flexibility and customizability. In addition, it can be ensured that the resulting solution exactly fits in the corporate design of a company. The holistic approach is the more flexible and customizable approach, but, at the same time, it is the most extensive alternative over all other discussed in this section. The approach to choose depends on the scenario, available budget, skills, and formation of the development team.

The following table summarizes the results from the current section about the different approaches to implement task-based UIs:

	ADF (auto-generated)	**ADF (manual approach)**	**Web forms**	**.NET**
Flexibility	Low	High	Medium	High
UI complexity	Simple	Complex	Simple	Complex
UX	Low	High	Medium	High
Implementation skills	Beginner	Expert	Beginner	Expert
Integration with BPM Workspace	High	High	High	Medium
IDE	JDeveloper	JDeveloper	BPM Composer	External (for example, Visual Studio)
Scenarios	Proof of concept	Various	Administration	Various

Best practice considerations – performance, extensibility, upgrade protection

Building task-driven applications is not easy as it can be seen from the sections within this chapter. As usual, the first steps are the most painful. Within this last section, some experiences from elementary implementation of best practices collected in real-world projects will be discussed, which can be used as hints for considerations about process and human task design when doing own implementations the first time.

General process design

How a process is designed is essential when building BPM applications. Ideally, a process's memory footprint is minimal to ensure platform stability and performance. This means that it carries as little business data as possible. In most cases, a technical identifier is suitable, which can be used to communicate with stateless service-evaluating process-flow-relevant data on demand. What applies to the processes applies to human tasks as well. The task payload should also be kept minimal. Business data relevant to later business decisions should be fetched on demand if possible. If, for some reason, business data is needed in a human task, the rule of thumb is to prefer complex data structures over simple ones. This is linked to the persistence strategy Oracle BPM Suite 12*c* uses to store the payload data. When the process state gets persistent in the underlying database, working with a simple data type leads to one row in one of the persistent store tables. So, when we define a task definition with 10 simple data definitions, this will end up in 10 rows, whereas when using a complex data type structure containing the 10 simple data fields, only one row in the table is needed to store the corresponding information. The tradeoff when using complex data structures is that task filtering on the deposited business data, such as a customer number, is not possible. This is only possible when using simple data types in conjunction with mapped attributes. In such cases, the business data will be mapped to the freely assignable public or protected fields of the task data structure. So, when designing human tasks and the corresponding data structures, the way tasks should be handled has to be considered because this highly influences the task and data structure design.

Implementing human-centric processes using Human Workflow components results in different design-time artifacts, such as the task definition, data structures, and possibly the needed UI components. Within a single composite, the defined human tasks can be reused in the processes, which are also contained in the composite. Usually, there is more than one composite containing different processes and using similar human tasks. In such cases, the aforementioned task artifacts will be duplicated because a new Human Workflow component has to be created. Doing so will decrease maintainability because changes in one human task usually involve changes in other similar human tasks too. To avoid such situations and to defuse the risk of potential errors as well as bad maintainability, similar human tasks should be identified and extracted into a reusable service, which is invoked from the corresponding processes. This ensures consistency with respect to changes and increases flexibility because of the modular process design. In addition, the development of new processes could be done faster and with fewer errors since available and verified services are reused.

Another approach, which goes a step further, is to implement a generic task handler component, which completely cares about human tasks, from the creation to the completion of tasks. In this case, only one human task definition is needed, with a generic payload, such as a technical unique identifier for loading business-relevant information from external data stores, when displaying the task form. Which approach to use depends on the business requirements and whether the human tasks are similar or different form each other. Finally, it is also a question of cost and benefit.

Explicit versus implicit modeling

Oracle Human Workflow provides more options than simply invoking a human actor to decide about critical business facts. As shown in the *Task identification and patterns* section, complex task assignment scenarios or task expiries and escalations could be depicted and are only a few features above the state-of-the-art human task functionality. In addition, options to extend the behavior provided to address special business requirements are provided by the platform. One example is the use of an external routing provider, where a custom Java implementation has to be provided, which implements the corresponding task routing logic. For cases that are not realizable using Oracle Human Workflow, standard BPMN activities in connection with human tasks can be used. Indeed, at this point, a new challenge arises.

When to use implicit product features provided by the Oracle Human Workflow component and when to do explicit modeling using BPMN 2.0 standard elements is often a crucial question within real-world projects. First things first: this question cannot be answered universally because it depends on different factors discussed in the following paragraphs. A short example will illustrate the challenge.

Within the RYLC car returnal process, generally two roles are involved: the car returnal agents and the maintenance staff. Depending on the decision of the car rental agent, maintenance may be involved or not.

When explicit modeling elements from BPMN 2.0 are used, the process model would look like the following figure:

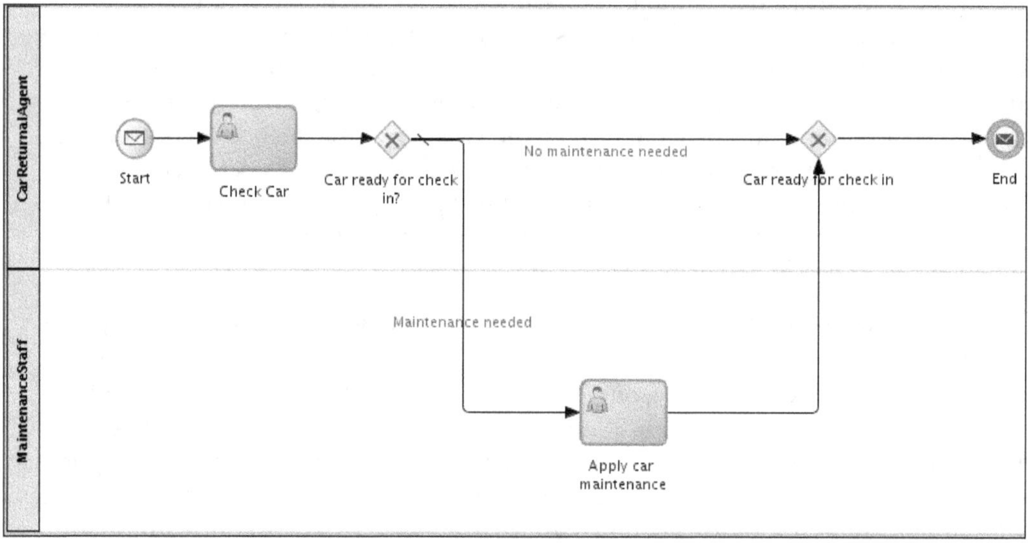

Figure 11

In contrast to the explicit modeling approach, the following figure shows the process model when using implicit Human Workflow functionalities:

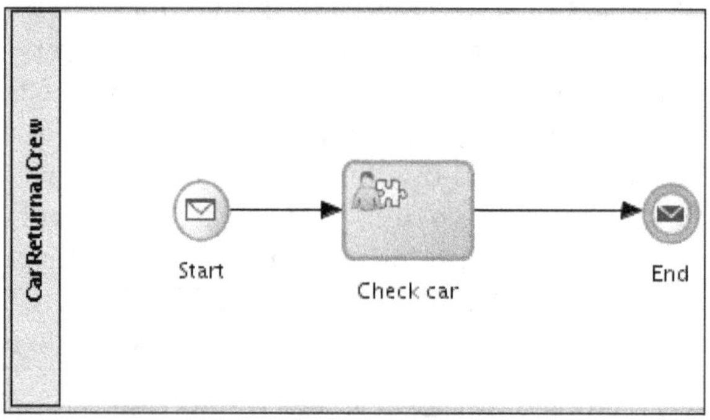

Figure 12

The original roles involved are subsumed under the **CarReturnalCrew** swimlane role. The task routing and assignment logic has been defined within the corresponding task definition by appropriately defining the routing slip.

There are further examples where we decide between explicit modeling and implicit feature usage, such as the definition of deadlines for human tasks. The Oracle Human Workflow component provides the possibility of defining such deadlines out of the box. BPMN 2.0 also provides the needed activities to model expiries of human activities by attaching a timer boundary event to the corresponding user task. Based on these examples, we are back to the original question: *Which approach is the preferable?*

Expressing a specific business requirement in a process highly depends on the underlying use case. Often, a process designer has to weigh different factors before deciding on one or the other variant of modeling a specific requirement. Factors that should be considered are as follows:

- Transparency
- Flexibility
- Performance
- Reusability
- Portability

One important factor is to guarantee transparency for business users. With the introduction of BPMN 2.0 and the related tight cooperation of business and IT, a technical process implementer has to take care that the business and the IT model of a process show as few deviations as possible. This is important to ensure and increase business-IT alignment, which is critical for the success of a BPM initiative because it is one of the key promises.

When deciding to use the explicit modeling approach, the process implementer is usually more flexible. The full power of a process modeling notation, such as BPMN, and its modeling elements can be used. Implementing the same requirements using the Human Workflow component's mechanisms is sometimes less powerful because the possibilities are limited to the features provided by a human task. On the other hand, functionalities such as business calendars are available out of the box by simply declaring them. In explicit modeling scenarios, this functionality has to be provided from the outside, for example, in the form of a separate business service that calculates deadlines in a specific scenario.

When doing explicit modeling, the clarity of the business flow is a great benefit of business-IT alignment, but process models tend to become bloated. Many tasks within one process diagram make it more complex. From a runtime perspective, this may also have performance implications. When using the implicit human task mechanisms, for every human task at the minimum, a task definition as well as the corresponding data definitions, in the form of XSDs, is needed. If a similar human task is needed by further processes, the corresponding task artifacts have to be duplicated. This will end up in a maintenance nightmare. Modularization into reusable building blocks, such as subprocesses implemented as standalone composites, as described at the beginning of this section dealing with general process design, is recommended to avoid overloaded process diagrams and acceptable performance. In addition, in real-world projects, the approach to model complex scenarios explicitly in the business process flow has proven to be more flexible and more consistent as regards the business model of the process.

Process modeling notations, such as BPEL 2.0 and BPMN 2.0, are standardized, so from a portability perspective, the explicit modeling approach is definitively the preferable one. Hence, in the case of a platform change, the porting of the process models is less difficult when using standard elements of a modeling notation. The description of human interactions and the corresponding elements are not standardized yet. Specifications, such as WS Human Task and WS BPEL4People, deal with the standardized integration of human interactions within automated business process flows, but those are not real standards until now. So, today human task features are mainly vendor-specific functionalities.

To ensure comprehensibility for all process participants, it is an important goal in BPM projects to achieve business transparency. In addition, this is essential to guarantee compliance with legal restrictions regarding the traceability of business decisions. In an explicit modeling scenario, the implementer must themselves care about it. The comprehensibility of a task's history is automatically ensured by the Human Workflow engine so that every participant involved in a task routing slip can transparently see what happened within the task processing previously. Doing explicit modeling usually means that there is a sequence of tasks to depict the needed routing slip. The comprehensibility in the form of a task history has to be ensured manually to show consistently what happened during task processing.

When modeling complex human task scenarios, it is crucial to check the factors from mentioned previously to decide about the implementation in a concrete scenario. There is no right or wrong solution; it is always a tradeoff. Process implementers should be aware of the consequences with respect to transparency, flexibility, performance, reusability, and portability when deciding for an implementation approach.

Custom inbox applications

An inbox application is a central architectural component in BPM reference architectures, used usually by any BPM application that has human interactions defined in their corresponding processes. The inbox and the BPM applications should be tightly integrated so that switching between the applications is as less disturbing as possible and to provide a good UX. When it is decided not to use Oracle BPM Workspace and to build a custom solution, a connection to the Oracle Human Workflow engine has to be established to process the tasks.

Using the engine's client API, this can be achieved. Since this API is technical, it is recommended that you define an abstraction layer, motivated by the business requirements, providing only the needed functionality. The abstraction layer can be implemented, for example, as a JEE web service, which can be centrally provided and so is reusable. This approach ensures reusability because the interface is clearer, less complex, and guarantees that in case of API changes, only the abstraction layer has to be changed. The security in such scenarios can be achieved either using the **Oracle Web Services Manager** (**OWSM**) security policies in connection with identity propagation or by acting on behalf of a user. The second approach presupposes that every action is done by an administrator user that acts in the name of the real user. In this scenario, only the full credentials of the administrator user are needed, including the username of the currently requesting user. When working with applications roles, this approach is preferable because, otherwise, the assignment between the real user and the application roles have to be done by hand in BPM Workspace. The roles and rights management will become more complex since it has to be done in different places—in a company's identity store and BPM Workspace. To handle the credentials of the administrator user, it is recommended to use Oracle **Credential Store Framework** (**CSF**), which ensures authenticity. The credentials will be obtained from Credentials Store using a logical key at runtime.

To ensure the responsiveness of the implemented abstraction layer, the following recommendations should be considered:

- **Protocol**: The Oracle Human Workflow Client API provides different possibilities of communicating with it: SOAP, RMI, and local Java invocations are possible. In the case of remote communications, the use of RMI should be preferred over SOAP to avoid the XML marshaling and unmarshaling overhead.
- **Data sources**: Because the Oracle Human Workflow Client API queries information about the tasks from the underlying dehydration database, the corresponding connection pool size of the SOA data sources has to be increased so that all requests can be served. As a rule of thumb, the configuration should be adapted to a minimum of 150 connections at least.

- **Context caching**: Every operation on a task has to be authorized by obtaining a workflow context, which is a specific security token. To avoid unnecessary new creations of security contexts, it is recommended that you cache them for a duration of time and then destroy the contexts explicitly. This ensures performance and minimizes memory usage.
- **Paging**: To minimize network load, when querying a large number of tasks, it is advisable to do task paging on the server side and to load new task pages on demand.

Besides these considerations on creating a responsive and maintainable inbox application in general, the way of presenting information and handling of the inbox application is important with respect to the acceptance of the application. This is very important because as heard before, an inbox application is a central architectural element. In the following paragraphs, some basic hints are listed, which should be considered when designing and implementing BPM applications where the inbox application is a BPM application. These are based on the thoughts put forth in the section dealing with UX.

- **Consistent behavior is recommended** throughout an application and is important to ensure simplicity and self-learnability of an application. If a click on the **Save** button causes the application to persist the data displayed in the current form, and another **Save** button in addition causes the current form to be closed, it is confusing because the user is not able to anticipate what happens when using a third **Save** button.
- **Homogenous and unique look-and-feel** for all applications and products within a company to is necessary to give users the feeling of working with only one application. In addition, this is important to generate a recall value so that users from outside the company can clearly associate applications and products with a company.
- **Standard widget usage** is necessary to process similar tasks within an application to ensure consistent handling and self-learnability of a system. If a multi-select has to be done with checkboxes once and the other time with a pick-list, it is confusing for the user and decreases its productivity.
- **Universal technology usage** should be homogenous to beware of the applications from looking heterogeneous. For similar contexts of use, the same technology should be used to provide a familiar handling as well as look-and-feel to the users.

- **Clear navigation** is required to avoid situations where users feel lost when working with an application. At every moment, it has to be clear how to come from A to B and back again. Furthermore, it must be ensured that the navigation is consistent for similar use cases.
- **Transparent feedback** for users should be provided at each point in time so that it is clear what is currently happening or what has happened in the background. This is, for example, important in BPM applications, where the processing happens mainly asynchronously in the background with the process engine. Information about a process's state and the state of the background processing should be visible from the user interface.
- **Promotion of flexibility** by providing different or alternative ways for users during task processing is important so that users can use the one alternative that seems to him most intuitive at first sight.
- **Customization opportunities** should be there in an application to enable users to adapt an application with respect to their own needs. Simple examples of the customization opportunities could be things like setting the individual language for a user or saving user-defined column configurations for a result list. Every user is unique and has their own preferences. Applications should consider and support this to support the efficiency during task processing.

From an architectural perspective, BPM applications are usually built in a modular way following a service-oriented approach, ensuring that new processes can be modeled more effectively using already available components. In most cases, the modularization works well and shows the expected effects. Regarding the frontends, this approach is often not considered, so UI components, such as pages or even whole page flows are duplicated over different BPM applications. This results in so-called frontend silos, which are less flexible and difficult to maintain. To resolve this situation, the modular approach used in the backend has to be adapted for the frontend. In an ideal world, reusable UI components should be accessible centrally in some kind of repository, from where these can be looked up. The centrally managed components should be as general as possible so that they can be used from different frontends independently from a concrete implementation technology. So, when a specific frontend looks up a UI component from the repository, the application itself takes care of the concrete flavoring of the needed component. This approach will lead to a universal, modular substructure from which all BPM applications can benefit.

Unfortunately, for real-world projects, the described approach is often not suitable, because it leads to a complex and hardly manageable environment. UIs in BPM client applications can be highly complex. So, the extraction of common components is difficult because of specific validations and UI behavior. As an example, take the case of a project, where the UI forms had different complexities starting from very simple, with only a few input fields, to highly complex, where one form had at least 400 input fields. Due to details about form validation and UI behavior, where, for example, components have to be disabled in specified cases, the creation of common components was limited. This led to higher implementation efforts when implementing the forms, but in the end, these additional efforts were justifiable. A fully generic UI component repository would have meant more effort regarding implementation, testing, and extensibility. Maintenance, extensibility, and changeability of the final solution were satisfactory although no fully generic approach was used.

As already stated, the aforementioned points are lessons learned from real-world projects and should be used as food for thought to avoid pitfalls in the areas we were talking about within this section. Hence no ready-to-implement solutions were presented, but elementary things that have to be considered to ensure smooth startup in own projects using the power of the Human Workflow component within Oracle BPM Suite 12*c*.

Summary

In this chapter, we covered various aspects of the interaction between a human individual and human-centric business process flows as well as the possibilities that Oracle BPM 12*c* provides to implement and automate such processes.

In this context, we have especially worked out how important and intuitive UIs are today to enable users to do daily work effectively and to ensure user acceptance of a process-driven application. In addition, it has been discussed what these newly arising aspects concerning UX mean from an application developer's perspective.

Besides these more conceptual aspects, we also showed the possibilities Oracle BPM 12*c* provides to incorporate human interactions with automated business process flows as well as the various options Oracle's Human Workflow component offers to define task routings, escalations, and more. In conclusion, we made some suggestions about design practices, you learned from numerous BPM implementations concerning the general process design, modeling techniques, and about different approaches to implement a custom inbox application, which is a central architectural component in every BPM reference architecture.

This chapter has a number of key takeaways. First, potential users of an application should be included as early as possible when designing and implementing user interfaces to understand the way users work as well as their pains and needs. Second, Oracle BPM Suite 12*c* provides various flexible and powerful abilities to provide strong as well as easy-to-adapt BPM applications depicting human-centric business process flows. Third, with the ADF and web forms technologies, a seamless, intuitive, and effective integration of human individuals in automated processes is possible; other UI technologies can also be incorporated with little effort. Fourth, when developing highly human-centric applications, keep in mind the transparency, flexibility, performance, reusability, and portability of the process modeling approach.

In the next chapter, we will introduce business rules and their meaning regarding the quality of business decisions within a company. You will learn how to discover, automate, and manage rules as well as how Oracle BPM Suite 12*c* can support you to successfully automate your business rules and incorporate them into your business processes.

8
Business Rules

Business rules are an essential and omnipresent building block in nearly every business process. Business rules define how a company's business works by describing business policies or key business decisions. So, they are the fundament on which the business logic and processes are built. Thus, rules should be considered as shareable and centrally managed BPM artifacts like other essential resources, such as service and data descriptions, used in the context of defining process-driven architectures.

Ideally, the management of business rules is done centrally and independently from the business flow logic, for example, in a **Business Rules Management System** (**BRMS**). The separation of the decision logic from the business process flow logic is essential to ensure comprehensibility and flexibility of business processes.

Unfortunately, the decision logic is often implemented as part of the business process flow logic today! Within this chapter, we will show why this is not a good approach.

In the previous chapter, we discussed how to involve human actors in automated business processes to fulfill decision requests. This chapter will outline how IT can support a transparent enterprise decision management by automating business decisions. Even if human decision making is not replaceable completely, as shown in the previous chapter, in this chapter, we will come up with ideas about when decision automation is possible and effective. We will do the following:

- Describe the characteristics of business rules and their relation with BPM
- Explain how to identify and assess business rules, that is, business rules candidates
- Discuss how to design, organize, and implement business rules
- Depict the Oracle Business Rules' design time as well as runtime architecture and its concepts
- Discuss best practice approaches to implement business rules

Why business rules within BPM are important?

Before understanding why rules are important within BPM, let's have a look at what a business rule is and what its characteristics are.

About rules

A business rule is an atomic assignment, which takes either `true` or `false` as its value. Rules have to be kept simple and not contain programming logic. Rules are declarative expressions, usually in an *if-then* style notation, consisting of a condition and an action. The action is only evaluated if the defined condition is met. Because of these characteristics, rules are easily readable and understandable for nontechnical people, regardless of the knowledge background, compared to the rules logic implemented in Java, for instance.

The following snippet shows a simple example for a business rule. It shows the characteristics previously discussed:

```
IF
  rentalCar.milesDriven > freeMiles
THEN
  return (rentalCar.milesDriven - freeMiles) * 0.5
```

The rule, taken from the car rental scenario, is used during invoice creation and deals with the calculation of additional fees for a car rental case if a customer exceeds the maximum number of free miles. As a result, customers will be charged for every mile that was driven over the free miles limit, with $0.5 per mile. The rule comes up in the aforementioned *if-then* style notation, where we have a condition, which is the Boolean expression after the `if` keyword, and the action is executed only when the condition evaluates to `true`.

After this short excursion to the characteristics of rules, let's get back to the actual question as to why the business rules are important within BPM.

Rules and BPM

Business process flows are usually not straightforward because daily business isn't so either and additionally, it changes rapidly today. This is challenging for companies and makes business process flows become more complex due to new requirements defined by the business or restrictions coming from the market that have to be incorporated with existing process models. The implementation of such changes can be done by adapting the business process flow to meet the changed conditions.

As an example, let's assume that the marketing of our car rental agency intends to ensure customer retention by providing discounts to particularly good customers that have the customer status **platinum**. The resulting business requirements are handed over to the IT, which applies the changes to the car rental process. The excerpt from the following process shows the changes to the process model:

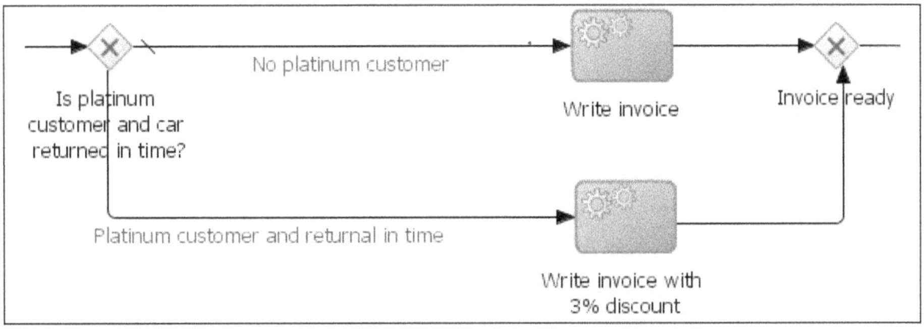

Figure 1

Before writing the invoice, the customer status is checked. If the customer is a platinum customer and the car has been returned in time, a total discount of at least 3 percent is granted to the customer. On the basis of the service-oriented BPM approach, the cost and time to bring the changed process into production is adequate; marketing is happy.

At first sight, everything seems to be fine. But it is not! What if the marketing campaign is limited, the granted discount is changed, or the campaign is extended to other customers too? The answer is that the process model has to be adapted every time the requirements change. This is a design failure because intentionally it was planned to change the invoice creation, that is, the underlying calculation rules, depending on the customer status.

Admittedly, the example is a little exaggerated. What should be demonstrated is that business decisions are often hidden within business processes and their flow logic that might lead to the following risks and problems:

- Risk of duplication
- Missing transparency
- Inconsistencies in rule usage and definition
- Inflexibility of processes
- Mixing of flow and decision logic
- Increased process complexity

The risks of duplication as well as lack of transparency may be fatal because both likely cause inconsistencies regarding rule usage and rule definition. Depending on a company's business, rules will change more or less frequently. When rule changes have to be applied, all concerned places must be changed. The challenge is to find these out. Furthermore, it is costly in terms of time and resources. Resources are usually rare, so a detailed analysis of rule usage is nearly impossible. In consequence, only a shallow analysis can be done, increasing the risk of inconsistencies because not all concerned processes, and, therefore, not all rules defined within will be adapted. This may cause serious consequences for the business, such as monetary or image losses and further legal sanctions, when being noncompliant with legal restrictions.

A further challenge arises from the release and change management when changes to rule and process artifacts have been applied and should be transported into production. When rules are defined within business processes, the flow and business logic are versioned and packaged together in a single application. So, a change in a rule causes a new process version and vice versa. Furthermore, a redeployment of the process application is needed. This causes two major challenges:

- The migration strategy for already running process instances
- The versioning of rules and process changes

Usually, business process services are stateful and long running. Therefore, when redeploying a process due to changes in the contained business rules, one main point is to clarify what should happen to the already running process instances. Questions that will come up about this point are:

- Should new rules directly be used?
- Should new rules be used by new instances only?
- Should new rules be used until a specific date?

Depending on the affected processes, dealing with the corresponding business cases and process owners may be complex and time consuming and has to be repeated every time a business process is changed. Additionally, different processes may be concerned with a single rule change, so different migration strategies could be required.

For the reason that rule changes cause new process versions, the comprehensibility regarding the changes is restricted. Rule changes, which affect more than one business process, may lead to different versions for business processes. This is confusing since the reason for the new process revisions is a change in the same business rule. Depending on the frequency of changes within the business rules and the chosen migration strategy to run process instances, several versions of the same business process may be deployed in parallel. From a governance point of view, this is not acceptable in terms of an accurate business processes life cycle management and the corresponding release management.

Additionally, business processes are obviously more inflexible. The processes' complexity may also grow when extensive checks using several attributes from the corresponding process data objects have to be performed. Testing these changes in isolation without retesting the whole business process flow is impossible in this scenario. Furthermore, the error analysis at runtime is difficult and lengthy.

In summary, it has to be concluded that the way the decision logic is implemented within business processes has an impact on the flexibility, maintainability, and the future-proofing of process-driven applications. The benefits that companies hope to gain from a holistic BPM strategy, such as an increase of business agility or transparency in terms of the business process flows, are not achievable over the long term, when business rules are not centrally managed. A more flexible approach is needed, which optimally supports a company's BPM strategy.

> It is essential to separate the business process flow logic and the decision logic to ensure comprehensibility as well as transparency regarding changes in flow or decision logic.

The separation of the decision and the business process flow logic allows the separation of responsibilities referring to process modeling as well as the decision logic declaration. To assure reusability and to avoid duplication of already existing rules, these have to be combined and centrally provided in a service-style fashion. Taking these few points into account when developing process-driven applications will guide companies to the expected success, with process transparency on the one hand as well as flexible and easily adaptable applications and processes on the other hand.

The information from the current section points out why rules are important within BPM. This is because the business logic explained in rules define essential policies and constraints of the business that a company is running. Rules are important for decision support, regardless of whether these are handled with fully automated decisions or manual ones. Flexibility and easy adaptability is important due to the dynamic nature of most companies' daily business. The time to market for changes applied to the business policies and constraints must be as short as possible in order to ensure competitiveness.

How to design rules and how to organize them

As mentioned earlier, rules are an elementary part of business processes within a company. So, the challenge is to identify the rules, separate them from the business flow logic, and organize them as services in an SOA-based style to ensure consistency and business agility. This approach sounds easy, but it isn't, as we will see in the following paragraphs.

Discovering rules

Identifying potential candidates for business rules within a business process seems quite simple because potential indicators for decision points are expressed as control structures, such as gateways in a BPMN 2.0 process or if activities in a BPEL 2.0 process. Other potential rule candidates might be found at code locations where decision preparations or complex calculation rules are implemented. However, these are only a few possibilities; in the real world, business rules are omnipresent. The use of the designation rule candidate is conscious since not all identified locations or decision points and the corresponding conditions are supposed to be declared as business rules—and this is the next challenge. Why? This will be explained in the following paragraphs.

When searching for potential business rule candidates, it is not sufficient to use static, straightforward-looking criteria, such as implementation-specific constructs as a hint. Such an approach would be very technical and, therefore, in itself not convenient to achieve the right level of granularity. To put it bluntly, using only technically-motivated criteria will end up in a mess of rules that nobody can overview and maintain. Additionally, the so classified rules are not suitable to generate business value.

Other, more business-relevant criteria have to be taken into account when rule candidates are evaluated in terms of their suitability for a business rule implementation. These might be:

- Volatility
- Reusability
- Impact
- Compliance

Some rule candidates have a static character and are expected to stay constant for a long time. Rating whether a person is of what age is an example of such a static constraint. In itself, this is not necessarily a business constraint that has to be externalized in the form of a business rule. However, business rule candidates from other business contexts, such as regulations or constraints from the human resources sector, might potentially change more frequently. To ensure business agility, it is important to externalize business constraints that exhibit dynamic characteristics; the static ones are less interesting.

Another label for potential business rule candidates is reusability. Business constraints that are specific and exclusively used by a single business process or within a specific business service can be kept internally. There is no necessity to provide such business constraints centrally unless it shows frequently changing characteristics. When business restrictions are shared and used by multiple consumers, a central implementation seems essential to allow central management of these rule artifacts. This assures consistency in business rule usage and avoids different, redundant rule implementations.

Wrong decisions made or prepared by systems on the basis of wrong or outdated business constraints could have more or less impact on the business depending on the current business context. When a car rental system rents a car to a person without a valid driving license, it is unfortunate but not existence threatening for the car rental agency. However, when a banking system determines wrong credit rating information for a customer who applies for a multimillion dollar credit, it may have far-reaching consequences for the financial institute. As it can be seen from these examples, wrong or outdated business constraints and restrictions as well as a bad information base may have significant consequences for the business of a company. So, when identifying potential business rule candidates, it has to be evaluated which impact the corresponding logic has on the business and, accordingly, it should be decided whether to keep those rules locally or centralize them.

Hence, business constraints are often based on legal regulations that they can change frequently as mentioned before. So, when the corresponding regulations change, the implemented business constraints must be adapted within as short a time as possible, especially for large, listed companies, which are subject to particularly strict regulations, for example, the **Sarbanes-Oxley Act** (**SOX**). The Sarbanes-Oxley Act is a US regulation enacted in July 2002 as a reaction to different corporate accounting scandals (for example, Enron and Worldcom) and is intended to ensure accuracy and reliability of corporate disclosures (read more at `http://www.soxlaw.com/`). It is important to ensure compliance with the corresponding restrictions. Furthermore, the business logic implementing the constraints has to be flexible and easy to change to avoid stiff penalties and loss of reputation. Therefore, business rules, which should ensure compliance with legal restrictions, are exemplars for centrally managed business rules because all of the aforementioned business characteristics are applicable to business constraints in this area.

The points mentioned previously show that the discovery of potential business rule candidates, which should be implemented as centrally managed business rules, is not straightforward. The different business indicators' volatility, reusability, impact, and compliance have to be considered and can't be evaluated in isolation to find out whether it is adding value to externalize, that is, centralize a business constraint or not because there are intersections between these criteria. It is obvious that not every business constraint must be necessarily implemented as a centralized business rule. Additionally, not all decisions, which have to be made within everyday business, can be defined as a fully automated business rule. Depending on the business case, the decision logic may be often highly complex or individualistic and can vary from case to case. Trying to implement the decision logic so that a machine can evaluate it is nearly impossible due to the variety of cases. Furthermore, the information base today is not only limited to business information owned by a company. Information is provided through a variety of channels, such as mobile or cloud, and in addition, from different platforms, for example, social platforms such as Twitter and Facebook, that are often not incorporated with a company's IT systems. So enterprise decision modeling will become more complex because more and more information has to be considered when it comes to making far-reaching decisions. A classic example is insurance cases where every case is different and for that, needs special treatment in terms of insurance payments, and so on. If a policyholder reports hail damage, the first thing to find out is whether it was really hailing the day the claim occurred. Weather information from every day in the year is usually not available from the internal systems of an insurance company, so this information has to be obtained from external sources.

The key takeaway from this part is that not every decision, based on business constraints, must be implemented as a business rule if it is not necessary and value-adding from a business perspective or if the affected business use case is too complex and varied. This could be evaluated by examining the available business constraints about their volatility, reusability, impact on the business, and their significance for compliance on the one hand and the corresponding business cases on the other hand.

Designing and organizing rules

If an adequate number of candidates has been identified, it has to be documented, revised, and finally implemented so that the now centrally provided business rules could be used from business processes and services. To ensure transparency and comprehensibility, the business rule management has to be incorporated into the BPM life cycle like other BPM-relevant assets to achieve transparent life cycle management. Furthermore, an explicit rule ownership must be defined to guarantee a dedicated responsibility for rule usage monitoring and evolution.

Regarding the methodology, how rules are documented and implemented, different approaches exist depending on the usage context.

Documentation could basically be done in a nonstandardized form using Excel sheets and Word files. This is the most common way business rules and business requirements are defined today by business analysts. A better approach would be the use of a standardized notation, such as activity diagrams of the **Unified Modeling Language** (**UML**) standard. The goal is to formalize decision models and make them easily interpretable by a machine and translatable into a machine-understandable format. Ideally, the new **decision modeling and notation standard** (**DMN**), approved by the **Object Management Group** (**OMG**) in December 2014 is used to define decisions in a standard-based fashion (more details are available at `http://www.omg.org/spec/DMN`). The purpose of the standard stated in the specification is to provide the constructs that are needed to model decisions so that organizational decision making can be readily depicted in diagrams accurately defined by business analysts and by (optionally) automating the process.

The benefit while combining BPMN and DMN is obvious. With DMN, business analysts have a notation to express decisions, their connections, and the requirements for the decision logic. Furthermore, it defines how to describe the decision logic in a finely granular manner so that it can be validated and automated. An example of how DMN looks and how it might be implemented is depicted in the following graphic:

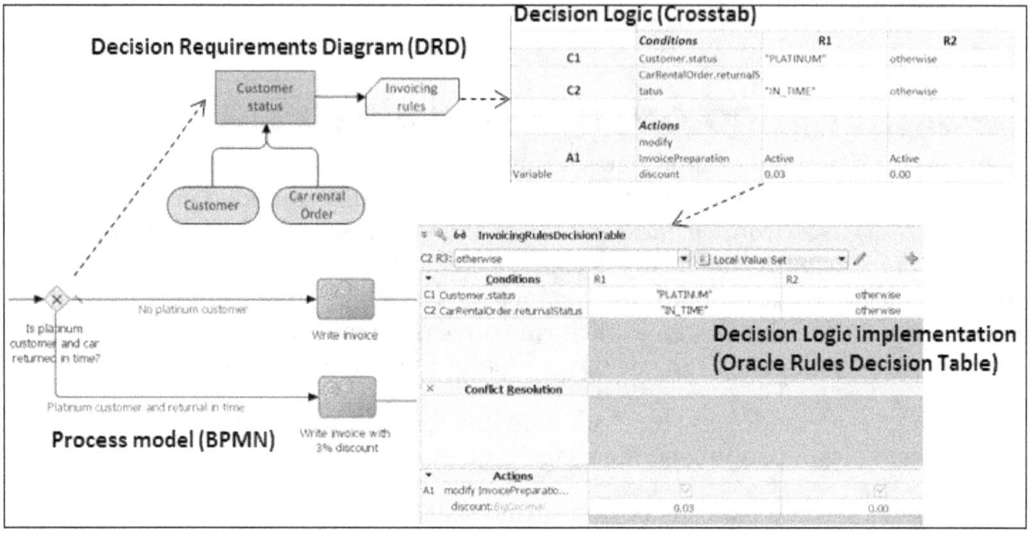

Figure 2

The DRD and the crosstab are described in the DMN specification. The depicted decision table that might be used for rule implementation is a specific artifact within Oracle BPM Suite 12*c*; DMN requirement modeling is currently not supported from within the platform.

Nevertheless, DMN helps to bridge the gap between business and IT in terms of business rule modeling—a key factor for success because a uniform vocabulary is available. Going this way, the alignment between business and IT is as close as possible. This ensures a consistent and transparent business rule management.

Analogous to definition and documentation, the implementation of business rules can be done using different technologies. For reusability reasons and according to an SOA-based approach, business rules should be encapsulated as services, exposing their functionalities in a standardized way. The implementation technology doesn't matter here and is not restricted. Business rules may, for example, be developed in Java or in the form of stored procedures in a database. The alternative to such classic, development-centric, and technical implementation approaches where IT specialists are needed to initially implement as well as evolve rules in later phases of a project, is the use of a so-called **Business Rule Engine** (**BRE**), which is responsible for business rule execution. The rules are less implemented but declared, for example, in the already mentioned *if-then* style. Such nearly zero-coding approaches are more business user friendly.

The organization of business rules is important to retain an overview of the defined rules. Furthermore, grouping them is indispensable in terms of the identification of dependencies as well as relationships between single rules and rule groups. In case of changes, the affected rules must be found quickly to do the adjustment within a short time to bring the adapted rules into production. Because companies are different in terms of the businesses they run and the organizational structures they have, it is impossible to define a general applicable structure. In general, it should be ensured that the granularity of the structure is neither too coarse nor too fine to guarantee clarity and to make business rules manageable. Additionally, the definition of explicit responsibilities for business rules are needed from a governance perspective.

It is important that the business rule groupings are aligned with the organization of business processes to ensure consistency and transparency. The assets could be structured using organizational units, which is a very coarse-grained classification. Responsibilities are clearly defined following this approach. The challenge with such a coarse-grained approach is that over time, areas with a mess of rules might arise where management becomes hard and confusing.

A more fine-grained approach could be to use business domains or business entities, such as products or services that a company is offering. Following this approach allows fine-grained usage monitoring and access control. The definition of responsibilities is not as clear as when using organizational units for business rules organization criteria, but from an IT perspective, change and release management are easier to handle because the potential impact on other components can be better estimated.

Regarding the design of business rules, it is obvious that the main challenge is to bridge the gap between the documentation from the business side and the implementation of executable business rules from the IT perspective. As of today, no holistic solution to overcome this challenge is available. DMN seems to be the required solution, but the adoption of the standard will take time. So, rule definition and implementation have to be done using an approach that keeps the gap between business and IT as small as possible. Later in this chapter, the approach of using a BRE, which potentially delivers a good balance between business and IT models, will be discussed in more depth looking at the Oracle Rule component within BPM Suite 12*c*.

Using rules

Oracle's business rule component, which is compliant with the **Service Component Architecture** (**SCA**) specification, allows us to define and manage business rules within process-driven applications. At runtime, Oracle's BRE, which is part of the common service infrastructure, executes the defined rules. At design time, the business rule implementation is done using a rules component that is very versatile. By integrating it with the other SOA components, different use cases can be supported:

- **BPMN component**: These rules helps in modeling business decisions and depicting conditional behavior
- **BPEL component**: These rules have a similar usage as the BPMN component, and in addition, it is used to set up dynamic routings from within Oracle's Phase activity (a specific BPEL extension activity) to dynamically determine endpoints
- **Mediator component**: These rules dynamically evaluates endpoints within routing rules based on the business data passed in the incoming message
- **Human workflow component**: These rules helps in modeling complex approval flows and managing the workload as per the task assignment for employees
- **Case management component**: These rules helps in evaluating the activation of case activities or withdrawal of a manual case activity; it marks milestones as achieved or revoked

Additionally, it is possible to integrate the business rule component with nearly every other type of application that can invoke web services.

The following sections will focus on using business rules in the context of BPMN processes to support automated business decisions. As a first step, the basic architecture of Oracle BRE is explained as well as what the important elements are when defining business rules within a business rule component.

Design-time architecture

Before understanding the architecture of Oracle's BRE, a few basic concepts regarding the definition of business rules within a business process application should be clarified. As mentioned earlier, the definition of business rules is done within a business rule component. The base of every rule component is the so-called **rule dictionary**, which can be built using the following elements:

- **Settings**: These define the base settings for the rule dictionary, such as the rule evaluation algorithm.
- **Facts**: These define data objects on which rule evaluation happens and also define more business user-friendly aliases to use in verbal rules. At design time, fact types will be created on the basis of business data objects (that is, XML Schema, Java classes, and ADF business components). At runtime, concrete instances of these types will be created and populated from within the business process' runtime data objects.
- **Functions**: These are predefined functions that could be used from within rules or decision tables. Custom functions can be created using Oracle Business Rules **Rule Language** (**RL**), a high-level, Java-like syntax.
- **Globals**: These are global value definitions for use in rules or decision tables, that is, to define thresholds; they may be constant.
- **Value sets**: This is a list of ranges or list of values of a specific type (such as a Java Enumeration). It can be associated with a fact property of the same type to constrain values assigned to fact properties in the rules definition, decision tables, or variable initial values and function argument values.
- **Links**: These link an existing rule dictionary from the current or another application with the actual rule application. Alternatively, look up rule dictionaries via **Metadata Service** (**MDS**)
- **Decision functions**: These are declaratively defined functions without using Oracle Business Rules RL. They can be used to expose a ruleset or a combination of different rulesets in a web service fashion.
- **Translations**: These provide localization opportunities for rules and their corresponding artifacts.
- **Test**: This allows the definition of design-time tests and test suites that can be executed without deploying the corresponding composite.
- **Data explorer**: This provides an overview of all data objects (user defined and predefined) used within the rule dictionary.
- **Business phrases**: These define rule tests and actions using a **domain-specific language** (**DSL**) for rules, allowing more business user-friendly rule definitions. These are used when defining rules with verbal rules (for an explanation, see the following section).

The actual implementation of rules is done within a ruleset, which is a container to organize rules into a logical group that defines a unit of execution. A ruleset may have an effective date and might be defined as active or inactive. The same configurations are possible at the rule level.

A single rule can be defined using different approaches depending on the preferences of the author of the rules. The three basic approaches are as follows:

- **If-then rules**: Here, business policies or constraints are expressed in the already mentioned *if condition then action* declarative style
- **Decision tables**: Here, business policies or constraints are expressed declaratively in a more business user-friendly crosstab style. It is more appropriate and clearly arranged to define rules that have more complex conditions.
- **Verbal rules**: Here, business policies or constraints can be expressed using native-language-like sentences that are either precomputed from the facts model or self-defined using the business phrases option. These are built upon *if-then* rule constructs—a new feature provided by BPM Suite 12*c*.

A new feature about decision tables allows us to export business rules to an Excel file. This file enables us to edit the rules as well as the corresponding value sets using specific Oracle Business Rule macros. Rules, conditions, and buckets can be created, updated, and deleted. Once rule authoring is done, the changed Excel file can be re-imported. The differences between the Excel sheet and the current implementation will be displayed and can be accepted or ignored.

The design-time definitions of a rule dictionary can be done in a business rule component using Oracle JDeveloper's rule editor. As an alternative, BPM Composer could be used, which is more business user-friendly. Both tools are tightly integrated via the **Process Asset Manager** (**PAM**), which cares about the synchronization of development artifacts between both development environments. Essentially, it interfaces with a source control system to provide source control integration to BPM Composer, references MDS for runtime artifacts, and also integrates with **Oracle Platform Security Services** (**OPSS**), to check permissions. PAM allows seamless collaboration so that parallel development is possible. More details about PAM can be found in the official Oracle documentation (`http://docs.oracle.com/middleware/1213/bpm/bpm-develop/bac_bpmpd.htm`).

Runtime architecture

From the runtime perspective, the architectural structure of the Oracle Rules Service engine looks like the following figure:

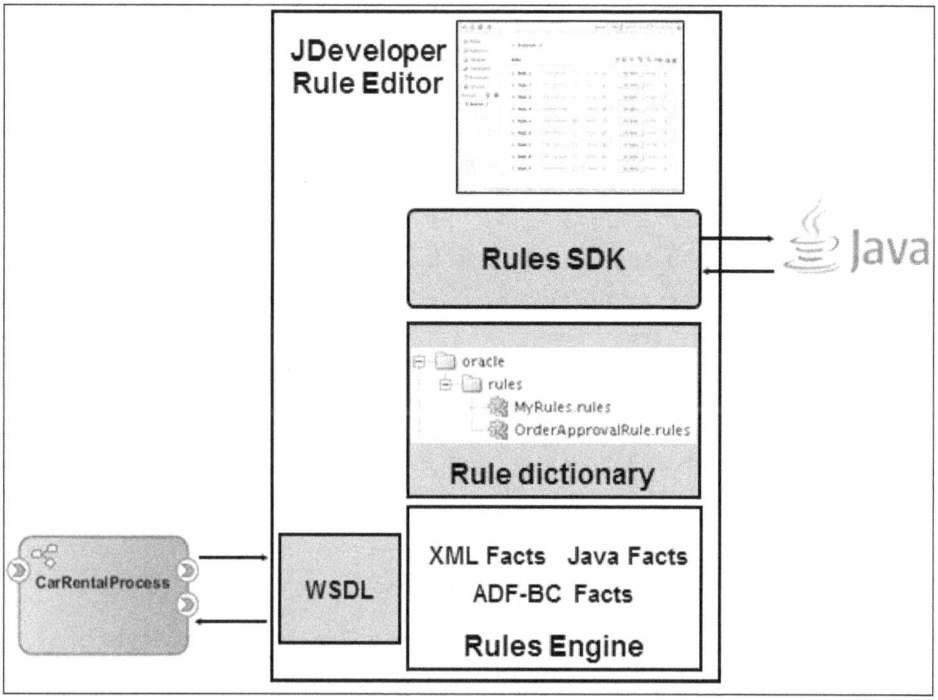

Figure 3

The BRE itself and the deployed dictionaries are accessible via the web service interface or, alternatively, using a native JSR94-compliant Java API provided by the Rules SDK. In addition, the SDK provides functionalities to define, validate, and debug business rules. JDeveloper also uses the provided interface to define the design-time artifacts, such as rulesets and the other artifacts contained in the rule dictionary. In addition, the Rules SDK allows the implementation of custom business rules editor user interfaces.

The Oracle BRE is a so-called inference rule engine, which, by default, uses the RETE algorithm, which was designed and published by Dr. Charles R. Forgy in 1982. It is an effective pattern-matching algorithm used by business rules engines for optimized rule processing on the base of the available working memory. To understand the basic concepts used by the Oracle BRE, let's have a look at how rule processing is done internally.

Once a business rule component is called, the current working memory populated with incoming facts is evaluated against the defined rules. If a rule's condition is set to true on the basis of a fact held in the working memory, this rule is taken on the so-called agenda. After completing the matching process, the agenda is processed by executing the defined actions for the corresponding rules. Afterwards, if the working memory changes due to the rule action execution, the described process restarts until no more changes to the working memory are recognized. The aforementioned procedure describes what is meant by rule inference; changes to the working memory made by one rule may trigger other rules in a later cycle. The advantage of this principle is that the order in which rules are defined doesn't matter because rules get evaluated in each case.

Depending on the complexity and number of facts held in the working memory, this way of rule processing may be inefficient. Most information contained in the working memory has a static character and is not updated during rule processing. An only small bits of information, such as customer status information, is changeable, and that is the place where the optimization of the RETE algorithm jumps in. After the first run, when all facts contained in the working memory are evaluated against the defined rule base, the subsequent runs only consider changed facts within the working memory. So, a smaller part from the working memory is analyzed on every pass.

A simplified example underneath should clarify the description of rule processing and demonstrate what is meant by rule inference.

Let's assume a ruleset, which is involved in the invoicing process of RYLC and contains, among others, the following rules:

Rule number	Condition	Action
1	`IF Customer. CustomerStatus == 'Gold'`	`THEN Invoice.Discount = 0.015`
2	`IF Customer. CustomerStatus == 'Platinum'`	`THEN Invoice.Discount = 0.030`
3	`IF Customer.History. RentalsPerYear >= 30`	`THEN Customer. CustomerStatus = 'Platinum'`
4	`IF RentalCar.milesDriven > 500`	`THEN Invoice. AdditionalFee = (RentalCar.MilesDriven - 500) * 0.5`

Furthermore, let's assume the working memory containing the following rental information:

```
<Customer>
  <CustomerID>123</CustomerID>
  <Firstname>John</Firstname>
  <Lastname>Doe</Lastname>
  <CustomerStatus>Gold</CustomerStatus>
  <History>
    <RentalsPerYear>30</RentalsPerYear>
  </History>
</Customer>

<RentalCar>
  <CarID>321</CarID>
  <MilesDriven>456</MilesDriven>
</RentalCar>
```

When rule processing starts, all defined rules will be evaluated against each data object contained in the working memory. After this initial run, rules 1 and 3 are taken to the agenda, and so the corresponding actions will be executed. The action of rule 3 changes the customer data object by setting the value for the `Customer.CustomerStatus` element to `'Platinum'`. The BRE recognizes the update within the working memory and restarts the process of business rule evaluation. The difference is that this time, the `RentalCar` object won't be considered because no changes have been applied to the data object. After the second run, only rule 2 is taken to the agenda, and after the defined action is evaluated, no changes to the current working memory have been applied. The rule processing ends at this point, and the defined results will be delivered. In this example, the result is that the customer becomes a platinum customer, getting 5 percent discount on its invoice.

Besides using the RETE algorithm for business rule evaluation, Oracle BPM 12*c* provides an alternative, non-RETE algorithm. This algorithm has a more optimal memory usage and may have to evaluate a ruleset only once to get back with the corresponding result. This might potentially improve performance during rule evaluation against the default RETE algorithm. The configuration and which algorithm to choose can be defined as per the rule dictionary in the settings section.

As the explanations in the current section show, when defining a business rule component to establish central rule management, the knowledge about the architecture is essential to define a future-oriented, robust, and reliable fundament for the business processes. Knowing the basic concepts of rule processing helps to define better rule-based, and process-based applications, preserving the business continuity and agility.

Best practices

Besides the knowledge of the internal architecture and processing logic about business rules, it is important to have an idea about how rules can be designed and what the do's and don'ts affecting rules negatively are, that is, about execution performance or maintainability. Within this section, some basic aspects regarding the definition of rule-based applications will be introduced that should be considered when practically starting with a project.

Defining the interface

Defining business rule services basically starts with the definition of the service contract, which means defining input and output data structures, operations, and so on. At first glance, this is not surprising because the contract-first implementation approach does not differentiate the definition of other non-rule services. The basic characteristics of a business rule service are statelessness and a synchronous interaction style. The latter means that the defined business logic can be processed efficiently and with good performance to ensure the responsiveness of the service. The service interface is the first place where optimizations of service responsiveness can take place. One point that should be considered when defining business rule services is to exchange only the data that is needed to evaluate the rules. Remembering the runtime architecture of Oracle's BRE, it is obvious to do so to avoid unnecessary growth of the working memory. Keeping the memory footprint as small as possible is important for building robust and scalable business rule services. Besides the amount of data, which is passed to the rule engine, the complexity of the data objects itself is another point with respect to the processing performance of business rules. If the data objects are highly complex and deeply nested, rule processing and the evaluation of the rules' conditions accordingly take more time. So, it is recommended to keep the exchanged data object's structure simple and flat to support the effectiveness of rule processing and ensure the responsiveness of a business rule service.

Service design

How business rules candidates could be discovered and how business rules may be implemented and organized was already discussed in the previous sections. As already mentioned, the processing effectiveness, and, thus, the service responsiveness, are basic aspects. Furthermore, the business rules should be declared clearly readable and easy to understand.

As explained, the Oracle rules engine uses a RETE or alternatively a non-RETE algorithm for evaluating rules. The rule conditions and actions should be kept simple and should not be deeply nested. Defining the conditions or even the corresponding actions in a complex and deeply nested fashion is counterproductive regarding the effectiveness of rule processing and the business rules' comprehensibility. In addition, rules become more error-prone and the definition of regression testing is more difficult referring to the test coverage of the possible evaluation variants.

In the earlier section, when discussing basic points with respect to the interface design, one recommendation was to exchange a minimum amount of data that is needed for the rules processing. Invoking other systems from within a rule component, that is, for fetching additional data from external data sources needed for the rule execution should also be avoided, because it might be time-consuming. Using a BRE for implementing massively data-intensive rules should be avoided, to keep the memory footprint of a corresponding rule session as small as possible. The service's responsiveness will be affected by doing so and the working memory will be blown out, which is inappropriate concerning the stability and scalability of a business rule service.

If business rules are very data intensive, a business rule engine might be the wrong place for implementing those rules. In such cases the implementation technology has to be redefined to ensure the service quality. Restrictions on that are given by the design principles for SOA services, that is, to have a clear service contract exposing functionalities in a standard-based, central way.

Rule management

In Oracle BPM Suite 12*c* Business Rule, services are regularly implemented as a business rule component within a composite. A composite is a versioned artifact, so if rules are modified, the version of the concerned business rule service should also be changed to show transparently that the rules have been adapted. Older versions of a business rule service should be retired to ensure consistent usage. In Oracle BPM Suite 12*c*, this can be easily done using Enterprise Manager's Lifecycle options for deployed composites (read more in the official Oracle documentation at `http://docs.oracle.com/middleware/1213/soasuite/administer/soa-composite-deployment.htm#SOAAG3564`).

From an organizational perspective, the service life cycle management, which should be clearly defined within a BPM governance initiative, is not as simple as it is on the technical side. It has to be seriously considered and should be closely coupled with change management to ensure comprehensibility of rule changes. Who has changed rules, when the changes were applied, what was changed—that is important information regarding legal regulations referring to the transparency of changes all over a company's processes and the corresponding components.

The adaption of rules means that an important part of the business logic is changed. This adaption must not affect other components that are using these rules and the changes made to the rules are compliant with the business requirements. To ensure this from a technical side, testing is essential. In Oracle BPM Suite 12*c*, design-time rule tests can be defined within a business rule component, which can be executed in JDeveloper. As an alternative, standard Java JUnit tests, be defined using Oracle Rules SDK functionalities. Using this common way of testing enables the possibility that the defined tests might be executed automatically every time a business rule application is built.

Oracle BPM Suite enables the user to manipulate business rules at runtime using the SOA Composer application, which gets deployed out of the box with every BPM Suite installation. When applying changes to business rule services at runtime using the SOA composer, it must be kept in mind that the changes have also to be applied to the design-time artifacts because an automatic way of synchronizing changes between runtime and design time doesn't work. Another point is that the service version stays untouched. So, there is a risk that the changes are kept undocumented and are not visible to the service consumers. In addition, no regression testing could be executed at runtime.

Example – adding rules to BPMN and BPEL

To be more flexible and agile due to environmental influences, RYLC decided to introduce a BRE to separate volatile and frequently changing decision logic from the business process flow logic. As a first prototype, a use case from the invoicing area should be implemented. The invoicing procedure has to be adapted to make RYLC's offerings more attractive to existing customers that should benefit from loyalty. This should support the strategic business goal to increase market share.

In tight cooperation with the business, a process implementer starts realizing the business rules using a business rule component. To do so, the developer adds a business rule task from within the BPMN process model. The following screenshot shows this:

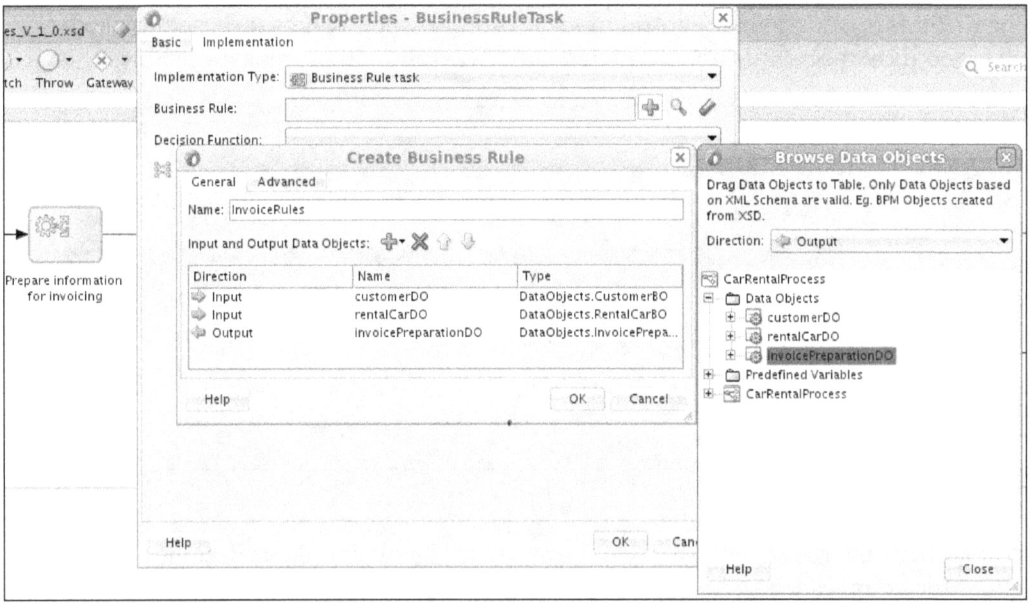

Figure 4

> When a business rule task is used, the rule implementation component has to be collocated in the same composite as the BPMN component.

In the next step, the rule developer has to fill the automatically created rule dictionary with life. The input and output data objects for the business rule component are defined in the step before they become facts and are automatically available within the dictionary. Before creating the rules, global constants are defined, which allows a consistent usage over different rules and rulesets within the dictionary and enables central modification for such values if these have to be changed due to new business requirements. The following screenshot shows this:

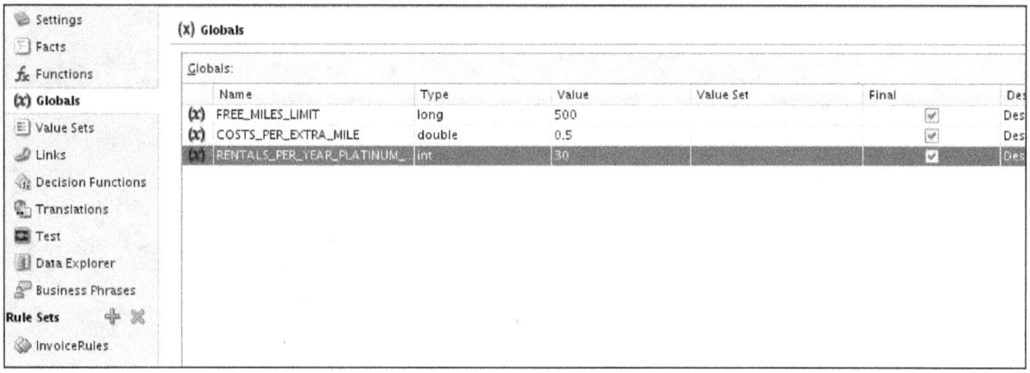

Figure 5

Afterwards, the rule declaration can be started. The business requirements of RYLC about the changes to the invoicing procedure define that for the invoice creation, it is important to find out if a customer is provided a discount depending on their status and to check whether additional fees have to be charged to the customer. Furthermore, the current customer status has to be checked to provide the right discount and to ensure customer satisfaction.

The rule developer decides to choose the **verbal rule approach** to implement the business rules to make them more readable for the business users. Based on the facts, standard business phrases are pregenerated and available. So, the rule definition may directly be started. Alternatively, custom business phrases could be defined to hide the complexity of rule condition tests and actions. Using custom business phrases makes the used expression more self-explaining, as shown in the following screenshot:

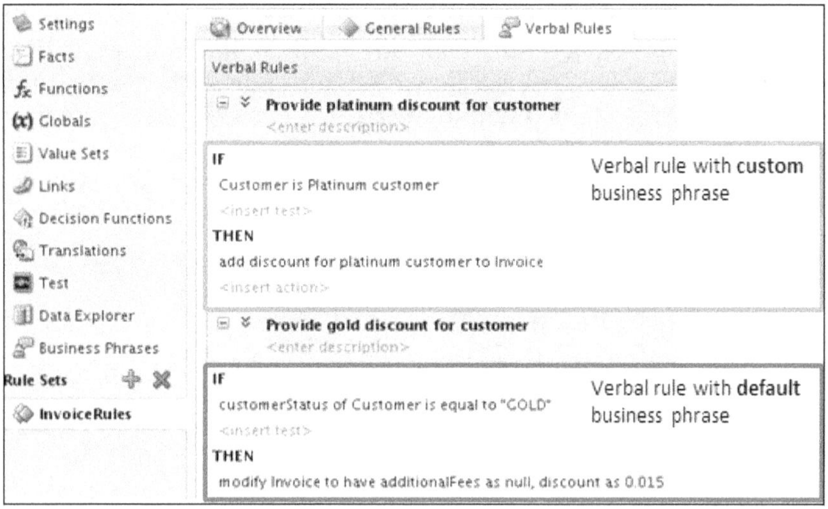

Figure 6

The upper rule, dealing with the discount for platinum customers, uses custom business phrases, while the lower one uses standard business phrases. The upper rule is self-explaining and more like a real sentence than the lower one. In cooperation with RYLC marketing, which is responsible for the corresponding rules, it is decided to use custom business phrases. The resulting custom business phrases are displayed in the next screenshot:

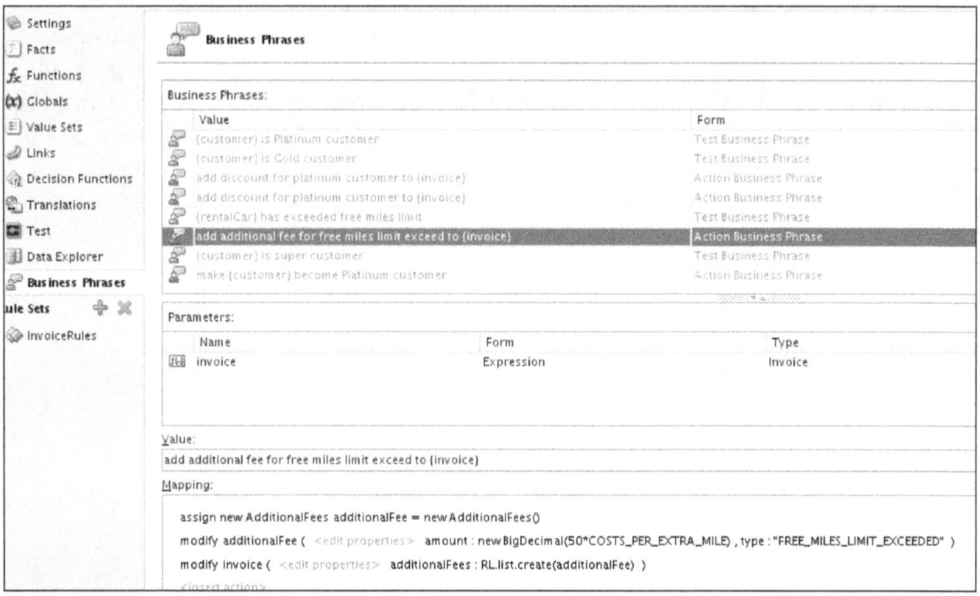

Figure 7

After implementing the rules on the basis of the defined business phrases, the business rule-based approach is fully realized. The final BPMN diagram does not contain conditional branches, as the following figure shows. The information needed to create invoices is implemented within the created business rule component and is invoked by a BPMN rule task.

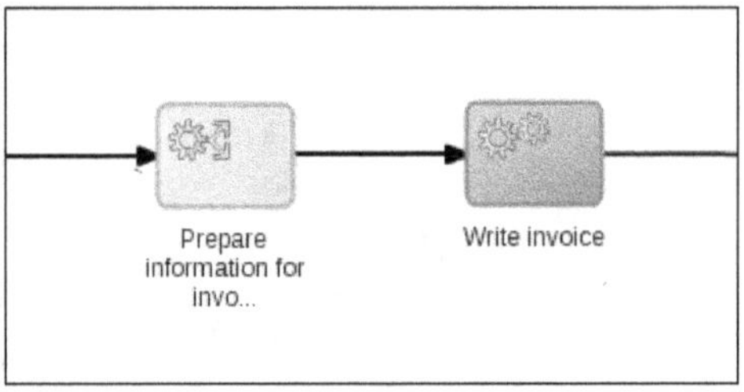

Figure 8

Now, when the invoicing rules changes due to new requirements provided by RYLC marketing, only the underlying ruleset has to be changed. The process, that is, the process flow logic, remain untouched.

During an implementation review, the RYLC BPM architect notices that the implemented logic to create an invoice is also needed by another process. So, they decide to do a refactoring to comply with RYLC's SOA architecture. They instruct the developer to do the refactoring and provide the decision logic as a separate standalone service.

During the refactoring, the responsible developer takes the two BPMN activities **PrepareInformationForInvoicing** and **WriteInvoice** that are together responsible for creating an invoice. The developer uses BPEL as the implementation technology. After the refactoring, the business process will change so that only one service call task is needed to create a invoice. Incorporating a BPEL process with a business rule component works straightforward and analogous to the BPMN variant.

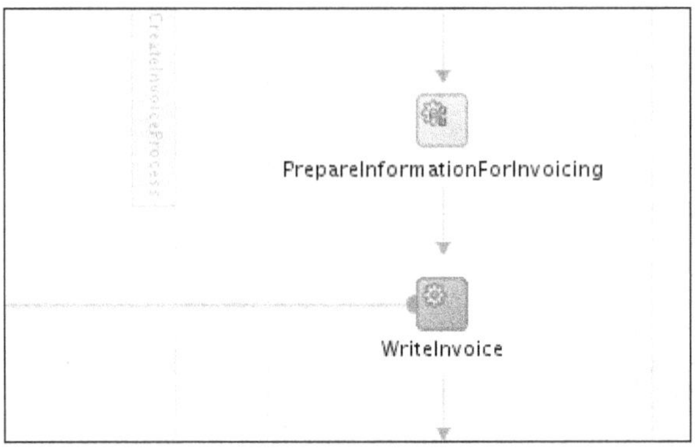

Figure 9

Using a business rule activity in BPEL allows the invocation of a specific rule dictionary. The facts will be populated from within the BPEL process' context, which receives the information from the calling BPMN process. After the invoice has been created, the BPEL process returns a success message to the caller. The CarRental BPMN process changes as a result, as the following figure shows, and contains only one service call activity:

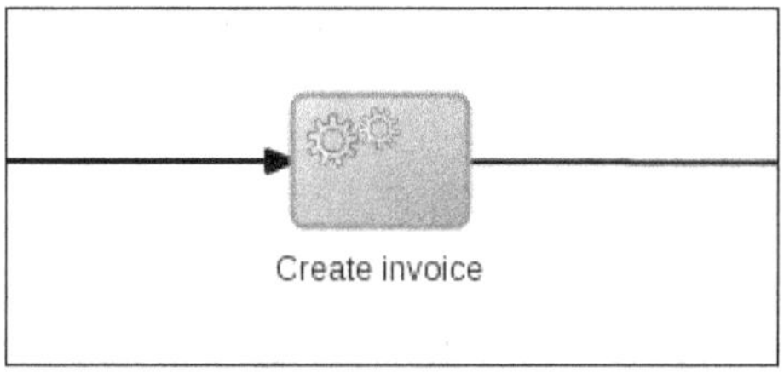

Figure 10

Summary

Within the current chapter, different aspects of the topic of business rules and especially their role regarding business processes and BPM have been discussed. There are a number of key takeaways from this chapter.

Business rules define basic policies and constraints therefore they are central, valuable elements when we define process-driven architectures. Also, business rules should be easily readable as well as understandable. Besides, they should be declared and not implemented like other business requirements. The separation of business rules and decision logic is essential to ensure business agility, flexibility, and transparency. Further, business constraints that are business rule candidates have to be chosen carefully by evaluating the criteria for volatility, reusability, impact, and compliance. Furthermore, an integrated approach is needed when designing business rules to bridge the gap between business and IT. Also, in Oracle BPM Suite 12*c*, rules can be defined using a business rule component, exposing the functionalities in a standard-based way as a web service.

Oracle's BRE is basically an inference rule engine using the RETE algorithm to optimize rule processing. With 12*c*, a new non-RETE algorithm comes up. Oracle Business Rules takes a big step towards the business by providing more business user friendly functionalities.

Besides the aforementioned points, a few best practices about interface and service design, as well as the management of rules, were introduced that should be considered when starting a new business rule project to build future-proof, rule-based applications. Additionally, the inclusion of a business rule component within the RYLC showcase has been made to demonstrate how to use basic elements of Oracle rules for the definition of a simple business rule service.

In the next chapter, we will introduce basic concepts about **Adaptive Case Management** (**ACM**) to depict dynamic, nonstatic business processes. You will learn what ACM can do to improve and optimize your business processes, when it should be used, and when it doesn't make sense and finally how to implement dynamic processes using Oracle BPM Suite 12*c*.

9
Adaptive Case Management

In early 2014, Gartner predicted that most of the work in the very near future will be mainly driven by knowledge. This is where **adaptive case management** (**ACM**) will help us build better IT solutions to optimally support the new kind of work challenges we are facing. This chapter gives all the overview information that is needed to fully understand the ideas behind ACM. In this chapter, we will cover the following topics:

- Overview of Adaptive Case Management
- Characteristics of ACM
- ACM and business analytics
- Adaptive Case Management in Oracle BPM Suite
- Modeling a case
- Building your own case UI on top of the Case API
- Sample - ACM at RYLC
- Best practices

By the end of the chapter, you will know what ACM is about why and when you should apply ACM principles in your work, and you will have an impression of how the Oracle ACM tooling works.

The people do matter – not the machines

A typical driver to automate processes is the striving for higher efficiency. We have heard such statements again and again in our history—coined and impressively put into practice in industrial manufacturing by Henry Ford. That was a golden time for *production workers*. But today, people sit in front of their screens getting irritated when they are forced to go through the identical-looking task lists and screen sequences, which feels like wearing a straitjacket.

They make it difficult, or even impossible, to work in a way that is innovative and suited to the situation. Increasing efficiency is no longer achieved by simply automating routine tasks (that is already mapped in today's standard ERP software). It is rather a question of providing today's knowledge workers with an optimal workplace that allows them to make the best possible decisions for the company. This means that people have to be the focus of business process management initiatives again—as participants in the process that are not fully controlled by the process model but contribute actively and directly to the improvement of the process model.

This is a classic situation today. The business unit employees are happy because their process for engaging external employees is running exactly as they specified it should run in a sequential process model. In detail, this process comprises a variety of assessments and approvals at different management levels. The exact sequence can be very well expressed in the Business Process Model and Notation (BPMN) 2.0 modeling language or in event-driven process chains (EPC). These models are understood by business units and can be easily changed. At the same time, they are the basis for a precisely executable IT process. This kind of success in local workflows suggests that BPM is a success and nurtures the belief in business-IT alignment through BPM. But why do the results of BPM projects often feel not right to so many stakeholders? Why are automated processes not finally breaking away from the limited space for improvement at the micro level, or within departments, and pushing forward into the enterprise area?

The rise of the knowledge worker

Here's a glance at the past. Henry Ford and Frederick W. Taylor successfully followed a management approach that broke work down into simple tasks to enable the complexity of the overall job to be managed. In this way, the giant task of manufacturing a car was broken down into many individual subtasks that only required a few movements each. Each production worker had to carry out precisely defined steps. There was no room for acting independently—and it wasn't necessary either. Drawing on Taylor's vision, several authors in the BPM management discipline have been promoting flowcharting as a way to optimize business processes since the 1980s. These kinds of *normative* BPM projects ideally enable business departments to analyze business processes, document them, and easily change them if needed. However, this only functions well for *normative processes*, the flow of which can be precisely described before executing them.

In knowledge-intensive contexts, this kind of process is too inflexible to be able to map the complex reality. It would simply be too expensive, and ultimately unmaintainable, to model all conceivable variants of the process cycles, including all possible error and event conditions in advance—if you could ever really achieve completeness at all.

A further requirement of successful normative processes is that the people who take part in the process can work productively under close and strict management conditions. The process participants are taken by the hand and guided through a given process following the model. Just like workers on Taylor's assembly line, they have little scope to make decisions.

However, today we have transformed into a knowledge society. Tasks such as customer complaint management, processing damage claims, supporting job hunters, assessing legal issues, and research and development, all require a high degree of dynamic reactions due to their complex circumstances and new events that can occur unexpectedly. Big names in management, such as Peter F. Drucker and Thomas H. Davenport, describe the rise of the knowledge worker, who is proving to be far less controllable than the production worker.

Why do we deliver bad IT support to our knowledge workers?

Let's have a look at our current workplaces. We all sense one of two main problems in today's business world (if not both of them together).

First, we don't have good support through IT systems at all. There is a massive amount of information out there—in books, magazines, the Internet, several databases, and so on. The age of the Internet of Things will bring even more data that is simply available at any given time. That's the good news—we have access to all the data we need. At the same time, that's the bad news—we have access to *all* the data. For today's knowledge workers, it would be really helpful to have IT systems helping to provide the right data based on the current context we are working in instead of giving access to the whole world. The important term here is *context*.

The second problem some of us face occurs in companies that introduced rigid workflows to "automate" most of the work the people have to do. At least in forcing them to only do some things, somebody who designed the process in some other time period (long ago) thought it might be right. In our more and more knowledge-driven world, this makes sense only in rare situations where really no deviation from the process flow is acceptable. We all know the situation when we enter an administration department and ask the clerk a question. Sometimes, they don't even look at us. They don't won't to talk with us unless they have entered data in maybe 20 screens, which isn't of any relevance for our current question, but which is forced by the workflow-driven system.

We wish for an IT system that provides more flexibility and that honors the fact that a human being is sitting in front of the screen. This system doesn't try to force us into predefined workflows with no deviation, but it guides us where possible. The metaphor we are using here is that of a navigation system. The goal is important but not the exact way to reach that goal as we are used to being guided by a navigation system when driving to a destination. If we decide to drive a long way round, perhaps to get some cheap fuel or to visit a friend living next to the route, then we can decide to do this. Our navigation system detects where we are and tries to guide us to our destination—no matter how often we deny listening to the system. There is a second aspect here in this comparison. Perhaps the destination is new to us; we have never been to this town with these big roads and heavy traffic. Then, we are glad that the navigation system helps us and guides us. We listen to the advice because we are new in this specific context, or perhaps, we are driving to this destination 10 times every week. We know the way, the best short cuts, and more about this specific context than the system. However, anyway, we have the system running in the background, giving us advice in non-normal situations—for example, a traffic jam is in front, and we are rerouted far ahead; a wrong-way driver is in our area, so we want to get that additional guidance of the system to make better decisions even if we are professionals in our area.

How to involve a user in the processes?

Why are so many implementations of business process automation ignoring the fact that we write software mostly for knowledge workers? Perhaps it's the way today's BPM platforms interact with the user. In process languages, such as BPMN 2.0 and BPEL, the user is integrated in the same way. The process is running in the backend, wants to interact with a human and, therefore, puts a task in the inbox of the individual (or a group depending on some roles). After the human who has to work on the task finishes that work, the process continues. That's a pattern that's working very well.

Unfortunately, a lot of products bring their own inboxes. That's a nightmare for the user, who has to look into several inboxes to find all pieces of their work. So, it is crucial to our IT strategy to consolidate all these inboxes into only one (or prevent this situation from happening from the beginning). Having only one central inbox, normally divided into an *inbox service* in the backend and some UI components that can be reused in several situations, is the base for every task's management in BPM scenarios. We strongly advise you to use this unified task list approach.

To have this as the starting basis is very important because in both worlds of BPM—the rigid world and the case management world—we need task management as a major building block.

Defining a "case"

To be honest, we don't like the term *case*. It's simply too restricted. Let's first look at a definition of "case" taken from the book *Taming the Unpredictable*, which is the second book after the classic *Mastering the Unpredictable*, both worth reading: *A case is the coordination of multiple tasks, planned or unplanned, for a specific purpose.*

Again, here we have a strong hint about the importance of *tasks*. But, besides that, this definition stays quite unclear. We have tasks; maybe they were planned, or perhaps some of them are just emerging. And we have a goal—a specific purpose.

Looking at this, we can treat almost anything as a case, for example, an insurance claim, a patient in a hospital, an event (such as a conference), an identity theft investigation, a project, an asset (such as a building), a customer request, a customer, a contract, or any incident.

The term "case" is much too limiting from our perspective. We discussed this with Max Pucher, one of the authors of *Mastering the Unpredictable*, and he also confirmed that he would have loved to have another term. We have to keep "case" for now, but we want you to think of a scenario that allows a knowledge worker to be more efficient.

The following figure depicts the three layers of the case concept:

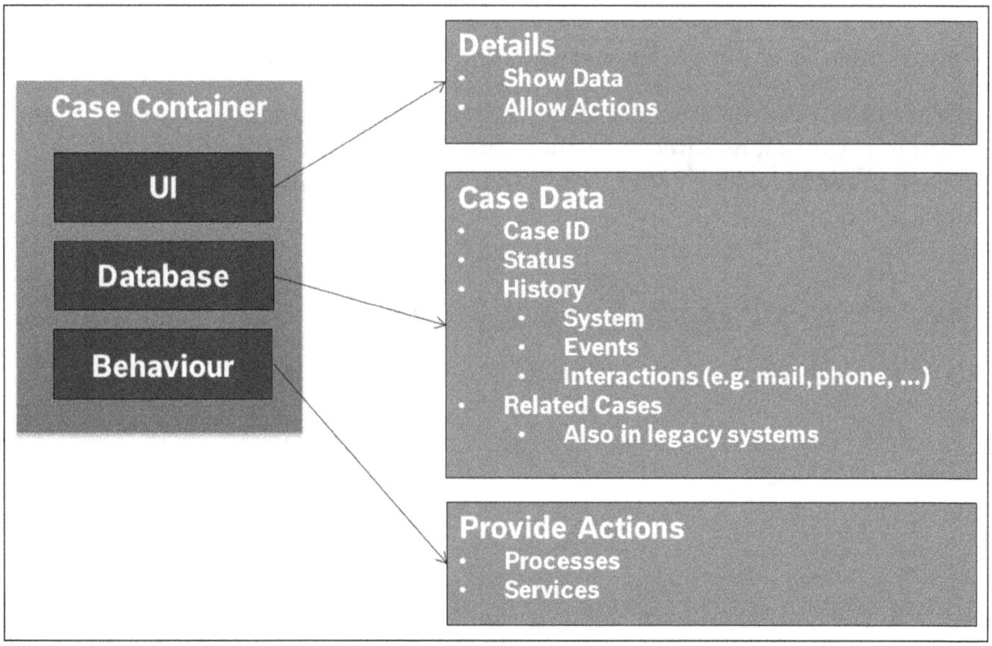

Figure 1

Case management is a natural evolution of BPM

When we talk about ACM, we often hear the questions, why is BPMN out now, and why should everybody do ACM from now on? Well, we think this is simply a wrong point of view. We see that BPM is a very important discipline in IT, addressing a lot of the problems we are facing today. BPM is also quite an old discipline, which started long ago with a lot of different workflow concepts and technologies. ACM is a natural evolution of the BPM stories because day by day, the kind of work we have to perform in the companies is changing.

We strongly suggest that you see ACM as a new tool and concept in the BPM world: *normative BPM* and *adaptive BPM* represent two equal branches of BPM. Every business and IT architect should know both of them to decide which to use in concrete scenarios.

In today's IT world, the normative processes in the sense of process automation with BPEL or BPMN work well. It's up to all architects that work in BPM environments to deal with the concepts of the adaptive processes in order to be able to design optimal solutions for the requirements in knowledge-intensive contexts.

In the normative BPM world, you define every activity and every transition between the activities at design time. This is necessary because most BPM engines work based on tokens, which means the whole model has to be known before deployment. Otherwise, the token can't "flow" correctly through the process.

In the adaptive BPM world, most of the activities are also designed at design time. The difference is that no direct transitions are defined. Oracle uses a rule engine approach to control which activity can run in a specific context. We will see a few examples of how these rules are defined later in this chapter.

The characteristics of ACM

The characteristics of ACM are explained in the following sections.

System interactions

In the classical, rigid BPM world, according to *Mastering the Unpredictable*, processes are designed top down normally with a cost or industrialized focus. The process types here are straight-through processes, structured processes, and dynamic processes. Dynamic processes are interesting because they allow a bit of the flexibility we are looking for in the ACM world. This flexibility is reached using extracted rules for gateway decisions, using mid process event communication, or by reading lists of activities (for example, from Excel) that define a specific context.

This view is complemented by the bottom-up approach, which brings the people in. They have a more quality-based, adaptive focus, and system interactions are more emergent than designed. That's where social collaboration and case management meet in the middle with the dynamic processes.

Is the exception becoming the norm?

In classic or rigid BPM, you normally start with the happy path and then add variants and exceptions as needed. In today's business world, it is very likely that you find more and more deviations from the standard process—all having their own justification. This makes your process models more and more complex. You find yourself adding gateway after gateway. When you show these models to a business person, they can't even imagine anymore what the happy path might have been. You make exceptions for a specific customer, a specific kind of claim, or a fraud detection. You can also make exceptions if you didn't find a corresponding contract or address, some pictures have bad quality, a letter can't be delivered, there are weaknesses in the expert evidence, the requested documents are missing, and so on. Our world is complex. So, maybe you realize that you will have more exception flows than standard flows. Maybe you realize that the exception is the norm.

In this case, you found a strong indicator that the rigid BPMN might not be the (only) right tool for you and that you should have a deeper look at case management.

Data centricity versus process centricity

About 15-20 years ago, the paradigm of object orientation was introduced. With the rise of the processes, this concept became less important (from a process view) because the process was the new big thing. The process is the first artifact to be designed, and the process manipulates data, typically sitting behind service interfaces.

With case management, this again shifts. With the upcoming case concept, the data becomes more important than the processes. Why? This is because you collect everything relevant to reach a specific goal in a specific context inside a case. From this point of view, a case is a kind of big container for data that was or will be important to some extent for the case worker. However, of course, processes are very important here, too. A case management system allows the knowledge worker to do their work by starting activities accordingly. These activities might be implemented as processes themselves.

Having said that, the focus of work is on the case; the goal is to close the case to reach a defined outcome. This means that you change the state of the underlying data by acting on the case, by starting activities. This shifts the case through different phases until the desired goal is reached.

Multiple stakeholders

In a classical BPMN process, you may have several stakeholders that interact with the process. Typically, you will find them modeled as roles in the business process diagram. If you only have a small set of involved roles/stakeholders, this might be a sign that the BMPN solution is the right one for you. However, if you find a lot of stakeholders with very different requirements in viewing the different states of the case, this might be a good hint that case management could be the right option. In the case management world, every stakeholder could have their own user interface with very specific adjustments to their concrete role. Of course, they could all share the same generic UI, which will behave differently based on the permissions in the case management engine.

Task management

We already stressed the importance of a solid task management block in the BPM and ACM spaces. With our new knowledge, we can now look at another difference. In the BPM world, tasks are initiated by a process, and the users have to work on these tasks to make the process run further. In the ACM world, we have the notion of a to-do list or a checklist. This is perhaps because there are several tasks to be completed to reach a goal. However, it is up to the knowledge worker to decide in which order they should be processed. Maybe some of them can be left out, some should be pushed up, and others pushed down. The case management engine tries to guide the knowledge worker by suggesting useful next steps. The knowledge worker is not forced into flows, they (perhaps) know better as an expert.

Building blocks

The heart of a case management solution is the case management engine. Within Oracle, this engine is part of BPM Suite, which provides both BPM disciplines in one joined core: BPMN and ACM. This is a real advantage because you have all options available according to the specific solution you are building. The case management engine is the container for the cases with its activities and data. But something more is needed.

We need access to a task engine for task management, as described previously. Oracle provides a rock-solid Human Task engine as part of SOA Suite, which is fully integrated in the ACM environment.

Of course, we need a classic process engine because a lot of activities in our cases will be implemented as processes with BPMN. This is a quick win within Oracle BPM Suite, which combines these two worlds anyway.

As we need a lot of data when working with cases, a service bus for integration is very helpful. In SOA Suite, we have two components available, which can take on this role: the mediator when working within a service component architecture (SCA) composite and the service bus (fully integrated into JDeveloper now) when dealing with external services.

A specific sort of data is unstructured data, typically put into a document management system. WebCenter Content is the first choice in Oracle scenarios. Of course, other **document management systems** (**DMSs**) can be integrated as well when they support **Content Management Interoperability Services** (**CMIS**).

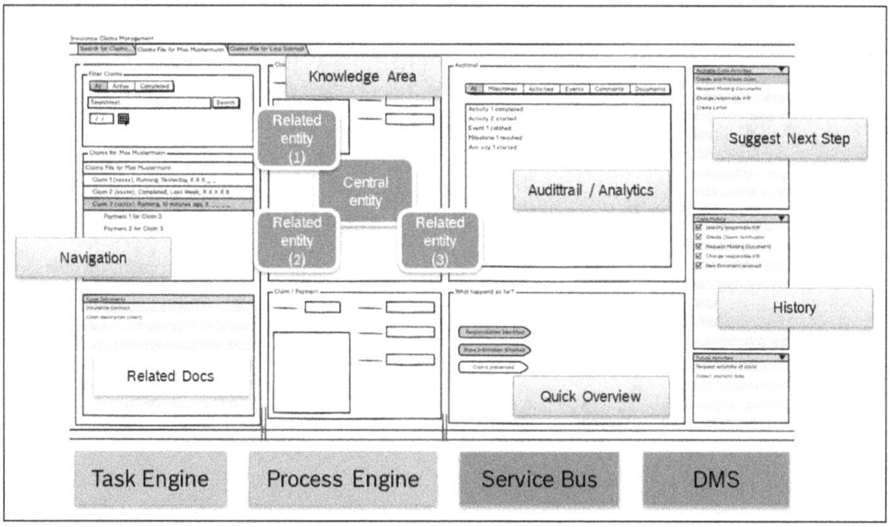

Figure 2: Building blocks of a case management solution

The ACM user interface

In traditional BPM projects, the user is typically considered to be something like an asynchronous service. If something can't be fully automated, a task is generated for a user and the process waits until it gets an answer. After the user completes the tasks, the process recognizes that it has to go on with processing—as it would do with any other asynchronous service. Depending on the requirements, the complexity and design of the forms that are presented to the user can be anything, from a simple and generated UI to a complex wizard-like or free-floating UI. But normally, we have simple UIs in workflow projects.

The user interface in an ACM scenario is especially important. The user can't even see that his UI is working against a case management engine, but the knowledge worker can sense that ACM only matters for IT and for flexibility. However, the knowledge worker, on the business side of things, only sees the UIs. So, UIs have to be simply perfect, not "casy". An example of a bad UI design from the knowledge worker's perspective is the case UI that Oracle delivers as a generic UI within the case engine. It simply puts all things you can read via the Case API onto a screen. This is completely unsuitable for the business.

But the Oracle Case UI is great for fast prototyping and testing purposes; there, you need it from a system architect's perspective. For real UIs, please use real UI designers to provide the best experience for the end user.

Technically, the Oracle Case UI is an ADF application that could also be used within the WebCenter portal. The Case API, in general, is open, as will be described later, so you can use whatever UI technology you want to build the best UI for your scenario.

In our projects, we mainly use a wireframe tool called Balsamiq. This is a great tool to design mocks of your UI without implementing anything, which is very helpful while discussing requirements with the stakeholders. Visual thinking works so much better than having only some features in an Excel sheet.

When you look at the figure in the *Building blocks* section, you see the wireframe we used to build a technical pilot to demonstrate that all we need from the Case API is available and working together.

In the top-left corner, you see a navigation area displaying cases and subcases. In the knowledge area, there is information for the case-related data and documents. The **Audittrail** section allows you to browse everything that happened to your case, such as started or completed activities, changes in milestones, data, comments, and so on. An additional milestone view gives direct feedback as to which phase the current case is from a processing perspective, for example, to give a quick overview when someone who is just looking for fast information looks into the case.

On the right-hand side, you see the area for the guided navigation. Here is one window displaying all activities that are possible to execute now. One window shows the activities already completed, and the one at the bottom shows activities that might be executable in the future, but for now, they are not, because some rules say so.

Here, we find the main ACM concepts in the UI. We don't show all activities to the user but filter the view as best as we can based on the context, which is built by the rules. This prevents the user from seeing information that is not useful in his current state. This shows the guiding concept. The activities could be rated, and they could say things like "Well, you can run me. But 80 percent of the best performing people in your organization choose another option here. You can run me. But be aware that there might be a better option."

All these are UI aspects and demonstrate the importance of the UI in knowledge worker scenarios.

The "A" in ACM

There is a lot of discussion going on in the ACM community about the true meaning and value of real adaptability mainly because different groups understand different things when they say things have to be *adaptive*.

So, we have different levels of adaptability, which we have to distinguish between:

- **The anticipated flow of work doesn't fit; another "way" must be allowed**: This is the basic "adaptability" that comes with ACM. If you find that the way you are following through a set of activities is wrong, you can adjust this with ACM. Just change the rules controlling the activities, and you are done. This is also possible to some extent with BPMN when you use rules to control your gateways. But, of course, ACM is more flexible because activities don't have to have a direct transition unlike in BPMN, where it is necessary. There is, however, an exception. There are "dynamic" BPMN solutions, where you use an activity to "load" work steps, for example, from an Excel file. So, something is possible here with BPMN, too, but things are more natural to ACM.

- **A work step that was anticipated is not yet in the "plan"**: This is an important concept in ACM, which will be introduced when we discuss CMMN (Case Management Model and Notation) in the *Modeling a case* section later in this chapter. The underlying idea is simple. As a designer, you think of all the activities a user should be able to execute to reach a goal. You know that there are activities that are used by everybody, so you make them required for the user to execute. But, you already know of a set of activities that are not used in every case instance because they deal with special circumstances. But the point is that you already know them; therefore, the designer provides them as discretionary items. This results in a clear view in the UI, where all required activities are shown directly and all discretionary items are hidden from the options a user can choose from. If necessary, the user drags such a hidden work step into the current plan and executes the discretionary item.
- **A work step is completely missing**: This is a common problem in the process and ACM worlds. The user, while executing his process or case, determines that an additional activity would be needed here, which is not in the system yet, not even as a discretionary item. This may be because the user experiences this situation several times and simply wishes to have the additional working step for the future for reasons of convenience. Or maybe it is critical to the business that even other knowledge workers, maybe not-so-experienced ones, should take this additional step also into account that was identified once by an expert user and then implemented by IT for all to benefit from its existence. Or, for compliance reasons, this step really has to be documented in the system. With this requirement, we reach the boundaries of what ACM engines can achieve.

There are some options now, which are as follows:

- **Create ad hoc tasks for a person/role**: This is an activity that the Oracle engine always offers to the user. Just to document that some work is done and by whom, you create an ad hoc task for someone, which is tracked by the system.
- **Use and parameterize e-mail work step**: If you want to communicate with someone by e-mail and want this to be tracked by the system, you use this kind of activity. Oracle also allows this to be present to be chosen by the user.
- **Send a notification to the governance team**: This is the preliminary stage to get a new activity designed and implemented by IT. You call your governance team stating that a "real" work step is needed in your daily work and request a technical implementation (which may include service/process calls). Of course, it takes some time for the request to be accepted until you (and others) can use your new activity (either directly or as a discretionary item).

- **Use engine that supports "real" adaptability**: This is the holy grail in community discussions at the time of writing this book. There are prototypes out there that work completely based on ontology and allow the addition of new work steps, including code without redeployment. Of course, the IT is still needed to do this, but this would work much faster. But currently, no vendor supports this feature as far as we know.
- **Access to data that might be helpful in the context**: When working, for example, on investigative cases, you often have the requirement to browse data in your context. You implement this data within your case and then things are easy. But often, you need access to data nobody has thought about upfront. Then, good UIs allow you to embed BI views or allow jumps to third-party systems to collect the relevant data.

Having said all this on adaptability, you might get a feeling as to what sort of adaptability is useful for your use cases. In most situations, you get along with the basic adaptive features, for example, Oracle BPM Suite offers case management. There are cases, where you touch the boundaries. Hopefully, we will see more innovation to that end from the Oracle BPM team in upcoming releases. For most use cases we see in our projects, the current possibilities regarding adaptability are enough.

ACM and business analytics

Business Intelligence, or what is nowadays called business analytics, is a very important discipline in the area of ACM projects.

Emerging paths and process mining

There is an interesting book out there called the *Oregon Experiment*. In this story, an architect got the task to design the campus of a university. But, he didn't approach it as expected. The first thing he did was to order some bulldozers to clear the whole campus area between the new buildings. Then, he seeded grass everywhere and... waited. After some months, the grass grew and the students started walking their preferred ways. This resulted in an interesting pattern of emerging trails. Some of them were very small; some were bigger because a bigger crowd seemed to use them constantly. See the figure with the trails for an impression. The following image shows this. With this highly valuable information, the architect knew where to build the best and most effective ways because the people who use the "system" had shown him the preferred patterns.

What can we learn from this experiment for ACM? Well, one option could be to have an ACM quickstart as the architect had with his campus. When you think of classic BPM projects, you have to have lots of requirement workshops to gather all the information needed to implement usable processes with all necessary paths, deviations, and exceptions included. This takes a long time, and you don't know whether all the needs of your knowledge workers will be fulfilled.

As an alternative, you can just gather the basic set of activities necessary to solve a case. Then, you put these activities into a basic ACM environment with Oracle BPM Suite and let a special, selected group of expert users work with the system. After some time, you look at all the "case instances" in your system, which make the same kind of paths as in the preceding example.

You use a process mining tool for this. For example, we have very good experience with the Disco tool provided by Fluxicon. All the necessary information you need to feed the mining tool is already in the ACM database—each activity has a unique ID, a start and end timestamp, a display name, and information about who called it. Disco then generates an interactive map, where you see the main activity flows and the rare ones. You see the duration of the steps and analyze for optimizations. Like the students leading to emerging paths on the campus, you can use this information to fine-tune your ACM implementation. For example, add rules that some activities can be called after others have finished, and so on. With this approach, you get a very fast way of kicking off your ACM/BPM project with high value for the right people—the knowledge workers.

Figure 3: ACM can lead to optimized, normative processes

Image credits

The preceding image has been taken from the Internet (`http://www.nature.com/nature/journal/v388/n6637/fig_tab/388047a0_F1.html`).

Adding business analytics to the game

Using process mining to initially fill your ACM system with life is only one option. It gets even more interesting when we begin adding innovative business analytics technologies. Remember that our goal is to build IT systems that excellently support the work of the knowledge workers—the real experts, those who are still learning their job, or those replacing somebody during vacation or other absences.

Using business analytics, we can implement some guiding algorithms. Think of the most common one, such as Amazon's *Suggest Next Best Order* algorithm: you are looking at product A and get a hint from Amazon that other customers also bought products B and C after looking at A. This can be very helpful because it may lead you to very useful things that were not in your mind before. Coming to ACM, the most interesting things here are the *Suggest Next Best Action* algorithms. Think of a recommendation system that guides you along your way, just like a navigation system in the car. It does not force you to do things unlike classical workflows. It guides where it is necessary.

For example, it gives a hint like this: user A, you are choosing to run activity 17 in this context. You can do this. But be aware that 80 percent of the top experts use activity 42 in similar situations.

Such a guiding system is socially very compatible with people. They don't feel controlled too much because they can decide which path to take on their own. And they get the hints about how to get better at the things they are doing.

Think of an insurance company that regulates claims on a daily basis. Sometimes, they have to deal with mass claims, for example, after a heavy thunderstorm. In one of our project scenarios, the insurance company was confronted with a total claim amount of 600 million euros for only one single storm with massive hail for 10 minutes. Making regulation more efficient and guiding the knowledge workers in an optimal way can lead to a fast ROI for such ACM systems that optimize the work the knowledge workers are doing.

Another interesting area, where a lot of potential might lie, is in leveraging rating systems for ACM activities. You all know the holiday check portals out there with millions of ratings for hotels. They work very well at the beginning. But in the meantime, you even can buy ratings for your own hotel on the Web. So you are not sure to get the cool "five stars" hotel that was liked by 2000 users—maybe the ratings were faked. But what about getting such an advice from your friends or peers? Only 2 persons that tell you their opinion about the hotel might outperform all the 2000 ratings out there. It's a question of trust and credibility.

Oracle has built such a rating mechanism into its ACM engine. So, allowing the knowledge workers to rate some activities might lead to much more trust in their peers when deciding about the decision to take in the way of solving a case.

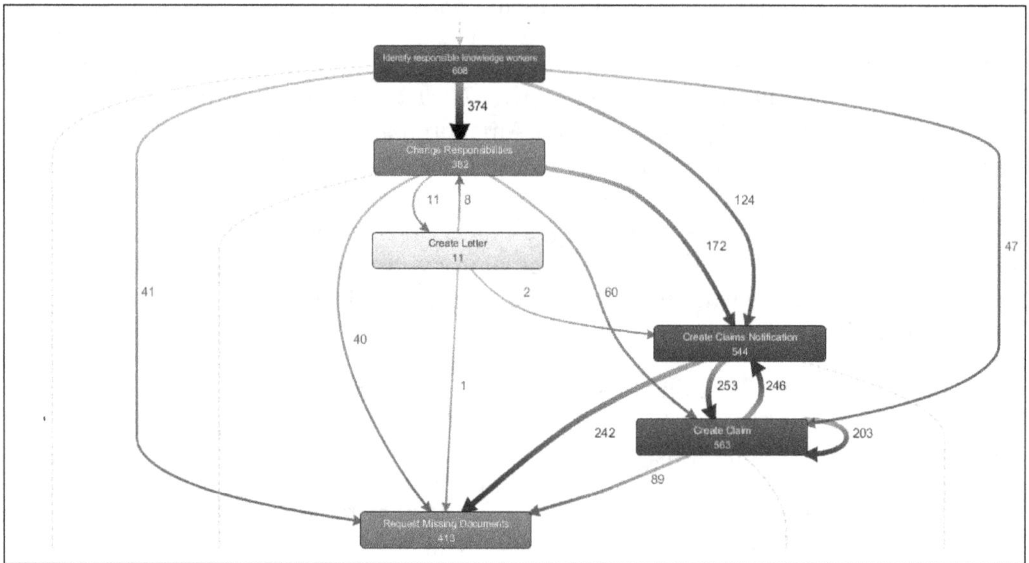

Figure 4: Emerging paths with process mining (simplified)

The basic concepts of adaptive case management in Oracle BPM Suite

Before we look at how to develop a case scenario in Oracle BPM Suite, we will have a brief look at the main concepts that will be represented in the tool.

- **Cases** need a BPM project in JDeveloper as a living space. We really like the fact that Oracle implemented the case construct like all main building blocks (BPEL, mediator, rules, human tasks, and so on) as an SCA component. This means that you can just drag and drop a "case" from the component palette into the composite diagram. You only can have one case per project, but that doesn't feel like a limitation. Once you have the new case in JDeveloper, you have to configure it.
- **Milestones**: This concept is really useful to give the user faster insight about the progress a case has made until now. In the system, a milestone is represented as a string. It is only a logical thing used to group a set of activities. But, there is no direct association between a milestone and an activity.
- **Outcomes**: They represent the goals that will be reached when closing a case. They are user-defined statuses represented as strings in the system.
- **Case activities**: The activities bring the behavior into the static case construct. To close a case, you have to reach its goal. Therefore, you have to perform some activities, normally in a nonspecific order. Think of a generic to-do list. Maybe you have to do all the tasks on the list to reach a specific goal. Maybe you only have to do some of them, to reach the same goal depending on your current context. A case activity is one entry on your to-do list. There are three representations of activity types: you can promote human tasks and BPMN processes to be case activities when they are in the same composite. Or, you can write custom activities in Java by implementing an interface and doing some configuration. Regardless of which type of activity you use as an implementation, you have to specify the same configuration details.
    - Activities have to be either manual, which means they are activated by a UI, or they have to be automatic, which means they will be activated by the Oracle ACM engine. When an activity has to be executed to reach the goal of the case, then it has to be required. If it can be activated more than once during the case life cycle, you have to make it repeatable. To make an activity only available to be manually or automatically activated depending on a business rule, you have to check **Conditionally Available**. And, of course, you have to define the permission as to which user or role is allowed to access this activity.

- **Case rules**: Here, we see a new use case for the business rules introduced in the preceding chapter. As mentioned in the introduction, BPMN processes have all the transitions between all activities designed during design time. These are the *lines* between the BPMN elements, which are used as paths for the BPMN engine during execution time to let the token flow through the system on the predetermined paths. The role of these transitions is taken over by the business rules in ACM. When a new case is created in JDeveloper, a business rule dictionary is generated automatically to store these rules. The rules control the possible flow of the activities described earlier. For example, activity 5 is only enabled after milestone A has been reached. Or, after completion of activity 6, activity 7 is started automatically. Or, after the occurrence of a specific user event, a milestone is marked as reached. Rules can be fired as a reaction to case events. Case events are fired for case life cycles, milestones, activities, data, documents, comments, or arbitrary user events. This allows maximum flexibility when designing the system.
- **Data**: Data plays an important role in ACM. We have the same decisions here as we have in BPMN. Data can be stored directly in the case as it is done in a BPMN process, of course, by specifying XSD types or using plain simple types. Beginning with 12*c*, you can also use flex fields when you need a more generic approach. Also, every activity can have input and output data, again as in BPMN activities. Of course, you can define your custom case container in an application-specific database to separate the data from the case instances, just as we normally do in BPMN world.
- **User events**: The user event concept is very useful and strong in ACM. You can define user events for arbitrary things that can happen and then react in the business rules depending on the context. In BPMN, you will have to use permanent listening event listeners, which then fire some actions against a running process instance. Within ACM, this is much easier because managing the unpredictable is built into the core. The combination of user events and business rules gives ACM much of its flexibility that is needed in knowledge worker situations. User events can be seen as outside events, typically business events that can occur during the whole lifetime of a case and can then trigger events inside the case. For example, a cancel event leads to a forced closing of an insurance claim case, maybe because the claim was taken back.
- **Stakeholders**: In BPMN, you use swimlanes to define which users or roles are allowed to execute activities. In ACM, you do the same thing. In the stakeholder section, you define the user or roles that are involved in working on the case—typically, the different kinds of knowledge workers.

- **Permissions**: Permissions are attached to case objects. These can be documents or data. The idea is to define who has what kind of access to objects. Public and restricted access to objects are created by default.
- **Translation**: This allows the managing of translations for all the wording you use in your cases.

Build a case in Oracle BPM Suite

As described earlier, the case component is introduced as a firstclass citizen in SCA with support for all the mentioned basic concepts and can be created, for example, by just dropping it on the composite diagram. As a result of the wizard run, JDeveloper generates a case component and a business rule component. Notice that even the case is exposed as a service. The following screenshot shows this:

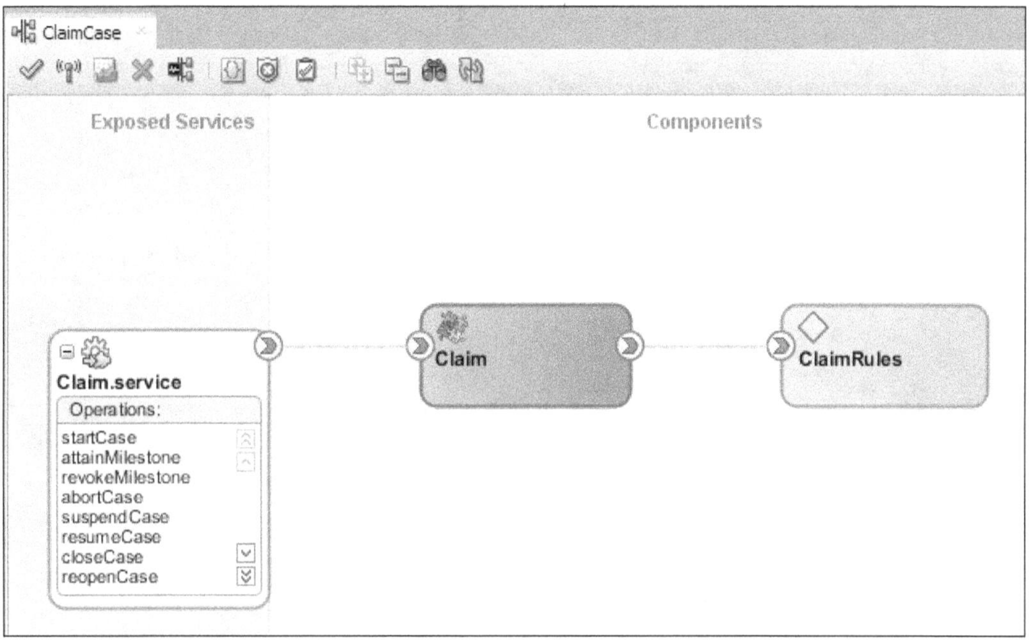

Figure 5: Composite.xml with the case component

A project can have only one composite, and a composite can have only one case. By double-clicking on the case, the case editor is opened. Here, you can define most of the configuration needed for the case itself: milestones, case outcomes, data and documents, user events, stakeholders and permissions, and translations. The following screenshot shows this:

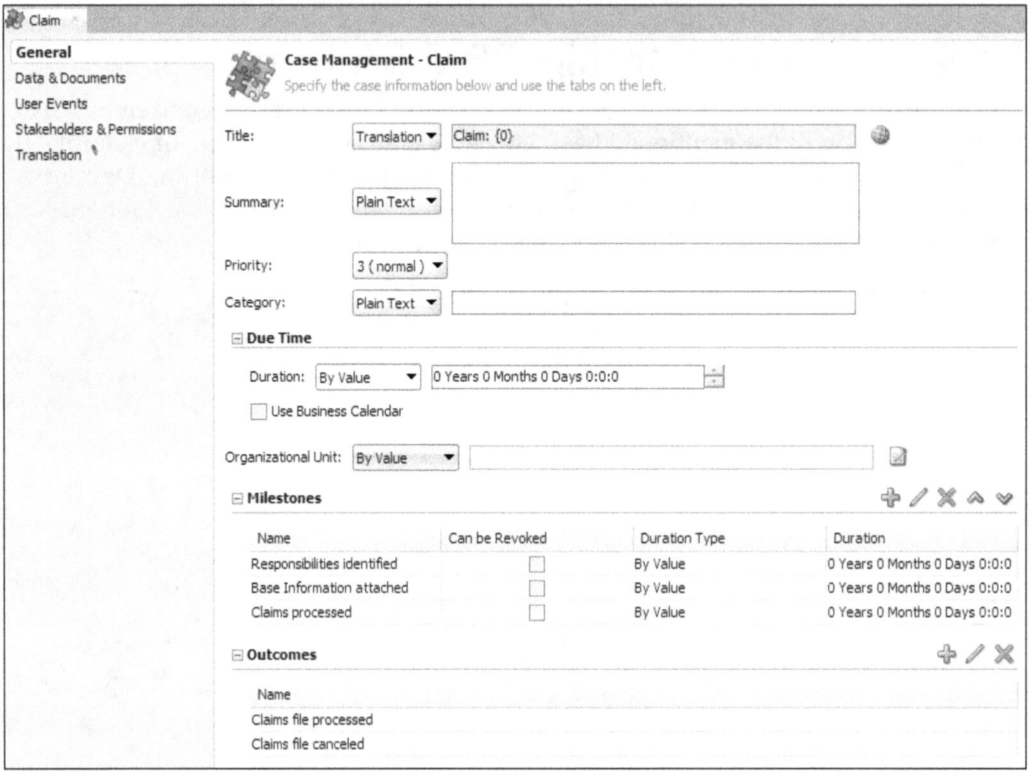

Figure 6: Definition of a case in Case Editor

Of course, the most important next step is to define and implement the case activities. You can open the *new* wizard, look for **BPM Tier**, and choose the **Custom Case Activity** option to create a first activity.

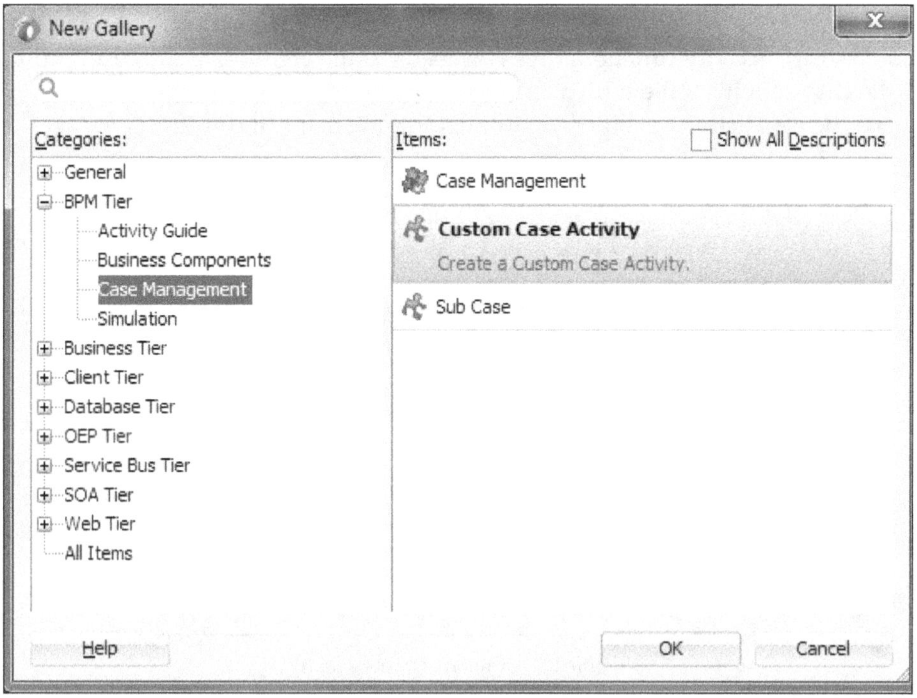

Figure 7: Definition of a case

You may wonder why only **Custom Case Activity** is being shown here. This is because the other two possible activity types (BPMN process and human task) have to be created inside the project in their normal way and then promoted as a case activity. We want to show here how to promote a human task as a case activity. Just create a normal human task in the project called **EvaluateClaimNotification**. Then, click on the **Promote as case activity** functionality. This leads to the creation of the configuration file of the case activity, a file with a `.caseactivity` extension. Double-clicking on this file opens the case activity editor. The following screenshot shows this:

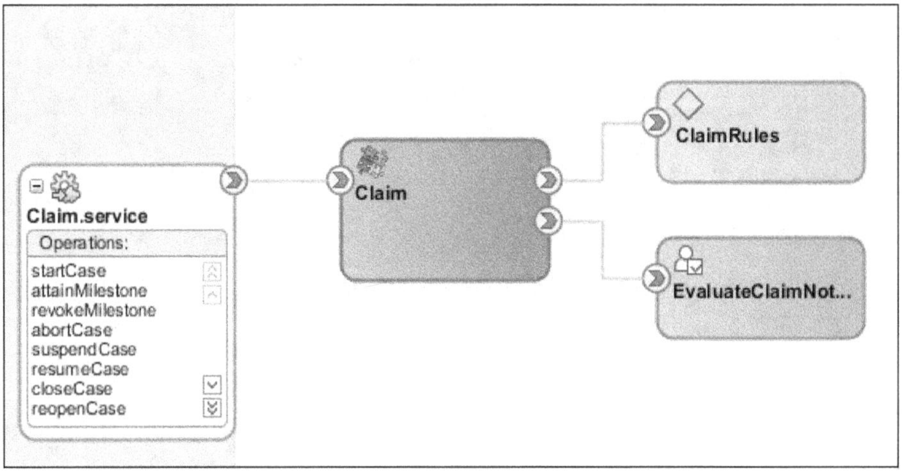

Figure 8: Definition of a case activity

Having configured a case activity typically isn't enough. You may want to specify when this activity can be called or what other things should be triggered after that activity is run. For example, the business rule needs to be configured because the checkbox **Conditionally Available** is marked during the creation phase.

The rule editor has a set of predefined functions, facts, and bucketsets:

- **Predefined functions**: For example, `reachMilestone`, `activateActivity`, `withdrawActivity`, and `revokeMilestone`
- **Facts and bucketsets**: For example, `TMilestoneEvent` and `TEventType`

The rules in ACM are equivalent to the transitions between elements in BPMN business process diagrams. They configure the behavior of the system, allowing only those activities to be executed where the appropriate rules evaluate to do so. For example, you can react to things like `ACTIVITY_EVENTS` (do something when the state is "completed") to trigger new activities or milestones. You also can react to `USER_DEFINED_EVENTS`, which allows nice and flexible communication with different parts of a system in the ACM engine. You can react to `MILESTONE_EVENTS`, typically to trigger case activities that should become active after having reached a specific milestone. The following screenshot shows this:

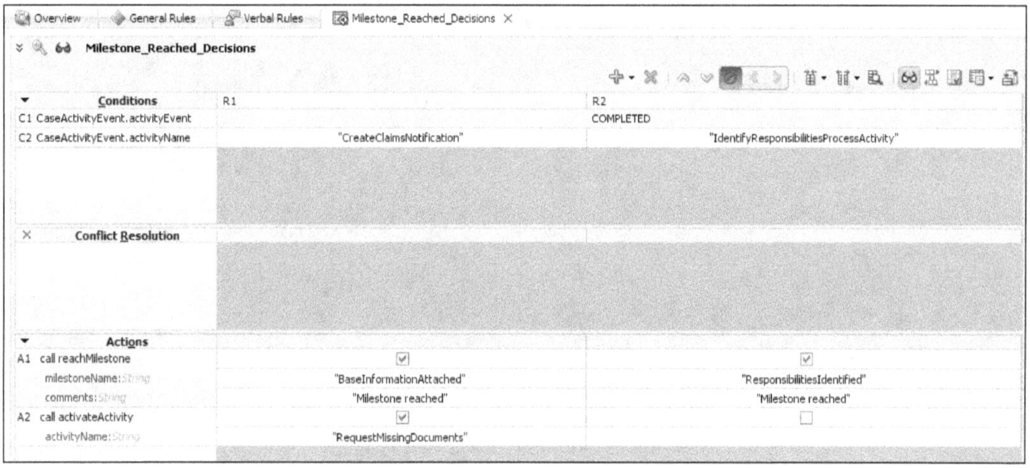

Figure 9: Definition of a case rule

A big advantage of the Oracle Fusion Middleware platform is the consequent use of **Enterprise Manager (EM)** to monitor the whole system, from higher views down to the composite level. As is possible with BPEL and BPMN, you can also see the "flow" of a case in Enterprise Manager. This is very helpful because here you can see what happened to your case instance and when, including error tracking and rules evaluation. The following screenshot shows this:

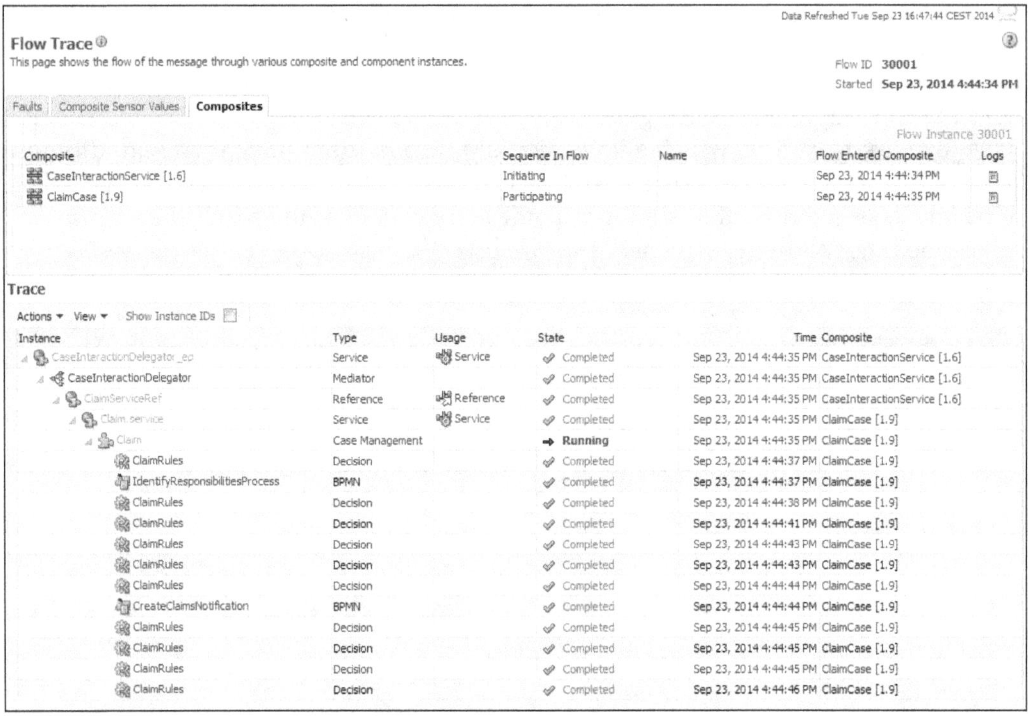

Figure 10: Monitoring case instances in EM

Maybe the most important component within an ACM project is the user interface. This is because in ACM, everything is about delivering optimal IT support to our knowledge workers. What does a knowledge worker see from our ACM world? Well... nothing but the user interface. A knowledge worker doesn't care about what's behind the scenes. He's only interested in a UI that perfectly supports his needs. Just as Oracle delivers a generic Worklist application to interact with the human tasks, beginning with a UI patch of Patchset 6 for BPM Suite 11*g*, the company also delivers a generic case UI as presented in the following figure. This UI is really useful for demonstration purposes and for testing during development. But, as with the generic Worklist application, we do expect every company to write their own UIs. So, the generic case UI can be seen as a good starting point for how to use the Case API to write your own user interface. We will describe how to do this later in this chapter. The following screenshot shows this:

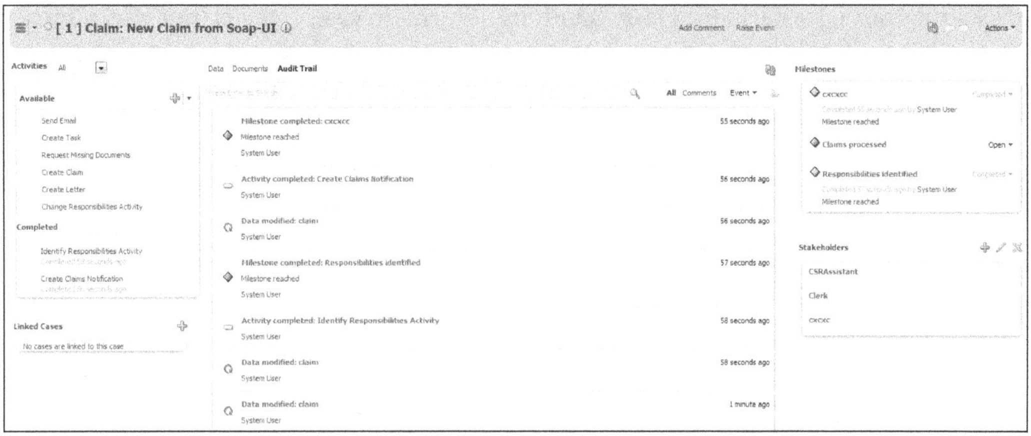

Figure 11: Generic case UI

Modeling a case

Until now, we learned a lot about case management. When it comes to real, live scenarios, the next question is how to gather the requirements for your case? And, how can this case be modeled? Well, the easiest path to gather all the needed requirements is to use a simple mind map. In our sample shown here, after long, long discussions, we found that we would like to go with a master-detail relationship between two case types, as shown in the following figure:

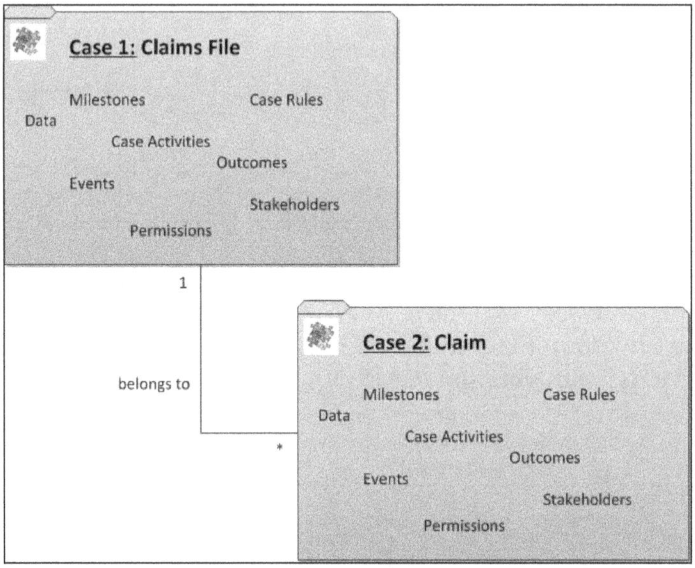

Figure 12: Master-child relationship between two cases

It's an insurance scenario for claim handling. The main case is the claims file, which carries the base data of the contract owner and other such details. Let's say there was an accident where you damaged two other cars and maybe a street light. Then, the owners of the two cars and the government responsible for street lights want to get their money back from you. These are three claims which all belong in your claim file, which makes the overarching peg. The following figure shows this:

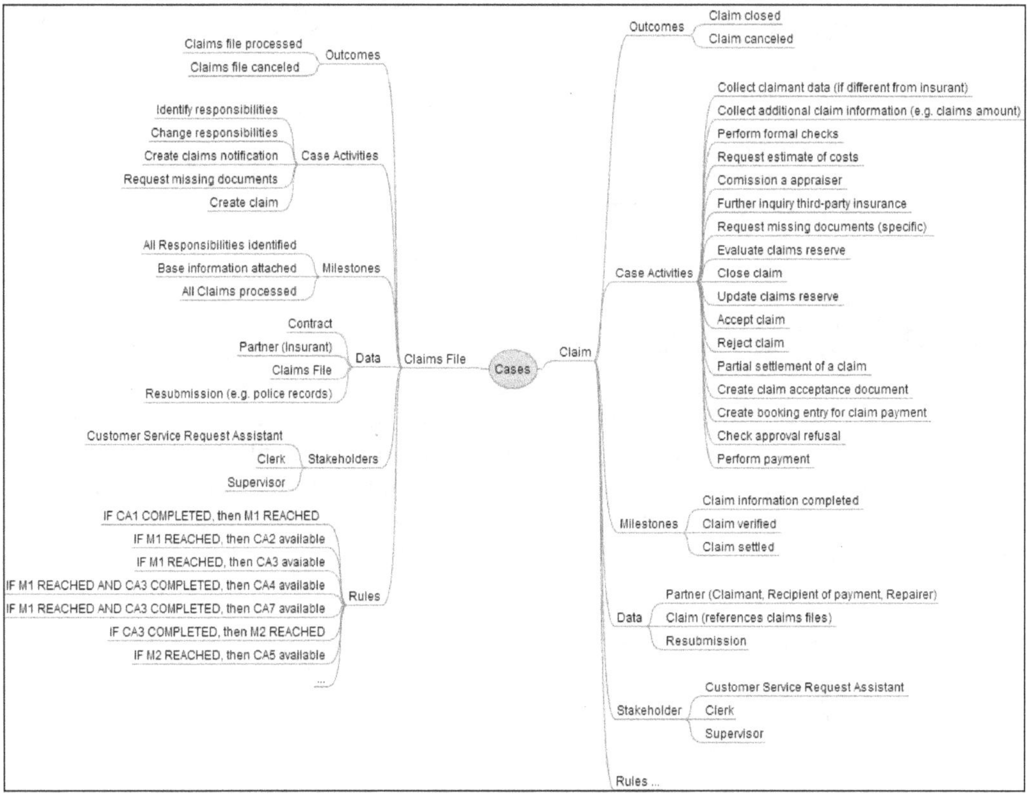

Figure 13: Gathering the requirements for a case with a mind map

Then, we simply put every artifact we identified into this map, grouped by the types of concepts necessary for Oracle ACM. As a lesson learned, we will introduce additional stages to group the activities, just as they are introduced in **Case Management Model and Notation** (**CMMN**), which we will cover in a bit.

We haven't been too happy with the mind map idea because we have a strong IT background and had the feeling that something better than a simple mind map must be available. Therefore, we tried another kind of diagram, which is completely custom built with no standard behind it. Here, we can already see three stages that group together a set of activities and milestones. For example, in the **Claim Evaluation** stage, we see three milestones and some activities grouped by milestones. Also, we see the stakeholders here to make it clear who is able to execute what action. This diagram turned out to be very useful because it gave much more insight at first view than our mind map. The following figure shows this:

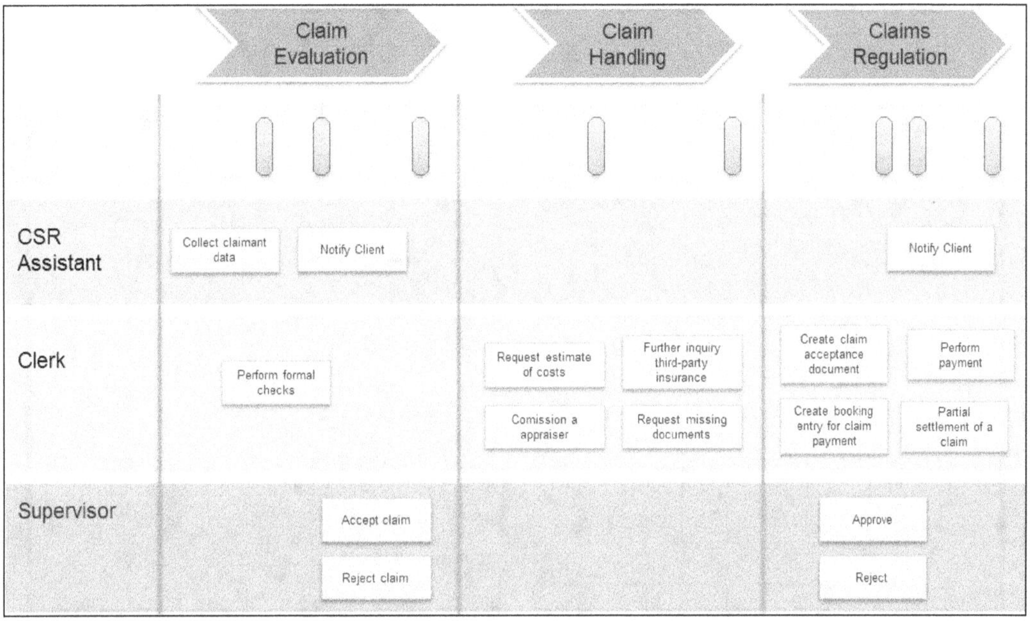

Figure 14: ACM diagram provided by Oracle

When all this information is available, building the case in JDeveloper is much easier than working only with Word file information. However, it turned out we can even do a bit better.

There is a brand new OMG standard out there that was released in May 2014. It's designed very closely to the ideas of BPMN and even the name reflects this: Case Management Model and Notation (CMMN). When you read the specification document, you will find the same main example that we use here. But interestingly, that's not because we used the sample from the spec, but the spec team, which we were in contact with during our first ACM pilot using CMMN, decided to use our example in the spec. Thanks for that; we liked this.

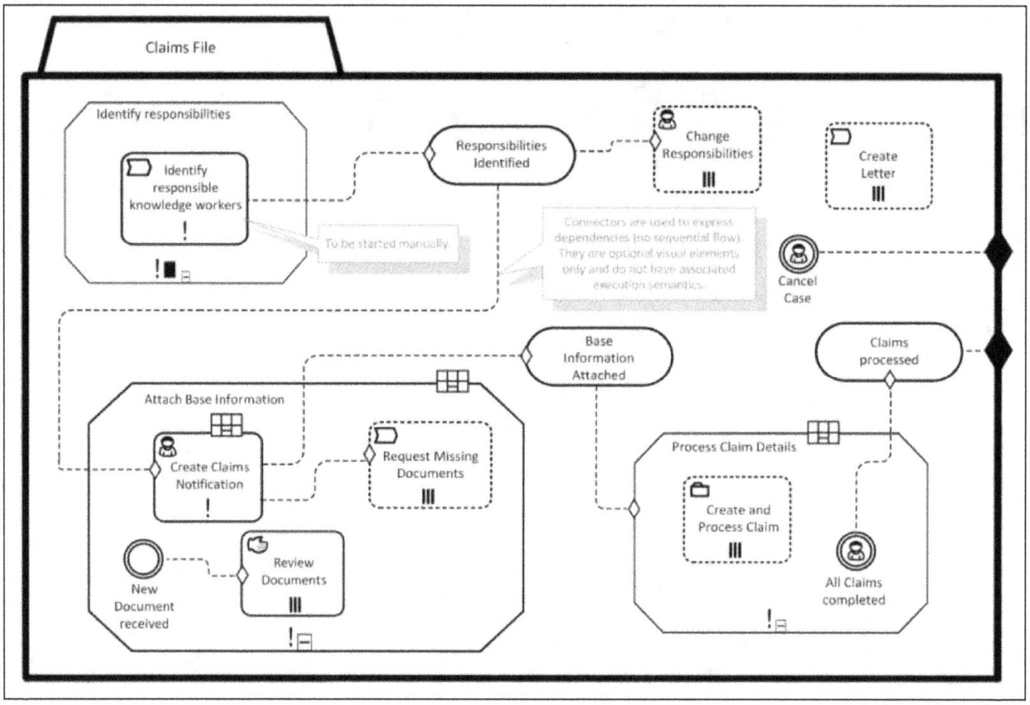

Figure 15: CMMN model of the Claims File case

So, in the next figure, we see a CMMN diagram of our Claims File case. It is again grouped into three stages, which are top-level elements in CMMN. This gives us a very good feeling about the structure of the case. But CMMN provides a more detailed level. We see that the activities are typed, for example, as process activities (calling a BPMN process), as human tasks (realized, for example, with Human Workflow), or as case activities (calling another case). Another level of detail is expressed via the used decorators. The black rectangle means autocompletion of the stage level. So, the first stage named **Identify responsibilities** is completed when all inner components have been completed. The exclamation mark means that this activity is required to be executed before the parent component is allowed to close. The three vertical lines indicate repeatable activities. At this point, you may realize that Oracle was involved very deeply in the standardization process of CMMN because most of these elements find a 1:1 representation in the current JDeveloper. We will hopefully even get the stages concept in a future release and a full CMMN import feature.

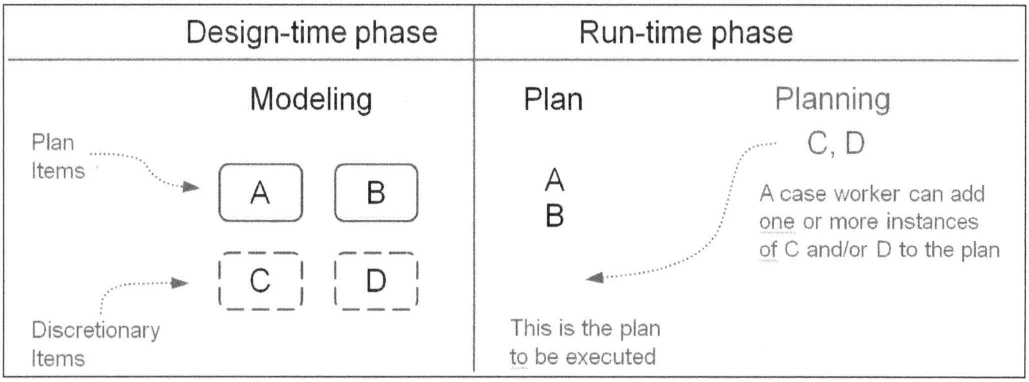

Figure 16: Discretionary items in CMMN

An important element in CMMN is the discretionary item. We had lots of discussions on how to interpret this construct. The preceding figure does a good job of explaining the use case. Looking at the design-time phase, someone will model all the activities they knows of. Activities **A** and **B** are plan items, while **C** and **D** are discretionary items. You notice them by the dotted lines instead of the non-dotted lines around the classic activities. The explanation of this is understandable when looking at the runtime phase. There, activities A and B are "in the plan", meaning these activities are rendered as actions that can be activated in the UI (if the context applies). The discretionary items **C** and **D** are not shown in the default plan. However, the knowledge worker can decide to drag these two in the working plan, if necessary, in his context. You see in the next figure how this looks in the generic case UI that Oracle provides.

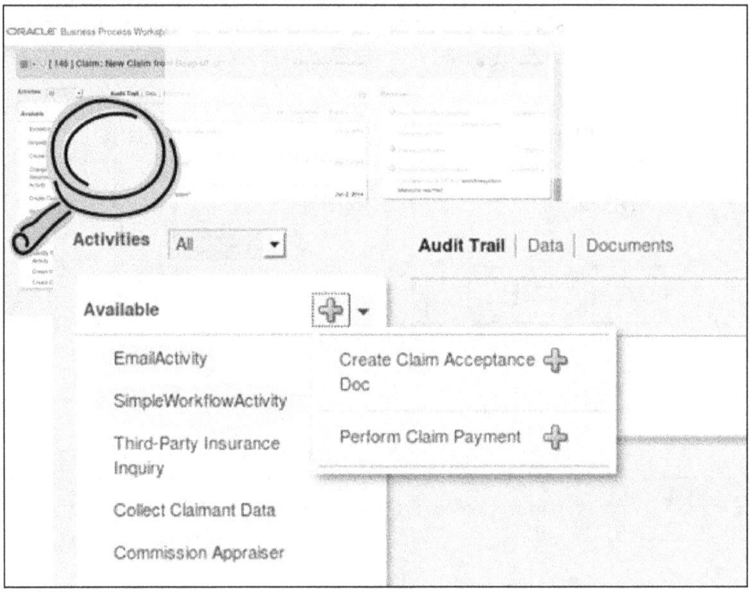

Figure 17: Adding discretionary items to the plan via the green plus

The idea behind this is having a UI that is clearest to the knowledge worker, which can filter away all the not-really-necessary working steps to make the people in front of the system more efficient.

Now that we have learned the basic concepts of CMMN, there is one question remaining: how to read this CMMN diagram? It's not as intuitive as it could be. Please look at the figure with the caption *CMMN model of the Claims File case* for better understanding. Let's look at all aspects in detail.

First, the whole Claims File case is activated via the generic case UI or some special kind of **Claims Management User Interface**. Then, the UI calls the API to get the actions that can be activated. The activities **Identify responsible knowledge workers** and **Create Letter** are displayed. The event listeners **New Document received** as well as **Cancel Case** are ready to catch incoming events. Note that the line drawn from the first milestone does not ending in a sentry at the second stage but ends on the first activity within the second stage. This activity has a sentry with a rule stating that the first milestone has to be completed before the activity gets activated. Otherwise, the first activity **Create Claims Notification** in stage 2 would be available in the UI, too.

The knowledge worker then manually starts the process task **Identify responsible knowledge workers** from the case UI. This will trigger an automated BPMN process to determine the responsible knowledge workers behind the scenes. After this activity is completed, the stage **Identify responsibilities** closes itself (note the AutoComplete decorator). The milestone **Responsibilities Identified** is completed because its sentry is evaluated to true (rule: the activity **Identify responsible knowledge workers** is completed). Now, the UI again asks for actions that can be activated. The human task **Change Responsibilities** (repeatable) and **Create Claims Notification** are now available and can be started.

Then, the knowledge worker starts the human task **Create Claims Notification**. This results in the milestone **Attach Base Information** being completed because its sentry is evaluated to true (rule: activity **Create Claims Notification** is completed) and the human task **Request Missing Documents** becomes available in the case UI. The **New Document Received** event can still be received (note that the stage **Attach Base Information** has no AutoComplete decorator and no exit criterion). The stage **Process Claim Details** becomes active because its sentry is evaluated to true. In the UI, the case task **Create and Process Claim** (repeatable) becomes available and can be started by the knowledge worker multiple times to trigger other (detail) cases.

After receiving the user event **All Claims completed**, the milestone **Claims processed** is completed because its sentry is evaluated to true (rule: event received). Then, the goal of the case is reached and the case instance and its stages are closed.

As illustrated, CMMN expresses a lot of details that makes the diagrams quite hard to read. On the other hand, having a CMMN diagram like this makes life for the ACM developer very easy because he needs all the detailed information anyway.

Building your own case UI on top of the Case API

We won't go much into detail here because there are a lot of good blog entries out there describing how to build your own user interface on top of Oracle Human Task Engine and already some describing the same activity for ACM.

The first things to keep in mind when you start your own ACM-UI project are the API Java documents that can be found in BPM Suite documentation and, of course, as a sample in the generic Oracle user interface based on this ACM API.

You can choose whatever UI technology fits your requirements best. The most native way in an Oracle technology stack would be to use ADF and maybe WebCenter Portal as the surrounding web framework. But, you are not limited to that. For example, for one project, we wrapped the Oracle API behind a REST service layer, and then we built a HTML5 user interface using AngularJS against our new API. We did that mainly to demonstrate what's possible on that side of the technology stack. You can see the wireframe for this UI in the following figure. When building this UI, we made the experience one important point to explain to the developers who are new to this area: they first thought that they would have to read, for example, the activities that can be activated and then manage them on their own in the UI. Apparently, that's conceptually a completely wrong way of thinking. ACM user interfaces typically have to be quite "stupid".

To display the activity history in the following figure, there must not be any management of called activities in the UI layer. The UI (well, the controller) just has to call an ACM API method that reads all activities visible to the user in the security context and set a filter to read only "completed" activities. That's all. This is also true for the window displaying the activities that can currently be activated. Again, no management of this kind of information must be found in the UI layer. It's just a call against the same API method using different filter criteria.

To activate an activity that can be activated, you click on it, render the necessary form to read the related input data as described in the ACM model, and again call the "activate" API method. After that, the UI has to refresh itself and ask the server again whether something that should be displayed has changed. That's what we mean by having a "stupid" UI. It has to ask the server via the ACM API for nearly everything that's of interest.

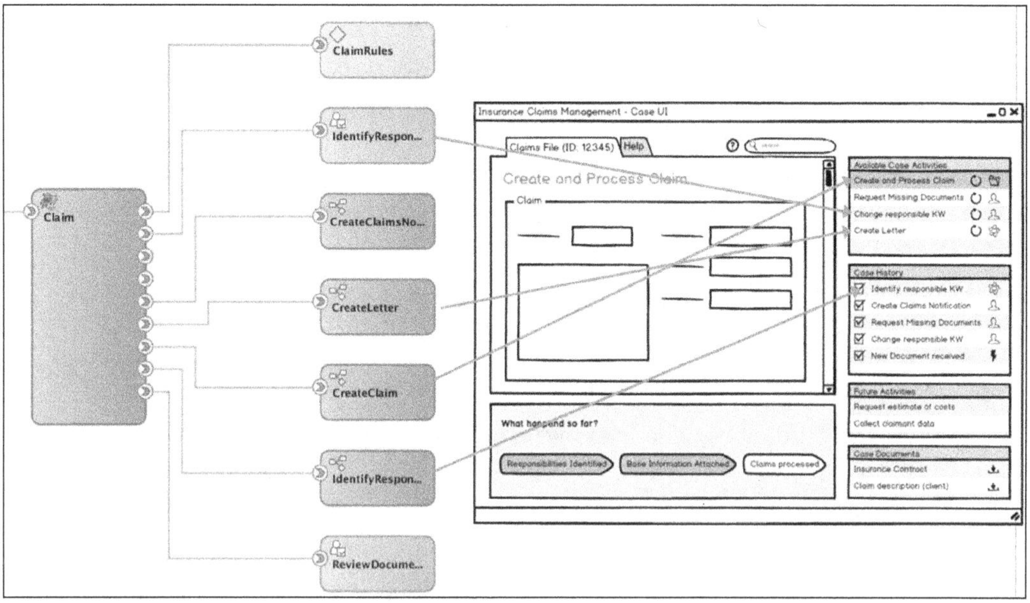

Figure 18: Relation of backend case concepts and their activation via UI

In this figure, we can also nicely see how the concept of a case in SCA maps to a user interface. As mentioned earlier, activities can be one of three types: BPMN processes, human tasks, and custom built with Java. All of these activities are displayed in the composite editor in JDeveloper, linked to the case itself with wires. We also see the **ClaimRules** component, which carries all rules to control which activities can be activated and in what state. So, it becomes very clear that the UI simply has to render these activities so that they can be "started" by the user. If it is an underlying BPMN process, this process gets started and may manipulate data that the UI could display. If it's a human task, a user or group will find a task in their task list. That's very simple from the ACM user interface point of view.

Of course, things will get a bit more complicated when you start building UIs that don't look so "casy". By that adjective, we mean UIs that look much like our wireframe or the generic Oracle ACM UI.

Sample – ACM at RYLC

For our concrete scenario in RYLC, we have built the following use case. RYLC has a department that is selling insurances to everyone who rents an RYLC car. This department uses a very, very old claim-handling tool with lots of business logic in the service layer. The UIs are very old, but it would be much too expensive to rewrite this tooling (several million dollars). Additionally, there are a lot of other small tools involved in the claim regulation process.

RYLC has identified the following problem areas:

- Limited traceability and missing reporting on the status of the hardcoded processes in the tool—generally regarding systems and case related
- Missing guidance of the users while working on claim regulation, especially over system boundaries
- Expert knowledge stays in the dark
- Process automation with normative process models is hard because of the high number of different claim types and their specialties in regulation
- Missing flexibility for mass claims (for hail damage during thunderstorm) when simplified processes have to be in place
- Exception handling is only possible by generating tasks and followups for the unified RYLC Worklist application
- Too many complex integration interfaces from the regulation tool to the other system landscape

Media discontinuity and island solutions (local Excel or databases), for example, sending pictures of an accident by e-mail or fax, connection of third-party garages, and so on

- Necessity to jump out of a normative process and involve a specialist for suspicion of fraud, mass claims, and substitute (illness, holidays, and so on)

RYLC discussed these problems with the IT department and found that a case management solution would address most of their problems in the long run. They agreed to deliver the following benefits:

- Strong benefit to the claim handling department
- Improved data quality and better base data
- Traceability of claim files over system boundaries
- Statistical analysis, for example, to develop new business models
- Optimized quality of decisions in the claim handling process
- Identification of potential for process automation (repeating activities)
- Integrated new systems, for example, making use of the portal (customer self-service)
- Faster integration of new employees
- Better customer satisfaction through faster support when substitutes have to jump in (illness, vacation, and so on)

Having identified all this, RYLC gave the order to build a case management system to address their needs. You can see artifacts of this building decision throughout this chapter. For example, in the *Modeling a case* section, you get a feeling of how the requirement phase started.

Based on the data we gathered in the requirements phase, we started building the pilot implementation with the building blocks and UI described until now.

Our main architectural idea behind this was the following. We didn't want to change the code base of the existing claim-handling application, but we wanted to provide a new and additional UI for knowledge workers. So, we injected event-generating code into the old system. That was very easy because it already had a very good architectural rework. There was a clear service layer that now additionally sends relevant events. These events are flowing through the system and can be handled on the ACM side.

In our first release, we built a completely passive ACM UI. We just caught all events from the outer systems, handled them in ACM, and got a nice case view as we would with a case dashboard. This fulfilled the requirement of transparency. In the next phases, we address the guiding requirements by making the new ACM view more and more active over time. Currently, when executing an activity on the ACM side, we send the user in the correct system to perform the task. Later on, maybe we will have all tasks completely implemented on the ACM side.

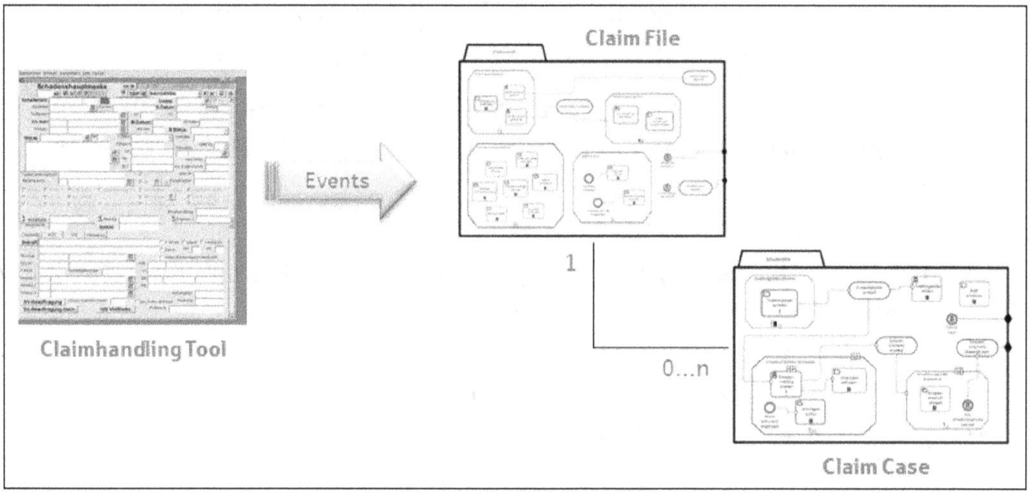

Figure 19: Connection of the old claim-handling tool with the new ACM world

Best practices

Even though case management is quite new to the Oracle BPM stack, we already found some patterns that we consider could be valuable as best practices. Here you will find a list of these things.

Using custom activities for fast prototyping

When starting an ACM project, it is useful to deliver a working user interface to the customer as fast as possible. The user interface may not be the most important component in an ACM architecture, but it is typically the most important component for the stakeholders you build the whole system for.

Our advice is to do some rapid prototyping, perhaps using lean concepts, such as delivering early and the minimum viable product. Therefore, you need a fast way to implement higher amounts of activities with minimal overhead. Adding a whole and empty BPMN process or configuring a whole human task for each activity is not the best option in this early phase of the project.

Using one simple Java class that implements the interface, marking it as a custom ACM activity, is much more beneficial here. You just add these custom activities via the *new* wizard, choose the same Java class for all, and then make your individual activity configurations. This will save a lot of time during rapid prototyping.

Using data in cases

A lot of simple samples demonstrate the use of process data in BPMN processes. This can already be seen in ACM samples. Well, this works very well. The BPM engine takes care of all the data and assures that it is persistent when process or case instances are dehydrated to the database. That happens, for example, when they do an asynchronous service call and then go to sleep until the engine wakes them up again with the answer they are expecting. So, what is the problem then?

We see two sorts of trouble that you might get into:

1. Your case (or process) has read some data from a database and falls asleep for a longer time. How can you know that the data inside the process or case instance is still valid when woken up after a longer timeframe? Typically, you can't rely on the old data, so we strongly advise you to only carry such data in an instance that is the only related instance. In general, don't carry any data in an instance at all. Read it all when you need it, and remember that the engine might send your instances to sleep longer than you expect.

2. You have some compliance restrictions in your environment. For example, you have to save all relevant data for the timeframe of 10 years. Do you think this is easy? Yes, the engine is taking care of that. Just back up your dehydration store for longer than 10 years and you are fine. Wait, do you have a bad feeling about that? We do too... 10 years is a long timeframe for software products. In that time, you will have to do several updates to your dehydration store. Of course, normally, this will work seamlessly. But, there is another drawback; when the dehydration store gets too full, Enterprise Manager becomes very slow and APIs start answering at much lower speeds. That's why purging the dehydration store is a very important topic for the team running your infrastructure. When you purge, of course you delete a lot of data (that's the goal of purging). So, make sure that you never purge the wrong data—the one that carries your business information that's relevant to compliance. Otherwise, you will externalize your case data completely to a business database carrying only "your" relevant data. That's what we strongly advise for process and ACM projects.

Cases and subcases

As we described earlier, we found several situations where we want to have master-detail relationships between cases. The question is about how to link cases together. Oracle provides a linking feature, but that's more a businesslike feature. For example, if a knowledge worker recognizes that a claim case is related to the claim of a third person, then he could mark the cases as related. That's fine but not the concept we are referring to here. We are talking about real master-detail relationships.

To provide a solution, you can easily use the execution context of the case components to store linking information and then provide a custom API method that reads, for example, all child cases for a given parent case. This has proven to be very efficient in our current projects.

Use the identification key property to map business identifiers to a case to distinguish the master from related details cases. It's much faster searching via the case header than querying other concepts.

Bringing order into different rulesets

The flexibility of ACM brings with it a higher degree of complexity on the rule side. To get a maintainable structure, we advise that you order all rules in decision tables:

Put everything that sets a milestone to the "reached" state into the `Milestone_Reached_Decisions` decision table. Put every rule that leads to the activation of other activities into the `Activity_Activation_Decision` decision table. And, put all reactions on user events into the `User_Defined_Event_Decisions` decision table. Perform the same operation with reactions on data changes and other things that come to your mind. The following screenshot shows this:

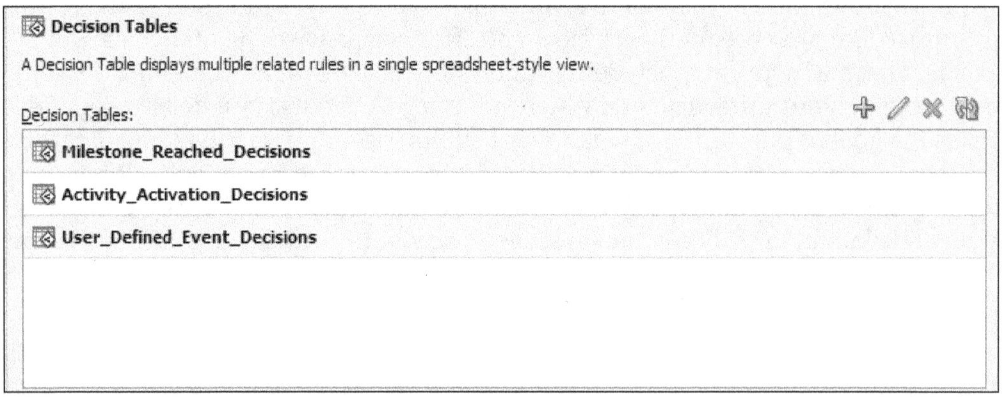

Figure 20: Decision tables for the different artifacts

Working around the missing stages concept

We introduced the fact that CMMN introduced a stage concept that is currently not reflected in JDeveloper. We hope to get full CMMN support soon. Until that happens, we propose to use even more decision tables to separate the rules by virtual stages.

Using ACM in BPMN or better BPMN in ACM?

Obviously, the main concept of ACM is that BPMN can be used to implement activities. That both ACM and BPMN can be handled by the same core is a very big advantage of Oracle BPM Suite.

However, we often hear the question whether the opposite can be true, too. Would it be an option to have processes realized in BPMN that need some flexible case handling in the middle? Yes, perhaps that could happen. However, we advise you to start with the case concept from the beginning because that's the more natural way of doing things. We advise you not to force people to work on activities (in BPMN) but to stimulate them using the most useful activities in the current context with ACM. That becomes especially true for specific kinds of people; for example, think of a judge who is supported by an ACM system. They would never accept a rigid workflow system to tell them exactly what to do and when.

Engaging a UX designer in your ACM project

ACM, technically speaking, only matters to IT. All the things that deliver the great value of ACM work under the hood. Only the developers get to see these details. It's a bit similar to the famous German Nomos watches produced by hand in Glasshütte. In their manual, you can read about the beauty of the inner life of these watches, closing with the comment: "What a pity that only the watchmaker will have the chance to see this beauty in the very rare cases when the watch has to be maintained." This applies to ACM as well.

The business only sees the UIs sitting on top of the ACM engine and can feel the high flexibility of ACM because the UIs are behaving so well. Therefore, ACM UIs simply have to be perfect, not "casy". Please use a UI designer for this.

Granularity of activities

A common question is what granularity of activities should be used. We advise you to use activities that are too big rather than too small. You won't build a wizard-like feeling driven by the case. Such things have to be done within a single activity. Use human tasks or rigid processes as activity implementations where no flexibility is necessary for the knowledge worker.

Summary

ACM complements BPM by adding adaptive case handling concepts to the rigid world of fully automated processes. It's not ACM instead of BPM; you need them both. And, you need to apply each discipline where appropriate. So, please add ACM as a new tool to your architect's toolbox.

The area of ACM starts when things get too complicated with classic BPMN: when you have more exceptions or more variants then you feel it would make sense to model, you should think about using the ACM concepts.

To make our businesses more effective in our always accelerating world, we have to build much better IT support for our most valuable people—the knowledge workers. We have to give them a perfect work environment that enables them to make better decisions (be more informed), concentrate on core business, and deliver more BPM value to the business.

Processes today must not only support automatable routine work. Nonroutine work has to be supported, too. What's important here is that we don't talk about naïve pure atomization of everything; we talk about a coexistence of humans and machines and let them both do the things they can do best.

This chapter has many key takeaways. ACM can help to uncover the dark processes that are hidden in the heads of people and to make the work more transparent to not-so-skilled coworkers. BPMN reaches its limit when a proven best practice is built into a process in BPMN and then the best practice changes. So, don't only put single best practices in processes, but allow the unpredictable. Build for change. In ACM, simply a few rules have to be adjusted or removed when the best practice guiding mechanism changes. In general, ACM brings a lot of support for dealing with events. This allows us to change from sequential flows with BPMN to event-driven interaction, where more flexibility is needed. ACM is about empowering the people. People get back the importance they always should have had. Don't imprison the knowledge worker in rigid processes. Watch out if people aren't allowed to make decisions on their own.

In the next chapter, we will look into the new mobile capabilities that smartphones and tablets are introducing to the BPM world.

10
Mobile and Multichannel

In this chapter, we will highlight how BPM can benefit from the large mobile and multichannel wave, which we are still experiencing. Some of the topics we will cover are the following:

- Development of mobile solutions
- Cross-platform technology
- Mobile solutions and SOA
- Mobile solutions and BPM
- Oracle Mobile Tooling for mobile application development

The rise of mobile devices is changing our IT world from the ground up. A shift is in progress and is still accelerating. Smartphones and tablets make us smarter, and they are becoming more and more powerful. The speed of innovation is tremendous. It's a question of survival to have answers to all the questions that this development brings to our IT landscape—we have to embrace the mobile channel in today's economy to leverage possible new business benefits and to cope with the quick change of traditional business models.

There is real business value behind new mobile capabilities. It's not as if just because they are nicer and easier to use than the "old style" notebooks or PCs, people start consuming things from wherever they are at the specific moment. As an enterprise, you will have to have very good and highly usable offerings for all kind of mobile devices, for example, to buy tickets for events, cinema, theater, buses, trains, and flights, and to buy books, films, clothes, shoes, and consumer goods of every kind. We are entering the century of "data". The more you know about your customers, the more you can run analytics for the past and to predict the future; this way, your company will perform better.

Smartphones and tablets are only the beginning of this wave. Wearables such as watches, glasses, and others, will again offer new and astonishing possibilities. Technology will come close and closer to the human body. From a backend IT perspective, these simply are—again—new kinds of channels to access our data.

The Internet of Things (IoT), where billions of devices are connected to the Internet and sending data to the backend IT, is not the future: it's already here.

Development of mobile solutions

It's obvious that our way of thinking is changing with the upcoming of mobile devices. But even more interestingly, the classical development of web application is also changing. For several years now, there has been no real innovation in how to implement web applications. We saw JSPs, then JSF, and then several AJAX-enhanced solutions. But now, with the HMTL5 movement, new development is grabbing new ideas, and developers apply the HTML5 way of thinking everywhere—making our software a bit more consistent.

Currently, we see a strong increase in customer plans to additionally address mobile channels. We will expect the mobile requirement to be a default one for every piece of software we develop— and that time is not far away. Passionate evangelists are shouting loud that for several use cases, a "mobile first" strategy would be even better.

Therefore, it's indispensable that we build knowledge on architectural and technical problems that arise while coping with the mobile challenge.

The challenges of mobile development

Developing mobile solutions is not simply developing applications for smaller screens. You have to cope with new challenges.

The biggest problem for sure is device diversity. Tons of different types of devices, vendors, operating systems, versions of operating systems, screen sizes, and so on are a real pain for developers who have to build good solutions.

What can we do to narrow down the development effort? To answer the question as to which platform currently is hyped and should be definitely addressed, you always find some statistics of relevant analysts. But these statistics differ from each other widely, and you always find the right statistics to prove what you want to prove. From the beginning of 2012, typically iOS and Android are listed as mainstream platforms. If it's possible to narrow down the decision to only two platforms, life becomes easier again. Then, you only have to cope with native development for these two platforms and address the different form factors and screen sizes. This seems to be acceptable from an investment perspective. In these days, perhaps Microsoft must be added as a rising player in the mobile market.

Unreliable connections are still a big problem. You can't assume that a mobile device has network all the time and that your user will interact with it. Therefore, you have to design your software for worst case scenarios. Typically, you will have to use device databases to store everything necessary and sync with your backend service when it's available again. Oracle has good support in this area with the Oracle Database Mobile Server product. With that, you can use a local database on the mobile device and set up sync mechanisms with several rules on overwriting and error correction for syncing with the enterprise database in the backend.

Scalability is an interesting topic, too. There will be situations where you can't predict the number of people who like to use your mobile software, resulting in high-load scenarios for your backend. Therefore, you have to make sure that your architecture is scalable enough to deal with an increasing number of users. If you only expect peak load scenarios, perhaps a cloud infrastructure would be the best way to scale fast and with low cost.

Security is an important discipline for all software that handles data. You can do the obvious things, such as using SSL connections between mobile clients and your backend IT. On notebooks, you typically encrypt the hard disk to prevent a lost or stolen device. You can't rely on the encryption mechanisms mobile devices provide today because the built-in algorithms can be hacked quite easily when somebody gets physical access to the device. And typically, the smaller the device is, the easier you lose it, which means a special kind of threat for your security officer. A common solution is to encrypt all the data on the application level to make sure that only encrypted stuff is saved in local cache mechanisms or local databases.

We already talked about the difficulties to program great applications for all the (unknown) different screen sizes out there. Today, we use strategies such as progressive enhancement, which are supported by a variety of mobile development frameworks. The idea is that an application detects it's possible screen size to be used and then "enables" richer functionality with the more screen space it finds. So, it's not like stripping down a big and rich desktop web application to a smaller screen but the other way around: you start simple and enrich when possible.

This directly leads to a discussion as to how to render forms for data input on a mobile device. Just providing the same fields that your rich desktop application offers is a bad idea in most cases. Navigating to all the form fields is as much a nightmare as the mini keyboard you have to use. So, taking this problem into account, use cases have to be designed for smaller screens. You have to use special widgets, such as date pickers and variants of combo boxes that your mobile OS provides, to simplify input of data. And, you have to make sure that you're doing your best to prefill as much of the fields as possible with data you already have. This data can come from linked data from the back end or from the sensors of the specific device. You can prefill the current date, time, address (via GPS location), or a context by looking into the calendar of the device and finding a scheduled meeting (as Evernote does).

Every mobile device has its own philosophy of user experience. For example, on iOS, you have the back button in the navigation bar at the top of the screen. Most Android devices have the back button at the bottom of the screen. Different gestures are used throughout the different operation systems that users get used to. For example, a user of iOS expects that clicking on an e-mail opens the text of the e-mail and a swipe fish to the right-hand side brings you back to the overview screen. Good practice in mobile applications is to adhere to these user experience specialties, which is another example of why rich desktop applications can't be migrated 1:1 to the mobile world—adjustments are necessary.

The renaissance of JavaScript

JavaScript is currently enjoying a renaissance. JavaScript used to be looked down upon because it was used mainly to "pretty up" websites and was not seen as a "real" language for professional application development. However, this trend has changed due to the enormous speed at which HTML5 has expanded. JavaScript is well on its way to becoming the language for application development and interface programming. Indeed, it can be said that JavaScript has the same significance for web development as Java for enterprise computing in the backend. For a programming language that is now 15 years old, JavaScript has many modern characteristics and is still evolving, for example, with ECMAScript 6 (see also the newest release of AngularJS). There are more and more tools that hide the actual JavaScript code from the developer, such as, for example, Google Web Toolkit, CoffeeScript, ClojureScript, or language approaches, such as Google Dart. However, sound knowledge of the basic principles is becoming more and more essential.

HTML5 – cross-platform technology

If you have the need to support a broader set of mobile devices, you wish for a cross-platform technology. The dream is developing an app only once and deploying and running it with or without minimal changes everywhere on every device. Does this sound familiar? Well, Java once lined up to address this "write once, run everywhere" philosophy. Unfortunately, we have to deal with the big players, and Microsoft and Apple have no suitable possibility of using Java within their platforms. So, we still have the browser. And really, in the meantime, HTML5 technology is omnipresent and tries to fulfill the cross-platform promise. Control remains with the central application, there is no need to download or update software on the end device, and, perhaps most importantly, apps continue to be developed in the same way as before. We are dealing here (in some key aspects) with the same "good old web development"—only for smaller screens.

A lot of people state that you can't distinguish mobile web apps built in HTML5 from native implementations, for example, on iOS or Android. And really, you have covered a long part of the way. HTML5 apps can look nearly like their native pendants. But they never get 100 percent down the pathway: native apps are always the last 5 percent cooler/prettier than their pendants in HTML5, which have to run in the browser and, therefore, have to simulate a lot of behavior. If the success of an app depends on achieving a high rank in an app store, winning against several similar approaches (mostly in B2C scenarios), and if it has to be downloaded as often as possible, then not choosing the native way of implementation might be a showstopper.

But for a lot of use cases, HTML5 apps are simply good enough. Then, you get the benefit of the cross-platform technology, for example, when there is no competing app or when 95 percent of the native look and feel is sufficient, which is typically more in B2B than in B2C environments. Here, the cross-platform idea wins so that you can cover a broad set of different devices with only one code base.

Today, most frameworks aren't good enough to really make a single code base run on every device. At least you can write your mobile-side business logic code in JavaScript and reuse this code on all the devices that you need to support. But for this approach, you still have to build your applications for every platform you are targeting. It depends on your requirements for the user experience.

HTML5 allows the use of several interesting features that were inaccessible to browsers in former times. For example, you find a simple API to interact with the device sensors for geolocation (you have to enable this for most scenarios before an app really is allowed to use this feature). A second great feature is the offline storage, to which HTML5 provides an interface. You don't have to install a database with your app for simple use cases but just use the built-in mechanisms HTML5 delivers. This makes customization and offline storage (when you have no network) much easier.

Updates of your apps

Another big advantage of the HMTL5 approach lies in the possibility of fast updates for your apps. The code always gets loaded from the server (if you don't want to cache something), which means that the current code always gets executed. After a code change, for example, a bug fix or the introduction of a new functionality, you simply deploy to your backend servers. In a native scenario, you would have to submit your changes to the appropriate app stores, where you have longer update cycles and maybe even new approval processes. This means a slightly higher risk in B2B scenarios, where critical updates have to rely on third parties. Of course, you can address this with private app stores under your own control.

Also, some hybrid options are thinkable. Native apps can download dynamic content and show it in dynamic app areas. This is very common today, when fast updates and the best possible user experience are needed.

Single-page web apps

What will change radically is the actual architecture of web apps. There is a general move away from the usual pattern of classic web applications, which are typified by the way in which page navigation is generally implemented using an MVC pattern that locates PageflowController on the server. Interaction with a website triggers a request that is sent to the web server, as shown in the following image:

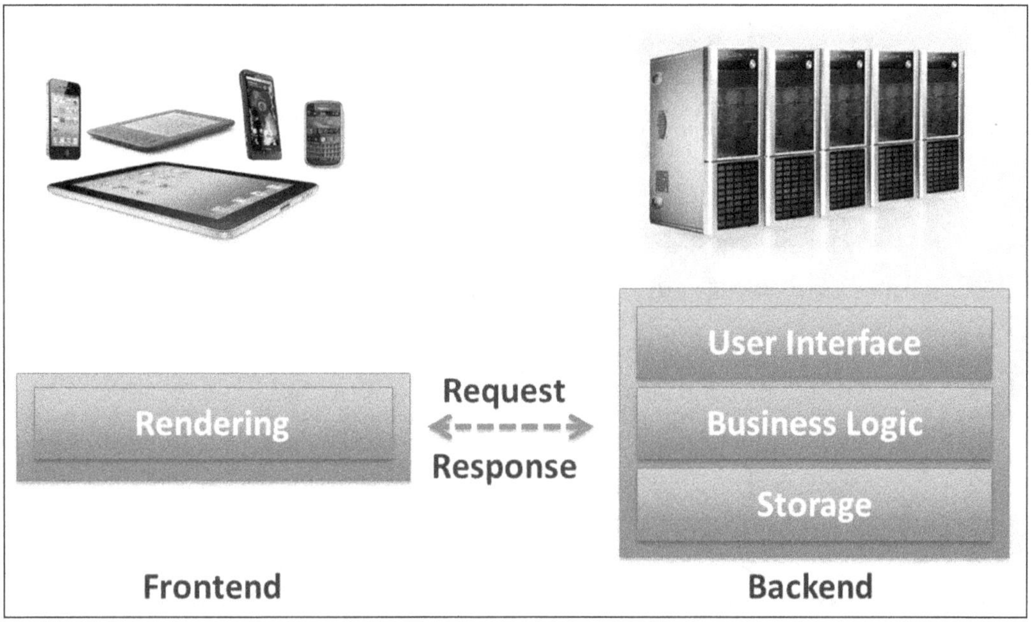

Figure 1

Here, PageflowController determines what page to display next and the server returns this page as a response to the browser. By contrast, with web apps, the client is more intelligent. Generally, the location of PageflowController is shifted to the client, usually realized in JavaScript. Here, it is usual to speak of single-page web apps:

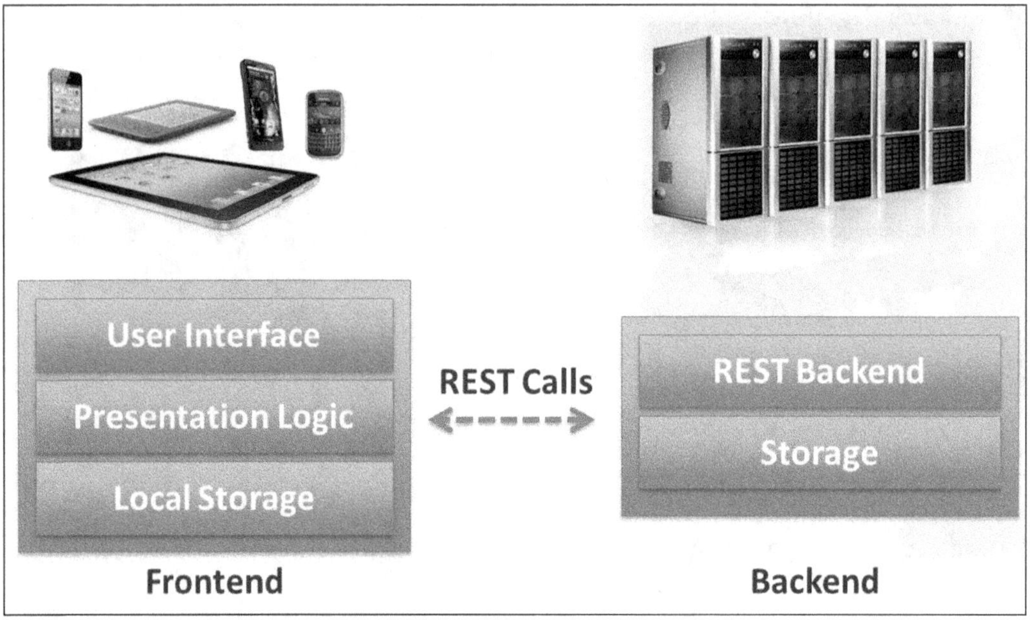

Figure 2

The name originates from the fact that when an HTML page is loaded, the entire web app is loaded at the same time, that is, a single HTML page, of which only a part is displayed. If a different page is to be displayed, PageflowController only shows a different part of the page already loaded on the client side. This eliminates the request response cycle to the server and back, which makes these kinds of applications react much faster than classical ones. This request/response cycle only occurs when services that are contacted through SOAP or REST are accessed in order to communicate with a backend. Later, we will see why putting an enterprise service bus (ESB) here is a good idea.

In concluding, single-page web applications behave and feel more like real client applications in the sense of client/server programming than like web applications in the sense of server-generated websites. Mobile web applications that are developed in this way integrate perfectly well into architectures where the backend gets exposed as REST services. JavaScript Object Notation (JSON) is used to communicate data. Another advantage is the potential offline capability and the option to wrap these kinds of applications into hybrid apps. Even classical, rich desktop applications will benefit from this new architecture pattern.

Hybrid apps

When we decide how to implement a mobile application, we realize that there is another animal on this planet. It's the hybrid species that combines some of the advantages of native apps with the advantages of HTML5 development. This is the way Oracle has chosen for Mobile Application Framework, formerly known as ADF Mobile. In a nutshell: you wrap your HMTL5 application into a container, and this container provides JavaScript APIs for the native features of a device to make them accessible in a standardized way. For example, you use only one and the same JavaScript call to get the GPS coordinates from the GPS sensor. The container knows which device you are running and calls either the iOS-specific native API or the native API of whatever device you use (if it's supported). This container typically is realized with Apache Cordova.

This is from the Apache website:

> *"Apache Cordova is a set of device APIs that allow a mobile app developer to access native device function such as the camera or accelerometer from JavaScript. Combined with a UI framework such as jQuery Mobile or Dojo Mobile or Sencha Touch or ADF Mobile, this allows a smartphone app to be developed with just HTML, CSS, and JavaScript."*

When using Cordova APIs, an app can be built without any native code (Java, Objective-C, and so on) from the app developer. Instead, web technologies are used, and they are hosted in the app itself locally (generally not on a remote HTTP server). Because these JavaScript APIs are consistent across multiple device platforms and built on web standards, the app should be portable to other device platforms with minimal or no changes.

Apps using Cordova are still packaged as apps using the platform SDKs and can be made available for installation from each device's app store.

Cordova provides a set of uniform JavaScript libraries that can be invoked with device-specific native backing code for those JavaScript libraries. Cordova is available for the following platforms: iOS, Android, Blackberry, Windows Phone, Palm WebOS, Bada, and Symbian.

Perhaps another name you have heard is PhoneGap. PhoneGap was created around 2009 by a start-up called Nitobi. In 2011, Adobe purchased Nitobi and with it, the rights to the PhoneGap brand. The open source core was donated to the Apache Software Foundation under the name Cordova. At first, the differences between Cordova and PhoneGap were minimal. But Adobe always had plans to build out a proprietary set of services around the PhoneGap ecosystem and has started to execute that plan with PhoneGap Build. So, when you start a new hybrid app project, you can either decide to use Cordova proper or enter Adobe's ecosystem and use the PhoneGap distribution of Cordova.

The bottom line is that hybrid apps allow us to build "real" apps for app stores and simplify access to device-specific sensors.

The shift in web development

With all the things we discussed until now, it is crystal clear that the "Web" is evolving very fast. Let's summarize this:

- **Documents to applications**: The classical approach was to send a browser request to a server, which delivered a HTML document. Now, we think more and more in terms of applications running in a browser and interacting with a backend.
- **Declarative HTML to programmatic DOM**: When we needed dynamic features in the past, we had to use HTML tags to express what we needed within declarative HTML documents. Today, we use DOM and manipulate it before a page is displayed. Many frameworks do several runs on the DOM tree to manipulate elements, for example, for progressive enhancement features.
- **Templates to APIs**: In the past, we needed templates and dynamically filled in the needed data. Today, we simply call APIs from the browser with AJAX calls against SOAP or more typically REST services.
- **Request/response to synchronization**: Classically, we had a client/server roundtrip for every page change on the client side. Today, we have the full MVC (Model-View-Controller) concept on the client side, so data in the application has to by synced with the backend (when the backend is available).
- **Thin client to thick client**: Our mobile clients are getting thicker again—we think of full-blown applications.

UX design

User experience design is something that is becoming more and more important. UI design is different for mobile as opposed to rich desktop portals. For example, we did a project to monitor the performance and incidents of radio extranet masts for a client. The desktop version was content rich, and a user would view this to see what incidents were approaching criticality. Map rendering was central to this and is where the user journey started. However, key users required access to the same functionality from their mobile device to be able to achieve the same task while on the move or out of hours. When designing and validating the user journey for mobile access, it was clear that although the task and the targeted outcome were the same, the way they reach that outcome should be different on the mobile device. Originally, the entry point should have been the map on the mobile device similar to the portal, but when the user journey was wireframed and reviewed, it became clear that the tasks on the move would be much better served with a tabular entry point that gave very quick access to the key information but would allow navigation to a targeted point of the map. The same services, same task, and same outcome, but a different journey, and hence, a different task flow for the light-touch interaction.

You can get an impression by examining this comparison between the rich desktop UI and the much smaller mobile UI here:

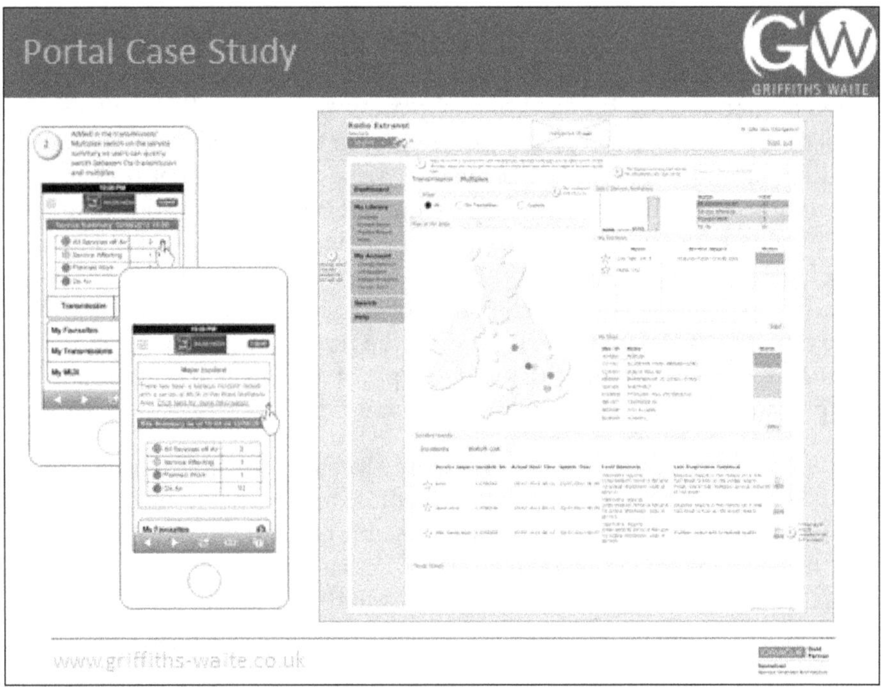

Figure 3

This gives only a small example of the need for good UX design when working on these kinds of applications. In BPM projects, typically about 80 percent of the time is used to build the applications based on the processes, and the user interface is the only thing that the user of our software will touch and feel. So, the most sophisticated processes will bring no benefit if the user experience bringing value to the end users is messed up.

Mobile solutions and SOA

Whether they are apps or mainly web-based, in enterprise contexts, mobile solutions almost always have to communicate with a backend. In simple terms, mobile frontends only offer a further output channel for applications that already exist anyway. Although true in principle, we see a lot of spaghetti architecture when mobile applications are built today, just as we saw 10–15 years ago before service-oriented design principles were understood.

All SOA principles that were built into our current system landscapes play out here now. You will be on the winning side when you can rely on basic principles that are implemented in your architecture, such as loose coupling, compositions, facades, and so on, so that service-oriented thinking in the backend comes fully into its own. New requirements can be implemented flexibly and quickly without major changes to the backend system.

Don't make the same mistake that we made so many years ago. Don't bring us into the hell of maintaining the "lots of cheap apps architecture". We all see lucky business people in several companies jumping onto the mobile train saying: "It's so easy to build a new app! I just bought three of these apps from a design agency. They look great and were so cheap!" Yes, they look great on first view and there's nothing wrong with being a lucky entrepreneur. But the price has to be paid afterwards. We have all learned lessons in the SOA days, where we saw how expensive the maintenance of systems gets when the principles of loose coupling are ignored, when one-to-one direct backend access is becoming the norm, and when applying changes to these kind of systems becomes risky and expensive. This hell of maintaining "lots of cheap apps architecture" must be absolutely avoided.

As described, sensibly applied SOA principles represent sensible countermeasures. It simply must not happen that a new "small" mobile app wants to directly access one of our backend databases. Sure, this would be a bit faster now, but we have to build an architecture for change so as to be able to react fast to changes that the future brings. So, the right answer to every new app is that it has to adhere to the unified mobile reference architecture:

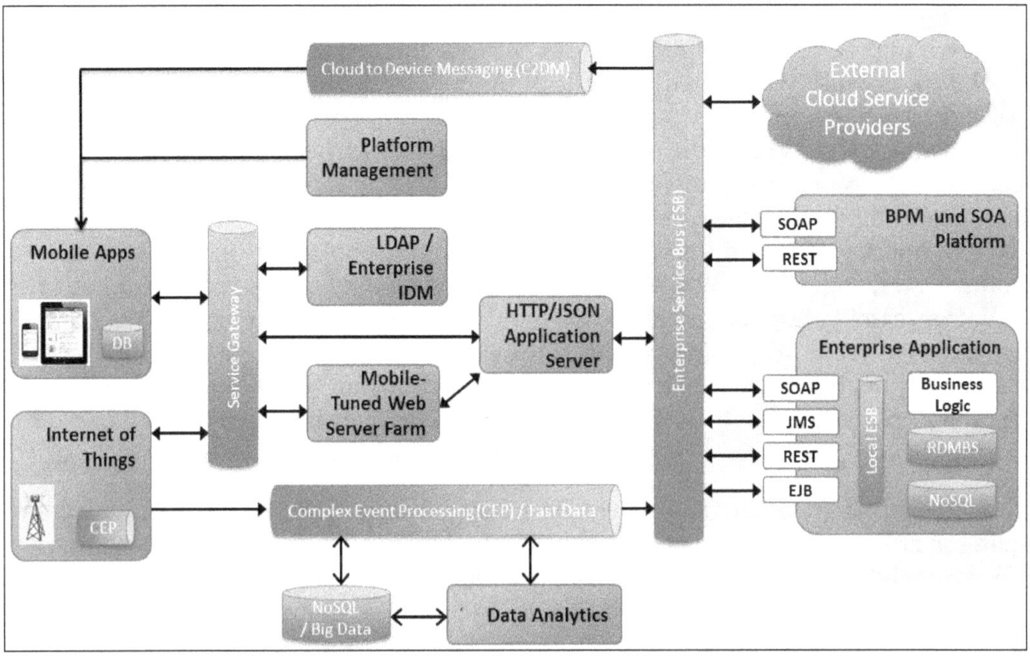

Figure 4

Of course, you see the introduction of an ESB (enterprise service bus). This ESB virtualizes all backend services, which gives you the flexibility to change the implementation or physical location of the services provided. It also allows the introduction of new service interfaces that are not backwards compatible by providing both service versions for a specific time. Additionally, we mentioned that mobile applications have an affinity for REST services. Again, the ESB helps here with its protocol transformation capabilities. For example, it can provide an additional REST interface for an existing SOAP- or JMS-based service. These are all topics that we want to address in the backend with the ESB to gain advantages from our service-oriented architecture (SOA).

But you can see more elements in the architecture and even more decoupling of the mobile app from the backend. The service or API gateway is responsible as a first line of defense against several possible threats, such as XML bombs, denial of service attacks, SQL injection, or brute-force hacking.

If you want to push messages to all your apps installed on devices out there, you need a cloud-to-device messaging component. Notifications have to be implemented and maintained on your own in a lot of scenarios. Of course, you will implement this component SOA-based.

The last interesting thing to note in the unified mobile reference architecture that is shown in the preceding figure is the new input channel capability of the Internet of Things. Because you have thousands or millions of devices sending data to your backend, these devices can't use standard service calls. This would be like a denial of service attack. Think of all the electric cars Tesla has sold. Each car sends data about battery and motor management to the Tesla backend. This is an enormous event stream. Or, think of all the cars our rental company has running—they all could send data to monitor, for example, the driving style of the people renting a car to make bonus advertisements to those who drive more carefully. For this massive amount of data streaming into our backend, we typically need new technology to deal with big data. An event processing engine can prefilter the event stream, detect patterns in the stream (such as accidents happened), and send this high-level business event to the standard backend to be handled there, for example, by calling a process in a BPM engine. Oracle provides an event-processing engine as part of SOA Suite.

The reference architecture could even be enhanced when you use business processes going over several software packages from vendors providing cloud solutions. If your mobile app integrates data from several cloud providers, it is even more obvious that it would be a very bad idea to do this integration within the app itself. Integration is a job for an ESB.

Another nice example for the real use of an ESB is the REST communication style that is favored by most mobile developers. Most of our services in our backends don't use REST today. We find a lot of SOAP services and also services exposed by EJBs or PL/SQL code directly in an Oracle database. Here, the ESB can be used as a protocol converter. You could, for example, use a database adapter in Oracle Service Bus to call your PL/SQL service in the database and use a proxy service on the bus that provides a REST interface. You even can autoexpose composite services as REST in the 12*c* version of Oracle Service Bus. This makes setting up the right kind of interfaces for the UI quite easy and fast without the need to rewrite unnecessary business logic in more than one location.

In the next screenshot, you get an impression of the basic functionality behind the following ideas:

- Easily expose any service or reference as REST
- Automated conversion from XML to JSON
- Map operations to existing services and bindings

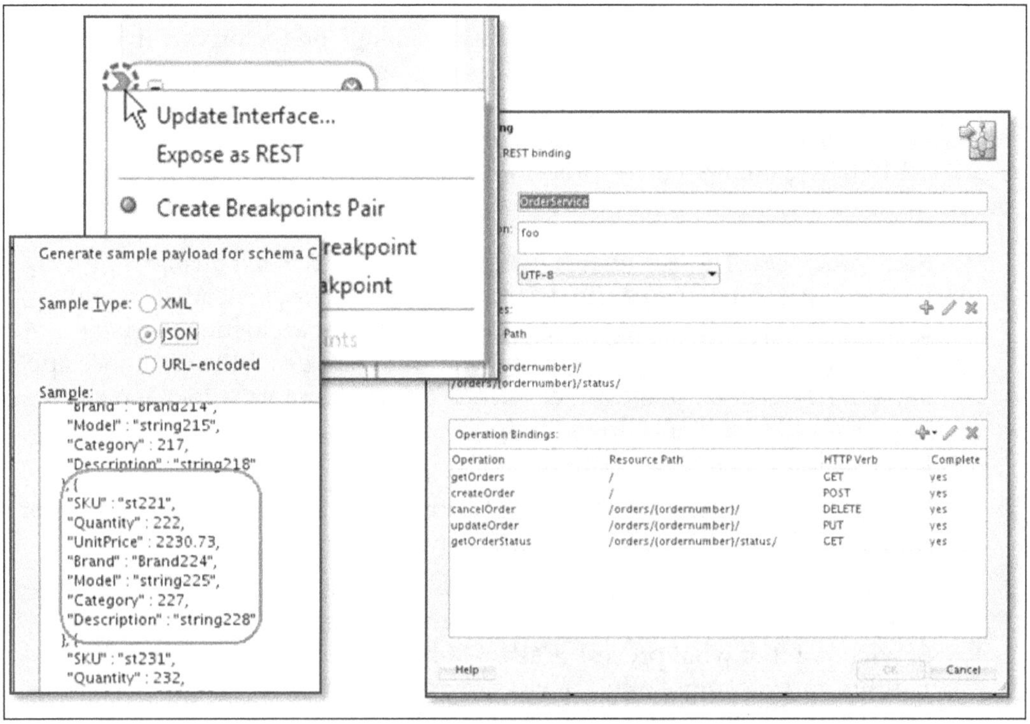

Figure 5

Mobile solutions and BPM

Mobile solutions are a major driving force behind process automation solutions. In this environment, there are no new technical options for mobile use. But a wide variety of options open up merely by enabling processes to receive input from people on the move, resulting in much faster throughput times. The advantages range from obviating the need to take notes on paper to simply being able to approve something while sitting through the coming attractions at a movie theater (this text does not discuss the influence of this technology on the private lives of these persons). The possibilities are very wide ranging, especially since the mobile devices' new sensors can be used—geolocation, card-based information, cameras, barcode scanners, or movement profiles, all of which improve process support. With regard to BPM, here understood as process automation, the following options arise concerning the use of mobile end devices:

- **Start processes**: There is no need to postpone the start of a business process until you get somewhere with desktop Internet access. Instead, it can take place on the spot. Remember the example of the car accident, where the claim process can be started right after the accident using the insurance app and taking a picture of the accident, including GPS information, and so on. This saves time and also provides opportunities for better data quality and accurate, up-to-date information.
- **Mobile task list**: Modern BPM systems involve people via e-mail inboxes or task lists. These can, of course, be made available on a mobile basis.
- **Mobile process images**: If an employee is frequently incorporated into more complex processes, it can be helpful to provide them with a clearer picture of what point or what process is affected by the decision they must take. For this purpose, mobile end devices can display process images, including visualization of the current status.
- **Alarms**: In emergency situations, systems that normally run independently require the attention of an expert. Here, alarms can be sent to mobile end devices that may already have preselected decision-relevant information, and that, therefore, permit rapid access to business, process, or system sequences.
- **Dashboards or mobile BI solutions**: The ability to access ongoing business on mobile end devices, in particular tablet computers, is becoming increasingly popular. In addition to the display of "normal" reports optimized for touch displays, use cases are, in particular, business-specific query options. For example, a store manager who scans an item on their shelf would immediately receive the price and brand development for this item in their own store, including a comparison with the prices throughout the store chain.

In all of these use cases, the aim at the highest level is to increase business efficiency by integrating the user into process flows earlier, more rapidly, or simply better.

However, there would be no point in coining the new term "mobile BPM" since there are no technical differences compared to other output channels to justify doing so. There are, however, a huge number of use cases that would benefit from a mobile implementation such that considering mobile solutions appears to make particular sense in the context of SOA and BPM. For BPM in particular, mobile use cases could become real drivers for development since smaller projects can supply a faster ROI on presumably expensive and complex central process engines.

Use cases

Sometimes, you just need examples to get inspired about how to leverage mobile devices, such as smartphones, tablets, and wearables, and to think about game-changing opportunities for your own business, for example, when combining these ideas with the capabilities BPM can deliver. Please find a nonprioritized listing here, categorized by possible fields of application:

- **Health**: There is the ability to connect new sensors, such as those for blood pressure, diabetes, and so on, to mobile end devices to be able to offer tricorder-like functionalities, with backend services
- **Smart home**: You have control over your own home as regards energy consumption, switching on energy-intensive consumers, remote control of heating, oven, lighting, alarm system, and so on
- **Transport**: You can view mobile train/bus schedules and buy tickets
- **Tourism**: There is access to onboard, cabin, and shopping systems on cruise ships; there is also support for tour guides
- **Logistics**: There is support for using barcode scanner and GPS information for specialist service providers
- **Inventory**: Elimination of paper and avoidance of media breaks lead to better data quality
- **Service level agreements**: Mobiles check whether goods are presented as agreed, whether there is compliance with features of relevant SLAs (cleanliness, punctuality, and so on), and whether there is compliance with contracts of any kind that are linked to the SLA
- **Sales and distribution**: There is access to sales material, catalogs, electronic forms, and so on often in visually attractive contexts
- **Warehouse**: There is immediate information on containers, pallets, boxes, packages, and so on

- **Facility management**: There are self-service applications that switch lights off outside of official office hours and report defective lamps, toilet flushes, and general damage to inventory; there are also information systems for climate and room control
- **E-government**: Public authority finders, mobile data entry for regulatory agencies, fault reporters (for example, dirt in public areas), mobile police stations, occupancy of parking spaces and parking garages, personalized vehicle license plates, garbage alarms for collection dates, and suspended bus services or school closures due to weather form part of e-governance; the objectives are addressing the target group appropriately, more efficient administration, crowdsourcing (citizen as the provider of input), and proximity to the citizen
- **Work planning**: Flexible update options obviate large volumes of quickly outdated documentation and rigid checklists
- **Marketing**: There is the use of augmented reality with supplementary real-time information for complex processes, for example, on advertising, which increases sales

Oracle Mobile Tooling

We are very happy to find interesting innovation in the Oracle Mobile development world. In the following sections, we will have a look at the most important offerings Oracle provides in the mobile space.

We feel that Oracle is positioned very well, putting together the SOA Suite, BPM Suite, Mobile Application Framework, Mobile Suite, Mobile Security Suite, and IoT strategies.

Oracle Mobile Application Framework

Oracle's **Mobile Application Framework** (**MAF**) is a commercial Java and HTML5-based environment for building and extending enterprise applications. Based on a hybrid mobile architecture, HTML5 provides common, cross-platform interfaces. Java is used to develop the application logic. Applications are installed on-device and offer access to native device services, such as camera, contacts, SMS, and GPS. This is done via Apache Cordova. Offline application use is supported with the added persistence and security of encryption in a SQLite database.

Leveraging Java and HTML5, the architecture's design enables developers to easily build and extend enterprise applications for iOS and Android platforms from a single code base. Developers do not need to learn a new platform-specific language. They can build mobile apps once and deploy them to multiple operating systems with support for various form factors, such as smartphones and tablets. Oracle takes care of monitoring and supporting the latest operating system releases. Given the popularity and flexibility of Java and HTML5, this architecture empowers enterprises to leverage their existing developer skill sets. Anyone with Java skills can readily build mobile applications.

The framework leverages a headless JVM to enable developers to build cross-mobile-device applications by leveraging the Java language. The applications install and run on both iOS and Android devices. The framework also offers a set of over 50 components that are used to define user interfaces that render in HTML5 on the devices. In addition, the framework includes a controller layer, built-in security, encrypted SQLite database for local data storage, and device feature (GPS, camera, contacts, and so on) integration.

Oracle Mobile Suite

Oracle Mobile Suite bundles Mobile Application Framework (MAF) to develop mobile applications together with Oracle Service Bus to abstract from backends. Also, some adapters are part of the bundle. The many advantages of this approach are described in the *Mobile solutions and SOA* section within this chapter.

Oracle Mobile Security Suite

We were not deeply discussing the security challenges in the mobile space until now. Oracle Mobile Security Suite offers a really interesting answer to most of the security challenges we face. The concept of a secure client-side container is introduced. This means that you don't deploy your mobile application via a standard app store anymore. You have a secure container app loaded to your mobile device, and you deploy your applications into that secured container. This works seamlessly, for example, with your MAF applications. The advantage is that your app runs in a controlled environment where you can forbid several "bad" things, while the full functionality of your device stays intact, for example, for parallel private use.

Oracle API Gateway

Oracle API Gateway can be used as an additional layer of security that filters all service calls before they reach your enterprise service bus. This, for example, allows the inspection of incoming traffic for several vulnerabilities, including denial of service attacks, XML bombs, and much more.

The key features of the API gateway are as follows:

- API security: There is threat protection for XML, SOAP, REST, and JSON; identity and access control; API key authentication; data-level privacy and integrity; content payload inspection; and compliance
- Centralized cloud connectivity: Proxy and manage interactions with cloud services, restrict, throttle, and manage web services and REST APIs
- There is API management for mobile and cloud, connecting mobile devices to enterprises, and map between data formats such as XML and JSON
- Centrally protect and manage API keys
- Virtualize and route cloud traffic
- Audit and monitor cloud usage

Mobile use case for RYLC with MAF

RYLC currently is selling only directly to end customers at central points, such as airports, train stations, and ports. Now, more sales channels will be addressed, especially smartphones seem to be interesting. Further on, the guaranteed quality of rental cars shall be improved by checking the cars in a better way with mobile device support (cleanliness and maintenance interval). This should lead to better customer satisfaction. The first release of the RYLC mobile app should deliver this functionality:

- Login/logout
- Show profile of logged-in user
- Show rental history of logged-in user
- Submit new car rental

The screenshot shows the Oracle Mobile Application Framework (MAF) flow for ordering a rental car via a mobile device:

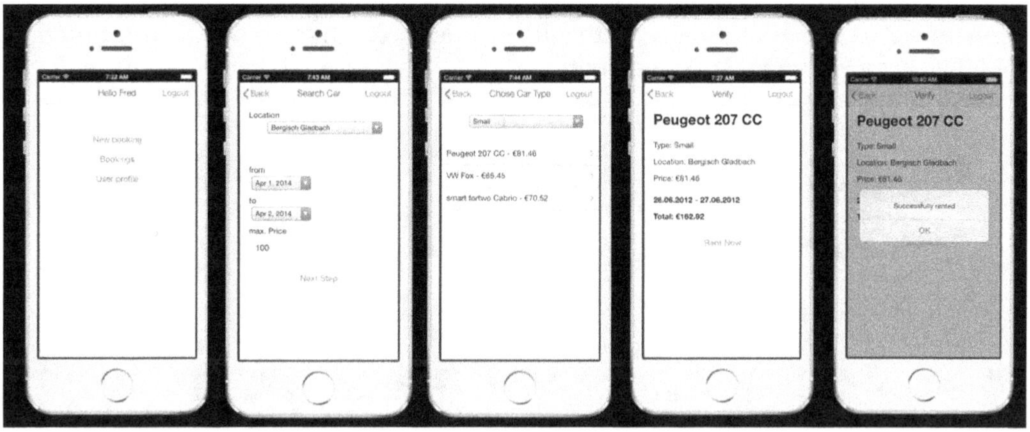

Figure 6

You enter your location (prefilled by GPS when identical to your rental location) and the date and time. On the second wizard page, you can choose the type and class of car. Screen 3 displays details of the option you chose, and screen 4 shows the success message for your order.

Building these kinds of apps is very easy and fast when applying a good framework delivering all necessary features on the enterprise scale. As described in the *Oracle Mobile Tooling* section, here we leveraged Mobile Application Framework to build the mobile application and deployed it to the native app formats so that the resulting apps can be published in Apple App Store and also in Google Play Store.

Of course, we made use of Oracle Service Bus, which is part of Oracle Mobile Suite, to make sure all our calls into the backend are secured, load balanced, and decoupled from "private" backend functionality. This is visualized in *Figure 7*. We also used the protocol transformation features of the service bus here and autoexposed business services on the bus additionally, with a REST interface, which makes consumption in mobile UIs more suitable to developers.

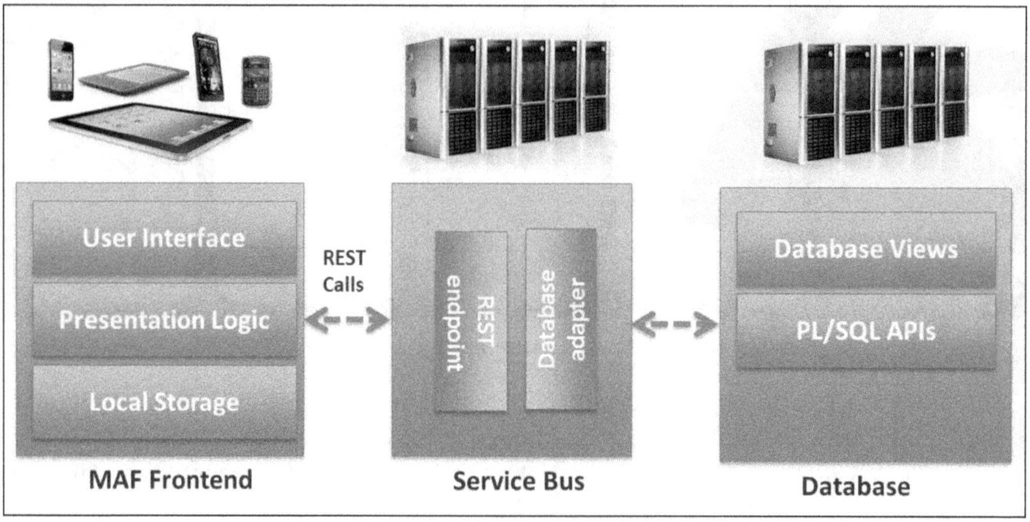

Figure 7

As illustrated in the architecture diagram, we also made use of the **CQRS** pattern, which is short for **Command Query Responsibility Segregation**. We had a very common discussion with the owner of the main application database when we started building this mobile use case. The offer we got was to use some "mobile views" in the database to read reservation data from the database. For writing our reservations to the database, the initial offer was to write to a staging area table in the database, where some logic gets the new car reservations and persists them in the real application database after a processing time of several hours. This, of course, violated one of our initial requirements—to have real-time access to the reservation system.

We accepted the way of reading data from the backend via database views created for our use case. It was easy to read these views via the database adapter connected to the service bus and expose the functionality via REST. This was a quick way to get things up and running. We are aware that we skipped the step of building a real business service with a service façade and a canonical data structure. But this was our tradeoff for getting fast results and also guaranteeing a futureproof architecture, because, with upcoming mobile applications, the backend part can be refactored easily without affecting the frontends. This is true for modifications of the UI, which don't affect our backend.

To write the data down to the database, we finally agreed on getting an API in PL/SQL in the database. This API makes sure that all business logic checks are valid and, therefore, allows us to write in real time to the real application database. Again, we exposed this API via the database adapter on the service bus, and REST enabled the proxy service. This was a very fast and accurate way of addressing this problem of access to the reservation system. This pattern is known as CQRS, where reading the data is separated from writing the data.

Summary

On the frontend side, the technological future certainly belongs to HTML5, as described at the beginning of this chapter. We are witnessing a lot of new developments and innovation is this area, and hybrid apps (for example, the ones using Apache Cordova) are playing a more and more important role.

The mobile solution environment, therefore, represents a genuine opportunity for IT to move away from being a cost center and towards being a value-creating business enabler, creating new business opportunities via technological innovation. This will happen even faster when the IoT hype settles and when our backends are flushed with high-volume data and event streams in the century of data. Mobile solutions have a hard need for good backend integration technology to avoid maintenance hell. In general, upcoming mobile technology will push the need for fast integration to a new extent. Also, business processes will benefit highly from mobile support, which includes smartphones, tablets, and wearables.

This chapter has a number of key takeaways. New architectural patterns, such as the single-page web app, must be added to the architectural toolbox. There is little doubt that HTML5 is the future. Also, hybrid apps combine the advantages of HTML5 with access to native device features. Further, the chapter provides sage advice to help you avoid the "lots of small and cheap mobile apps" maintenance hell" by forcing a solid backend integration strategy. Finally, the chapter urges you to see mobile devices (including wearables) as enablers of the BPM technology because new business will be possible by leveraging the new possibilities of innovative technologies through business process automation.

In the next chapter, we will go into detail about how the new possibilities in event-driven architectures can boost our BPM projects.

11
Event Processing and BPM

In this chapter, we will explain what event processing is, why it is of interest to combine it with BPM, and how this can be achieved. Some of the topics we will cover are as follows:

- What is fast data?
- What is event processing?
- Key elements of event processing
- Different types of event processing
- Event processing versus Business Rule Management Systems (BRMS)
- Conceptual architecture for event processing
- How does event processing fit into a modern architecture?
- Event processing architectural patterns and their use cases in RYLC

Whether the business is logistics, healthcare, finance, or manufacturing, every organization has to deal with a lot of events daily. Events occurring, whether planned or unplanned, often disrupt the best designed and managed business processes, which then has an impact on the business results.

Today, event processing is often pragmatic, ad hoc, and improvised. But the proper management of events is becoming more and more important. Especially, the emergence of the Internet of Things (IoT) will account for a huge increase of events flowing into the enterprise to be reacted on.

To react quicker, businesses must be able to detect events when they happen and take appropriate action. This is where fast data solutions become interesting, offering to combine event processing with business process management to better support new business cases.

The high velocity of data from many real-time data sources, such as market data, the Internet of Things (IoT), mobile devices, sensors, click-streams, and even business transactions, are still largely unused by most companies today even though they might contain valuable but perishable insight—perishable because the insights are only valuable if we can detect and act on them immediately. The amount of data a company has to deal with will grow enormously over the next few years. This is exactly where event processing can help.

What is fast data?

To understand what fast data is, we first have to look at one of the hot topics of today—big data. Big data solutions address the challenge today's businesses are facing when it comes to managing the increasing volume, velocity, and variety of data. When people talk about big data, they often refer to the volume part. Velocity, on the other hand, is often only a second thought. Velocity is about the ability to store and process large amounts of data in real time. Big data technology might be capable of storing the information when it arrives, but because of its batch characteristics, it is not able to process it immediately and deliver results in real time.

That's where fast data comes in. Fast data is a term that was invented by Ovum's Tony Baer, who defined it as:

> "*Fast Data, the velocity side of big data, is not new, but technology price/ performance trends are making fast data applications more widely available.*"

Every company wants to be smarter about how they do their business. Velocity is a critical component to achieve this goal. By both capturing and moving data faster, it can be analyzed and acted on faster.

We will see that event processing offers all the means to support a fast data application.

> **Big data streaming analytics**
>
> Lately, Forrester has defined a new term for products that support fast data initiatives, the *big data streaming analytics platforms*. Forrester defines such a platform as "*Software that can filter, aggregate, enrich, and analyze a high throughput of data from multiple, disparate, live data sources, and in any data format, to identify simple and complex patterns to visualize business in real time, detect urgent situations, and automate immediate actions.*"
>
> Event processing is an important part of such a platform.

What is event processing?

Although event processing has been around for a while, it hasn't yet been used widely.

The goal of event-driven architectures is to process information in near real time by reacting to the publication of that information when it happens. Event-driven architectures lower the latency of information propagation while promoting loose coupling between components compared with sequential programming in traditional models.

Event-processing systems have several important fundamental aspects, some of which are as follows:

- **Push-based messaging pattern**: As discussed before, the traditional messaging pattern has been request-response—what can be called a *pull* messaging pattern because the client pulls information from the server by sending a request. In contrast, in event-processing systems, the event producers push events into the system when they occur.
- **Autonomous messages**: Events are signaled by notifications that are independent of other events (this doesn't mean that event consumers might not correlate an individual event with another event as part of the processing). Because of semantic encapsulation, events are not dependent on the event producer for their meaning, and each event consumer is free to interpret the event independently of others. An event contains information about the state transition it represents and any associated attributes.
- **Higher decoupling** : Compared to other architecture styles, event-processing solutions provide a much higher level of decoupling. The following list shows this:
    - Events do not transport any instructions about how an event should be processed. The representation of an event is simple and flexible, requiring minimal coordination between the event producer and the event consumer.
    - Event producers do not need to know which consumers are interested in the event. Event producers send information to the event channel, not to a specific consumer.
    - Unlike RPC-style interactions, event notifications do not include specific processing instructions.

  - System components can be added or removed with less coordination in the overall system. New components that want to respond to a given event in their own way can join the network without the event producer or any existing event consumer being affected. Existing components can be removed without the event producer and other event consumers being updated.

- **Receiver-driven flow control**: After an event producer sends an event notification, its role in determining what happens to that event is over. Downstream event consumers can ignore the event, handle it as appropriate for their domain, or propagate it to other consumers.
- **Near real-time propagation:** Event-processing systems work in real time. This is in contrast with fixed-schedule, batch-oriented architectures, which transport the information as batches in given and predefined intervals. Events propagate through the network of event consumers soon after they happen and can further affect how those consumers will interpret and react to future events from the same or different event producers. Event-processing networks thus allow a more natural way to design and create real-time information systems.

These important aspects of event-processing systems lead to architectures that are more flexible, agile, and scalable than the more tightly coupled traditional request-response designs.

When we know that an event has occurred, we can react to it in appropriate ways. Some reactions to events can be simple, while others can be more complex.

Event processing can be used to perform the following functions:

- **Visualize business in real time**: Dashboards, as a part of Business Activity Monitoring frameworks, can help people to visualize, monitor, understand, and make sense of large volumes of incoming information (events) from multiple sources in real time.
- **Detect urgent situations**: Event-processing platforms can be used to define simple or complex analytical patterns of urgent business situations, which happen in real time, and which must be acted upon as quickly as possible.
- **Automate immediate actions**: Event processing engines work quietly in the background, processing thousands if not millions of events until they detect an urgent situation (can be a risk or an opportunity). The occurrence of the situation can either be signaled through sending e-mail or text messages or by publishing a business event message, which can then be used to trigger a business process or a service call.

Event-driven thinking

In our daily lives, we are very used to thinking in an event-driven way; when the phone rings, we either answer or ignore it; when there is a traffic notice on the radio about a traffic jam, we try to find a way around it; and so on. But, if it comes to thinking about computerized systems, we are often programmed to think in request-driven ways, which basically means that we send a request to another system and assume and wait for a response. We are so used to that style of interaction that a request-driven way is even used for scenarios that are in fact event-driven.

Therefore, events are often treated as data and stored in a database, and they later ask queries to detect the situation we are interested in. The question is when and how often such a query will be executed. We can do it after every update, but if we are only interested if a customer calls our hotline three times within a single day—assuming that most of our customers only call us once a day, if at all—then, most of our queries will be needless as they don't detect the situation we are interested in.

The nature of event-driven use cases is that we don't know when and whether they are going to happen, but if they do happen, we often need/want to do something very fast.

The fact that people today often try to model and implement event-driven scenarios using traditional request-response interaction styles creates added complexity.

The four Ds of event processing

Reactive systems and, therefore, event-processing systems can be described by the 4D paradigm, which has been published by Jeffrey M. Adkins (`http://dblp.uni-trier.de/pers/hd/a/Adkins:Jeffrey_M=.html`) and stands for Detect, Derive, Decide, and Do.

The following diagram shows the base idea of that 4D paradigm—becoming aware of a situation and doing something about it:

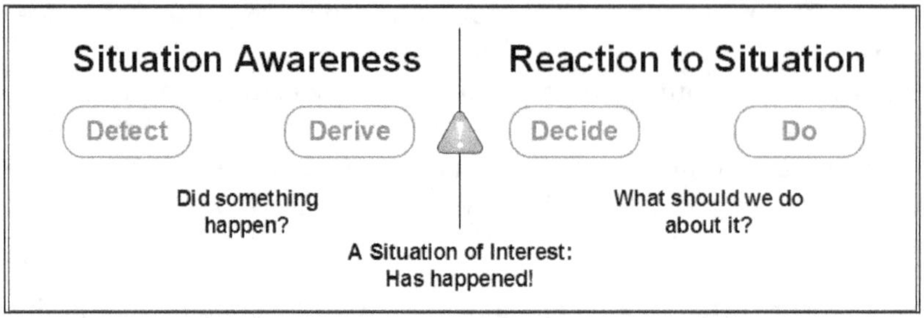

Figure 1

Detect: This is the act of detecting that an event of interest has occurred. This includes becoming aware of changes that happen outside a system's awareness boundary and bringing the knowledge about the event into the system. Some ways of detecting that an event has occurred are:

- A business user recognizes the change and enters it into a system. This is the classical case and the most flexible because humans often have the knowledge to detect change directly and easily.
- A sensor senses the indicators and creates the corresponding event in the system.
- A data feed allows events to be published into the system.
- When the business process under the system's control makes changes, it should publish these changes as (business) events.
- Connected things are becoming more and more self-aware of their inner workings and environment, so they can publish their own state changes.

Derive: This is the act of becoming aware of events that are not directly detectable by bringing together events with other events, data, patterns, and publishing the observation as a new, derived event. Some ways of deriving events are given here:

- A business user recognizes a pattern and enters the derived event or just reacts to it directly. This is often provided by dashboards and analysis.
- A software solution applies pattern matching over multiple events and data to find derived events. This is what typically an event-processing system provides.
- The Derive phase can be hidden in today's existing application code.

Decide: This is the act of determining the course of action that needs to be taken in response to the situation. This includes the background information needed to be collected to make the decision. Some ways to decide the importance of an event are given here:

- Sometimes, there is no decision needed, and the derived event (situation) is passed through
- A business person is doing a manual decision on behalf of the system
- Automated algorithmic decision via a decision management system

Do: This is the act of performing the course of action that was decided upon in the Decide phase. Some ways to act on the event are as follows:

- Sending a signal to either a person or a system, such as calling a web service or sending an alert
- Sending an order for a business user to do something, such as entering a new task to the Human Workflow system
- Cause an action or change a setting on an actor (could be an IoT device)
- Trigger the execution of a new business processes or trigger a single action within an existing business process

Detect and **Derive** are the responsibility of an event-processing solution.

Decide is sometimes handled by decision management tools or rule engines as their strength lies in decision tables and fact-based analysis. Simple decision logic can also be handled by an event-processing solution.

Do is sometimes handled by business process or workflow tools.

A reaction to a situation can be also be an event and feedback into the **Derive** phase, as shown in the next diagram:

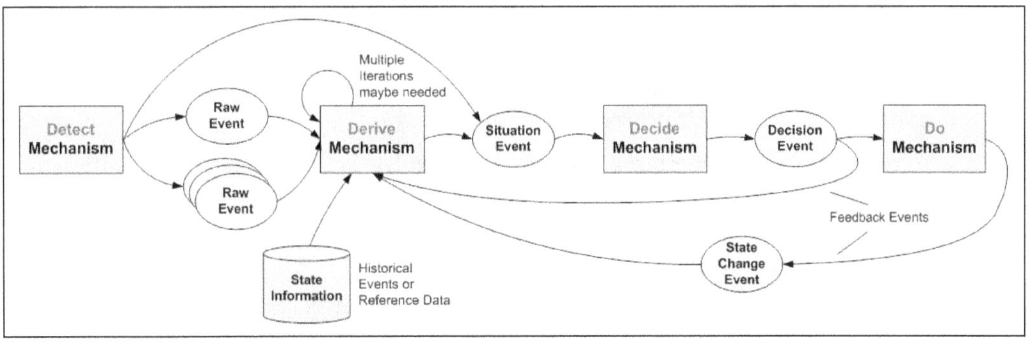

Figure 2

An event driven system is based on the 4D architecture.

The key elements of event processing

In this section, we will explore some of the basic principles and concepts commonly used when talking about and creating event-driven applications. These are the major building blocks for any solution that handles streaming event data.

First, here is a summary-level explanation for some of the key terms and concepts used:

- **Event**: An occurrence within a particular system or domain, an event is something that has happened in the particular domain. An event is atomic—it either happens completely or not at all. The word event is also used to mean a software entity that represents such an occurrence in a computing system.
- **Raw event (simple event)**: This is an event that is introduced into an event-processing system by the event producer and records a real-world event.
- **Complex event (derived event)**: An event that is an abstraction of one or more other events. This is generated as a result of event processing that takes place inside an event-processing system. Most complex events are created by performing CEP computations on base (input) event objects.
- **Business event**: This is anything that happens that is significant to the business of the given organization/company.
- **Event producer**: This is an entity at the edge of an event-processing system that introduces events into the system.
- **Event consumer**: This is an entity at the edge of an event-processing system that receives/consumes events from the system.
- **Event stream**: This is a set of associated events. A stream is often a temporally ordered set (there is a well-defined timestamp-based order to the events). A stream in which all the events must be of the same type is called a homogenous event stream.
- **Event hierarchy**: This is a model that represents the relationships between events that are at different levels of abstraction.
- **Event cloud**: This is a term used to describe the set of all the events entering an enterprise, together with the timing, causality, and other relationships between those events. The events enter the event cloud.
- **Event pattern detection**: This is used to search a set of events to find matches to event patterns.

- **Time window**: This is a bounded segment of an event stream. For example, the events in the last 10 minutes are a moving window.
- **Event-driven architecture** (**EDA**): This is an architectural style for event-driven solutions, further explained later in the sections.
- **Event processing network** (**EPN**): This is a conceptual framework for describing the structure of an event-processing solution. This is further explained later in the section.
- **Simple Event Processing** (**SEP**): This is a type of event processing, further explained later in this section.
- **Event Stream Processing** (**ESP**): This is a type of event processing, further explained later in the section.
- **Complex Event Processing** (**CEP**): This is a type of event processing, further explained later in this section.

Next, some of the preceding terms are explained in more detail.

Event-driven architecture

Event-processing architecture is an architectural style in which one or more of the components in the system are event-driven and minimally coupled. Minimally coupled means that the only relationship between the event producer or (source) and the event consumer (target) is the one-way transfer of event objects.

A business application implements an EDA if it complies with the following principles:

- **Loose coupling**: Event-driven systems must be loosely coupled to improve flexibility, promote agility, and reduce dependencies.
- **Pushes event notifications**: Event notifications are *pushed* to the consumer and not *pulled* by the consumer. The event producer decides when to publish the event/send the notification because it knows about the event before the consumer does.
- **Free of commands**: An event notification is a report of a situation, not a specific request or command. The consumer is free to decide how to react; the producer does not prescribe the action to perform.
- **Communicates one way**: Event notification is a fire-and-forget type of interaction. The producer sends the notification without waiting/requiring any feedback from the consumer.
- **Reacts immediately**: Here, the consumer does something in response immediately after it recognizes an event.

- **Handles high volume of events**: Real-time visibility and business intelligence requires high-volume event streams to be processed quickly in order to make in-time business decisions.
- **Modular and extensible architecture**: The architecture must be modular and support extensibility to allow additional capabilities to be added with minimal effort and change to the system.

Event processing network

An **event processing network (EPN)** is a conceptual framework that describes the structure of event-processing systems and the common features that they should all support.

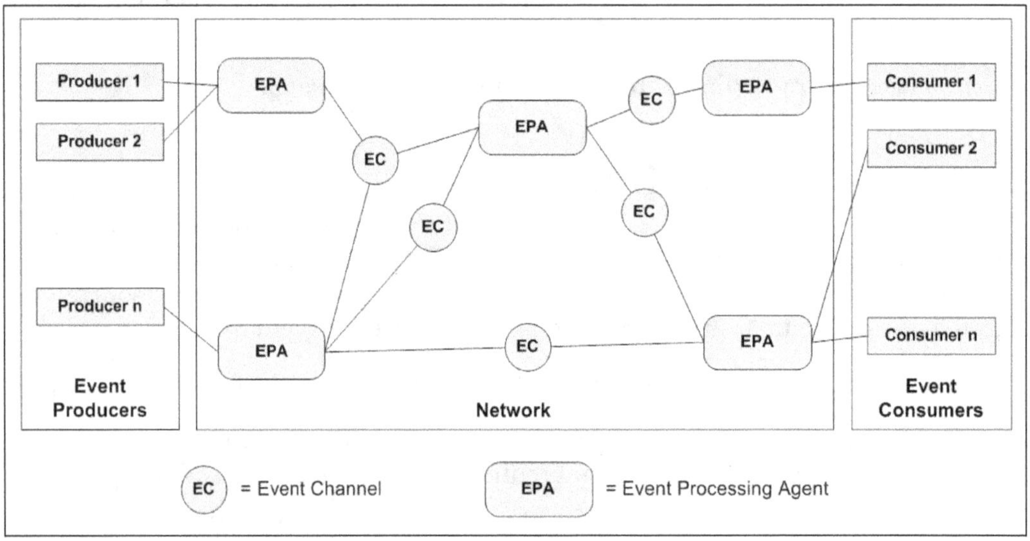

Figure 3

An EPN is defined by the following four components:

- **Event producer**: This gets information from outside the EPN and transforms them into events, which are placed on the event channel to be processed by an event-processing agent.
- **Event consumer**: This consumes the events the consumer is interested in and performs the action associated with the event (the *Do* of the 4Ds).
- **Event processing agent (EPA)**: This represents a piece of intermediary event-processing logic inserted between event producers and event consumers. An EPA receives events from event channels and does some processing on it, such as pattern detection, event filtering, and so on.

- **Event channel**: This is the transport mechanism for the events. Either a *push* or *pull* model can be used to transport the events over the channel, and the channel can also act as a buffer in between the other components.

An event processing network (EPN) does the following:

1. Gets a set of one or more events as an input.
2. Performs some processing.
3. Returns a (possibly new) set of zero or more events as output.

The main objective of the event processing network is, therefore, to receive events from event producers, pass them onwards to the network of event-processing agents for processing, and deliver the resulting events to the right consumers.

Types of event processing

Event processing can be categorized into Simple Event Processing, Event Stream Processing, and Complex Event Processing. The difference between the three is broadly determined by the processing complexity.

Simple Event Processing

Simple Event Processing (**SEP**) is the processing of ordinary or notable events that may initiate further downstream actions. The volume of events arriving here is rather small, and they mostly arrive as single events, which often, if not always, can be treated directly as business events. The operations needed in SEP are rather simple and match the functionality of a mediator, that is, filter, transformation, routing, enrichment, and splitting of events. The following diagram shows this:

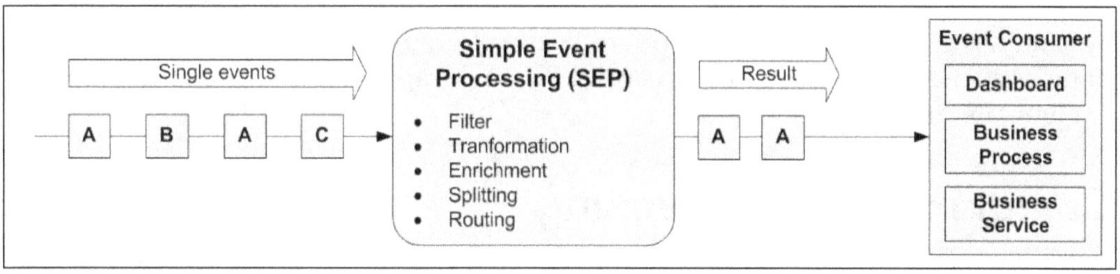

Figure 4

Events occur either individually or in low-volume streams. Single events can be regarded as an important change in state in a resource or in a business process. Events of this kind typically trigger processes in the systems that receive the message. This form of event processing corresponds exactly with the specification of **Java Messaging Service (JMS)**. Therefore, a typical example of SEP is JMS. Also, Oracle Event Delivery Network (EDN), which we will see later in this chapter, and Oracle Service Bus can very well support Simple Event Processing.

Event Stream Processing

Event streams are continuous input events that occur in high volumes. They are generally time ordered and do not end. They are almost impossible to process or analyze in real time with traditional relational database management systems. The following diagram shows the events arriving as stream and being analyzed by the Event Stream Processing (ESP) engine, without having to store the events in a data store:

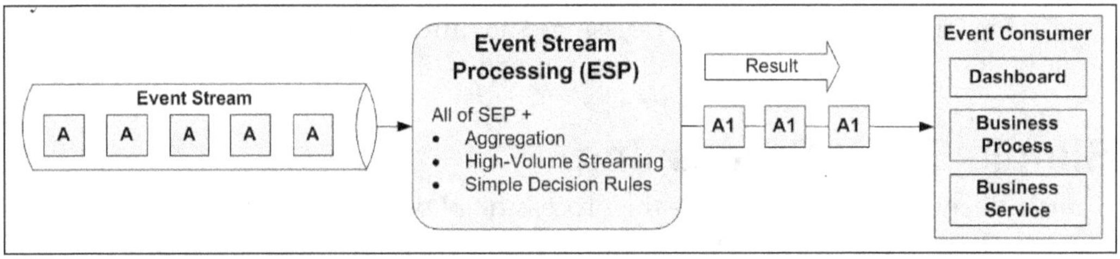

Figure 5

For example, stock quotes may be streamed at a frequent rate, but the consumer may only be interested when the stock price changes. **Event Stream Processing (ESP)** can identify the stock price change and raise a notable event to the consumer.

Similarly, there are situations where duplications need to be eliminated in a flood of events, such as in RFID streams. ESP can be applied in the scenario to eliminate duplicates.

Complex Event Processing

Complex Event Processing (CEP) is event processing that combines data from multiple event sources to infer events or patterns that suggest more complicated circumstances. This large amount of incoming events is also referred to as the event cloud. Typically, the processing involves applying a collection of evaluation conditions or constraints over all the events arriving through the event cloud. The events (notable or raw) might span different event types and might occur over a specified time period. Events might be correlated over multiple dimensions of interest, including causal, temporal, spatial, and other dimensions.

Complex Event Processing does not mean *very complicated processing of events*. It is processing applied to events that might sometimes be very complex or results in events that might be very complex, as shown in the following diagram:

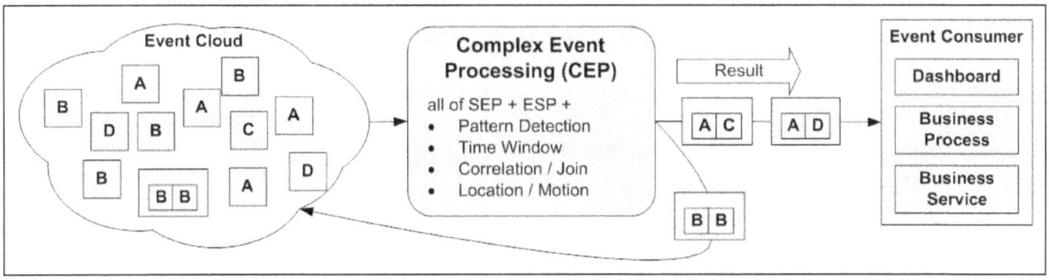

Figure 6

CEP requires a high-performance infrastructure that supports pattern recognition, time-window processing, and continuous query language.

Event processing versus Business Rule Management Systems

Due to the fact that some of the event processing systems/platforms are using the term *rules*, event processing is sometimes confused with business rules; however, these technologies are complementary, with little overlapping functionality.

Business Rule Management Systems (**BRMS**) are software systems that execute rules, typically in the form of condition-action or if-then, which are kept separate from the application logic. This means that rules can be modified without requiring a change in the application code. *Chapter 8, Business Rules*, of this book covers Oracle's Business Rule Management System.

Both CEP and Business Rule Management Systems support declarative business rules. The main differences between the two approaches are as follows:

- Event-processing functions are activated as a direct or indirect result of event occurrence; business rules are activated on request.
- A business rule system allows externalizing the decision logic from the core application logic. Event processing allows event filtering, transformation, aggregation, and event pattern detection directly on the event stream.
- Event processing has a strong relationship with temporal capabilities, that is, temporal contexts, such as various types of time windows and temporal patterns. Business rules typically do not support temporal aspects.

- The strength of a BRMS is the life cycle management of the rules. The business user can author rules, view rules, test rules, and simulate rules and IT can deploy rules. The life cycle is managed within a robust repository.
- The strength of rules in the CEP platform is speed. The weakness is the ease of changing the rules and business-user friendliness.

Synergies between event processing are also possible as follows:

- The routing and filtering of events in an event-processing solution can be backed by a business rule engine.
- Event-processing logic can be defined in a rule-based style.
- The detection of an important event / situation can trigger the evaluation of business rules; the BRMS is consuming events.
- The outcome of the evaluation of business rules (the action) can signal a new event to be handled by event processing; the BRMS is producing events.

This is illustrated in the following diagram, where Complex Event Processing is extended by a BRMS, which handles the evaluation of complex business rules on behalf of event processing and by that supports the Decide phase of our 4D paradigm.

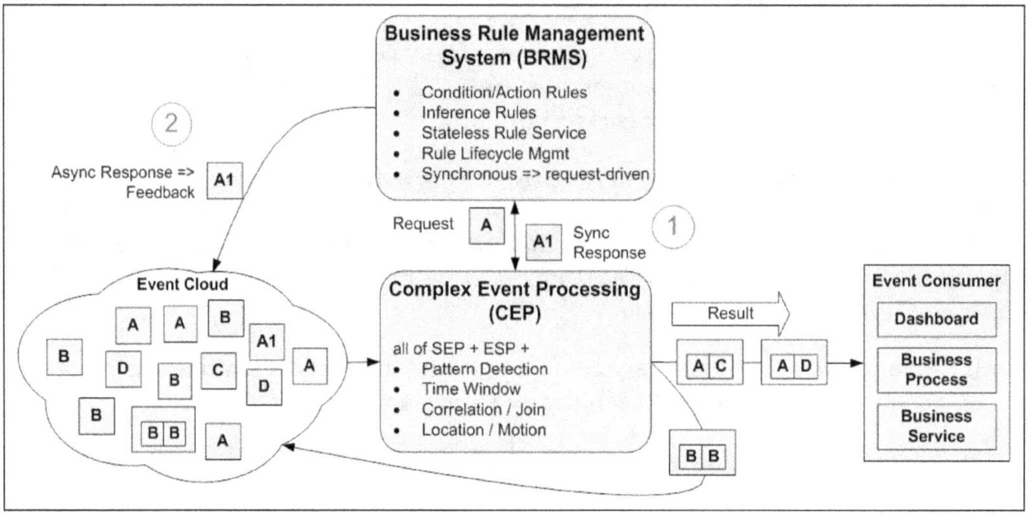

Figure 7

The interaction can either be synchronous, where the rule engine is integrated in a request-response fashion (**1**) or asynchronous, where the BRMS is more like an event consumer and feeds back its results (**2**) into the event cloud as new events.

Of course a rule engine can also be integrated in SEP and ESP in a similar way.

Conceptual architecture for event processing

The conceptual architecture builds on the concept of the event processing network, as shown in the following diagram. Any event-processing implementation should be achievable with this as the base set of components. However, not all of the components will be required for any given scenario.

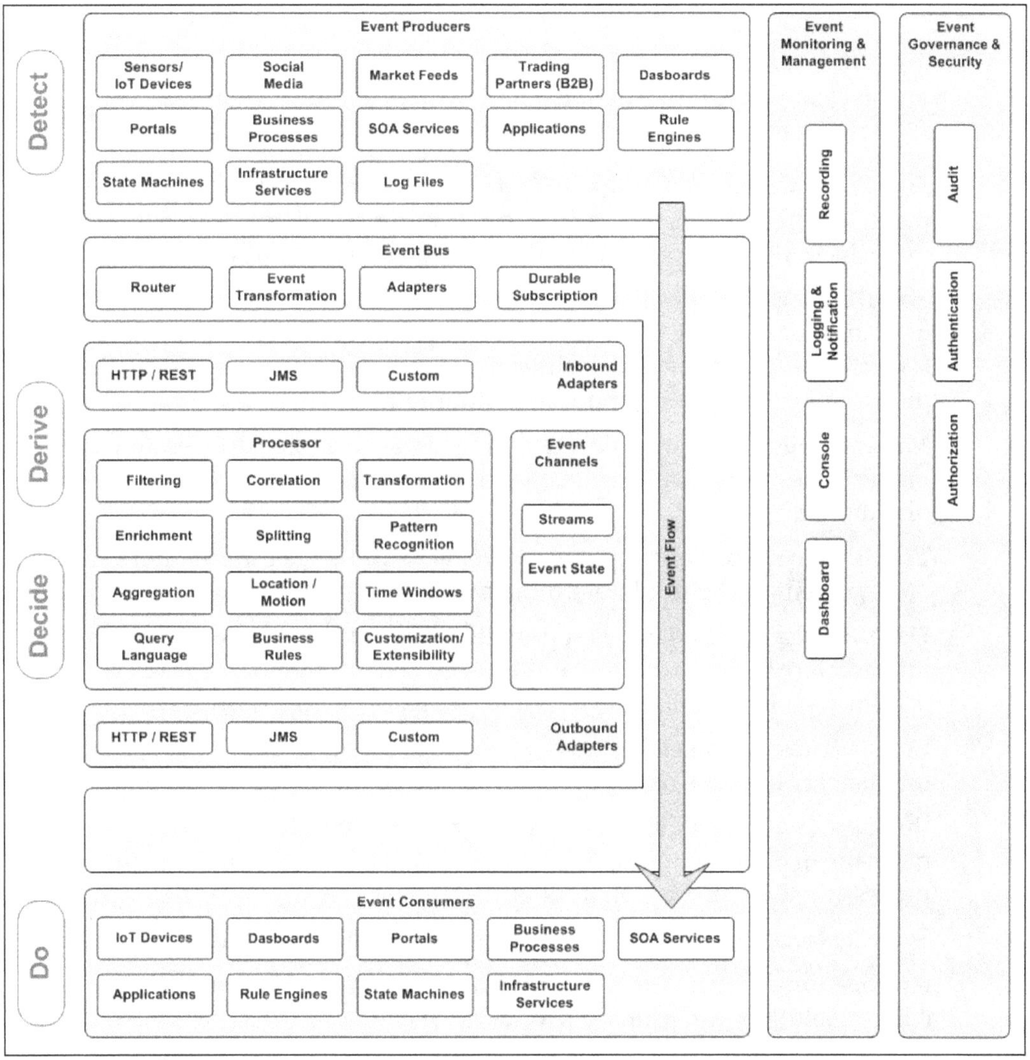

Figure 8

The event flow in this conceptual architecture is from event producers to event consumers, and the components shown in the preceding diagram are summarized here.

Event producers

Event producers are the systems or components that define the event and generate the event as the business change happens. Producers are also known by several other names, including event source, event publisher, and event provider.

An event producer does not include logic to manipulate events. Also, it does not include any decision logic on what to emit and when, and the events that are generated could be redundant or irrelevant. Typical event producers include:

- **Sensors / Internet of Things (IoT) devices**: These detect situations (things that happen) and generate raw events or originate events from data streams or business flows, for example, transmission of temperature.
- **Social media**: Today, citizens as well as authorities are increasingly using new, and more direct, communication channels, such as social news media, for example, Facebook and Twitter, and the capability to analyze such media, therefore, becomes more and more important.
- **Market feeds**: These include external feeds, such as stock prices and market interest rates, which are received by dedicated components and need to be distributed.
- **Trading partners**: These may send events to exchange information such as order, inventory, or fulfilment information.
- **Dashboards**: Agile enterprises provide ways to the business users to respond immediately to opportunities and threats. The reaction of the users is transformed into business events and published by the dashboard.
- **Portals**: These are a key producer of business events as they are a primary interface for business users. User actions can be translated into business events.
- **Business processes**: Either events are used as a loosely coupled interaction mechanism between multiple business processes, or they are feed into event processing to do process analytics.
- **SOA services**: A service in SOA can publish business events of importance.
- **Applications**: Either enterprise applications, such as ERP and CRM, or custom solutions are primary producers of events.
- **Rule engines**: These can publish an event as part of its processing.
- **State machines**: These generate events when changing state.

- **Infrastructure services** - These include monitoring, alerts, and management services and can produce important events that need to be acted on.
- **Log files**: These can directly be a source of events, where each line is treated as a separate event and sent in as input in a streaming fashion.

Inbound adapters and outbound adapters

The role of inbound adapters is to convert events from the source format into the format understood by event processors.

The role of outbound adapters is the reverse of the role of inbound adapters. Outbound adapters push out the outbound events using the appropriate protocol. For example, a JMS adapter can be used to publish events to a JMS queue or topic. This is especially useful when consumers want to receive offline events as they can use JMS Queue or JMS Topic durable subscriptions.

Event channels

Event channels are inbound or outbound conduits through which events are transported within the event-processing solution. Events can be transported using:

- **Streams**: Streams are the primary channels that receive and distribute outbound events. Among other things, streams are responsible for queuing event data until the events are delivered.
- **Event state**: Although an event state is technically not a channel, sometimes event streams may be persisted and consumed again later. This can either be through in-memory caching or in a persistent store, such as a NoSQL database.

Event processors

Event processors, also called event processing agents, consume normalized event data from inbound channels and process it using the rules predefined in the form of queries. The processors may generate new events to an output channel or simply execute the response action.

The kinds of operations that can be applied to the base events typically include:

- **Filtering**: The incoming stream of events is filtered to only keep relevant information.
- **Correlation**: Events arriving might not mean much individually until they are correlated with other events or contextual information. An event-processing platform should have the ability to resolve causal, temporal, or spatial correlations between events.
- **Transformation**: The format of incoming or produced events is sometimes incompatible with the consuming systems. Therefore, an event has to be transformed from one format into another.
- **Enrichment**: Events can be enriched with additional data retrieved from another event or data source.
- **Splitting**: Sometimes, it might be necessary to split an event into multiple events, for example, when one single event contains a lot of logically unrelated information and there are different potential consumers for these different parts of information.
- **Pattern recognition**: Event streams often contain interesting patterns that only emerge as new events arrive. A common pattern is when event A arrives at time t and another event B arrives at time $t + x$. Pattern operators allow us to define complex relationships between streaming events at different times to detect such patterns.
- **Aggregation**: This allows events to be consolidated either to remove duplicate events or to combine related events in order for them to be useful, for example, by adding fields or by arithmetically aggregated values.
- **Location/motion**: Event streams increasingly also contain geographic and localized location information, which can originate from a vehicle, a machine, or the mobile device carried by a person.
- **Time windows**: Streaming data flows in constantly in real time. To be able to detect situations, often a snapshot of the event stream over a given time period is needed. Time window operators allow us to define a time period and to include the streaming data in such a *window*. Time windows can then be used to perform time series analysis, such as running totals or moving averages in real time.
- **Query language**: A query language can be offered to code event processing rules, thus offering a certain abstraction. It allows the rules to be described in a SQL-like expression language.

- **Business rules**: These support the implementation of complex decision logic within event processing. They can be delegated to a dedicated decision management solution, such as a rule engine.
- **Customization/Extensibility**: Incoming and outgoing event streams might need to be integrated in a proprietary way, not directly supported by the event-processing platform. Therefore, the platform should be extensible/customizable and allow the integration of third-party libraries.

Event consumers

When performing tasks in reaction to an event, the event consumer has limited concern about the origins of the event. It is just aware that its invocation is a result of the event, along with the context of the event. Typical event consumers include:

- **IoT devices**: These are invoked to perform physical tasks, such as operating valves, switches, or alarms.
- **Dashboards**: These consolidate and visualize business information to business users based on the events they receive. These can be standalone dashboards as well as dashboards integrated in a full-fledged **Business Activity Monitoring (BAM)** solution.
- **Portals**: These consume events to display on portal dashboards or to react appropriately.
- **Business processes**: These can be started by significant business events, or they can wait in a quiescent state to be woken up by particular events of interest.
- **SOA services**: Similar to business processes, SOA services can be invoked by the occurrence of an event.
- **Applications**: Enterprise applications as well as custom solutions consume events to react to business opportunities and threats.
- **State machines**: Their state can be changed in reaction to an event.
- **Infrastructure services**: These include services such as e-mail services, alerts, monitoring, and management services. They can consume events that may need to be analyzed.

Event bus

The event bus or mediation layer provides the components to route and transform events before they arrive and when they leave the event-processing platform. The functionality you find here is what is usually provided by an **enterprise service bus (ESB)**; however, something even more lightweight could be used here in order to get the throughput and scalability needed when processing thousands or millions of events. The main functionalities provided by the event bus are:

- **Router**: This routes events based on routing rules defined on the event bus. Routing can happen based on the event header or event content values.
- **Transformation**: Events are transformed into another form or type by the engine on the event bus.
- **Adapters**: This allows various formats and protocols to be integrated and mediated at the event bus layer.
- **Durable subscription**: This saves event messages for an inactive subscriber (event consumer) and delivers these saved messages when the subscriber reconnects.

Event monitoring and management

The components in this layer deal with the system monitoring and management of the event-processing platform. The following functionality should be provided:

- **Logging and notification**: Two of the important aspects of monitoring the event-processing platform are to raise alerts and to log key infrastructure events.
- **Recording**: Events typically occur at a very fast pace and in real time, and real-time monitoring may not always help in revealing the necessary information for troubleshooting. For testing and debugging, events flowing through the event-processing platform should allow recording in an event repository for future playback.
- **Dashboard**: This provides insights into the event-processing platform and the applications deployed for monitoring and troubleshooting purposes.
- **Console**: This supports the deployment, configuration, and management of all resources and artifacts needed for event processing.

Event governance and security

The components in this layer deal with securing and protecting the event-processing platform and the event data by providing the following capabilities:

- **Authentication**: This verifies that the user is who they claim to be
- **Authorization**: This is the process of granting or denying requests to perform actions on a given resource by a party
- **Audit**: This provides a record of activities or transactions that have occurred in the system

Self-contained versus claim check event messages

A fully self-contained message is purely a complete representation of a specific event. And the message can be published and archived as one. The message can either immediately or later be interpreted as the event without relying on additional data stores that would need to be in time-sync with the event during message processing. An example of a self-contained event message is shown in the following diagram:

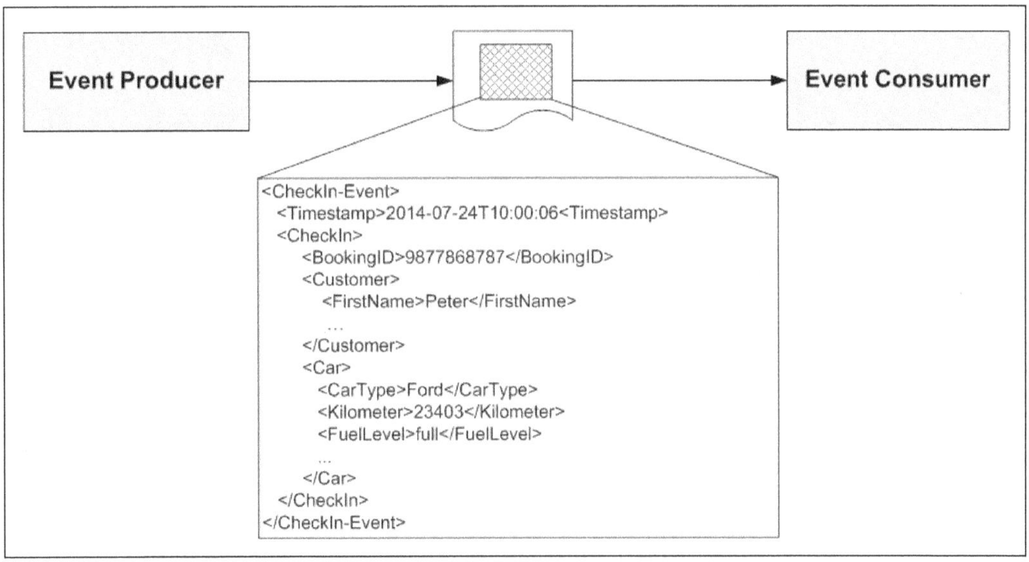

Figure 9

This is in contrast to only passing references to the data in the event, with the information itself being stored elsewhere. This is similar to the claim check pattern described for the integration solution, and that's why we use the term claim check event message here. The following diagram shows the same example with a claim check event message used:

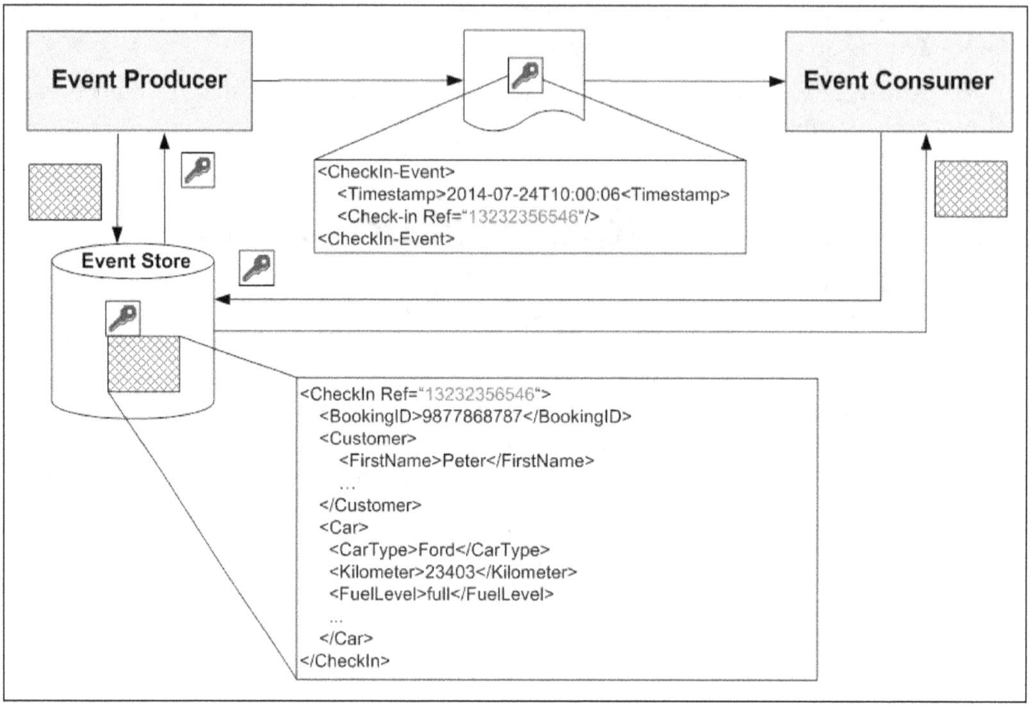

Figure 10

Depending on the event type, the strategy to choose might be clear. A raw event, for example, will mostly use a self-contained event message. But when modeling a business event, we have the choice between the two strategies. So, what are the reasons for choosing one strategy over the other?

The following table compares the two strategies:

Self-contained event messages	Claim check event messages
Very loosely coupled All information is passed in the message, and there are no other dependencies for the event consumer as well as the event producer.	*Less loosely coupled* The event consumer as well as the event producer are not only dependent on the event structure but have an additional dependency to the persistent event store where the additional data is stored. To reduce dependencies, access to the event store can be given through a service facade, which is through information services, perhaps using a RESTful API.
Large and potentially very large messages We have to pass everything we know of the given message; the messages can get rather large, which can have an impact on the network bandwidth, especially if we have many consumers of the event.	*Very small messages* Messages are tiny and consistent in size because they only hold the reference information. Of course, if detailed information is needed, then the full message has to be transported over the network as well but only on demand and with the ability to only read parts of the event from the event store.
Access to event information is quick and easy The event message contains all the information corresponding to the event occurrence. Therefore, consuming the event is all that is needed to act on the event.	*Access to information is more expensive and involves a second call* In order to act on the event after it has been consumed, the information needs to be retrieved from the event store.
Event represents state when the event took place The event message is immutable, that is, its state cannot be modified after it is created. Even if the message itself processes much later than it was published, it will contain the right information.	*Event only contains a reference to data stored somewhere else* In order to be able to retrieve through a reference the information at the time the event took place, an additional event store is needed, where the additional information is stored immutably. It is not sufficient to pass a reference to the operational data store because the information might change after the event has been published. Not only the information but also the structure of the information might change over time; the event store has to be able to reflect that.

Self-contained event messages	Claim check event messages
Harder to govern access to information Because we always pass everything we know for a given event, we might end up in a situation where not all consumers are allowed to see all the information. A solution might be to use different events for that, but if security requirements are too fine and granular, we might end up with just too many events. Another option, to encrypt the information, has a similar limitation; the more fine and granular it is, the harder it gets.	*Access to event information can be governed on event store access* Access to information can be governed through the data access (service) layer using the same principles as when securing services in SOA. Very fine and granular security requirements are, therefore, also hard to achieve.

For the implementation of an event store, a NoSQL database can be an interesting option as a simple key-value lookup is sufficient. A NoSQL database will offer the necessary scalability, and due to the relaxed schema handling, allows the structure of the event information to change over time without having to reflect that on the storage level. Immutability can be easily guaranteed.

Of course, we can also use a mixture of these two strategies, where we pass some information as *self-contained* and some other information through a reference.

How does event processing fit into a modern architecture?

The following diagram shows a high-level view of event processing in the context of a modern architecture:

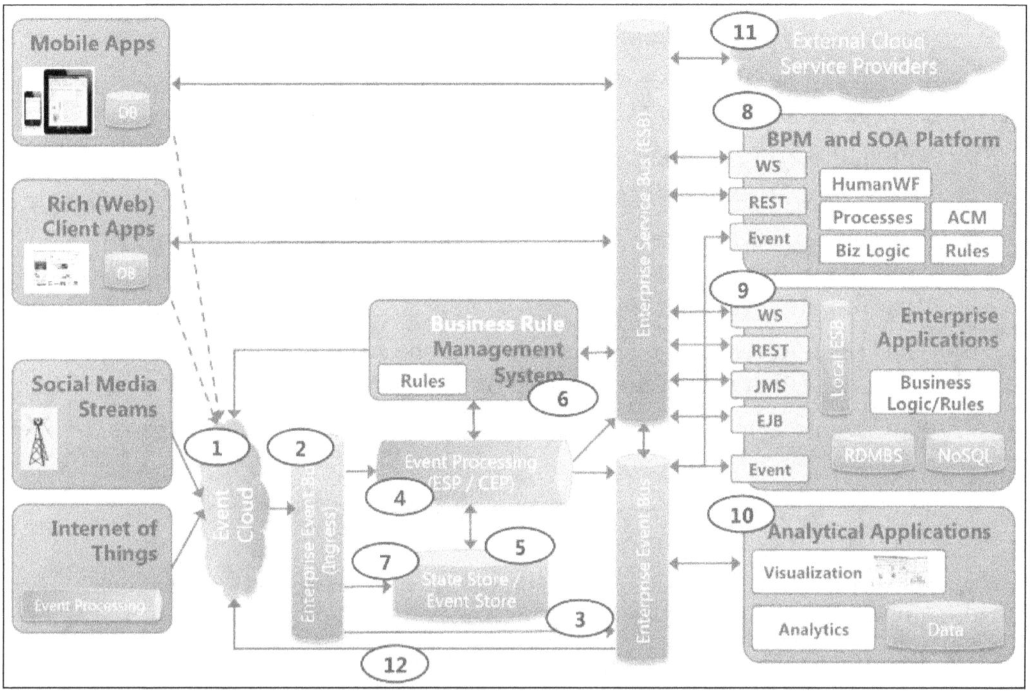

Figure 11

On the left-hand side, we can see the different systems acting as event producers. The following interactions can take place when an event is generated by one of the event producer systems:

1. The event is pushed into the event cloud.
2. Events are made available through the so-called enterprise event bus. In contrast to the enterprise service bus, the enterprise event bus only transports events. The ESB also handles service calls on an SOA system.
3. Events can be consumed directly by a consumer system on the right-hand side.
4. But, in most cases, events are handled by the event-processing component, which supports Event Stream Processing or Complex Event Processing.
5. The state and event store provide additional information to event processing—either historical events or reference data to support detecting derived events.
6. The Decide phase of the 4D paradigm can be supported by a rule engine. Rules can either return the decision or publish new events to the event bus.
7. Raw events as well as derived events can be stored in the event store for later use.
8. Events trigger a business service or a business process in order to act (the Do phase) upon the detected situation.
9. Events can be sent to an application in order to act upon the detected situation.
10. Events can be sent do an analytical application for visualization on a dashboard, so a business user can further analyze (Decide) the information and act on it if necessary (Do).
11. Events can also be sent to the cloud, potentially to a trading partner to act upon it.
12. Systems can send back new events (feedback), which are placed onto the event bus to be consumed by the event-processing component.

Does this sound interesting? But what about a platform supporting all this? In the next section, we will discuss what the Oracle Fusion Middleware product family can provide in the area of event processing.

Oracle Fusion Middleware products supporting event processing

Oracle Fusion Middleware provides a wide range of products to choose from. To support event processing as described in the preceding sections, the products listed here are available. The following diagram shows the architecture diagram from before but now with the Oracle products mapped to it:

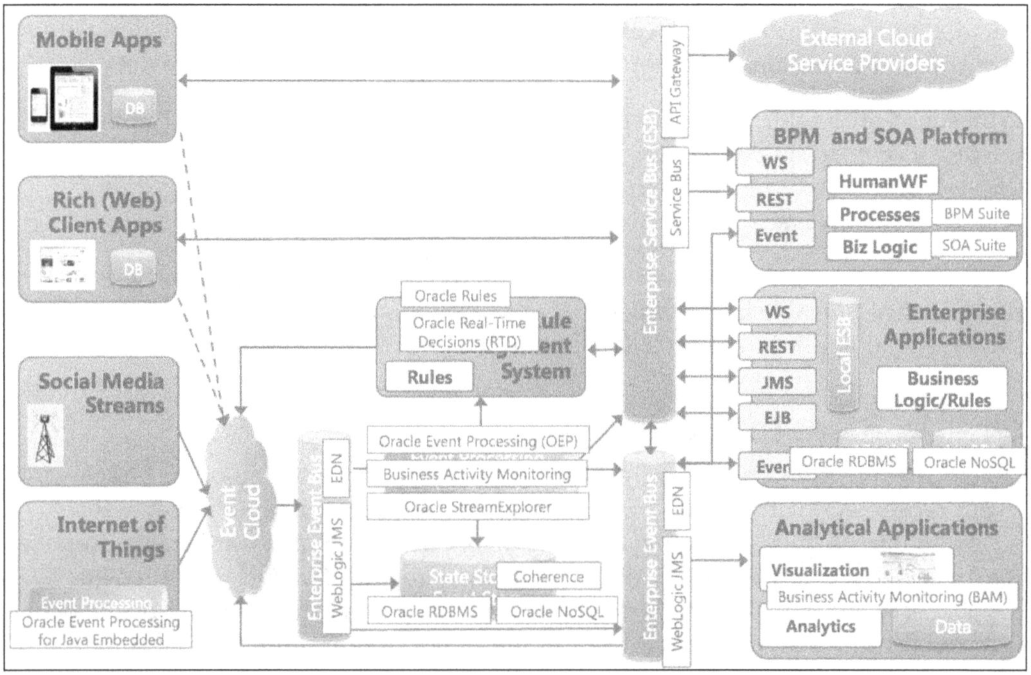

Figure 12

Oracle Event Processing

Oracle Event Processing (**OEP**) is a lightweight Java server for the development and deployment of event-driven applications. It is based on a separate OSGi application container and does not run on the WebLogic server. OEP provides a complete event-processing solution for building applications to filter, correlate, and process events in real time. It provides a rich, declarative environment based on Oracle Continuous Query Language (Oracle CQL), a query language based on SQL with added constructs that support streaming data, to improve the efficiency and effectiveness of managing event-driven solutions. OEP is based on the idea of an event processing network (EPN), which has already been introduced in this chapter.

OEP supports an active-active HA architecture.

Oracle Event Processing can be used to support both Event Stream Processing and Complex Event Processing.

Oracle Event Processing for Java Embedded

Oracle Event Processing for Oracle Java Embedded is an event-processing server designed to support event-processing applications in embedded environments often found at or near the event sources. These environments include sensors such as for environment conditions and moving sources, such as vehicles or mobile devices.

With event-processing applications deployed in these locations, events can be filtered at or near the event source, which reduces the network traffic flowing through other server resources, including Oracle Event Processing applications on enterprise servers.

Oracle Event Processing for Java Embedded only includes a subset of the functionality available in the Oracle Event Processing product. This subset supports the particular application needs of event processing in an embedded environment.

Oracle Stream Explorer

Oracle Stream Explorer offers an easy to use the visual face on top of the Oracle Event Processing platform. It abstracts away the development and deployment process completely by providing a web-enabled, intuitive, and simple user interface. It allows a business user interested in analyzing streams of events to implement event processing solutions without having to write a single line of code. A business user can directly start exploring the available event streams and visually add filters, aggregation over time, and joins with other streams and/or reference data. Additionally, a set of predefined event explorations, such as Top N, Up Rend, Duplicate Elimination, and many others, are available as so-called patterns. Behind the scenes, Oracle Stream Explorer transparently creates the necessary artifacts and deploys them onto the same Oracle Event Processing platform discussed before.

Oracle Business Rule

Oracle Business Rules is a lightweight business rule product that provides high performance and addresses the requirements of agility, business control, and transparency. Part of the Fusion Middleware stack, it integrates seamlessly across Oracle SOA Suite and BPM Suite stack.

Oracle Business Rules is further explained in *Chapter 8, Business Rules*.

Oracle Real-time Decisions

The Oracle RTD platform combines both rules and predictive analytics to power solutions that provide real-time automated decisions. It, therefore, supports the Decision phase of our 4D paradigm. Oracle Event Processing detects and identifies notable events that can then be passed on to Oracle RTD.

Oracle Business Activity Monitoring

Oracle Business Activity Monitoring (**Oracle BAM**) gives business executives the ability to monitor their business services and processes in the enterprise, to correlate KPIs down to the actual business process themselves, and most importantly, to change business processes quickly or to take corrective action if the business environment changes.

It offers a wide range of intuitive visualizations that you can include in dashboards, including tree maps, scatter charts, bubble charts, and KPI watchlists, and is, therefore, an optimal match for visualizing detected situations so that a business user can react to it.

Oracle BAM also provides real-time pattern matching, trend analysis, and rolling-window computation through a query engine, which is also based on Continuous Query Language (CQL), the same language which is also supported by Oracle Event Processing (OEP).

Oracle BAM is further explained in *Chapter 12, Business Activity Monitoring*.

Oracle Coherence

Coherence plays an important part in building reliable and scalable event-driven applications. It provides replicated and distributed (partitioned) data management and caching services on top of a reliable, highly scalable, peer-to-peer clustering protocol. Coherence has no single point of failure; it automatically and transparently fails over and redistributes its services when a node becomes unavailable.

Coherence can be used to store recent events for fast retrieval by Oracle Event Processing.

Oracle RDMS and Oracle NoSQL

Both the flagship relational database as well as the newer Oracle NoSQL database can be used to store additional data, which is necessary during event processing.

Oracle NoSQL is very scalable and can be used to store recent events, the resulting, derived events, and potentially, even all the raw events arriving from the event cloud.

Oracle Event Delivery Network

Event Delivery Network (EDN) provides a declarative way to use the power of publish-subscribe semantics within Oracle SOA Suite. The idea of EDN is to increase the decoupling between the different components within the service component architecture (SCA). Instead of directly coupling two components via a request/response interaction (service call), one component can publish an event that zero/one or many other components can subscribe to.

Events can be defined through the event definition language (EDL), so every event raised and signaled over EDN is a typed event represented by EDL.

EDN runs within every SOA instance. Raised events are stored by SOA Suite and delivered by EDN to the subscribing service components.

Since version 12*c*, Oracle Event Processing has also been supporting the interaction with EDN through EDN adapter nodes. Oracle Event Processing Network can either subscribe for an event from EDN or can publish an event to EDN.

EDN is an implementation of the event bus component of the conceptual architecture.

Oracle WebLogic JMS

WebLogic JMS is an enterprise-class messaging system that is tightly integrated into the WebLogic Server platform. It fully supports JMS Specification and also provides numerous WebLogic JMS extensions that go above and beyond standard JMS APIs.

WebLogic JMS also directly supports an event bus of the conceptual architecture.

Event processing architectural patterns

In this section, we will show how the different components of the architecture discussed before can be added together into architectural patterns in order to support certain use cases. We have identified the following patterns:

- Standalone event processing
- Event processing in front of BPM and/or SOA
- Decoupling processes/services through business events (potentially including some event processing)
- Analyzing BPM process behavior with event processing

These patterns are now explained together with a use case in our RYLC system.

Architectural pattern 1 – standalone event processing

In this pattern, event processing is used to implement a solution that captures and refines high-volume event data that arrives from other systems (either internal or external sources) and makes it available for later analytics. External sources can be a lot of things, from the so-called Internet of Things to social media streams. The purpose of such applications of event processing is to reduce the volume and improve the quality of event data through functions such as:

- Filtering out irrelevant information
- Eliminating duplicate events
- Discarding data that might be erroneous because it is out of range of possible values
- Putting the events in some meaningful order if they arrive out of order
- Enriching events by looking up data from a table in the memory or database
- Storing raw events, maybe unfiltered, in a database using potentially a NoSQL or in-memory datastore
- Making and recording calculations from multiple incoming events
- Sending (derived) events directly to analytical applications, that is, BAM dashboards

With this architectural pattern, there is no automated reaction to events. Instead, events (raw or derived) are persisted into a database and/or sent over the enterprise event bus to consuming applications, which present the events to business end users to be analyzed manually. The visualization of events is often through a graphical user interface, potentially a dashboard. The person analyzing the information might be engaged in some kind of business process, which may or may not be managed by BPM, but there is no direct interaction with a business process from the event-processing solution.

The following diagram shows this architectural pattern and the necessary interactions between the different components:

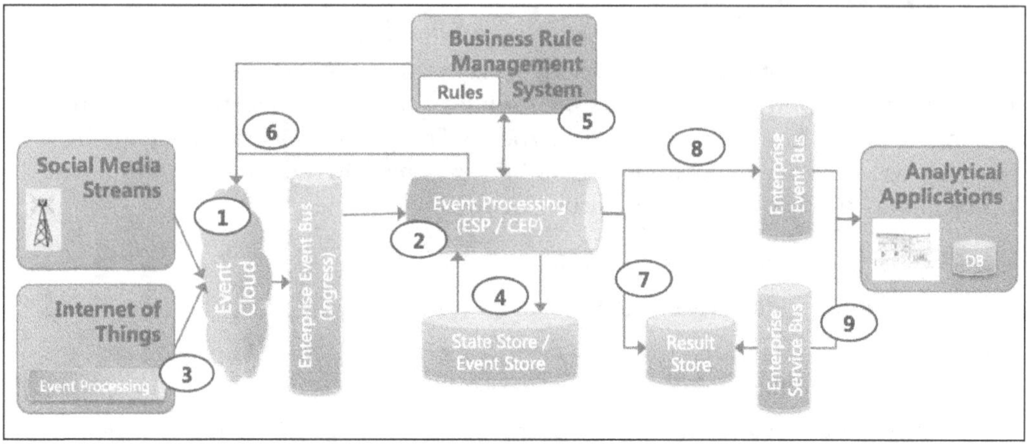

Figure 13

The following interactions take place between the different components:

1. Events arrive from the external and internal systems as Event Cloud and are made available on Enterprise Event Bus.
2. An event-processing platform (ESP or CEP, depending on processing requirements) consumes each single event and applies its event-processing rules.
3. Events can also potentially be preprocessed (filtered/aggregated/prioritized) on the event producer (IoT device) using an embedded and lightweight event processing technology.
4. Additional data residing in-memory (cache) and/or on a database can be joined with the incoming event stream.
5. Rules can also reside in an external Business Rule Management System (BRMS), and events can be evaluated against these rules. Optionally, the BRMS can generate new events.
6. The event-processing engine and the rule engine can generate events and feed them into Event Cloud to be analyzed as a new event.
7. Events / derived events can be stored in-memory or in a Result Store database for later retrieval.

8. An analytical application (such as a dashboard) gets the resulting events (derived/complex events) immediately through Enterprise Event Bus.
9. If not by the method employed in the previous point, the analytical application gets the resulting events by retrieving them from Result Store trough a data service provided on the Enterprise Service Bus.

Example in RYLC

RYLC wants to use and analyze social media channels, such as Twitter, to get a more direct interaction with their customers. The first attempt is, therefore, to retrieve all the tweets related to RYLC from Twitter through their streaming API and present it on a dashboard for analysis by the folks in the CRM department.

The following diagram shows how this solution can be built using the *standalone event processing* architectural pattern:

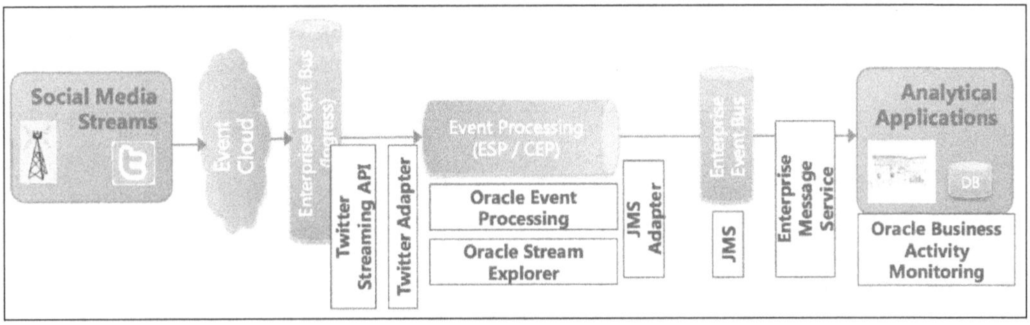

Figure 14

The solution uses Oracle Event Processing and its capability to implement custom adapters to connect to the Twitter API and stream in the relevant tweets. The tweets are analyzed by the Oracle Event Processing solution and aggregated counters, and sentiment analysis is performed directly on the stream. For visualization, a dashboard built on top of Oracle Business Activity Monitoring (BAM) is used. The integration between OEP and BAM can be done through a JMS queue and using the Enterprise Message Service functionality of BAM. Optionally, Oracle StreamExplorer can be used by a business analyst to analyze the event stream.

The following diagram shows a simplified version of an implementation of Oracle Event Processing Network inside the JDeveloper development environment. Using a custom adapter, the Twitter Streaming API can be accessed. The tweets are enriched with a sentiment indicator and then sent to Oracle BAM through a JMS adapter.

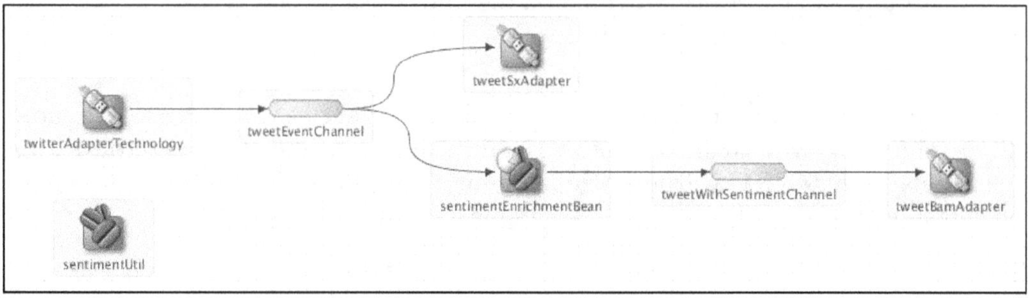

Figure 15

Additionally, the tweets are sent over another JMS adapter to be retrieved by Oracle StreamExplorer. The following diagram shows StreamExplorer in action:

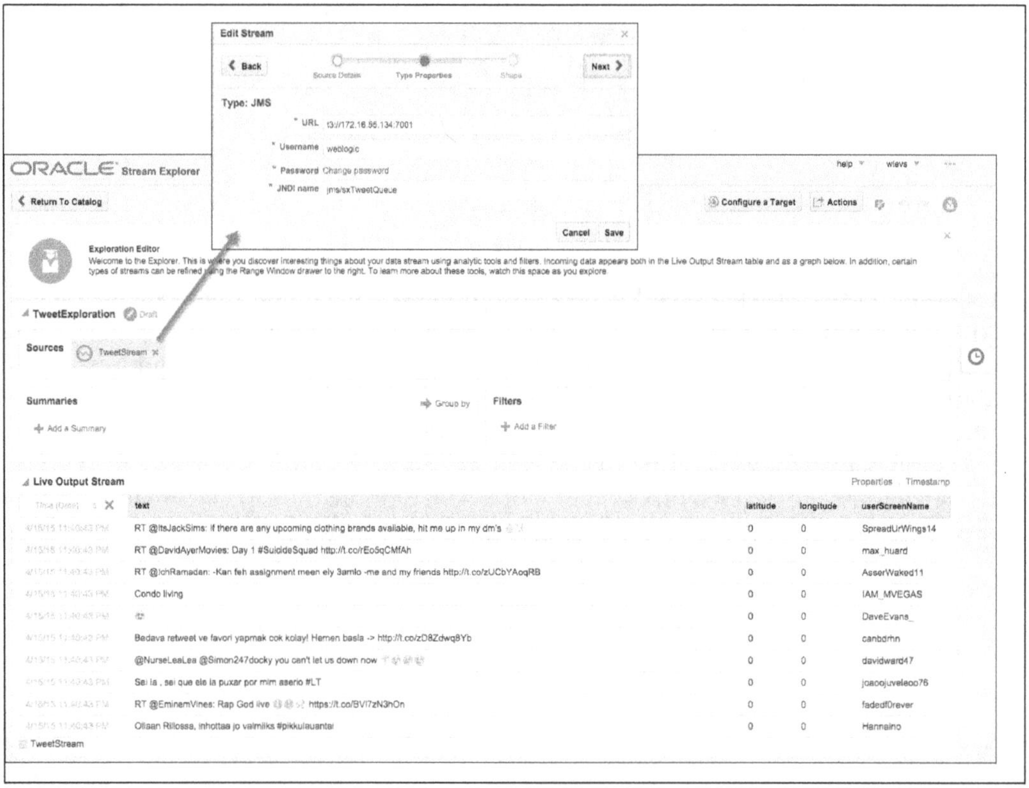

Figure 16

The following diagram shows how the data can be visualized on a dashboard using Oracle BAM:

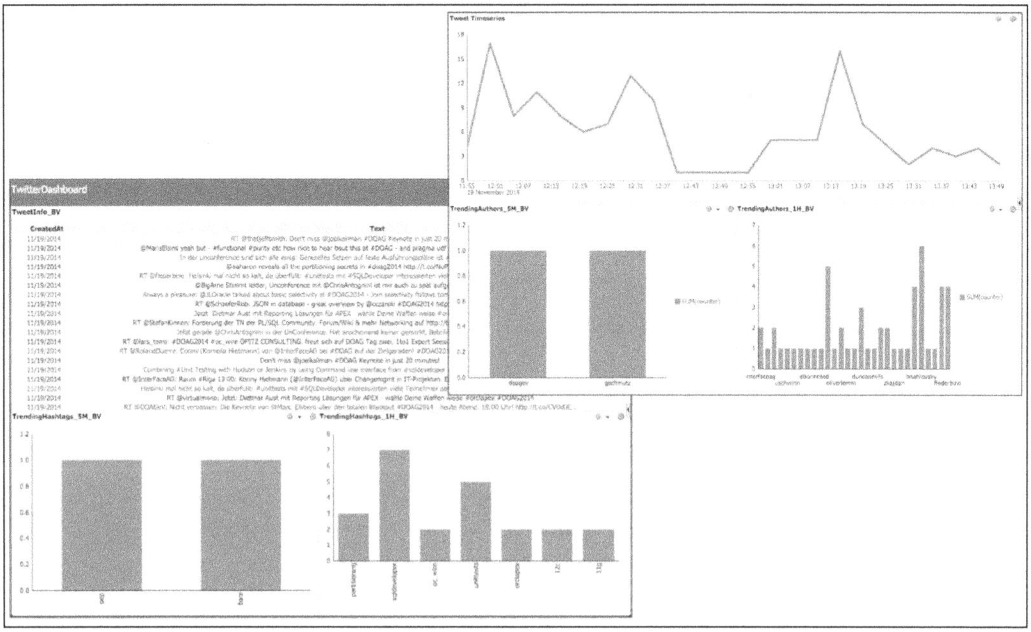

Figure 17

Architectural pattern 2 – event processing in front of BPM and/or SOA

This architectural pattern is similar to pattern 1, with the same idea of reducing the high-volume event data that is arriving from the event sources. But this time, the derived events (complex events) can be classified as business events, and they have a known corresponding action in the business. So, the actions on these events are either implemented as processes in a BPM suite or as services on an SOA platform. This means that the detection of such a business event will trigger an SOA business service or a BPM process, with the process either being started or a signal being sent to an already running process instance.

Using processes to define and execute reactions to certain events provides several advantages. Processes have a graphical presentation, which enhances understandability. Therefore, the reactions are easy to understand and maintain—much better than being hidden in a low-level implementation language. Furthermore, they provide a high degree of flexibility. Processes can be modified or adapted to new environments very easily. Additionally, they can be substituted by other processes in a BPM suite without affecting the event-processing suite if both systems are loosely coupled. This loose coupling also enables an event-processing suite to be integrated in any other system without affecting the BPM suite.

The following diagram shows this architectural pattern and the necessary interactions between the different components:

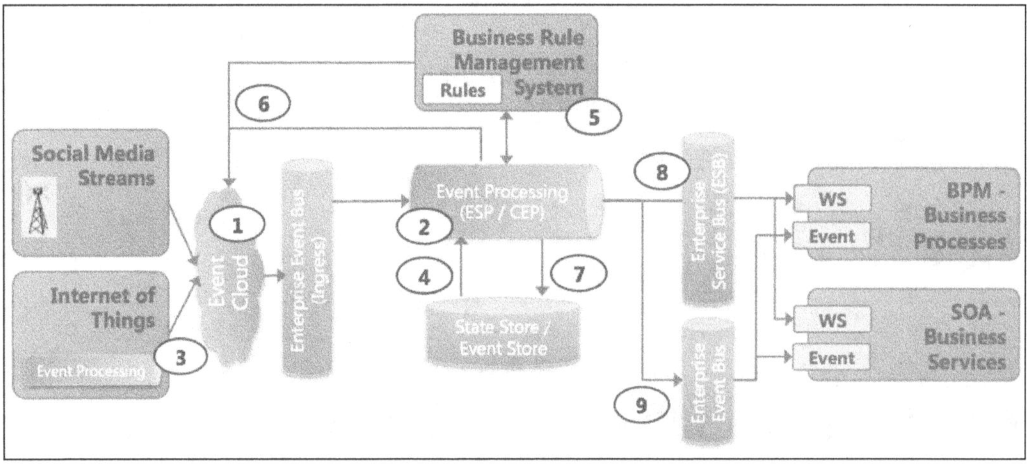

Figure 18

The following interactions take place between the different components:

1. Events arrive from the external and internal systems on Event Cloud and are made available on Enterprise Event Bus.
2. An Event Processing engine (ESP or CEP) consumes each single event and applies its event-processing rules.
3. Events can also potentially be preprocessed (filtered/aggregated/prioritized) on the event producer (IoT device) using an embedded and lightweight event-processing technology.
4. Additional data residing in-memory (cache) and/or on a database can be joined with the incoming event stream.

5. Rules can also reside in an external Business Rule Management System (BRMS), and events can be evaluated against these rules. Optionally, the BRMS can generate new events.
6. The Event Processing engine as well as the Rule engine can generate events and feed them into Event Cloud to be analyzed as a new event.
7. Events / Derived events can be stored in-memory or in a database for later retrieval.
8. Notable events (relevant for business) are either sent to a BPM business process (as an event or by invoking the processes service interface directly) for further processing.
9. Notable events can also be sent to a business service, again by sending an event or invoking the interface of the service directly.

Example in RYLC

RYLC wants to proactively detect problems during car rentals so that the customer is not stuck with a malfunction of a car. By constantly sending information about the car (such as engine data, actual mileage, current GPS position, and so on), RYLC hopes to better understand how the rental cars are used and hopes to be able to predict possible problems before the customer detects it. A proactive action could be to arrange a car replacement in the nearest office or perhaps offer to send a replacement car to the customer. Detection of the malfunction alert would be done by an IoT device, whereas the event would be classified in an event processing solution in the main center either automatically (directing customer to a nearby garage or sending a replacement car) or by a BPM process or case (maybe communicating back to OEP to find out the actual position of the car with respect to the distance from the nearest rental office along with a replacement car).

The following diagram shows how this solution can be built using the *event processing in front of BPM and/or SOA* architectural pattern:

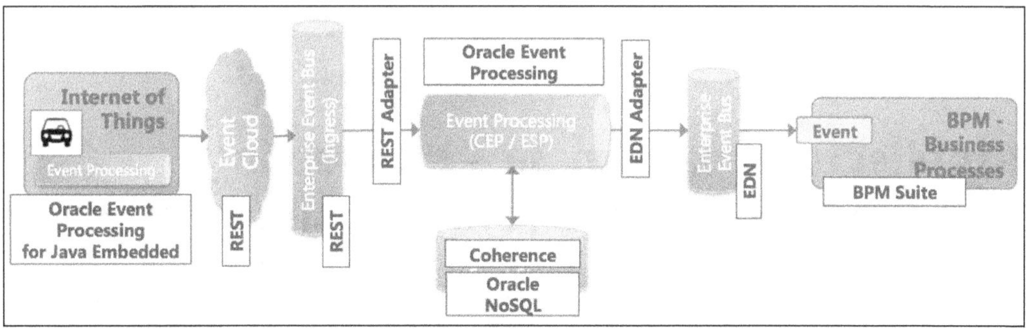

Figure 19

The solution uses Oracle Event Processing for Java Embedded on the IoT device in the car to implement a first filtering on the event raised by the different sensors of the car. Only notable and important events are sent over HTTP as a RESTful request to the Oracle Event Processing platform in the center. Here, the main detection, derive, and decision logic is applied. If a notable event is detected and immediate action is necessary, such as organizing a replacement car, a business process or a case is initiated using EDN as the business-event delivery mechanism.

The following diagram shows how an EDN event can be published from Oracle Event Processing. On the BPM side, we can subscribe to the event and use it to start a business process. The subscription is made by a mediator component, which then starts the BPM component.

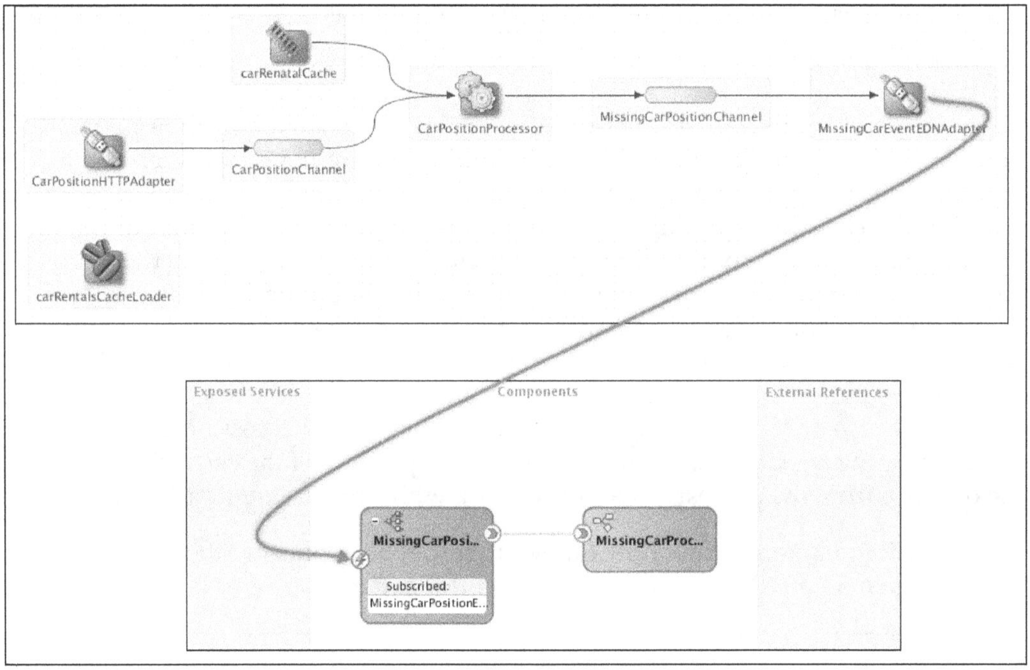

Figure 20

Architectural pattern 3a – decoupling processes/services through business events

In this pattern, events are used to further decouple systems/domains. There is no Complex Event Processing applied to the events, and there is also no derivation of new events.

The idea is to replace some of the traditional request-response interactions by events. That way, a BPM process or an SOA service no longer calls another BPM process or SOA service directly by invoking its service interface but, instead, is publishing an event on the enterprise event bus. Any party that is interested in the event can subscribe to it and will be informed after the event has been published. Such a subscription can be persistent, meaning that if a subscriber is unavailable, the event occurrence would be kept and delivered as soon as the subscriber is back online.

The following diagram shows this architectural pattern and the necessary interactions between the different components:

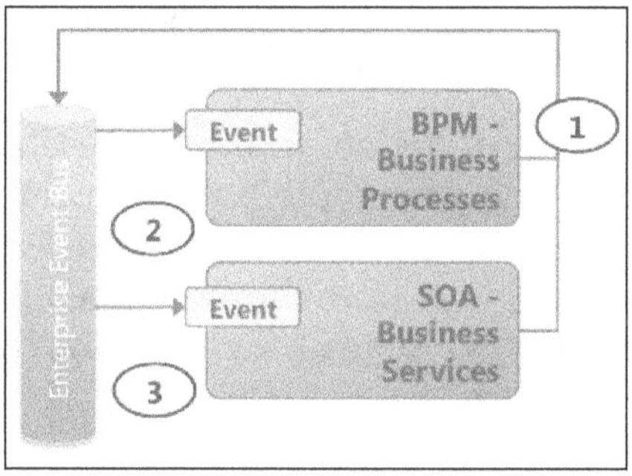

Figure 21

The following interactions take place between the different components:

1. A notable situation is detected by either a BPM process or an SOA service and published as a business event on Enterprise Event Bus.
2. One or more BPM processes, which have subscribed previously to the relevant business event, are notified about the event.
3. One or more SOA services, which have subscribed previously for the relevant business event, can also be notified about the event.

Enterprise Event Bus might offer a simple, static filter mechanism when subscribing to a business event.

Example in RYLC

When a customer returns the car at the end of the car rental, the check-in of the car is handled by the CheckIn business activity service. There are different parties interested in the CheckIn event depending on the event details, which are as follows:

- The *car rental* business process is the main interested party so that it can finish its processing with invoicing the customer.
- The *damage management* case has to be started if some damage has been reported in the CheckIn event.

- The *car cleaning and fueling* service is interested in any case. It takes care of bringing the car back in a state so that it can be rented out again.
- The *car repair* process is only interested in the check-in of cars, where either a repair or a regular service is necessary.

A traditional solution would store the event in a database belonging to the CheckIn service and then let all the other interested parties query the database for events of interest. This is a pull-based approach, where each party queries the database at regular intervals. The query can be written in a way that suits the interested party so that, for example, for the damage management case, only events with reported damage are returned. If we don't want the interested parties to check the database directly, then a data service can be provided instead.

The other solution is to do it event-driven, where all the CheckIn service does is publish a CheckIn business event. This could be done by invoking all potentially interested parties directly on a service interface, thus sending the event on a one-way interaction, with the downside of the CheckIn service being tightly coupled with event consumers. If a new party is interested in the event, the CheckIn service has to be changed as well to invoke the new service interface.

A better solution is using an enterprise event bus as described by the *decoupling processes/services through business events* architectural pattern and only publishing the business event on the bus. The CheckIn service no longer has to know and take care of the parties interested in the event; the event consumers subscribe directly and independently to the events they are interested in on the enterprise event bus.

The following diagram shows how this solution can be built using the *decoupling processes/services through business events* architectural pattern:

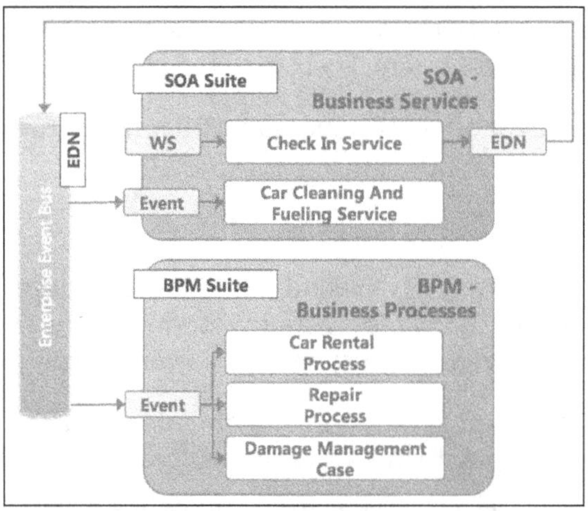

Figure 22

The solution is using Oracle Event Delivery (EDN) mechanism to publish the CheckIn business event from the CheckIn Service, using the self-contained event message strategy. The interested party subscribes via EDN and will be informed as soon as a CheckIn business event occurs.

If a party such as the CarRepair process is only interested in some of the events, the logic for filtering the right events can either be applied to the subscription (if it's a simple and static filter), or the event has to be thrown away by the consumer after consumption if the checked-in car needs no repair or maintenance. This is not really efficient and a lot of instances are created in the SOA or BPM suite just to find that an event is not relevant. To improve it, event processing can be added in between, which will apply the necessary filtering and perhaps aggregation of events and which is shown by the next architectural pattern.

The following diagram shows how the CheckIn service, implemented by a BPEL component, signals CheckInEvent using a mediator. CarRentalProcess, implemented by a BPMN component, subscribes to this event:

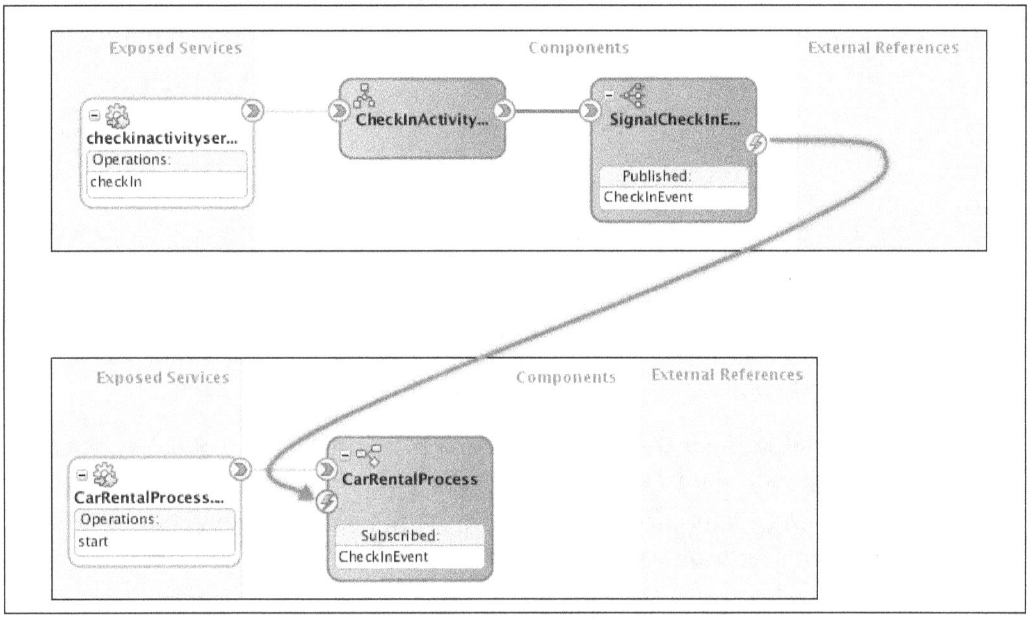

Figure 23

Architectural pattern 3b – decoupling processes/services through business events with event processing

This pattern extends the previous pattern 3a by adding event processing between the sender and the consumer of the business event. The purpose and the feature set of event processing here can be the same as shown in patterns 1 and 2.

The following diagram shows this architectural pattern and the necessary interactions between the different components:

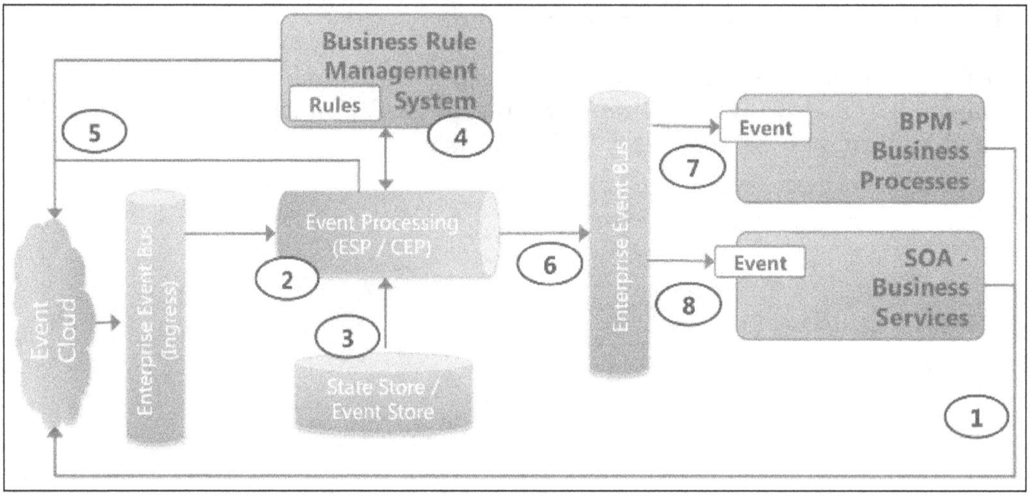

Figure 24

The following interactions take place between the different components:

1. A notable situation is detected by either a BPM process or a SOA service and the corresponding business event is published on Event Cloud.
2. An event-processing platform (ESP or CEP, depending on processing requirements) consumes each single event and applies its event-processing rules.
3. Additional data residing in-memory (cache) and/or on a database can be joined with the incoming event stream, that is, enriching the incoming event with additional information.

4. Rules can also reside in an external Business Rule Management System (BRMS), and events can be evaluated against these rules. Optionally, the BRMS can generate new events.
5. The Event Processing engine as well as the Rule engine can generate events and feed them into Event Cloud to be analyzed as a new event.
6. The resulting business events are published in Enterprise Event Bus.
7. One or more BPM processes, which have subscribed previously to the resulting business event, are notified about the event.
8. One or more SOA services, which have subscribed previously for the resulting business event, are notified about the event.

Architectural pattern 4 – analyzing BPM process behavior with event processing

With this architectural pattern, the sources of events are BPM processes and SOA services. In contrast to architectural pattern 4, events here are used to monitor and analyze the process behavior in real time by sending events to an event processing solution, which is extended by a monitoring dashboard. The idea here is to monitor the execution of business processes in order to detect exceptions, disparities across systems and anomalies, and to analyze system performance.

The event-processing logic can automatically detect situations and take appropriate action, for example, by reconfiguring a business process at runtime to automatically adapt to a given solution. Additionally, a business analyst can use a business monitoring dashboard to detect situations. In that case, he might use this knowledge to manually change some parameters of the runtime execution to change the behavior of the corresponding process.

The following diagram shows this architectural pattern and the necessary interactions between the different components:

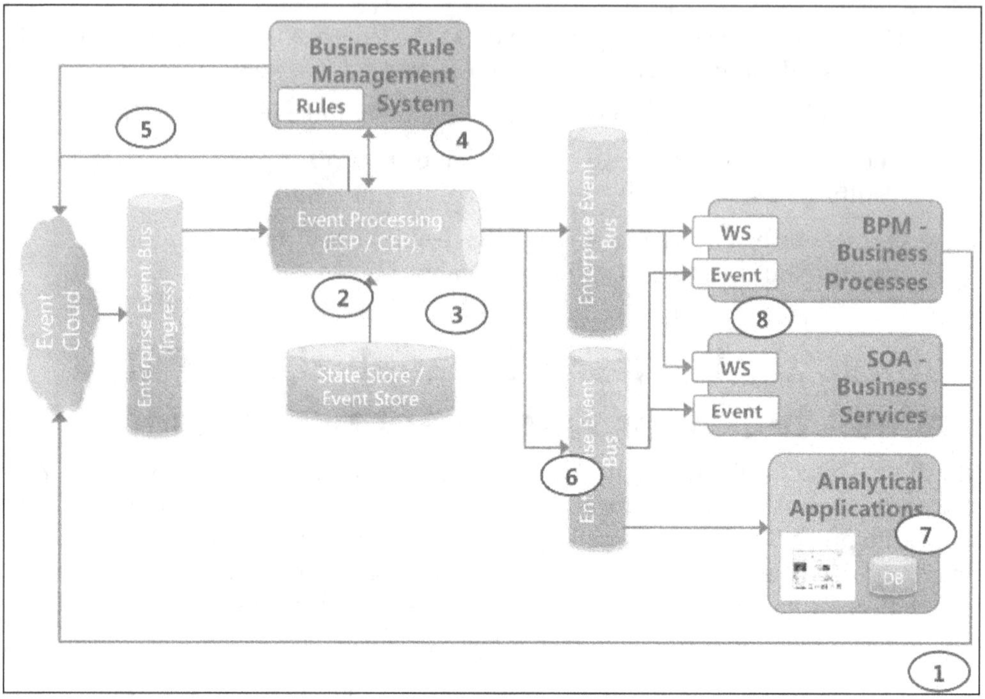

Figure 25

The following interactions take place between the different components:

1. At runtime, defined events are created by running business processes and/or business services and delivered to Enterprise Event Bus.
2. Event Processing consumes each event and applies its event-processing rules.
3. Additional data residing in-memory (cache) and/or on a database can be joined with the incoming event stream, that is, enriching the incoming event with additional information.
4. Rules can also reside in an external Business Rule Management System, and events can be evaluated against these rules. Optionally, the Rule engine can generate new events.
5. The Event Processing engine and Rule engines can generate events and feed them into Enterprise Event Bus to be analyzed as a new event.

6. The resulting notable events are published on Enterprise Event Bus.
7. The notable events are made visible on a dashboard.
8. The notable events can also result in an automatic adoption/optimization of the (running) business process, such as changing limits or ranges.

This architectural pattern is where Oracle Business Activity Monitoring really shines, and use cases for it will be covered in the next chapter.

Summary

In this chapter, you learned about the paradigm of event processing and how it can be used standalone as well as combined with the other components of Oracle SOA and BPM Suite. We covered a number of topics in this chapter. The idea of fast data and how event processing can support the processing of information in real time was discussed at length. The 4Ds (Detect, Derive, Decide, and Do) paradigm was put forth to describe event processing systems. The key elements of event processing and the basic principles and concepts used when talking about event processing applications were also talked about. The three different types of event processing—Simple Event Processing (SEP), Event Stream Processing (ESP), and Complex Event Processing (CEP) were also covered. The conceptual architecture of event processing and how event processing fits into a modern architecture was also dealt with. Oracle Fusion Middleware products supporting event processing were also discussed in detail. The different architectural patterns of event processing were also given due coverage.

In the next chapter, we will go into detail about how Business Activity Monitoring (BAM) can be used to monitor the behavior of a business process in real time, to detect exceptions, and to analyze process performance.

12

Business Activity Monitoring

Throughout the previous chapters, you were introduced to an approach to design an architecture supporting the definition, design, and execution of business processes. This approach has incorporated interactions with systems, events occurring, user tasks, mobile interfaces, complex cases, and business rules. This gives us a comprehensive solution to roll out a platform to support an organization's business architecture and processes. However, when implementing a business process architecture, the initial rollout of the solution should be seen as only the first step, as a preparation for the ongoing execution and continuous improvement of processes. The real success will be attained in sustained improvement of business operations and in the ongoing achievement of good business outcomes as business landscapes change and strategy evolves. Facilitating this execution is only part of the story; insight into that execution is required not just from an IT operations viewpoint, but also from a business performance perspective.

This chapter will show how Business Activity Monitoring (BAM) can help an organization gain insights—in real time—into business operations and outcomes enabling optimizations, efficiency gains, and ongoing improvements to business processes. In this chapter, we will do the following:

- Define the capabilities that a BAM platform should provide and the different types of insights that it delivers
- Clarify the difference between BAM and traditional data warehouse-based reporting solutions
- Introduce the Oracle BAM 12*c* product with the out-of-the-box process analytics included
- Describe how BAM integrates with SOA and BPM to monitor business processes and services in real time
- Present a methodology and best practices for designing and building BAM dashboards and supporting data objects

What is BAM?

BAM describes an approach, architecture, and the supporting toolset to push events and data streams from transactional systems and processes to a monitoring platform that will present information from these streams in a visual and insightful way. These visualizations provide awareness of the immediate situation and present critical business indicators to allow stakeholders and executives to respond accordingly in a timely manner before the impact of their actions is diluted. The timeliness in which BAM can bring the information to the attention of the user through alerts and dashboards greatly enhances the effectiveness of the actions taken.

A BAM platform will provide the following capabilities:

- **Sense**: The platform should be able to identify and be notified of changes of state in business operations, transactions, and processes; this could be the happening of an event that interacts with a case or process, update of some key data, progression of a business process to subsequent steps, an exception occurring, or a touch-point with the customer being initiated or received.
- **Aggregate**: Fragmented events will normally not give the full picture to a stakeholder about what is happening within business processes, so a BAM solution must filter uninteresting events and aggregate related events together to present composite business events that will closely represent what is happening in the business.
- **Visualize**: Stakeholders need to see at a glance what is occurring within business processes, and people react better to visualizations of data rather than the raw data itself, so graphs, charts, and innovative ways to present data is required to bring key trends, peaks, and changes to the users' attention. Change should be highlighted, with visual transitions identifying the extent of the change.
- **Respond**: Automating an action or giving information and context to allow a user to take direct action on the process or instances of the process (for example, movement of tasks from one Worklist group to another to level workload or the relaxing of rules to clear a business backlog with the associated risks monitored) or implement changes to affect the immediate behavior of a process and its stakeholders (for example, sending a communication to the team to socialize current performance against KPIs or adding a temporary step in the business process to perform quality checks if customer feedback shows a negative trend).

BAM covers multiple Analytics use cases, both tactical and strategic, allowing monitoring at both the process level and a more macro level of business indicators. The type of analytics that are implemented through a BAM platform can be summarized as shown in the following sections.

Operational analytics

Operational analytics give the BAM user oversight of the running of business processes. Such analytics are intended to give immediate visibility into the operational indicators that will determine whether business processes are likely to meet their goals within the targets set out. Operational analysis will help monitor the throughput of the process to identify bottlenecks and exception-prone parts of the process. With such analytics, the views in the dashboard are related directly to the process rather than the strategic view of performance. They are used as early indicators of process health, and often, issues outlined in these can be resolved by tactical actions, such as moving resources to help with a process exception or fixing a bottleneck in an automated task by reallocating work.

Oracle BAM 12*c* provides a set of out-of-the-box process operational dashboards, a supported data object model, and integration to the BPM and BPEL process engine. These give an immediate picture of what processes are not performing as desired, awareness of exceptions occurring, and a guide to how much inflight volume is occurring in the processes. There are also dashboards to show the trend of elapsed time of each process or task, volume over time, and a map of current bottlenecks. These dashboards are invaluable in ensuring that good business processes are built; an executable business process without measurement, monitoring, and facility of improvement only delivers a fraction of what is intended with BPM.

Business analytics

Monitoring operational metrics within a business process only goes part of the way in allowing business performance to be managed; it will only allow improvement at the local process instance level. Business analytics give the opportunity to measure, monitor, and improve business outcomes that are affected across multiple business processes and other ad hoc business transactions.

Within Oracle BAM 12*c*, custom business indicators and measures can be identified and maintained within the process and streamed to the BAM engine. These can then be filtered, aggregated, and visualized into KPI and business performance dashboards. These custom indicators can focus on the KPIs identified through the strategic analysis of the business as described in *Chapter 2, Modeling Business Processes for SOA - Methodology*. In addition, other event sources can be combined with process metrics to add to the full picture of what is occurring within the business; these events could be streamed from stream explorer, as described in the previous chapter, or sourced directly from applications (via services, database code, or JMS events).

Operational intelligence

Operational intelligence takes operational analytics a step further, and instead of just reporting what is currently occurring within a set of process instances, it adds context and rules to apply acumen and present a more knowledgeable view of operations. Operational intelligence utilizes the patterns and event-processing techniques described in *Chapter 11, Event Processing and BPM*, to combine analysis on the streamed events with historic and contextual information stored in BAM and relational data stores. Operational intelligence looks for patterns, trends, temporal changes, and the absence of events to derive a view on top of operations that will allow better-informed decisions to be made. Templates are available to report on data trending up or down, KPI thresholds being breached, performance of high-ranking occurrences, high-volume peaks, and missing or delayed events. The event correlation patterns that look at the absence of something occurring over a period of time, or in a sequence of other events, are very powerful in identifying issues before your customer does and should always be considered in event and dashboard design. Often, something not happening is as important as something occurring.

Strategic analytics

The aforementioned patterns allow BAM stakeholders to be proactive in responding to exceptions, trends, and patterns that may present immediate issues or opportunities to the business. Strategic analytics allow stakeholders to look for patterns and trends over time. This allows more strategic change to the processes to deal with potential issues, mitigate predicted risk, and implement longer-term improvement of the process. Within any BPM methodology, measuring the process performance is an essential part of process improvement—within improvement methodologies, such as Lean Six Sigma, a good measurement phase is critical in the success of a project. A major part of this improvement will include strategic changes rather than operational efficiencies. This may include changing the business process by consolidating steps or adding in check steps, altering product rules (for example, changing the parameters or structure for pricing models), or making off-system changes, such as organizational change. BAM is a very good method for capturing measurements of the process, allowing business process designers to alter the process and run simulations, using the new process in BPM, and observing the improvements or deteriorations in BAM. It is common for a BPM team to have a *model office* environment where scenario tests can be run on variations of the processes; BAM will be a key tool within that environment.

BAM versus BI

The question of the difference between BAM and business intelligence (BI) has often been asked, with organizations unclear as to when to present charts in BAM and when to use their BI platform. This discussion has often been triggered for the wrong reasons due to the tools in place in the organization or the structure of the teams; BAM is often owned by the SOA team, and BI is often owned by the reporting or application teams. Both of these tools are intended to give users an insight into business operations and performance—each from a slightly different perspective.

BI reporting systems traditionally extract data from transactional systems at a predetermined time interval to a separate data warehouse schema. This database is then interrogated by reports on requests to show data in an aggregated and list format, comparing historic data with recent data. The more recent the data, the more frequent the extracts needed to be, and, therefore, the more intrusive they were to the transactional system. However, the business constantly strives for more insight into the state of ongoing transactions and a finer level of granularity of task reporting. It was common for the data warehouse team to submit change requests to the transactional system in order to provide additional data or add extra persistence steps within the transaction to store finer data milestones. This broke a fundamental rule, that of a reporting system not impacting the system it is reporting on; if an organization is building functionality into applications or services merely to satisfy BI requirements, then the architecture is flawed.

It is the role of BAM to satisfy these real-time reporting needs alongside a BI solution. BAM will show the impact as events occur in your business processes and applications, whereas the strength of business intelligence tools is to show a more static view at a point in time (current, end of the day, end of the month, end of the year, and so on). BAM should focus the transition of the events onto the dashboards, highlighting change and the impact of change. With BAM, messages are streamed directly to the BAM server and then periodically persisted to a data store. Therefore, all caches are updated immediately rather than needing to await the persistence of new events and the rehydration of caches to refresh the dashboard views. This is how BAM can deliver fast updates to the users that are nonintrusive to the monitored processes due to a decoupling (via the event-processing engine) between the process execution and the consumption of the event in BAM.

With BI tools, the data is moved to the analytical data store or data warehouse first through a series of data integration steps (which could include BAM objects as a source) and then reports request the new view of the data when refreshed. BAM implements a push-based pattern for updates, whereas BI updates require a pull from client reports.

Oracle BAM 12*c* architecture

Oracle BAM 12*c* is built upon a scalable architecture that integrates natively to Oracle BPM, BPEL, and Event Processing seamlessly. The architecture is built to ensure that it can monitor processes in real-time without affecting the processes; it is designed to be a non-intrusive monitoring platform. The process or service transaction that changes the state of a metric visualized in BAM is decoupled from the act of persisting events to the BAM database and rendering metrics in dashboards. The Oracle BAM 12*c* architecture is represented in the following diagram:

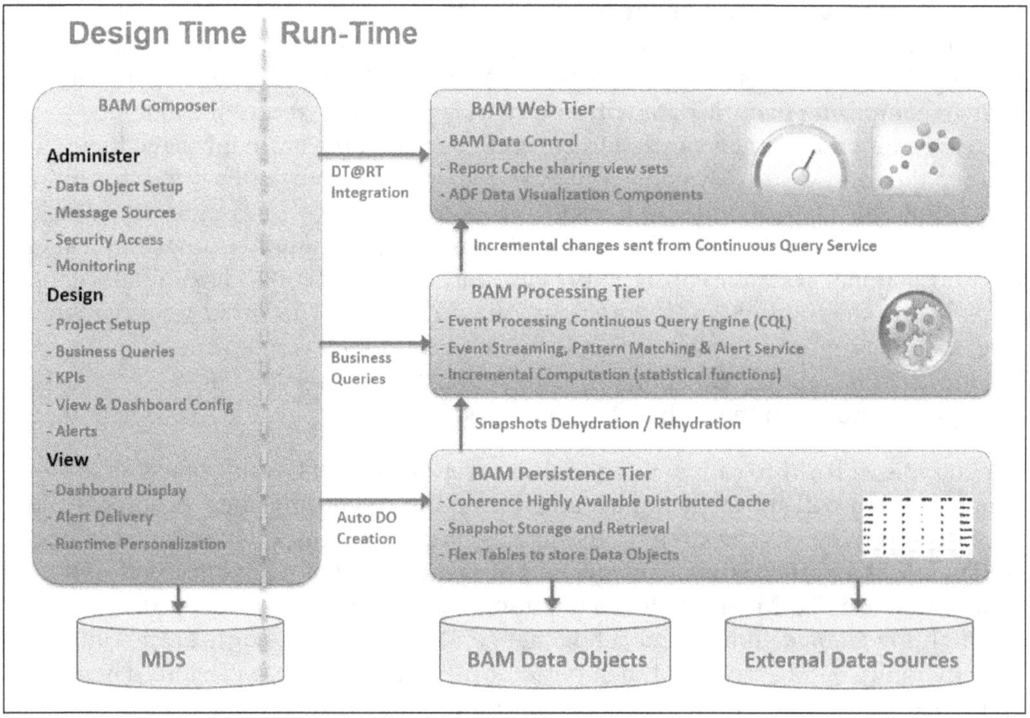

Figure 1

The BAM architecture is made up of the following components:

- **BAM Composer**: This is a design-time and runtime environment to model data, set up message sources, provide design views of data visualization components, compose BAM Dashboards, and administer the dashboards. Fine-grained security policies can be created in the composer to limit access at the project (a group of views), dashboard, view, data query, or data row level. BAM Composer can also be used to view runtime data, views, and dashboards. All the configuration setup in composer is stored in the Metadata Services (MDS) database as it is for process and rule configuration.

- **BAM Persistence Tier**: As physical data objects are saved within the composer environment, Flex Tables will be created within the SOAINFRA database schema. These will be populated with snapshots from the events that are streamed to BAM Processing Tier. A set of preinstalled process star schema tables are provided to support process analytics with further data objects created when metric collection is configured for a BPM or BPEL process. As data objects are modified, Oracle Coherence will cache the objects and present them to Continuous Query Service.
- **BAM Processing Tier**: The message sources, business queries, and alerts created in the design-time composer environment will be deployed to BAM Processing Tier on commit. This is a push-based system, based on the Oracle Event Processing engine streaming, that implements the filtering, aggregation, and pattern matching designed in business queries. The processing engine's continuous queries will identify thresholds for alerts and deliver them via a service for alerts that is integrated with Oracle User Messaging Service.
- **BAM Web Tier**: BAM Web Tier will interact with the design time via BAM Composer through a *design time at runtime* pattern that increases agility in the rollout of dashboards by removing the need for a traditional release cycle to deploy changes. The changes made in the composer will be immediately reflected in the runtime view on BAM Web Tier. BAM data controls, which are then created, can be used in custom ADF UI components as well as in BAM Data Visualization and table components. BAM Report Cache, within which all report views are managed, manages shared view sets amongst users. This will be incrementally updated by pushed updates from BAM Processing Tier.

BAM Process Analytics

Within Oracle BPM 12*c*, there is a set of prebuilt data objects (in the form of the process star schema), views, and dashboards to present common analytical information on the BPM or BPEL process. All data objects, queries, and views available in BAM Process Analytics can be customized or reused in other dashboards, so they form a great foundation for the business view of the processes, which is traditionally absent if the IT operations view of the processes in Enterprise Manager is all that is exposed to process stakeholders.

To enable BAM Process Analytics, you simply set an MBean configuration property within the BAM domain, as follows:

```
AnalyticsConfig/analytics/DisableProcessMetrics = false
```

In Oracle BAM, you are presented with a set of BPM Analytics sample views that are preconfigured within dashboards linked from a process launchpad, as represented in the following screenshot:

Figure 2

The following dashboards are preconfigured and should be reviewed and customized to deliver a business stakeholder view of the process:

- **Process Summary** lists each process and identifies which are overdue, due soon, or faulted. It will also show how many instances have been opened and closed within a chosen time period (defaulted to today).
- **Open Process Analysis** measures and compares the cycle times of the process instances to allow an estimation of how long a standard instance of the process will take to complete.
- **Closed Process Analysis** compares the current cycle times of processes with historical summaries, allowing degradation against the past to be performance tified.
- **Process Health** gives a simple color-coded view of active, faulted, and suspended processes, so you can see in which processes the current bulk of the activity is occurring.
- **Process Activity** monitors the progress of tasks, showing the ones that are overdue and due soon by task name, filtered by process. This dashboard is useful for looking at the task workload by assignee. Alerts can be set up to notify when a bottleneck for an assignee occurs so that you could configure an action (such as reassigning or unclaiming the task) to quicken the resolution of the task and allow the process to continue.

- **Trend Analysis** shows the historical transition of the number of process instances opened and closed over a selected time period and their associated process cycle times, allowing the process stakeholder to identify time-based patterns and trends.

For all of these dashboards, alerts can be configured with thresholds to allow notification of potential issues to process stakeholders. It is then advisable to provide a mechanism for the user to get more context on the individual process instances that are troublesome or require fine tuning. A link should be provided to the BPM process instance map for root cause analysis and to allow the user to see more details of the process data used in that instance.

Version 12.2.1 onwards, these dashboards are delivered with the Alta UI style. Alta UI is a design system that is used in Oracle cloud and mobile applications. It provides a fresh and uncluttered visual style that responds to desktops, tablets, and mobile devices. As BAM Process Analytics dashboards, and the views that they contain, are built to adhere to the Alta UI design guidelines and development standards, they are easily extended and integrated into your own ADF or Alta UI applications.

The BAM methodology

Designing a BAM solution should start with business aims and goals, identifying the desired business outcomes to measure and leading and lagging indicators for these, and KPI's to monitor. The dashboard is only part of the design and should be based on a clear and consistent design of data objects, view objects, queries and views. The following process should be followed to achieve a good design in a BAM implementation:

1. Working with business stakeholders, define the strategic business goals and the KPIs that specify success of these goals.
2. Identify the personas, their user experience map for using BAM, and the user journeys that contribute to the strategic business goals.
3. Understand the measurements (for example, quantity, amount, elapsed time, and so on) and metrics (for example, ratio, percentage, average, and so on) that influence the KPIs and should be captured. Defining to the dashboard data that relates to KPIs in isolation helps ensure these are related to the strategic business goals rather than just a visualization of data that the user deems interesting.
4. Define the reference lookup data that the measurements will need to be filtered and aggregated on.
5. Identify the attributes for which changes affect the KPIs (for example, change in status, time elapsing, new assignment, and so on).

6. Identify the points in the process, user journey, or external events that will change this data and cause variations or exceptions to happen that will influence business goals and KPIs.
7. Define the aggregations and structure of data that will be monitored.
8. Define the view that can visualize the aggregations and KPI's.
9. Identify the thresholds that will lead to action being required.
10. Define the action to take place, who is the owner of that action, and what supporting context is required.
11. Define the point at which the KPI would be back at acceptable levels and need standard monitoring rather than remaining in action mode.
12. Design a dashboard for each persona based on the views identified to visualize the metrics and KPIs. This should be done in an iterative fashion to meet user expectations.
13. Identify the points in the user journey and business processes that would benefit from BAM views being presented to the user.
14. Build ADF visualizations with BAM data controls for the views that are to be reused within the applications or portals that are part of the user's journey.
15. Monitor the usage of BAM and evolve the actions, including automating the initiation of rectification processes, changes to rule parameters, and shifting of workload between user groups.

Monitoring RYLC with BAM

Now that RYLC has a process-driven architecture in place to allow it to deliver service in a much more efficient manner and tailor rental deals to the customer needs; it is looking to build on the architecture foundations and grow demand through marketing activities. To ensure these are effective and to consider which countries react best to which campaigns, they are looking to build a BAM dashboard to track in real time the responses to a direct digital marketing campaign. They will target offers through Twitter, Facebook-sponsored links, direct e-mails, and a local television campaign. Over the course of a few days, they will consider the most effective lead generation technique and invest more heavily in that.

The aim is to build a set of views that can be used in a dashboard to monitor in real time the effect of the marketing campaign and tailor the campaigns accordingly to raise the profile of RYLC. The views should be directly related to the metrics that are critical to the success of the campaigns, which is not necessarily just how many leads the campaign has generated. To keep the views insightful and action-oriented, a number of analysis sessions were held with the marketing, sales, and operations teams to determine which key performance indicators are true measures of successful campaigns. These sessions focused on why each metric needed to be visualized in real time and explored any leading indicators to that metric. Common questions asked by the business process analyst in this scenario were the following: how is that metric related to the outcomes of the marketing campaign? What metrics really contribute to the bottom line success of the campaign? What are you going to do with that information to change the process or the campaign parameters?

The following metrics were agreed upon as the key measurements of success of the campaign, to determine whether action is needed to be taken on issues or opportunities and to identify the relative value of each campaign.

Metric	Description
Contact efficiency	This shows how efficient a contact is (how much revenue was generated out of a contact)
Campaign cost ratio	This shows the revenues generated by events and campaigns divided by campaign and event costs
Lead generation ratio	This shows the number of leads generated as a percentage of contact recipients reached
Lead generation total	This shows the number of leads generated over time from campaign events
Lead generation lag	This shows the average time for a lead to make contact after the campaign starts
Contact conversion rate	This is the ratio of response to a campaign to the completion of rental

User stories were produced that described which persona wanted to see which metric and for what purpose. Within the acceptance criteria, we defined any particular actions that would need to be taken based on the visualization, any thresholds or alerts that would lead to this action, and any context about the metric that was needed to inform better decisions. We, therefore, steered the team away from user stories that couldn't articulate any threshold or actions or had any direct relation to the key metrics that we were attempting to monitor in real time. A number of these stories would be better served via a business intelligence solution set up for executive reporting and strategic analysis working on data fed into the data warehouse overnight. As an example, a common story heard in all BAM analysis workshops relate to viewing the total number of items that show progress and value of the team, such as the following:

"As a RYLC sales advisor, I want to see the total number of cars rented this month."

These are confidence metrics and if used to make decisive actions to change behavior, then they are useful, such as showing a sales team the current progress against the target in the final few hours before an accounting period is closed. However, these behavior-related metrics are of limited value when monitoring the results of an ongoing campaign.

The rationale for this metric is not communicated, and at the moment, we are just sharing data, not insight that will improve business performance. To change the data into information, we need to add context, and to change information into insight, we need actions to be prompted. So, a good BAM user story may read as follows:

"As an RYLC sales advisor, I want to see the number of rental leads closed per hour segmented by marketing channel so that I can determine the trends in the quality of leads throughout the day and determine where the sales effort should be focused over the next hours of the day."

BAM data object design

Oracle BAM should only keep recent data in the schema; it does not replace DW and business intelligence schemas and reports that will include historical analysis in their reports and dashboards. BAM will provide transparency to the process but shouldn't be treated as a repository of all metrics that the team can think of. Also, ensure that any insight can be actioned; we want to avoid an explosion of alerts that do not give the context or opportunity to take action on the alert.

The BAM database design should focus on a star schema approach with logical view objects being layered on top of physical fact and dimension data objects. This design is common in analytical solutions, with fact tables consisting of the key entity attributes, measurements, and metrics of a business process. The fact tables will be flattened from their relational form with master attributes repeated and with rows simply detailing the analytical functions associated with a reporting solution. Dimension tables hold reference or lookup data that fact data can be filtered or aggregated on. In BAM data objects, these should also be flattened where possible to allow logical data objects to only have to join to one layer of dimension (for example, if sales areas are split up into countries and regions, then the country name would be repeated on each region row within the `REGION` dimension to facilitate drilldown through country and region).

The physical design should be structured in a way that metrics and attributes are only stored once and populated by each process or service that impacts the data. The logical design should map to the chart views that will be displayed and include aggregations, filtering, and the joining of dimension data and will represent a flatter view of the data to be monitored.

RYLC BAM data design

To produce views to visualize and provide alert on the metrics, two fact tables are created, one holding campaign data and one holding details of the contacts resulting from the campaigns. Dimensions are provided to filter and summarize the data by country, channel, vehicle class and the status of the contact that resulted from the campaign.

Campaign Fact holds details of each campaign's running count of prospects reached (this is estimated for some channels) and the cost of the campaign. A calculated field is included for the cost per contact (prospect reached / total cost) to make cost-related metrics easier to summarize per converted lead. The following diagram shows the Fact and Dimension model for Campaigns:

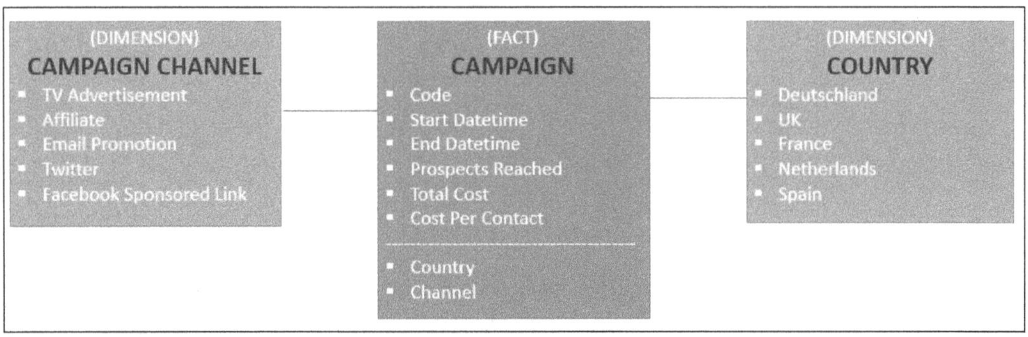

Figure 3

Campaign Contact Fact holds one record per prospect targeted in the campaign. **Contact Status** will progress with the sales lifecycle with a converted contact mapping to the first rental being agreed. In the data warehouse, further statuses will be added to signify whether the prospect turned into a repeat customer, but in the BAM schema, for the purposes of the campaign monitoring dashboard, the sales lifecycle ends with the first rental. The following diagram shows the **Fact** and **Dimension** model for **Campaign** Contacts:

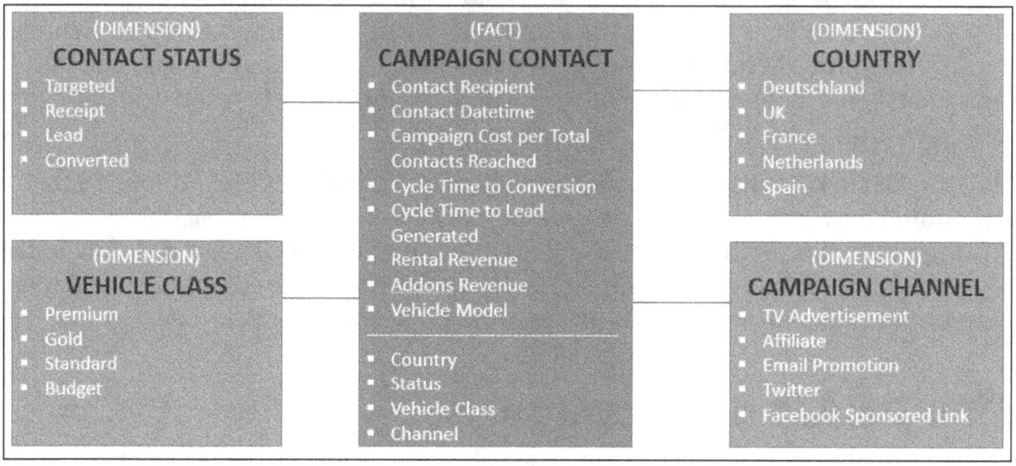

Figure 4

The following screenshot shows how a **Simple Data Object** can be created to store the **Fact** data:

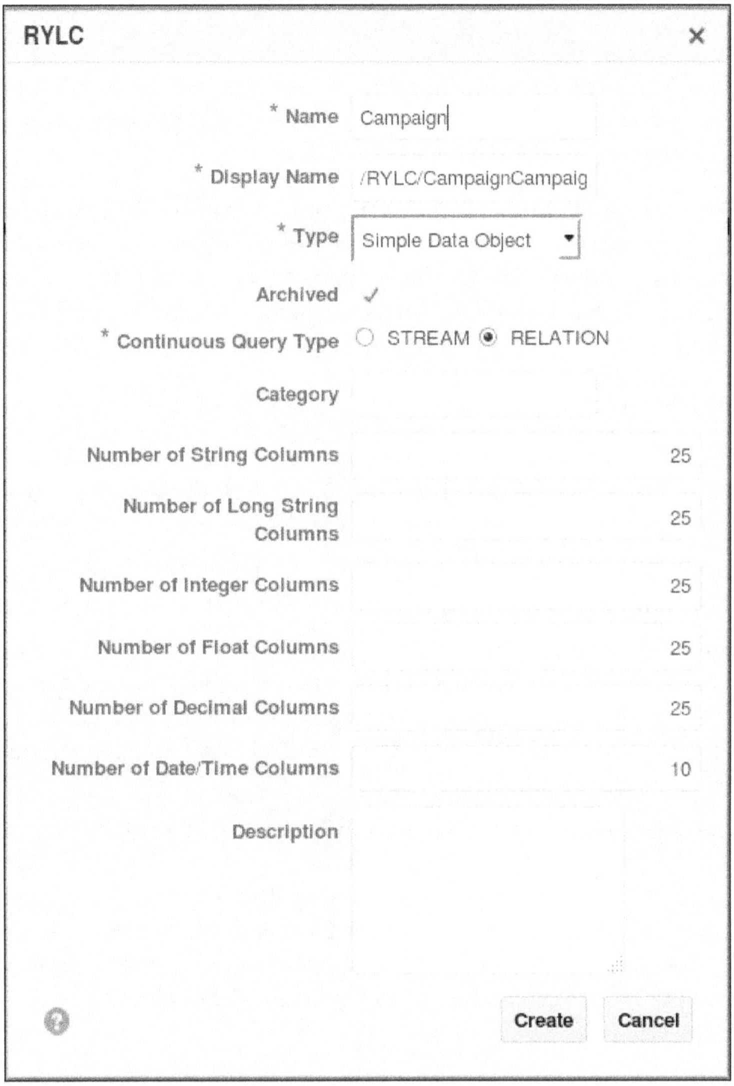

Figure 5

Physical data objects are created within the BAM RYLC project to represent these fact and dimension objects. We keep the dimension tables separate in the physical layer to ensure that these dimensions can be reused across a number of different logical data objects.

To create a data object the BAM designer clicks on the **Administration** tab in BAM Composer. The data objects are created once within the BAM repository and can be made available to multiple BAM projects.

Display Name contains a prefix to denote the folder that we will store the data object within `/RYLC/Campaign`. Note that the number of columns of each type represents the maximum number of each of the types as, at this point, a physical database table named `BEAM_nn` is created in the MDS schema, which contains flex fields to store data object columns.

There are four types of data objects within Oracle BAM 12*c*:

- **Simple**: This is to hold the base data of fact. This is what will be populated by the event stream. We will create `Campaign` and `Campaign Contact` simple objects to hold the details of the RYLC BAM data.
- **Derived**: This is a copy of the simple data object. This is often useful to archive data, keeping the simple objects focused on storing recent data.
- **External data object**: This points to data stored in a database outside of BAM. This is often useful to include reference data in the BAM schema, for instance, the master data for countries is likely to be stored in a reference data schema external to BAM, so we would create an external data object for the `Country` dimension.
- **Logical data object**: This is a read only view on top of other data objects. It is here that data objects will be joined together and calculated columns will be added. RYLC will join the fact tables with the dimension tables to pull the descriptions into the logical data object to allow descriptions rather than code from dimension to be used in the views. `CampaignVO` and `CampaignContactVO` are created to be used as view objects within RYLC views.

After creating the data object, columns are added in the **Administrator** view. If you want calculated fields to be consistent across all view objects, and all input to the calculation is local to the data object, then these can be added at this physical level; otherwise, if they are dependent on multiple data objects, they should be added in the logical data object. The RYLC BAM designer adds the columns to the physical data object. The following screenshot is an example of the main `Campaign` physical data object:

Figure 6

A physical data object is created for each dimension; the following screenshot is an example of `CountryDim`:

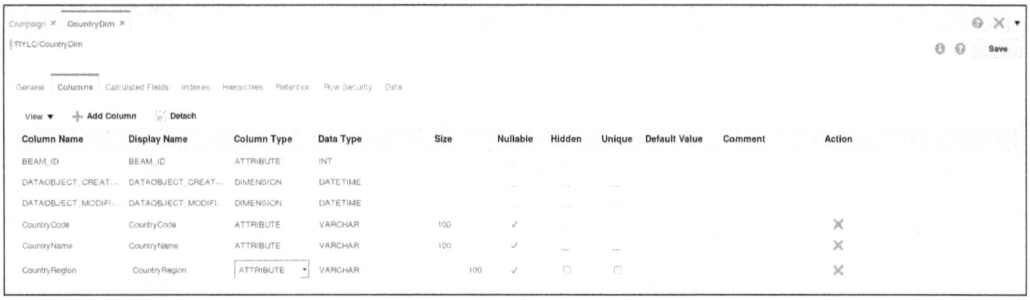

Figure 7

A logical data object is then created to merge the dimension details with the fact table; the RYLC standard is to suffix the name with VO to show that this is the data object that should be used in BAM views. The primary data object, `Campaign`, is linked to the foreign data object, `CountryDim`, and the join column selected. Joins to dimension tables should be on one single ID column, which, in this case, is `Country` / `Country Code`, which holds the short ID of the country (UK, DE, NL, and so on). The following screenshot shows this:

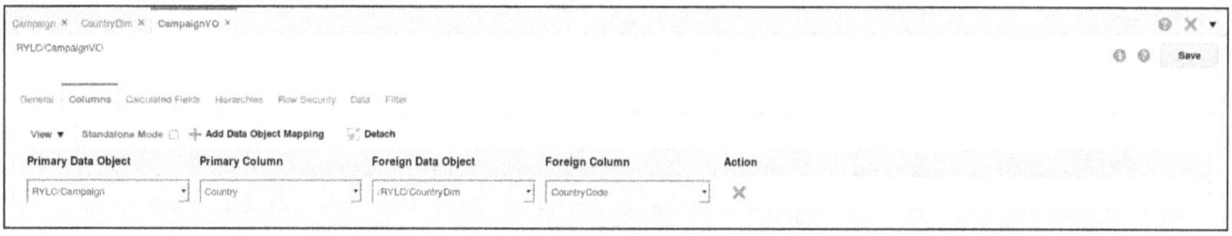

Figure 8

The logical data object can use all or a subset of columns from physical data objects, and, at this point, calculated fields can be added by selecting the **Calculation** tab. All columns are added to `CampaignVO`, including the dimension lookups, and a calculated field is created to hold the cost ratio for the campaign.

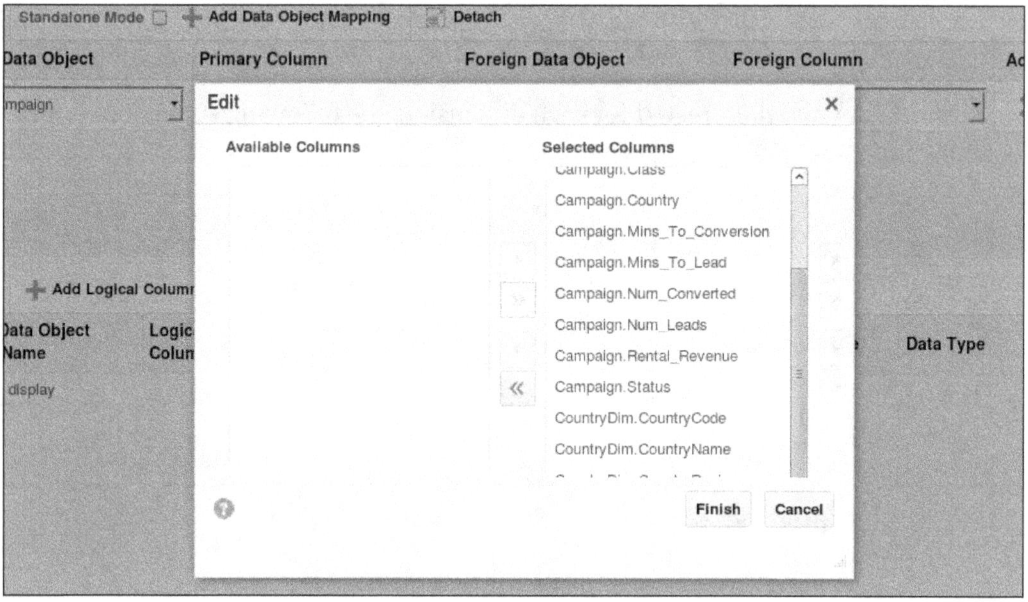

Figure 9

The following screenshot shows how a calculated field can be added using an expression based on fields currently included in the logical data object:

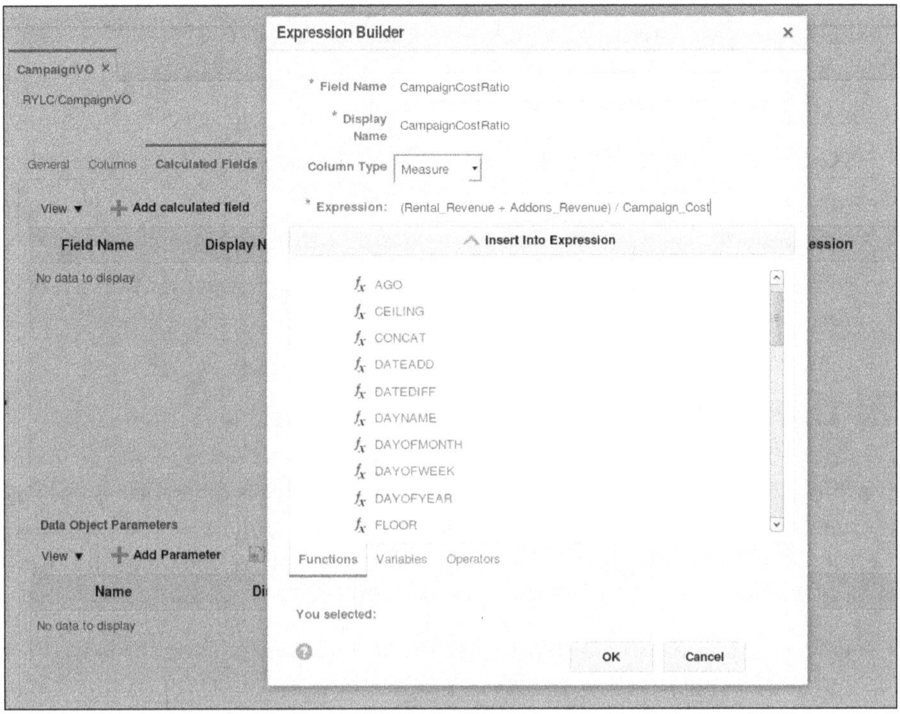

Figure 10

BAM integration with BPEL and BPM

It is very simple to enable out-of-the-box process analytic dashboards to provide monitoring views of process instances, allowing the operational management of processes; however, insight that matches the business goals, KPIs, and metrics will require more business context within dashboards, and events from the business processes and services will need to be mapped to the metrics they are affecting. This is where the traditional BAM approach of attaching sensors within BPM or BPEL processes is required to provide in-process data to the event that will be sent to BAM. The following steps are required to be taken to add sensors to the process to provide data for BAM objects:

1. Identify each process that may result in the change of a measurement or leading indicator. Add a counter or measure and identify the dimensions that this is based on.
2. Bind the counters or measures to the business process they are used within.

3. Add counter marks and measurement points at each step of the process where there is interest.
4. Add script tasks if you need counters on paths that do not have activities, such as monitoring the path taken through a gateway step.
5. Define data associations for business indicators by populating the dimension fields in the project's data objects.
6. BAM will create the data objects on the deployment of the process.
7. Add the data objects to the BAM project, and note that the activity data object contains activity instances and user-defined attributes.
8. Follow the steps in the BAM methodology to create logical data objects, views, queries, and dashboards.

BAM dashboard design

There is a design challenge in determining how to sense and process large amounts of data rapidly to determine what is going on within business operations. The BAM design must highlight the exceptions, correlations, opportunities, and trends in a clear and attention-grabbing way. It should not, however, simply be aesthetic and flashy. It should be of sustained use and be built on solid and consistent data foundations.

There is always a danger with a BAM solution of delivering dashboards that are received well in the first few weeks of use, as they are different from what has come before, but fade into obscurity as it is realized that the data cannot be trusted or the visualizations are not giving anything new—just the same data but now in real time. It is the quality and relevance of data as well as the visualization of data that brings value.

A common BAM analogy to car or flight dashboards does not tell accurately the story of the value and the requisites for BAM design as, within these examples, manual decisions are needed constantly. The driver and pilot use all the information presented, aggregate it with their knowledge and skills, and make a decision on what manual action to take next (hit the brake, change gear, change altitude, and so on). Hopefully with a BPM and BAM solution, the process is automated—what is in the user's control is less and the BAM user is not having to make every decision to steer the process.

Therefore, a more accurate analogy would be of driverless cars. A future dashboard in these vehicles would not concentrate on speed and revs but on confidence that the automation is making the correct automated decisions and alerting the driver only when manual input may be needed. Similarly, with a business dashboard, the design should provide confidence that operational efficiency is being maintained, that there is focus on improvements and on alerts as or before issues occur.

BAM dashboards should facilitate informed and aligned decisions to support automated business processes, with design finding an appropriate way of communicating the impact of change rather than just providing flash gadgets. The dashboards should be designed as operational scorecards of the process, thus showing opportunities for innovation and requirements for optimization of the process through measurements, alerts, and supporting context.

It is important in dashboard design that the right chart is used for the right purpose; otherwise, the visualization could be misleading. For example, pie charts should only be for percentages or the splitting of a distribution into dimensions, that is, the relationship between the part and the whole, rather than comparing multiple values together. For instance, a pie chart of the number of complaints showing that 95 percent of customers are contented with the service and 5 percent are not does not reflect true insight into the data. The visualization would not get across the fact that 5 percent complaints is high; it will appear as an insignificant value in a pie chart. A range gauge would better serve this purpose as you will be able to add a further indicator—the threshold as to when the level of complaints is not acceptable.

If the dashboard does not convey the meaning of the metrics at a glance, then the view is using the wrong visualization tool. The layout, font size, and color of metrics should be used to emphasize the most important metrics. It is also important to review designs with customers of the dashboard with example datasets to ensure that the views are validated from the data quality perspective as well as the usability testing perspective.

Dashboards should progressively reveal more information about a metric. The user should first identify the need to pay attention to a particular view in the dashboard, then be given a drilled-down view with more context to attempt to focus on the root cause of the issue or opportunity. A further drilldown or link should then be provided to be able to take action on the insight that has surfaced. This pattern of glancing to see the headline changes, scanning the context in more detail, and drilling down to the transaction or instance level to commit to action is of value when considering dashboard design.

The following pattern should be followed when structuring a set of analytics screens for a user journey:

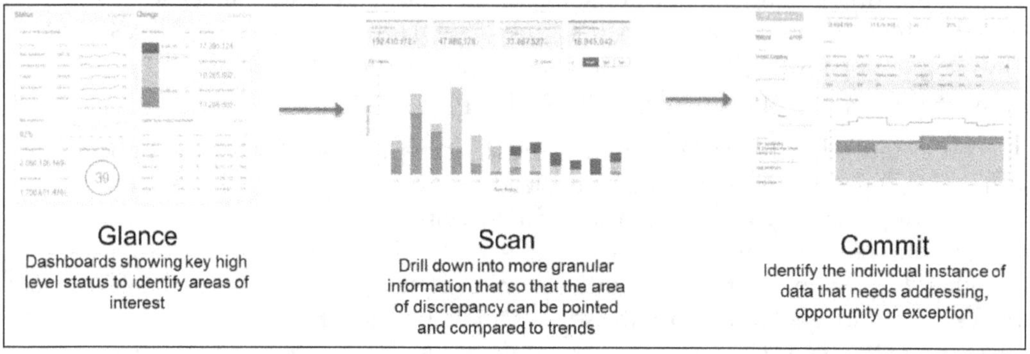

Figure 11

The RYLC BAM dashboard

The RYLC BAM designer now switches to design mode to build visualizations and includes all the RYLC data objects into a new BAM project. The marketing users want to see at a glance how the latest campaigns are progressing. They want to see some headline confidence figures to ensure that rental figures across their key global markets are responding to the marketing blasts. They also want to see the country and channels where the campaigns are being run effectively to leverage that market further.

We do not attempt to show all the data we have on the dashboard; this should be an entry point to allow further drilldown. We also build the dashboard fairly rapidly and work with the users to determine how they want it laid out. For more permanent BAM views, ADF visualization will be built based on the BAM data control and be made available in their portal and core rental applications. The following screen shows a sample dashboard to monitor RYLC campaigns:

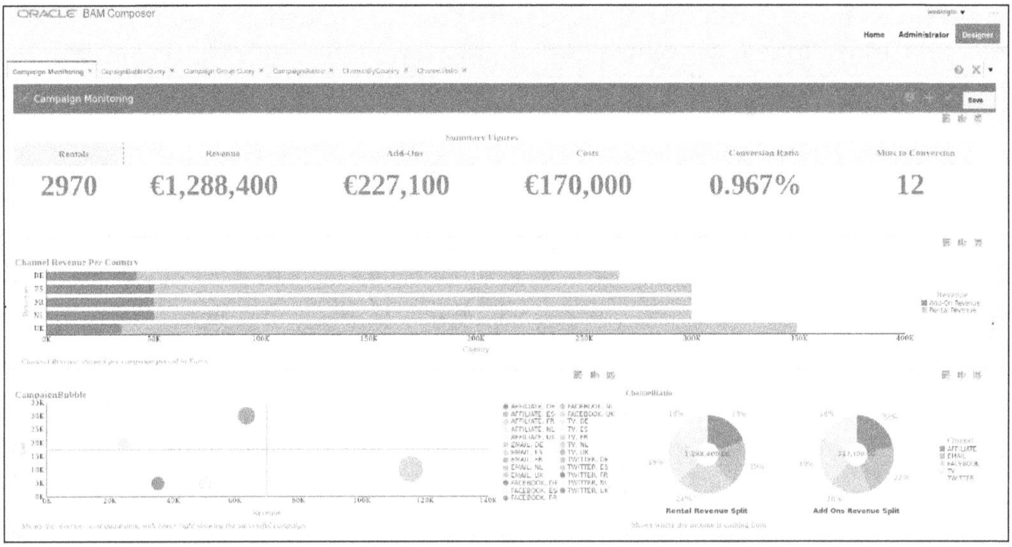

Figure 12

The dashboard will update in real time as new rentals are made. The charts are designed to bring key opportunities and issues to the users' attention. It is designed in the marketing campaign executive persona, but the base data objects are now in place to allow the fast creation of specific views for other personas. We will not dilute this view by adding other metrics for other personas' interest.

The top view comprises collapsed lists used to give a quick view of aggregated data. The next view shows the channel revenue per country, allowing an at-a-glance view of where the campaign is effective from a revenue point of view:

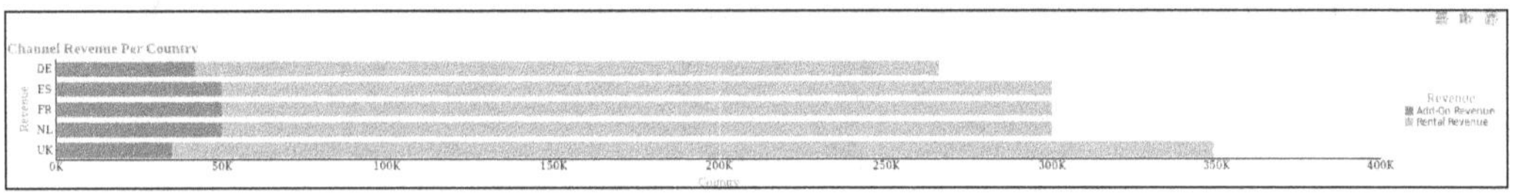

Figure 13

It also allows further drilldown to see what is effective in this country. The actions may be to run a subsequent campaign straightaway or look into countries with less traction, understand why the campaign was not quite suitable, and run a variation. A threshold is added as to where the target revenue is in relation to the actual value.

Once an overview of effectiveness by country is achieved, the user will want to look at specific campaign details and understand which channel is driving leads and revenue. The prospects to lead effectiveness views are decided to be implemented in a specific drill-down dashboard rather than crowding this one, which is the executive view and, therefore, focused on revenue. A bubble chart is provided to see which campaign is proving the most valuable by plotting the cost of the campaign against the revenue. Four quadrants help the user see immediately where they are getting the most value from the budget spent on the campaign. You can see in this example that the Facebook advertisement campaign in the UK is in the leading bottom-left quadrant:

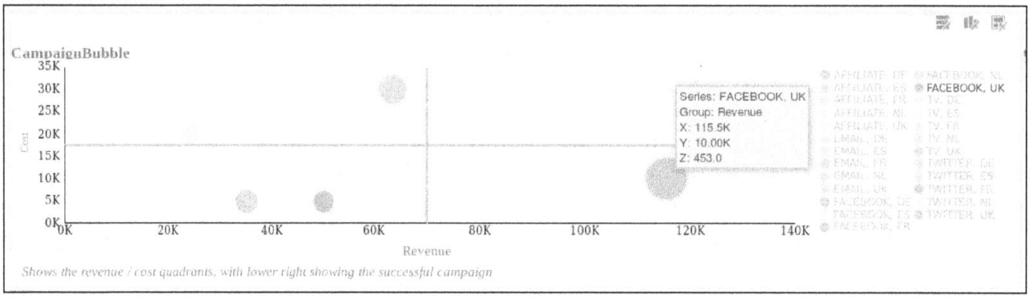

Figure 14

To understand whether the marketing channel success is consistent across other markets, a ring pie chart is provided here to show the split of total revenue by channel. RYLC wants to promote add-ons within this campaign and are running a number of offers, so a second ring pie chart is provided to show the add-on revenue split too.

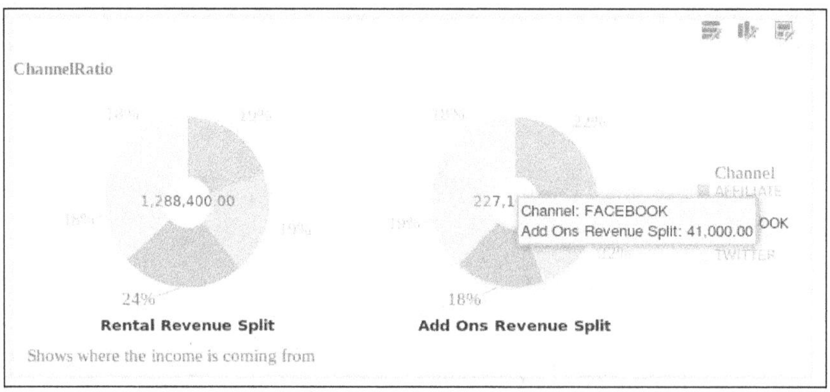

Figure 15

BAM best practices

BAM can add value to most BPM projects; however, BAM dashboards are often added as an afterthought, delivered as a bonus view onto the process with little design consideration for the dashboards being an integral part of the BPM solution.

The following best practices should be followed to ensure the BAM solution is built upon a good design.

- Each dashboard should be designed for a specific user persona; mixing contexts together to produce a dashboard that satisfies all will take up valuable space and may take away clarity from the information being showed.
- Each view within a dashboard should have clear and concise meaning—only metrics that have a correlation should displayed together in views. Don't mix unrelated measures as artificial links between the metrics will be assumed; for example, complaints located next to *discount* could give the impression of a false correlation between the two.
- Define a clear threshold showing when the metric needs attention and highlight the key information to the user's attention. BAM views without thresholds should be challenged to determine when the user is expected to pay attention to the view.
- Determine the action or drill through, which presents further information. If a dashboard view does not have an action, then it should be challenged; even off-system manual actions can be guided by suggestions within the application with supporting context displayed. BAM analysis sessions are often dominated with enquiries, such as shown here: *what will you do if the metric falls to an unacceptably low level? What question is being answered by showing that visualization of the data?* It is only when this extra level of information is provided that the true value of BAM is realized.
- BAM is a push-based technology, so the more active data in a given view, the greater the performance overhead, so do not crowd a dashboard with too many views of data.
- Ensure that the views in a dashboard or drilldown have the same time lag for updates. Different views will be compared, so if some metrics are fed from a downstream system that is updated asynchronously from the process, you may see inconsistent and outdated information as you drill down to the details.

- Filters must be considered and planned upfront. These should be designed as dimensions in the data model.
- Wherever possible, do not use BAM to show lists of large volumes of data. All data within BAM comes from the active data cache, so loading huge lists into this will have a detrimental effect on performance. BAM is for real-time data; users should not be expected to scroll through a list of records. In the RYLC scenario, it is OK to show how many rentals have occurred in the past 24 hours, but there is unlikely to be a valid BAM use case to list all these rentals. The design of the view should consider why the user is asking for the detailed list and only then show the instances from the list that satisfy this requirement; for example, an RYLC user may want a list to show rentals where the first choice wasn't available or where a free upgrade was offered to allow immediate follow-up with the individual rental or sales advisor.

When designing dashboards, avoid the following design pitfalls that will render the dashboards difficult to use or make them misleading and ultimately lead to a difficulties in adopting them:

- Too much information is displayed, presenting an overload of data without clearly guiding to the insight that is intended to be taken from the dashboard.
- There is no context for the data, or bad measures are being selected, giving no clues for the user as to what to do with the data. It is only when the context is added to data that information is produced, and it is only when comparisons, trends, or thresholds are added that insight can be taken from the data (*data + context = information, and information + guidance = insight*).
- The same data should not be represented in different visuals. Consistency of visual style is important to implicitly give further context as charts are displayed, for example, the value of rentals should be consistently showed in one style of chart and color scheme throughout the application, whereas the volume of complaints should be shown in a different style and color scheme.
- Wrong charts might be used for display of data. Common examples include combi-charts showing uncorrelated data and pie charts hiding issues with small slices that are over unacceptable thresholds.

- Too much detail with a low level of granularity being displayed in the initial high level dashboards results in the user not being able to get insights, just raw data. The user should be taken on a journey with the starting page highlighting the areas for attention, with drilldowns progressively taking the user to the cause of the issue.
- Examples of bad dashboard layouts could be layouts leading to the eyes being focused on one area or ones where certain areas are too cluttered with others being too sparse. Do not place data on a dashboard just because there is space left if it does not add value or is not relevant in the dashboard context.
- Dashboards that are designed to check work rather than react to insights seem useful initially, but their use will fade away and add less value over time. If the user cannot answer the question of what they will do with the data being displayed, what decisions it will support, or what actions it will take, then it may just be information in vain, for example, the number of cars rented today may give the RYLC team confidence, but unless there is clarity on what actions this will lead to, there is less value in this figure alone being displayed on the dashboard. It would be much more beneficial to add context to this figure to show a spark line of cars rented over the last month, comparisons against this period last year, or rentals against target.
- Overuse of color lessens the value of color where it's important. BAM tools make it easy to implement different color schemes throughout the dashboard. However, it is essential that a visual language is produced with consistency of color throughout—with bold colors used when data thresholds are breached or when metrics need to stand out. Red and green should be used consistently. Often, red has undertones of poor performance rather than just low metrics, so it must be used carefully. Often, shades of similar colors become useful when designing dashboards that show subtle changes in performance.

Summary

In this chapter, we saw the importance of monitoring the process within a process-driven architecture. The design of monitoring is crucial to support well-informed decisions to improve efficiency and innovate within business processes. Following the best practices set out in this chapter will give longevity in their use and allow the reuse of views in multiple dashboards and ADF visualizations that are part of the core application task flows. Tying dashboard views, dashboards, and alerts to business goals and performance indicators allows continuous improvement and constant refinement of the process and rules within the business. A process architecture is not complete unless you can initiate a cycle of monitoring and improvements, so BAM and process analytics become key components of the BPM solution.

There are many key takeaways from this chapter. First, there are multiple types of analytics that are provided with BAM; understand which type suits the measurements and insights you wish to present to business users. Further, use out-of-the-box process analytics to provide insight into the operational running of business processes. Furthermore, BAM and BI work together in giving tactical and strategic views on top of current and historical data; they should both be complementary parts of your IT architecture. Also, design your BAM data structures for ease of access, not for relational storage. Use flat structures to store the effects of events with dimension tables used for reference data that the user will use to filter and aggregate.

- On a parting note, put thought and rigor into the design of the dashboards and views, highlight the key events that occur, and provide insight rather than cluttering the dashboard with all the information available

Index

Symbols

A

B

F

G

H

I

J

K

L

M

O

P

R

S

Thank you for buying
Design Principles for Process-driven Architectures Using Oracle BPM and SOA Suite 12c

About Packt Publishing

Packt, pronounced 'packed', published its first book, *Mastering phpMyAdmin for Effective MySQL Management*, in April 2004, and subsequently continued to specialize in publishing highly focused books on specific technologies and solutions.

Our books and publications share the experiences of your fellow IT professionals in adapting and customizing today's systems, applications, and frameworks. Our solution-based books give you the knowledge and power to customize the software and technologies you're using to get the job done. Packt books are more specific and less general than the IT books you have seen in the past. Our unique business model allows us to bring you more focused information, giving you more of what you need to know, and less of what you don't.

Packt is a modern yet unique publishing company that focuses on producing quality, cutting-edge books for communities of developers, administrators, and newbies alike. For more information, please visit our website at `www.packtpub.com`.

About Packt Enterprise

In 2010, Packt launched two new brands, Packt Enterprise and Packt Open Source, in order to continue its focus on specialization. This book is part of the Packt Enterprise brand, home to books published on enterprise software – software created by major vendors, including (but not limited to) IBM, Microsoft, and Oracle, often for use in other corporations. Its titles will offer information relevant to a range of users of this software, including administrators, developers, architects, and end users.

Writing for Packt

We welcome all inquiries from people who are interested in authoring. Book proposals should be sent to `author@packtpub.com`. If your book idea is still at an early stage and you would like to discuss it first before writing a formal book proposal, then please contact us; one of our commissioning editors will get in touch with you.

We're not just looking for published authors; if you have strong technical skills but no writing experience, our experienced editors can help you develop a writing career, or simply get some additional reward for your expertise.

[PACKT] enterprise
professional expertise distilled
PUBLISHING

Getting Started with Oracle SOA B2B Integration: A Hands-On Tutorial

ISBN: 978-1-84968-886-4 Paperback: 332 pages

Implement Oracle B2B solutions effortlessly with the help of one of the most knowledgeable Oracle author teams ever assembled

1. Design, implement and monitor B2B transactions quickly using this clear, detailed and practical guide.
2. Wide coverage and detailed discussion of Oracle B2B functionality and features for the new and advanced users.

WS-BPEL 2.0 Beginner's Guide

ISBN: 978-1-84968-896-3 Paperback: 388 pages

Design and develop WS-BPEL executable business processes using Oracle SOA Suite 12*c*

1. Develop BPEL and SOA composite solutions with Oracle SOA Suite 12*c* and JDeveloper 12*c*.
2. Understand Human interaction in BPEL and learn how to add human tasks to a BPEL processes.
3. Automate business processes with WS-BPEL 2.0.
4. Implement and develop compensation and compensation handlers in BPEL processes.

Please check **www.PacktPub.com** for information on our titles

www.ingramcontent.com/pod-product-compliance
Lightning Source LLC
LaVergne TN
LVHW080008210926
848481LV00011B/2973